❖

A LIBRARY OF PROTESTANT THOUGHT

❖

A LIBRARY OF PROTESTANT THOUGHT

❖ ❖ ❖

❖ ❖ ❖

FERDINAND CHRISTIAN BAUR

ON

THE WRITING OF CHURCH HISTORY

Edited and Translated by

PETER C. HODGSON

New York

OXFORD UNIVERSITY PRESS

1968

PRINTED IN THE UNITED STATES OF AMERICA

A Library of Protestant Thought

A LIBRARY OF PROTESTANT THOUGHT is a collection of writings intended to illumine and interpret the history of the Christian faith in its Protestant expression. It is as variegated in its literary forms and theological positions as is the movement it mirrors. Tracts, letters, sermons, monographs, and other types of literature comprising the heritage of Protestant thought find a place in this series. Works that were originally composed in English, whether in Great Britain or in the New World, and works that were originally written in other languages, many of them not previously translated into English, are included. But it is neither necessary nor desirable that every segment of Protestant theology, piety, and ethics receive equal space. The trite theology, the conventional piety, and the platitudinous ethics always bulk larger in any tradition, also in the Protestantism of the past four centuries, than does the creative output of the religious spirit. The latter is our primary interest in this Library. While we have not felt obligated to grant them equal attention, we have included works that are typical of the more commonplace literature of the Protestant tradition. On the other hand, some works which logically belong in this series have not been included because they are readily available elsewhere.

In keeping with the fundamental purpose of this Library, the voices of Protestantism are allowed to speak for themselves, with only as much introduction, commentary, and exposition as will in fact allow them to do so. Wherever feasible, documents are reproduced in their entirety. A few representative selections have been preferred to more numerous but shorter passages, for the Library tries to depict the structure of thought rather than the genetic development of a man or a movement. Nevertheless, the variety of Protestant forms precludes a uniform treatment throughout. Our aim has been to be representative rather than exhaustive and to employ the best available tools of critical historical scholarship. Despite its ambitious scope, A Library of Protestant Thought is not an encyclopedia of Protestantism. It is a series of volumes from which not only clergymen and theologians, but students of philosophy, history, literature, political science

v

and other disciplines can gain a more balanced view of how the Protestant mind has thought and spoken since the Reformation.

The Board is grateful to the Hazen Foundation for an initial grant enabling it to begin its work; to the Sealantic Fund, Inc., for a grant making possible Board meetings, consultations, and editorial assistance in the preparation of specific volumes; and to the Oxford University Press for undertaking the publication of the Library.

THE EDITORIAL BOARD

Abbreviations

ANF	*The Ante-Nicene Fathers: Translations of the Writings of the Fathers down to* A.D. *325.* Ed. Alexander Roberts and James Donaldson. New York, 1885–97.
CSEL	*Corpus scriptorum ecclesiasticorum Latinorum.* Vienna, 1866—.
Epochs	F. C. Baur. *The Epochs of Church Historiography.* Tübingen, 1852. (Citations are to the page numbers of the translation contained in the present volume.)
GCS	*Die griechischen christlichen Schriftsteller der ersten Jahrhunderte.* Leipzig, 1901—.
H.E.	*Historia ecclesiastica.*
LCC	*The Library of Christian Classics.* Philadelphia, 1953—.
LHD	F. C. Baur. *Lectures on the History of Christian Dogma.* Vol. I/1. Tübingen, 1865. (Citations are to the page numbers of the translation contained in the present volume).
Loeb	*The Loeb Classical Library.* London and New York.
NPNF 2	*A Select Library of Nicene and Post-Nicene Fathers of the Christian Church.* 2nd Series. Ed. Philip Schaff and Henry Wace. New York, 1890–1900.
PG	*Patrologiae Cursus Completus: Series Latina.* Ed. J. P. Migne. Paris, 1857–66.
PL	*Patrologiae Cursus Completus: Series Latina.* Ed J. P. Migne. Paris, 1878–90.
RGG	*Die Religion in Geschichte und Gegenwart.* 3rd edition; 6 volumes; Tübingen, 1957–62.
Schaff-Herzog	*The New Schaff-Herzog Encyclopedia of Religious Knowledge.* Ed. Samuel Macauley Jackson, et al. 12 volumes. New York & London, 1908–14. Based on the 3rd edition

of the *Realencyklopädie für protestantische Theologie und Kirche*, ed. J. J. Herzog and Albert Hauck (Leipzig, 1896–1913).

ThJ   *Theologische Jahrbücher.*

TZTh   *Tübinger Zeitschrift für Theologie.*

ZThK   *Zeitschrift für Theologie und Kirche.*

Table of Contents

ix

❖

FERDINAND CHRISTIAN BAUR

❖

General Introduction

1. Baur as Historical Theologian

The purpose of this Introduction is not to provide a general survey of Ferdinand Christian Baur's life, works, and theology, or to engage in an analysis of the historical framework and contemporary significance of his thinking. These tasks have been addressed in two recently published books.[1] My concern rather is to analyze Baur's conception of the hermeneutical principles underlying the work of the historical theologian, with special attention to the development of these principles in the two texts selected for translation in this volume. I want to pursue somewhat further than has hitherto been done an understanding of Baur's "speculative" hermeneutic, and especially of its grounding in his analysis of "Spirit" as the dynamic principle of history and as the subject matter of Christian dogma.

Before undertaking this analysis, however, a brief summary of his career, as well as of the present state of Baur studies, is in order. Ferdinand Christian Baur was born of Swabian parents in 1792 and was educated by his father, a pastor, until the age of thirteen, at which time he entered the lower theological seminary in Blaubeuren, his boyhood home. Four years later, in 1809, he became a student in the evangelical-theological seminary at the University of Tübingen. During that period, the theological faculty was still conservatively oriented, and for a time Baur remained under its influence. It is evident, however, that shortly after returning to Blaubeuren as a member of its faculty in 1817, he had read Fichte, Schelling, and especially Schleiermacher (whose *Glaubenslehre* was first published in 1821–22), and had been deeply influenced by the new direction given to theology by their thinking, as can be seen

1. Wolfgang Geiger, *Spekulation und Kritik: Die Geschichtstheologie Ferdinand Christian Baurs* (Munich, 1964), and Peter C. Hodgson, *The Formation of Historical Theology: A Study of Ferdinand Christian Baur* (New York, 1966). On Baur's life, works, and theological context, see especially chaps. i and ii of the latter work; on his present significance, see chap. vii of Geiger and chap. vi of Hodgson. The major concern of both these works is an analysis of Baur's conception of historical theology (or, as Geiger prefers to call it, his "theology of history").

3

especially from his first major book, *Symbolik und Mythologie, oder die Naturreligion des Alterthums* (1824–25).[2] In 1826 he was called to the evangelical-theological faculty at Tübingen as full professor of theology, and there he remained for the rest of his life.

Whereas Baur's teaching at Blaubeuren had been primarily in ancient history, philosophy, and religion, at Tübingen his energies were first directed to New Testament studies and patrology, resulting in several articles published in the 1830's. The most important of these was an analysis of the conflict between Paulinizing and Judaizing parties in Corinth, which appeared in 1831.[3] In 1833 he became involved in a dispute with his colleague on the Catholic faculty at Tübingen, Johann Adam Möhler, over the proper understanding of the distinction between Catholicism and Protestantism. In his reply to Möhler, *Der Gegensatz des Katholicismus und Protestantismus*,[4] he refers for the first time in any of his writing to the philosophy of Hegel. In a footnote, he criticizes the use of Hegelian dialectic in the theory of the church's historical development advanced by the Catholic church historian Adam Gengler; and a few pages later he proposes a means of transcending and reconciling the present antithesis between Catholicism and Protestantism (both of which are "one-sided") by turning to a "purified and spiritualized conception of tradition," based upon Schleiermacher's consciousness theology and the new philosophy "that places speculative thinking in the closest connection with the activity of Spirit objectified in history, since it regards history as the vital progression of the concept, or allows Absolute Spirit to press and work its way to its own consciousness only through the mediation of history"—i.e., the philosophy of Hegel.[5]

The influence of Hegel was especially felt during the next decade and

2. Complete information on Baur's writings is contained in the bibliography at the end of this volume.

3. "Die Christuspartei in der korinthischen Gemeinde, der Gegensatz des petrinischen und paulinischen Christenthums in der ältesten Kirche, der Apostel Petrus in Rom," *TZTh*, V:4 (1831), 61–206.

4. First published in the last two numbers of the *Tübinger Zeitschrift für Theologie* for 1833, and then issued separately as a book in 1834. A second, revised and enlarged edition appeared in 1836. Citations are from the first edition.

5. *Gegensatz*, 421–23, 431–32. In view of these references, my dating of Baur's first encounter with Hegel's philosophy (see *The Formation of Historical Theology*, 23–24) must be advanced by a year. See also Geiger, *Spekulation und Kritik*, 42–43. In the second edition of the *Gegensatz* the material on Gengler was reworked and expanded into an appendix, "The Hegelianism of Recent Catholic Theologians," in which F. A. Staudenmaier was also included. Aside, however, from these two references to Hegel, there is no evidence of any substantive influence of Hegelian categories and conceptions in the first edition of the *Gegensatz*. Appar-

a half, when Baur turned with extraordinary productivity to the study of the history of Christian dogma. He brought out his great monographs on the doctrines of reconciliation and the Trinity and incarnation, followed by his textbook on the history of dogma, and gave final form to his lectures on the history of dogma.[6] During this period he also continued his Pauline studies, which reached a climax in 1845 with the publication of his *Paulus, der Apostel Jesu Christi.* Thereafter, his attention turned increasingly to the Gospels and the critical study of the teaching and ministry of Jesus.[7] This coincided with a new emphasis upon the fundamentally moral character of the religious relationship between God and man and upon the freedom of the believing subject, as distinguished from the more purely conceptual and speculative interests of the "Hegelian" period.[8] Finally, during the decade of the 1850's, Baur became heavily engaged in church historiography: first his methodological prolegomenon, *Die Epochen der kirchlichen Geschichtschreibung* (1852), then the first two volumes of his church history lectures, *Das Christenthum und die christliche Kirche der drei ersten Jahrhunderte* (1853; second edition, 1860), and *Die christliche Kirche vom Anfang des vierten bis zum Ende des sechsten Jahrhunderts* (1859). The last three volumes of this series, including a history of theology and the church in the nineteenth century, were published after his death in 1860.

Baur has been and will continue to be a highly controversial figure;

---

ently, Baur's first real acquaintance with Hegel was based on the latter's *Lectures on the Philosophy of Religion,* published by Marheineke in 1832—an acquaintance that was not fully appropriated until Baur's *Die christliche Gnosis, oder die christliche Religions-Philosophie in ihrer geschichtlichen Entwiklung* (1835), where Hegel received major attention, along with Schleiermacher and Schelling. In other words, by the time Baur first came under the influence of Hegel, he was in his early forties, and already a mature scholar in his own right.

6. *Die christliche Lehre von der Versöhnung in ihrer geschichtlichen Entwiklung von der ältesten Zeit bis auf die neueste* (1838); *Die christliche Lehre von der Dreieinigkeit und Menschwerdung Gottes in ihrer geschichtlichen Entwiklung* (3 vols., 1841–43); *Lehrbuch der christlichen Dogmengeschichte* (1847; 2nd ed., 1858); and *Vorlesungen über die christliche Dogmengeschichte* (ed. F.F. Baur, 3 vols., 1865–67).

7. See especially *Kritische Untersuchungen über die kanonischen Evangelien* (1847); *Das Markusevangelium nach seinem Ursprung und Charakter* (1851); *Vorlesungen über neutestamentliche Theologie* (1864); and various articles in the *Theologische Jahrbücher* and the *Zeitschrift für wissenschaftliche Theologie.*

8. The shift in emphasis is first clearly seen in an article published in 1847 in the *Theologische Jahrbücher* on the distinction between Reformed and Lutheran doctrine. I am not persuaded, however, by Geiger's argument concerning a fundamental dichotomy between "speculative" and "ethical" phases in Baur's theology. *Spekulation und Kritik,* 77–87. See below, n. 10.

both his own precise theological position and his significance for contemporary theology are in dispute. During the past decade fresh interest in Baur has emerged, primarily in Germany,[9] in part because of a new recognition of the contemporary significance of Hegel's philosophy, and also because of a general awareness that the theologians in the era following Schleiermacher and Hegel were confronted by many of the same problems that have become so vitally important to us today: the problem of the radical historicity of the Christian faith, the hermeneutical relation between past and present or between text and interpreter, the quest for a non-supernatural understanding of the relation between God and world, the focusing of theology upon anthropology without simply surrendering language about God but indeed making it possible in a new way, and the first lineaments of a "secular" theology, with its positive assessment of the conjunction between Christianity and the modern world. Most of these themes were obscured to a greater or lesser extent in the final, Ritschlian phase of nineteenth-century liberalism and in its twentieth-century heir, dialectical theology; but they have returned to haunt us with renewed vigor in the second half of our century. Among the post-Hegelians, none addressed these problems with greater sensitivity and daring than Ferdinand Christian Baur. Just because his problems are also our problems, his resolution of them remains controversial and debatable. The most recent phase of Baur criticism makes this abundantly clear.[10] Of course, there can be no question simply of repristinating

9. See the secondary materials listed in the bibliography at the end of this volume.

10. It is appropriate at this point to make a few remarks about Geiger's impressive study of Baur, *Spekulation und Kritik*. This work came into my hands after the manuscript of my own book had been completed, and I was unable to take it into account there. Geiger's interpretation of Baur and evaluation of his significance differ from mine in important respects. Our differences of interpretation can be traced ultimately to a differing orientation toward the network of problems mentioned above—mine a more fundamentally positive orientation, Geiger's a more fundamentally negative or critical one. The latter reads nineteenth-century developments in general and Baur in particular from a right-wing Barthian perspective, and makes critical demands of Baur which, as Heinz Liebing puts it, can only be regarded as anachronistic.

Geiger readily grants Baur's theological significance in forcing theology to confront the problematic of history with a radicalism never before approached (242–43). He agrees with Dilthey and others that Baur is the greatest theologian in the epoch between Schleiermacher and Ritschl. But he intends deliberately to stress our present-day "difficulties" with Baur rather than our "agreements" (243–44), for the latter's greatest significance is to be found precisely at the point of his greatest

Baur. We must rather learn to confront these problems in our own way, learning from his treatment of them and from both the strengths and the weaknesses he shared with theological idealism and liberalism. To do theology in Baur's spirit (as he himself would insist), we must not return to the past but venture into an unknown future. But the venture into the

---

difficulty, namely, his resolution of theology into history (246, 234-39). Geiger fears that Baur has identified the content of Christian faith too undialectically with *human* self-consciousness, thus reducing theology to anthropology, to a product of the history of *human* Spirit; nothing transcendent, supernatural, other-worldly remains of Christianity (79, 84, 89-90, 96-107, 225-27, 230-33, 245). Baur does, to be sure, guard himself against the pan-anthropologism of the left-Hegelians by means of his shift to a fundamentally *ethical* idealism in the last phase of his thinking, but only at the price of a certain degree of theological impoverishment (76, 81-84, 88, 229). In any event, the only genuine alternative to Baur's historicization of theology (his significance is that he forces us to recognize this) is to be found in a new theology of the *Holy* Spirit, a theology that does not merely give an account of *faith* or religious *consciousness*, a theology willing, in other words, to risk a greater "embarrassment" or "difficulty" in order to surmount the "difficulty" occasioned by Baur (246-47).

By way of criticism of this thesis, and of crystallizing the major differences in interpretation between our two works, three comments are in order. First, throughout Geiger's study, a reductionism is evident in his analysis of Baur's theology of Spirit. This can be accounted for by his tendency to read Hegel in the tradition of those for whom Hegel's philosophy of Spirit is ultimately nothing more than an elaborate humanism. This tradition finds it difficult to take seriously Hegel's conviction concerning the reality of the Absolute, or his statement (e.g., in the *Philosophy of Religion* and the *Encyclopedia* [1827], § 384) that God is Absolute Spirit. Hence for this tradition Hegel's Absolute Spirit must be reduced to the absolute primacy of finite consciousness. At this point I can only call attention to the fact that another interpretation of Hegel is possible, and in my judgment more defensible. Furthermore, I think it can be adequately demonstrated that in Baur's theology, Spirit is a category which transcends finite, individual, empirical men, and is fully exemplified only by God as Absolute Spirit, who is the inner ground of the process of history as such, and of man as finite Spirit—of man whose destiny, to be sure, is to be reconciled with God and to become one with him, but whose present condition is one of estrangement and separation. For Geiger, however, such statements by Baur as that "the eternal, self-subsistent God revealed in his Son and Spirit is also a God present to man and immanent to human self-consciousness" (*Dreieinigkeit und Menschwerdung Gottes*, I, 101), are untenable (see Geiger, 226), for he believes, as does Barth, that there is no way to prevent God thus conceived from collapsing into a projection of human consciousness; the attempt to distinguish God and man within such a unity is doomed to failure. This is admittedly a complex and crucial problem for Baur, and my earlier discussion of it in *The Formation of Historical Theology* was not entirely adequate. Accordingly, and with Geiger's criticism in mind, I have attempted to address myself to Baur's theology of Spirit in some detail at a later point in this Introduction (see below, 21-31).

In the second place, Geiger believes that a fundamental shift occurs in Baur's thinking between 1852 (*The Epochs of Church Historiography*) and 1853 (the first

future can be charted, to some extent, by learning from those whose work placed them at the cutting edge of theology in their own time.

The theme of this volume is Baur's conception of the hermeneutical principles upon which historical-critical theology must be founded, and the two documents selected for translation herein represent the major sources for his development of that conception. For Baur, hermeneutical questions were not separable from the task of historical "reflection"

---

volume of the church history)—a reversion to Kant's ethical idealism away from Hegel's speculative philosophy, as can be seen especially from his portrayal of Jesus in the church history as a mere teacher of "universally valid moral truths," whereas in the *Epochs* he still describes the founder of Christianity in speculative categories as the embodiment of divine-human unity (see Geiger, 64–91). I acknowledge that there is a shift in emphasis in Baur's later theology (see above, 5, and *The Formation of Historical Theology*, 20–22). But it does not suddenly occur between 1852 and 1853 (Zeller, for example, dates it during the late 1840's). Nor does Baur surrender his interest in a speculative interpretation of history; rather, he develops more independent categories of interpretation and in that sense frees himself from Hegel's influence. Most important, in Baur's treatment of the historical Jesus in his lectures on church history and New Testament theology during the 1850's, it is not true that the philosophical-theological and historical-critical components in his understanding fall irreconcilably apart, as Geiger contends. Rather, the Jesus of history who emerges from Baur's later critical studies is the precise embodiment of his theological conception of the Redeemer as the one in whom the Idea of reconciliation, of God-man unity, achieves the fullest actualization conceivable for a single individual. The substance of Jesus' message, according to Baur, is not simply the moral freedom and autonomy of the human subject. Free moral subjecthood or "consciousness" is rather the *medium* or *locus* of the reconciling relationship between God and man—the actualization of divine-human unity—which *is* the fundamental content of Jesus' teaching as well as the significance of his person. He is the one in whom the unity of God and man is normatively actualized precisely in virtue of the unique quality of his moral person. In this respect, Baur's Christology is closer to Schleiermacher than to either Kant or Hegel. (This point is argued at some length in *The Formation of Historical Theology*, 100–121, 221–34; see also below, 244, 252.) The return-to-rationalism thesis is also rendered implausible by Baur's thoroughgoing criticism of rationalist theology and historiography, which continued to the end of his career (e.g., see *The Epochs of Church Historiography*, chaps. IV, V; and *The Formation of Historical Theology*, 39–43). Finally, the alternative Geiger proposes does not take adequate account of the situation in which theology has found itself since the beginning of the nineteenth century, namely, the injunction laid upon it to develop a coherent "secular" theology, in which God and the world are neither identified nor separated into qualitatively incommensurable realms. Baur, together with Schleiermacher, Hegel, and others of his age, clearly recognized this need, even if his own solution now seems inadequate from our point of view. But the alternative to Baur cannot be a return to the *status quo ante*.

(I am happy to acknowledge that the reflections contained in this footnote are indebted in part to a colloquy at the Perkins School of Theology in March 1967, at which Professor Klaus Penzel presented a penetrating review and comparison of Geiger's study of Baur and mine.)

(*Betrachtung*) or "comprehension" (*Auffassung*), which included both critical and participative-responsive elements. Indeed, the critical quest for the *Sache* behind the text was occasioned and determined in part by the need to participate in and respond to the self-interpretation of the *Sache* for the present; and the latter was possible only on the basis of the former. In other words, the total process of historical understanding, as Baur conceived it, was hermeneutical in character.[11] Nevertheless, it is characteristic of Baur that he did not address himself to hermeneutical questions in a separate systematic treatise on historical method, but only in the form of critical surveys of the disciplines in question. The classic instances of this procedure were *Die Epochen der kirchlichen Geschichtschreibung* [The Epochs of Church Historiography] (1852), which served as the methodological prolegomenon to his church history, and the lengthy Introduction to his *Vorlesungen über die christlichen Dogmengeschichte* [Lectures on the History of Christian Dogma] (1865–67).[12]

The background to these two texts needs to be considered briefly. (1) Prior to the publication of the *Epochs* as a separate volume, Baur treated methodological questions in a "General Introduction" to his earlier church history lectures.[13] Here he dealt with the conception, methods,

---

11. I am not persuaded by Geiger's argument that Baur lacked hermeneutical interests because he did not use the terms *Verstehen* ("understanding") and *Hermeneutik*. See Geiger, *op. cit.*, 238. Baur employed other terms with hermeneutical significance, such as *Betrachtung* ("consideration," "reflection"), *Auffassung* ("comprehension," "understanding"), *Darstellung* ("presentation"), *Nachdenken* ("rethinking"). Baur's "criticism" (which Geiger says displaced interpretive interests) was in fact hermeneutical in character, since its ultimate intention was to let the subject matter, the given, interpret itself to the knower. For further discussion of this question, see below, 17–20, 23–26, and *The Formation of Historical Theology*, 167–69.

12. The *Epochen* is readily available in a reprint edition published in Stuttgart–Bad Canstatt by the Friedrich Frommann Verlag, 1963, as Vol. II of *Ausgewählte Werke in Einzelausgaben*, edited by Klaus Scholder. Also important for Baur's treatment of historical method and hermeneutical questions are the Introductions to *Lehrbuch der christlichen Dogmengeschichte* (1847), *Kritische Untersuchung über die kanonischen Evangelien* (1847), and *Vorlesungen über neutestamentliche Theologie* (1864); the Prefaces to *Symbolik und Mythologie* (1824–25), *Die christliche Lehre von der Versöhnung* (1838), and *Die christliche Lehre von der Dreieinigkeit und Menschwerdung Gottes* (1841–43); and "Die Einleitung in das Neue Testament als theologische Wissenschaft. Ihr Begriff und ihre Aufgabe, ihr Entwicklungsgang und ihr innerer Organismus," *ThJ*, IX (1850), 463–566; X (1851), 70–94, 222–52, 291–328; *An Herrn Dr. Karl Hase: Beantwortung des Sendschreibens "Die Tübinger Schule"* (1855); and *Die Tübinger Schule und ihre Stellung zur Gegenwart* (1859; 2nd ed., 1860).

13. A manuscript of these lectures, probably dating from the 1840's, is contained in Signature Mh II 166 h in the University of Tübingen Library.

principles, sources, tools, uses, and value of church history, in addition
to a "survey of the major phases in the history of church historiography" (about forty pages in manuscript). This is the antecedent of the
Epochs, which however was completely reconceived and greatly expanded before publication. There is no anticipation in the lecture manuscripts of the concluding chapter of the *Epochs,* where Baur first developed the category of "Idea" in conjunction with a theology of the
church. (2) Although the *Lectures on the History of Christian Dogma*
were not published until 1865–67 (by Baur's son, Ferdinand Friedrich
Baur), the lecture manuscripts on which the published edition was based
date from an earlier period, probably the mid-1840's (1843 to 1847).
This period can be determined by comparing the structure and contents
of the manuscripts used for the published edition with a set of student
notes of Baur's lectures taken by C. Sarwey in 1842–43, and with the
two editions of the *Lehrbuch der christlichen Dogmengeschichte* [Text-
book of the History of Christian Dogma] (1847 and 1858).[14] The evidence from this comparison indicates that the basic *Lectures* manuscript
was written sometime between the student notes of 1842–43 and the
first edition of the *Lehrbuch,* even though subsequent revisions and
emendations to the manuscripts were made at various points. There is
further evidence in that the works discussed in Section VI, Part 10 of
the Introduction, "The Most Recent Literature in the History of
Dogma," date no later than the early 1840's. If this dating is correct, the
Lehrbuch was written somewhat later than the basic *Lectures* manuscript, even though it was published much earlier. In structure it paral-
lels the *Lectures* very closely, but with some interesting minor variations
(which indicate a more mature text). The contents, of course, are much
more compressed, and are presented almost in outline form. The first
edition of the *Lehrbuch* contained only 284 pages, as compared with the
2,353 pages of the printed edition of the *Lectures;* the second edition of
the *Lehrbuch* had 396 pages. Section IV of the Introduction to the
Lectures, "The Periods of the History of Dogma," is not found in the
Lehrbuch at all. Section VI, Part 12 of the *Lectures,* "The Speculative
View of History," is not in the *Lehrbuch* but is replaced by a concluding final section, "The Interest in the History of Dogma," part of which
I have included in a footnote at the conclusion of the *Lectures* text.[15]

14. The Sarwey notes and the lecture manuscripts are contained in Signatures Mh
II 154 and Mh II 166 m, University of Tübingen Library.

15. See below, 364, n. 45. This note, and n. 44, page 362, contain in addition two
other passages from the *Lehrbuch* that supplement the discussion in the *Lectures.*

Not only do these documents represent Baur's two most important methodological introductions; they are also mutually complementary, by virtue of Baur's conception of the intrinsic connection between church history and the history of dogma. The latter discipline is properly considered a part of a larger whole, church history. At the same time, it is the hermeneutical key to the study of church history, for it uncovers the internal "spiritual movement" to which the "external phenomena" of church history "are attributable as their ultimate basis." [16] Dogma, as a conceptual phenomenon, is peculiarly appropriate as a historical "form" or "manifestation" of the Idea constituting the essence of Christianity, for this Idea in turn is a conceptual reality, the self-actualization of thinking Spirit. Dogma is the conceptual objectification of finite, human Spirit, as the latter participates in the rational process by which Infinite or Eternal Spirit lives and by which the reality of history as such is constituted. Dogma is thus the most "intrinsic" of the forms of the church, for it shares most directly in the nature of the reality actualized in it. The history of dogma thus warrants separate treatment. It introduces us to the category of "Spirit" as the dynamic principle of history, without which church history and Christianity could not be understood, for Christianity itself is grounded in the nature of Spirit. In his church history, however, Baur moderated the primacy he had attributed to dogma in his earlier studies. The church history affords new significance to the "external" forms of the church, such as ecclesiastical polity, missionary activity, political-cultural relations, and worship and ethics; but it includes as well an extensive treatment of dogma. The history of dogma is now fully internalized by church history.[17] At the same time, Baur did not simply transfer the interpretive categories developed for the study of the history of dogma to the broader and more complex field of church history. Rather, he formulated new categories expressly for an understanding of the historicity of the church; they are based, however, upon the earlier analysis of Spirit and cannot be understood apart from it. Hence in the discussion to follow we shall examine Baur's historical method as an integrated whole, displaying successive stages of refinement.

16. *LHD*, 261–62. Citations of the *Lectures on the History of Christian Dogma* and the *Epochs of Church Historiography* are to the page numbers of the translations contained in this volume.

17. *Das Christenthum und die christliche Kirche der drei ersten Jahrhunderte*, v–vi.

2. *Beyond Supernaturalism and Rationalism*

In both the *Epochs* and the Introduction to the *History of Dogma*,
Baur attempts to demonstrate the intrinsic connection between the theological stance of the historian and the way he treats his subject matter.
The task of historical knowledge or "historical presentation" (*die geschichtliche Darstellung*) is that of "setting forth the objectively given
for subjective consciousness," of enabling "what has objectively taken
place" to become "subjectively known." [18] Historical knowledge represents the dialectical movement and tension between object (or subject
matter, *die Sache*) and consciousness, in which each is modified and
shaped by the other. The task of subjective consciousness is to follow
the movement of the subject matter itself, to become one with it so far
as possible, to become a true and adequate reflection of it, to transcend
its own merely subjective perspective. But this is a never-ending and
never-realizable task. For the historian can grasp the subject matter in its
objective reality only from a perspective that enables him to grasp the
principle of unity or "Idea" joining together the mass of individual
phenomena; the understanding of the principle of unity depends, in turn,
upon how one conceives "the starting point in which the Idea that is to
be realized through its entire temporal manifestation is clearly and definitely expressed." The historiography of the Christian church is based
ultimately on a "fundamental perception" of the church's constitutive
point of origin, and of the Idea that comes to decisive manifestation in
that point of origin and functions as the principle of unity binding together into an intelligible whole the disparate phenomena of church history. This "fundamental perception" is a function of the historian's theological vantage point or dogmatic orientation; as this perception changes,
so also does the whole picture of church history. [19]

Now, when we examine the history of church historiography and the
history of the study of the history of dogma, we can discern, according
to Baur, two basic dogmatic vantage points which have guided historical
theology in the past but are no longer intelligible as its foundation in
their "older, absolute sense": supernaturalism and rationalism. [20] *The
Epochs of Church Historiography* can be described both as a sustained

18. *Epochs,* 46–47; cf. *LHD,* 335–36.   19. See *Epochs,* 47–49; *LHD,* 269–70.
20. *Epochs,* 48–49.

polemic against supernaturalism and rationalism, and as the quest for a "speculative" hermeneutic that transcends the inadequacies of these two "obsolete" theological and church-historical stances. The same can be said for the Introduction to the *History of Dogma*.

1. *Supernaturalism* in its various modes exhibits, according to Baur, two fundamental characteristics. The first and more important is its historical dualism—which indeed has proved to be the most pervasive weakness of church historiography in all its epochs. It lies at the heart of the old Catholic view of history, but is perpetuated in Protestant orthodoxy, pietism, and "neo-supernaturalism" (e.g., Neander) under different guises. It also appears in rationalist historiography, freed of its supernaturalist clothing. Fundamentally, dualism results from the conceptual inability to grasp the history of the church as a unified, internally coherent total process, which contains within itself the principle of its own nature and development. Consequently, the church tends to split apart into its supernatural essence and its contingent human manifestations; in it transpires the endless conflict between God and Satan, light and darkness, truth and heresy, rationality and irrationality. At the basis of this conceptual inadequacy is a failure to understand the proper relation between God and history—a relation in which history in general and historical Christianity in particular are to be seen as the outward patterning of the inward dialectic of the divine life itself. "The historical process, in which Christianity comes to historical manifestation, is simply an element of the general process which is the life-process of God himself, in which the Idea of God explicates itself in the distinction of its moments. . . . Historical Christianity is simply an element of the same course in which the process immanent to the nature of God explicates itself historically." [21] "God" and "history" are not two mutually incompatible spheres of reality; rather, each is intelligible only in its relation to the other. Explicit statements of Baur's "pantheism of history," [22] such as the one quoted above, occur with relative infrequency in his total corpus; nevertheless they are the clue to his conception of history as a whole and to the force of his polemic against dualism.

From this it follows that the "supernaturalism" to which Baur objects in traditional church historiography is not the belief that the church has its ultimate foundation in the reality of God, or that God is the infinite,

<hr>

21. *Vorlesungen über die christliche Dogmengeschichte*, III, 352–53. See *The Formation of Historical Theology*, 54, 134–41, 145–48.

22. Geiger, *Spekulation und Kritik*, 45.

eternal Spirit in which finite nature and Spirit have their being and life; rather he sees that supernaturalism as the failure to understand the proper mode of relation between God and history. God does not impinge upon history as an extrinsic, alien force or personal agency by means of miraculous interventions into the "natural" course of affairs; he is rather the ground of the process of history itself—a spiritual process sharing in the life of God as Spirit. God is not simply to be identified with the finite process of history; he transcends it as its infinite ground. It is certainly true that Baur never managed to describe the character of this transcendence very clearly—a deficiency he shared with theological idealism in general. Nevertheless, his rejection of "supernaturalism" is to be understood as the rejection of an inadequate conception of a *relation*, not as the denial of the reality of God as such. In Baur's vocabulary, "supernaturalism" is a term synonymous with "miracle," the latter having come to be understood as the disruption of the historical nexus by the suprahistorical actions of an alien deity, a *Deus ex machina*. Miracle is believed to occur whenever the hand of God intervenes directly in the affairs of history, whether to inaugurate the Christian religion in the figure of a supernatural God-man and to preserve his followers from harm, or to punish the enemies of the church.[23]

Antecedents of the dualism characteristic of old Catholic historiography are already to be detected in Hegesippus, the earliest of the church historians, who sees the course of the church determined by the antithesis between "authentically apostolic truth" and "heretical falsification."[24] This dualism is sharpened and given classic expression by Eusebius and his successors. The antithesis between truth and error, between unchanging dogma and constantly new forms of heresy, is seen to have its real foundation in the cosmic struggle between God and the Devil. Only the Devil is a worthy antagonist of God, an antagonist of such cunning and suprahuman strength as to require for his subjugation the incarnation of the divine Logos himself.[25] Here dualism is given a purely supernatural foundation. The same cosmic conflict underlies the church historiography of the Lutheran *Magdeburg Centuries*. The only difference is that its visible epiphanies have exchanged roles. According to the Protestants, after the establishment of the Roman primacy, the work of the Devil becomes localized in the Papacy and the magisterial

23. See *Epochs*, 62–63, 103–104. Cf. also Baur's rejection of theories concerning the "miraculous" beginning of Christianity in his criticism of Neander and Gieseler.
24. *Ibid.*, 52–53.   25. *Ibid.*, 60–62.

office of the church, which consistently distort and destroy the true doctrinal standards of early Christianity (though these have been restored to purity by Lutheran dogmatics). Heresy is now seen to have infected the church from within rather than from without.[26] Gottfried Arnold generalizes the internal agency of Satan to include not simply the Papacy but also "the clergy" or "the priesthood" as a whole, Lutheran as well as Catholic. Furthermore, he does not share the confidence of the Centuriators in dogmatic formulation as a means of preserving truth. Rather, the true witnesses of God are reborn Christians, those "individuals who carry true and vital Christianity in their hearts in faith and love, without dogma and school theology." [27] For the ancient church historians, the conflict is between Catholic truth and pagan heresy; for the Centuriators, it is the Lutheran dogma of *justificari sola fide* against the papal magisterium; for Arnold, it is inner piety versus clergy and doctrine.

The second characteristic of supernaturalism is its failure to recognize genuine change within the continuity of historical development. If history transpires merely at the point of intersection of two irreconcilable and transcendent antitheses, then nothing really "happens" other than their steady interaction under new guises. Genuine novelty, change, and variation are excluded in principle from historical development, in favor of an eternal repetition and monotony. The interacting principles are not modified and enriched by their mutual contact, for they are already complete at the beginning of the process. "In the entire historical sequence of the church everything remains as it was from the beginning, and no change can take place by which the substantial forms of the church might be essentially altered." [28] From the Catholic perspective, so long as the principle of darkness remains external to the institution and dogma of the church, i.e., localized in heresy, paganism, persecution, then no genuine change transpires within the church itself. It is significant, Baur notes, that the first histories of dogma were really histories of heresies: dogma itself has no "history." [29] But when heresy ruptures the church from within, as it did in the sixteenth-century Protestant Reformation, then we experience a "fall" of the church, a devolution, not a historical progression.[30] From the Protestant perspective, as we have

26. *Ibid.*, 91–94, 96–98, 101.   27. *Ibid.*, 120, 133.
28. *Ibid.*, 96. Cf. 94–95, 214, 219, 221–22, and especially 115, where Baur summarizes the problem of continuity and change in historical development and suggests a way of relating these two factors.
29. Cf. *LHD*, 336–42, 345, 360–61; and *Epochs*, 59–60.
30. Cf. *Der Gegensatz des Katholicismus und Protestantismus*, 422–23.

seen, the internal rupturing of the church occurs at a much earlier date, and the "fall" is pushed steadily further back: for the *Magdeburg Centuries,* it occurs with the achievement of Roman primacy in the Western church; for Gottfried Arnold and C. E. Weismann (as later for Ritschl and Harnack) it comes in the second century, with the transition from apostolic Christianity to dogma and episcopacy; [31] and for some of the Protestant rationalists, such as J. S. Semler, it is to be found as early as the apostolic age, which already represents a corruption of the original, purely moral religion of Jesus.[32]

2. *Rationalism,* for different reasons, is also unable to discern continuity and development within history. Its atomistic procedure disintegrates history into isolated and disconnected moments. There is no objective meaning or purpose of the whole; the contingency of outer circumstance and autonomous individuals replaces the dualistic antithesis of cosmic principles. Chance assumes the role of Providence.[33] When history loses comprehensive meaning and intelligible continuity, then its study becomes "pragmatic" in character: it is utilized for purposes of moral-religious edification, or for the demonstration of convictions about life believed to be true by the historian.[34] Underlying the pragmatic attitude is a pervasive subjectivism. On the one hand, the historian reads his own subjective interests into history, which becomes a vast field on which he can either construct his own ideal picture of the rational functioning of the cause-effect nexus, or demonstrate that the actual course of events is a manifold tissue of irrationalities, interspersed with a few rays of light (not the least of which is the new *Aufklärung*).[35]

On the other hand, the subjectivism of Enlightenment historiography is to be seen in its concentration upon the subjectivity of the individual as the locus of true religion and as the focal point of historical process, as exemplified in the pragmatic psychologism of L. T. Spittler, the interest of G. J. Planck in the intentionality of individuals, and the important role accorded to free individuals in shaping the course of history by J. S. Semler and C. W. F. Walch in the eighteenth century and by August Neander in the nineteenth.[36] Of this subjectivism, Baur regards his con-

31. *Epochs,* 138.   32. *Ibid.,* 158–59.

33. Cf. especially Baur's discussion of L. T. Spittler, *ibid.,* 180–81.

34. This is the central theme of chaps. IV. and V of the *Epochs;* see especially the discussion of Semler and Walch, 166–67.

35. *Epochs,* 187, 189–98, 201. In this respect rationalism perpetuates the dualism of the older supernaturalism, even though the cosmic presuppositions have eroded away. It is now the irrationality of history that stands in seemingly irreconcilable antithesis to the rationality of the historian. Cf. *ibid.,* 202.

36. Cf. *ibid.,* 166, 181–82, 196–98, 210–211.

temporary Neander as an especially instructive example. For Neander, as for his theological mentor, Schleiermacher, the interest in individuals stems from a romantic conviction that religion is a matter of subjectivity, of feeling, and therefore that "all religious manifestations can be judged only in accord with the immediacy of the religious consciousness from which they proceed." This means, Neander thinks, that it is impossible to ask what Christianity is objectively in itself, apart from its subjective appropriation in acts of religious consciousness. But then the occasion is provided for the historian's confusion of his own subjectivity with that of past historical figures, and for the appeal to a supernatural essence of Christianity lying beyond historical comprehension and development.[37] Baur insists that historical study can be concerned only with that which objectifies or expresses itself outwardly in historical actions, not with inner religious piety.[38]

A final weakness of Protestant rationalism is its failure to grasp the historicity of the church in its own internal structures and dynamic. The conception of the church is "externalized" and "secularized"; it is construed on the model of the state and other human societies (as with Mosheim and Planck), or its division into historical epochs is based on political history and other factors extrinsic to the unfolding of its own Idea (as with Spittler and Hase).[39] In short, there is still lacking in rationalism an objective penetration into the reality of the subject matter itself, namely the Christian church in its own peculiar historicity.

3. A Speculative Hermeneutic

What is required to complete the task of church historiography is a movement beyond the abstract dualism of the older historians and the equally abstract empiricism of pragmatic rationalism to a speculative grasp of the unity and dynamism of history (against dualism) and its comprehensive meaning (against empiricism).[40] "Speculation" is a way of thinking critically about the given of history, a thinking in which the historian transcends his subjective vantage point and the given presents *itself* in its own objectivity. Speculative thinking is two-

---

37. *Ibid.*, 211–12, 225, 227, n. 31, 227–29.

38. See *Epochs*, 130–31, where Baur criticizes Gottfried Arnold. The same criticism is brought against Semler and Planck.

39. Cf. *Epochs*, 146–48, 176, 178, 193–94, 236.

40. Cf. *Epochs*, 241, n. 1, and *Lehrbuch der christlichen Dogmengeschichte* (3rd ed.), 56 (quoted below, 363, n. 44).

directional or reflexive in character: it is a movement from the historian through the text to the subject matter, but at its climax it occasions a reversal in the flow of meaning such that the subject matter now unveils itself to the interpreter in its objective truth and meaning, and becomes the subject rather than the object in the act of knowing.[41] The task of the historian is to "transpose himself into the objective reality of the subject matter itself," so that "instead of making history a reflection of his own subjectivity, he may be simply a mirror for the perception of historical phenomena in their true and real form." [42] Gadamer has pointed out that the root meaning of "speculation" is "to mirror" (from the Latin, *speculum*). "Mirroring," he writes, "involves a constant exchange. . . . The mirror image (*Spiegelbild*) is essentially bound to the view of the thing itself (*Anblick*) through the medium of the observer. It has no being of its own. It is like an 'experience,' which does not exist itself, but yet allows the thing itself to appear reflectedly (*spiegelbildlich*). It is like a doubling, which nevertheless has only a single existence. . . . 'Speculative' signifies opposition to the dogmatism of everyday experience. Whoever does not relinquish himself directly to the binding character of phenomena or to common opinion in its fixed determinateness, but knows how to reflect—or, put in Hegelian terms, whoever recognizes the *Ansich* as a *Fürmich*—is a speculative thinker." [43] The reflexive character of speculative thinking is suggested by the term *Betrachtung* (from *betrachten*, to "view," "consider," "reflect upon"), which, together with *Auffassung* ("understanding," "comprehension") and *Darstellung* ("presentation"), is a major category for Baur's description of the work of the historian.

The basic presupposition of speculative thinking is a coherence between Absolute Truth (the reality of which is affirmed) and *consciousness* of the Absolute. This coherence is grounded in the nature of the Absolute itself. Absolute Truth "would not be the Absolute were it not

41. Cf. the following definition of speculative method in *Dreieinigkeit und Menschwerdung Gottes*, I, xix: "The nature of speculation is . . . rational reflection [*die denkende Betrachtung*] upon the object with which one is concerned; it is the posturing of consciousness in relation to the object in such fashion that the object appears as that which it really is; it is the striving to place oneself in the objective course of the subject matter itself and to follow it in all the moments in which it carries itself forward."

42. *Epochs*, 241. Cf. *LHD*, 335.

43. Hans-Georg Gadamer, *Wahrheit und Methode: Grundzüge einer philosophischen Hermeneutik* (2nd ed., Tübingen, 1965), 441–42. He then attempts to show that language as such has a speculative structure, and therefore is the medium of hermeneutical experience. (*Ibid.*, 442–51.)

the Absolute for subjective consciousness as well." Spirit accomplishes itself (becomes Absolute Spirit) in the coming-to-consciousness of finite spirituality, which is a moment in the process of being-in-and-for-itself (*an-und-für-sich-Sein*) of Absolute Spirit. "The speculative standpoint is concerned with the consciousness of the Absolute; but the subject can be conscious of the Absolute only because it is essential to the Absolute itself to give this consciousness." Hence it can be said that *knowledge* of the Absolute is the Absolute itself.[44] The movement from interpreter to subject matter is a movement in *critical* thinking, for it is evident, at least since Kant, that reality is grasped, not in raw immediacy, but only as it is filtered through the medium of consciousness and the critical categories of the mind, categories that are intended precisely to free the knower from the confusion of his own subjectivity with what is given in experience.[45] Critical thinking is required because our apprehension of the given is always inescapably conditioned by our subjectivity of vantage point and the relativity of our position in space and time (it is precisely this that requires church history to be rewritten from each new theological perspective). But at the same time the movement represented by critical thinking is embraced by a more "essential" or "primordial" form of thinking (to employ for the moment a Heideggerian terminology), a "rethinking" (*Nachdenken*) in which the historian traces or follows (*nachgehen*) the objective, essential course of the subject matter in such fashion that the subject matter presents itself rather than remaining merely an object of human conceptualization. Speculative thinking, properly understood, includes simultaneously both elements in the dialectic of thinking—the *critical* movement from consciousness through text to subject matter, and the *essential* movement from subject matter to consciousness. Speculative thinking, in other words, embraces both elements in the hermeneutical circle by which understanding is accomplished. Speculation *is* hermeneutical in character; and hermeneutic, for Baur, is accomplished by the speculative method. Such a method, furthermore, is "phenomenological," for it intends, by means of a critical movement from consciousness to subject matter, to permit the subject matter, the given, to "appear," to present itself to the knower as it is in itself. Only by means of speculation can the genuine *objectivity* of the subject matter be grasped in such fashion that it is not something simply

44. *LHD*, 364.
45. Cf. *Lehrbuch der christlichen Dogmengeschichte* (1st ed.), ix–x (quoted below, 364, n. 45).

alien and extrinsic to consciousness—e.g., the external unity of ecclesiastical dogma—but rather *intrinsic* to its very nature, the ground of its
own being as finite Spirit. That which presents itself phenomenologically
does so as a datum of consciousness. Hence Baur's method can be characterized both as a speculative hermeneutic and as a critico-idealistic
phenomenology.[46]

46. The speculative-hermeneutical circle, as conceived by Baur, can be summarized somewhat schematically as follows: historical understanding (*Auffassung*)
or reflection (*Betrachtung*) is accomplished by the movement from critical thinking,
through which the interpreter transposes himself (*sich hineinstellen, sich versetzen,
eindringen, eingehen*) into the subject matter (*die Sache*), to essential thinking,
which reproduces, rethinks, or re-presents (*reproduciren, nachdenken, darstellen*)
the inner, essential continuity (*der innere wesentliche Zusammenhang*) of the given
of history (*das geschichtliche Gegebene*), a thinking which follows or traces
(*folgen, nachgehen*) the objective course of the *Sache* as it moves itself forward
(*sich selbst fortbewegt*), in such fashion that the *Sache* is permitted to present
itself or to appear as that which it really is (*als das erscheint, was es wirklich ist*).
The description of the second of these elements in the speculative process as "essential thinking" (*wesentliches Denken*) is of course dependent upon Heidegger; but
there is some warrant for it in Baur himself, since it is the "inner essential (*wesent-
lich*) continuity" of the *Sache* that is to be made manifest in such a *Nachdenken*.
Baur himself describes the first element in the speculative process as "critical" in
character. (For the texts in which this technical terminology appears, see *The
Formation of Historical Theology*, 162–69. Of special importance are *Epochs*,
46–48, 241; *LHD*, 283, 305–306, 335–36; *Dreieinigkeit und Menschwerdung
Gottes*, I, xviii–xix; and *Lehrbuch der christlichen Dogmengeschichte* [1st ed.],
ix–x.) The similarity in both terminology and point of view between Baur and
Dilthey is worth noting. Instead of *Auffassung* and *Betrachtung*, Dilthey normally
uses *Verstehen* (although *Auffassung* often serves as a synonym for *Verstehen* in
the Dilthey corpus). In place of *sich hineinstellen* and *sich versetzen*, Dilthey uses a
similar term, *sich hineinversetzen;* and in place of *nachdenken* and *nachgehen*, he
employs *nachbilden* and *nacherleben*. (Cf. Wilhelm Dilthey, *Gesammelte Schriften*,
VII [4th ed., Stuttgart, 1958], 213–16, 233–34, 261–62). The shift in terminology, especially from *nachdenken* to *nacherleben*, reflects Dilthey's movement
away from an idealistic to a more broadly experiential or empirical framework, and
his interest in individual human lives rather than in Spirit as the given of history.
(In his latest writings, however, Dilthey returns to a more idealistic conception of
"life" as "Spirit.")
   Concerning the phenomenological character of speculative thinking, Baur himself
says that history—specifically, the history of dogma—is to be understood as a
"phenomenology" of consciousness, for it confronts the one, unchanging given of
theology—the truth of reconciliation—only in the changing modes of dogmatic consciousness. In the Introduction to *Dreieinigkeit und Menschwerdung Gottes*, I, 107,
he explains the nature of "development" in the history of dogma as follows:
"Dogma in itself remains the same; but the posture of consciousness in relation to
dogma differs in each period, and the moments that make up this difference determine the character of the periods [of dogmatic development]. The whole history of
dogma is to be comprehended from the point of view of phenomenology."

As thus conceived, a speculative method would transcend and indeed heal the antithesis between Catholic and Protestant conceptions of historical theology dominant since the Reformation. It is quite clear from concluding introductory materials in both the *Lectures* and the *Lehrbuch der christlichen Dogmengeschichte*, as well as from the early monograph, *Der Gegensatz des Katholicismus und Protestantismus*, that Baur regards the future of theology as resting not simply with Protestantism, but only with a Protestantism that has appropriated for itself the authentic Catholic insistence upon the "objective unity" or "universal principle" that underlies the various and individual phenomena of history—hence a Protestantism that transcends rationalistic subjectivism. Catholicism has grasped the objectivity and unity of the church's history. But it conceives of an objectivity that is extrinsic to history, one that is laid upon it from above, by virtue of the supernaturalistic world-view that underlies Catholic historiography; and the unity is such as not to permit genuine diversity, novelty, and freedom in historical development. Conversely, Protestantism has grasped the subjectivity and diversity of the church's history. But it is a subjectivity that readily collapses into subjectivism, and a diversity that has lost the underlying unity. "The one-sided, restricted, and limited character of these two opposing and mutually self-negating vantage points can be transcended only in the Absolute of the speculative conception." [47]

On this basis it is now possible to understand more fully the meaning of the fundamental category, "Spirit" (*Geist*), as Baur learned it from Hegel. An important clue is to be found in Baur's criticism of Neander's attempt to locate the ultimate basis of dogmatic development in "the universality of human nature." For Neander (as well as for Schleiermacher), human nature subsists only in single individuals, and history itself is made up of a network of interacting individualities. Hence the universality of human nature, which Neander proposes as the principle of the movement of history, is merely an abstraction, a classification of discrete and autonomous entities. In itself, it has no reality; it is a psychological, not an ontological category. The principle of the movement of history must rather be understood as "the *concrete* universal, thinking Spirit, whose immanent moving principle is in the nature of thinking itself, and which strives toward the freedom of its self-consciousness in

---

47. LHD, 362–64; *Lehrbuch der christlichen Dogmengeschichte* (3rd ed.), 55–58 (quoted below, 363); and *Der Gegensatz des Katholicismus und Protestantismus*, 422–36.

the single individuals who are the living members of the organism of history." The absolute truth contained in the thinking of Spirit transcends the contingent forms assumed by this thinking in the consciousness of individuals.[48]

Thinking Spirit, as the concrete universal, is the "organism of history," to which single individuals are subordinated as "living members." It is a category that transcends human subjectivity; it is the concrete, fundamental, universal reality in which human existence is grounded. Spirit is that which *is;* it is Being-itself, the Being-process by which beings are and history is founded. The process of Being subsists in knowing *(Wissen)* or consciousness *(Bewusstsein)*; it is constituted by the dialectic of thinking *(das Denken)*. To be is to think, to know, to-be-conscious *(Bewusst-sein)*. "Thinking" is not to be understood as lifeless abstraction; it is rather that which constitutes the vitality, the historicity, the concreteness of Spirit. God is Absolute Spirit, infinite and eternal consciousness. But man also is Spirit, finite Spirit, finite consciousness—which is, however, *implicitly* identical with infinite consciousness. This identity became *virtually* explicit in Jesus Christ, who thus inaugurates the final or absolute *epoch* of world history; and it will become *universally* explicit in the final consummation of humanity and the cosmos in God. Man in his *actual* state is not one with God but is estranged from him; the implicit unity of divine and human Spirit is man's destiny or *telos*, not his present condition.[49]

Hence "Spirit" is a broader and more fundamental category than either "God" or "man." [50] It describes that quality of conscious Being which God and man have in common, yet exemplify in different modes. God and man are bound together in the nature of Spirit. Spirit actualizes itself in the becoming-explicit of their implicit unity and interdependent reciprocity. Reconciliation, according to Hegel, is accomplished by "the spiritualization of man, or coordinately, [by] Spirit becoming actual through its embodiment in an existing being, in man. Absolute Spirit comes into existence in history in its progressive self-reflection in human consciousness. It is the nature of Spirit . . . to be 'for Spirit,' in the 'true infinite' of self-reflection." [51] "Spirit is . . . the living process in

---

48. *LHD*, 289–90. Italics in the quotation are mine.

49. Cf. Stephen D. Crites, "The Gospel According to Hegel," *The Journal of Religion*, XLVI (April 1966), 248, 250, 255, 258–59.

50. It is the explicit recognition of this that I find lacking in Geiger. See above, 6, n. 10.

51. Crites, *loc. cit.,* 250.

which the *implicit* [*an sich*] unity of the divine and human nature becomes *explicit* [*für sich*], is brought forth." [52] History, says Baur, is the work of Eternal Spirit; it is "the eternally clear mirror in which Spirit perceives itself, views its own image, in order to be what it is in itself [*an sich*] for itself [*für sich*] as well, for its own consciousness, and to know itself as the moving power of historical becoming." [53] To indicate the distinctive meaning of the term *Geist* in Baur's usage, it will be translated consistently in the texts included in this volume as "Spirit" with a capital *S*, including the many instances where Baur refers to Spirit in its human, finite, subjective modality.

At this point we can perhaps understand more fully Baur's place in the history of hermeneutic. He sought to transcend the romanticism of Schleiermacher's hermeneutic—its psychologism, subjectivism, and individualism, especially as exemplified in the church historiography of Neander, and only partially modified later in Dilthey's theory of historical understanding—by developing a conception of the historical process as a whole, a theology of universal history,[54] on the basis of which the relation between the past text and the present interpreter could be properly understood. On the one hand, the text itself must be understood in its historical context, its *Sitz-im-Leben*, and in its distance from the present—a fact which Schleiermacher tended to ignore, as a result of his conception of psychological immediacy, but which Baur stressed in his emphasis on historical mediation of a text and in the development of what he called "tendency criticism"—the critical endeavor to establish the historical milieu and theological orientation of the text vis-à-vis its content, other texts, and the history of tradition.[55] On the other hand, both text and interpreter are encompassed by a more comprehensive reality, the life of Spirit in history, which is actualized in the process of

52. G. W. F. Hegel, *Vorlesungen über die Philosophie der Religion* (ed. Georg Lasson; Leipzig, 1925–30), III(1), 38; quoted in Crites, *loc. cit.*, 250.

53. *Lehrbuch der christlichen Dogmengeschichte* (3rd ed.), 59, quoted below and discussed, 365, n. 45. See also *Dreieinigkeit und Menschwerdung Gottes*, xix.

54. Cf. Wolfhart Pannenberg, "Hermeneutik und Universalgeschichte," *ZThK*, LX (August 1963), 90–121. My reflections in this and the following paragraphs have been occasioned by this article. See also James M. Robinson's treatment of the history of hermeneutic in *The New Hermeneutic* (ed. J. M. Robinson and John B. Cobb, Jr.; New York, 1964), 1–77.

55. Cf. Baur's criticism of Schleiermacher's "abstract literary criticism" of the Gospels and his failure to develop a truly "historical comprehension" of the biblical texts, in *Kritische Untersuchungen über die kanonischen Evangelien*, 28–40. On "tendency criticism," see *ibid.*, 71–76, and *The Formation of Historical Theology*, 196–201.

thinking. The task of the interpreter is to participate in the thinking of Spirit of which the text is a concrete expression. The "horizons" of both text and interpreter are encompassed by a more comprehensive horizon, that of history as it is constituted by the self-mediation of Absolute Spirit. On the basis of this encompassing horizon, the interpreter is able to *comprehend* (*auffassen*) the subject matter of the text, the reality to which it refers, without simply reducing the text's peculiar embodiment of this reality to an aspect of the interpreter's own self-understanding, thus obliterating the autonomy of the past, which for Baur clearly has a priority and independence over against the present; the past is that *from which* the present attains self-understanding when the past is mediated with the present by means of historical thinking.[56]

The medium in which "comprehension" or "understanding" (*Auffassung*) is accomplished is thinking (*Denken*). As the process of the self-expression, self-mediation, or self-manifestation of Spirit (in which the interpreter participates "speculatively"), thinking can be regarded as a formal equivalent to language (*Sprache*) in its relation to Being (*Sein*) for the hermeneutic of Heidegger and those influenced by him—when language is understood in its fundamental sense as *Logos*, the process or power of gathering into presence and hence of making manifest or letting-be-seen, which functions as a basic ontological structure or "existential" of Dasein's Being-in-the-world. Likewise, Idea (or concept) and speech (*Sprechen*) have similar functions, as the concrete, outward expressions in human activity of thinking and "presencing" (language as *Logos*) respectively. The *spoken* word is to serve as the instrument of *Logos*, whereby Being comes to expression, just as Spirit actualizes itself historically in the Ideas or concepts that serve as the tools of its life-in-thinking. Hence, *Geist, Denken,* and *Idee* (*Begriff*) stand in the same structural relation to one another for Hegel and Baur, and have the same relative functions, as *Sein, Sprache* as *Logos,* and *Sprechen* do for a Heideggerian phenomenology of language.[57]

56. Cf. *Paulus, der Apostel Jesu Christi,* I, 4; and *Die christliche Lehre von der Versöhnung,* vii.

57. Heidegger himself hints at this correspondence in "Hegels Begriff der Erfahrung," *Holzwege* (Frankfurt, 1950), 105–92; cf. William J. Richardson's masterful analysis in *Heidegger: Through Phenomenology to Thought* (The Hague, 1963), 331–60, especially 334–39, 350–53, 355–58. With neither Hegel nor Heidegger is Spirit or Being to be thought of as a metaphysical ground or first cause somehow residing "behind" thinking or *Logos*. Rather, Spirit for Hegel, very much like Being for Heidegger, *is* the event of coming to consciousness (for Heidegger, the coming

This correspondence helps to account for Baur's anticipation in an idealistic framework of some of the themes of the new hermeneutic: its stress on the interpreter's participation in the self-unveiling of the sub-ject matter (*die Sache*) by his again bringing to expression in his own speaking and thinking the *Sache* of the text; the importance of "primal" or "essential" thinking as an element in historical understanding (the movement from subject matter to text to interpreter, correlative with the "critical" movement from interpreter to text to subject matter); hence the essential fusion of historical-critical and participative-responsive functions in the hermeneutical circle that constitutes the total process of understanding; the concomitant transcendence of the subjec-tivism and anthropocentrism—the "objectifying thinking"—of the older hermeneutic; and finally the conception of language itself (or, in Baur's framework, of "thinking" itself) as interpretation. At the same time, Baur brought his hermeneutic into the "horizon" of a comprehensive theology of history, which served as its speculative foundation. His theology of history, although deeply indebted to Hegel, represented a modification of the latter at two important points. First, he stressed the *finitude* or *historicity* of the thinking of human Spirit, by pointing to the relative vantage point of the historian, the need to base historical interpretations on empirical data,[58] and the fact that historical knowl-edge can never simply be transcended in the absolute knowledge of philosophy,[59] any more than that the historicity of the Christian faith can be absorbed into philosophical *gnosis*. Second, he insisted against Hegel upon the *openness* of the future. He did not believe that the history of theology and philosophy had come to an end with Hegel's system, but that they would indeed continue beyond the Hegelian syn-

---

to presence) by which beings are. The difference between them is that Hegel ulti-mately identifies God and (Absolute) Spirit, whereas Heidegger does not identify God and Being. This does not mean for Hegel, as Heidegger implies in "Die onto-theo-logische Verfassung der Metaphysik," *Identität und Differenz* (Pfullingen, 1957), that Spirit finally becomes a metaphysical object after all, but rather that God is defined as the universal consciousness-process in which finite human spirituality shares—which is the source of the difficulty in understanding God as "personal" (in the biblical sense) in Hegel's scheme. Heidegger is correct in recognizing that God and Spirit/Being cannot simply be identified. Being is rather to be understood as the *Word* of God.

58. On these two points, see above, 12, and below, 32.

59. Indeed, Baur believed that in the era following Hegel theology must turn to historical-critical questions with renewed vigor. Cf. *Vorlesungen über die christliche Dogmengeschichte*, III, 356.

thesis in quite powerful antitheses, which already were apparent. He left the future open and renounced any claim to prophecy.[60]

With this analysis of Baur's general hermeneutical principles as background, it is now possible to examine his application of these principles to the study of the history of dogma and church history. We turn first to the history of dogma. His treatment of this discipline involves an analysis of the function of dogma in relation to Spirit, which in turn is based on a conception of "revelation" as the self-manifestation of Absolute Spirit in and to finite human Spirit. Although Baur ordinarily avoids the category of "revelation" because of its supernaturalistic connotation, it is not entirely excluded from his theology. He says, for example, that "revelation is an act of Spirit in which an objective reality confronts subjective consciousness as an immediate given, and becomes for the subject the object of a faith whose content is the Absolute Idea. Moved by the power of the Absolute Idea, the entire thinking activity of the subject feels the compulsion to become absorbed into this objective reality, given as an immediate divine power, in order to bring its content into consciousness—as it were, to lay it out in all its components for the representative consciousness." [61] Revelation, in fact, marks the essential point of difference between religion and philosophy. "It is characteristic of religion that Spirit knows the truth which is the content of religion only as something received, something absolutely given—an external revelation which, even though it contains nothing in contradiction to thinking reason, nevertheless has at least its historical origin outside of reason; and on this account it exists only in the form of representation, as something immediate, which is not yet mediated with thinking consciousness. In philosophy, on the other hand, Spirit knows the truth as something immanent to itself, as the result of its own thinking." [62] The constant threat to philosophy is subjectivism, the confusion of truth

60. See *LHD*, 265; *Vorlesungen über die christlichen Dogmengeschichte*, III, 359. See also Heinz Liebing, "Historical-Critical Theology: In Commemoration of the One Hundredth Anniversary of the Death of Ferdinand Christian Baur, December 2, 1960," *Journal for Theology and the Church*, III (1967), 68. These modifications are similar to those proposed by Pannenberg as essential to the appropriation of Hegel's philosophy of history to contemporary hermenuetic; see *loc. cit.*, 109–110, 116, 120–21. Baur's reasons for modifying Hegel are not identical with Pannenberg's, however, nor does he share the latter's constructive interests in a theology of universal history oriented to the future. Rather, his modifications of Hegel represent his instincts and his caution as a historian, and his sense for the radical historicity of human experience.

61. *LHD*, 298; cf. *Paulus, der Apostel Jesu Christi*, II, 175–77; and *The Formation of Historical Theology*, 120–21.

62. *LHD*, 320.

with the estranged subjectivity of finite Spirit. Religion, and above all Christianity as the absolute religion, transcends the subjectivism of philosophy in its claim that truth is not simply immanent to man but is rather given to him by God in a revelatory historical event that stands outside subjective consciousness, confronting the latter with the truth of its own being. Christianity frees Spirit from everything particular and subjective, bringing it into unity with the Universal, the Absolute, which is the principle of Christianity. It occasions "a revolution out of subjectivity into the Objective, into Being itself, i.e., a return to God. Consequently, Christianity appeared in the world not as philosophy but as religion. As divine revelation in the form of religion it was something absolutely given, which in its immediacy could be the object not of thinking and knowing but above all only of faith. Thus Christian dogma has its starting point in faith. It is itself faith in a representational mode; and all thinking connected with dogma has its final, determinative principle only in faith, regardless of how free it might otherwise be." [63]

If the danger to philosophy is that of subjectivism, then the danger to a religion of revelation is that of an unmediated objectivism. The given of revelation must not be allowed to rest in the immediacy of *representation* (*Vorstellung*) and unreflective belief, but must be mediated with subjective consciousness through a reflexive articulation in thinking, in the process of which the reality of revelation, the confrontation of Spirit with Spirit, is perpetuated and consummated. This is the function of Christian dogma, which, although it remains ultimately bound to the content of faith, nevertheless brings dialectic to bear upon this content, thus mediating it with the subjectivity of the believer. The task of dogma is to effect a transition from belief as immediate assent to extrinsic truth, to faith as the co-presence in consciousness of divine and human Spirit (faith in its authentically Protestant conception).

Baur's conception of dogma in relation to Spirit can perhaps best be summarized by saying that it is the fundamental means by which human Spirit assimilates into consciousness the absolute truth of Infinite Spirit, a truth that is mediated, according to Christian faith, by a historical revelation with its source and center in the person of Christ. The task of Spirit is to assimilate into subjective consciousness the objective truth conceptually formulated in dogma, a truth not alien to Spirit but rather of its very essence.[64] By virtue of its cognitive character, its affinity to

63. *LHD*, 329, 322–23; cf. "Das christliche des Platonismus oder Sokrates und Christus," *TZTh*, X:3 (1837), 91, 153–54.
64. See especially *LHD*, 305–306; also 298, 333.

the rational nature of Spirit, it can be said that dogma is the *basic* manifestation of the self-revelation of Absolute Spirit in history. It is the conceptual articulation of a fundamentally conceptual reality. Hence in
dogma the church finds the first and most important of the "forms" of
its historical life. On the basis of traditional usage, Baur says, the term
"dogmas" is to be understood to mean "the doctrines or teachings
[*Lehren*] of the Christian faith, in so far as they contain the absolute
Christian truth." Dogma is the conceptual formulation of the absolute
truth of Christian faith, a formulation that must be stated as precisely as
possible in virtue of the absolute significance of its content. It is the
reflexive articulation of faith's experience of being confronted—both in
history and in consciousness—by the Absolute, a confrontation that
transpires in the event of revelation.[65]

"Dogmatics" is a form of dogma; concretely, it represents the "system
of dogmas" (or doctrines) determining and expressing the content of
Christian faith for a given age. A dogmatic system accomplishes its task
by bringing to a halt for the moment the ceaseless movement of the history of dogma, and by giving expression to "the constant element in the
true Christian consciousness," "its immanent substantial content within
the variable forms of the changing consciousness of the times." Dogmatics would be impossible "without the awareness that something firm
and enduring exists in the midst of what is constantly changing and moving." Its task is to give expression to this enduring content—what Baur
sometimes calls "the one implicit dogma" or "the one Christian consciousness"—as it takes form around a specific dogmatic focal point in a given
age (such as the doctrine of the Trinity for the third century, the doctrine of sin for Augustine, and the doctrine of man for nineteenth-
century Protestantism), and in a conceptuality intelligible to the era at
hand. A dogmatic system succeeds so far as it articulates the foci of dogmatic consciousness for the time in which it stands, which means that it
should never simply be an aggregate of historical materials, an *ersatz*
history of dogma, as are so many putative dogmatics. On the other hand,
the dogmatician must recognize "that everything permanent and enduring is only temporary, and that what for the present seems to have a still
firm solidity must sooner or later revert to the flux of history." This
means that dogmatic systems must be reformulated around new foci and
with new categories for each new age. Baur judges that Schleiermacher
is the contemporary dogmatician who most adequately recognizes both
the relativity of dogmatics and its task of bringing to expression the en-

65. Cf. *LHD*, 269–70.

during truth of the Christian faith by formulating it in language and with a systematic focus intelligible to the Christian and cultural consciousness of his era.[66]

If dogma cannot be understood apart from its systematic formulation in dogmatics, then the "history of dogmatics" belongs within the history of dogma as one of its essential concerns. The history of dogma, in other words, is not limited to the official creeds, confessions, and symbols of the church, but includes theology in all its forms. For Baur, the history of dogma really encompasses the history of Christian thought as a whole—the continuous process by which the given of revelation is reflexively articulated in the thinking of finite Spirit, first objectively in abstract formulas, but then subjectively as it is progressively mediated with the self-consciousness of Spirit. In other words, Baur possessed a much broader conception of the nature of dogma and its historical range than did most of his contemporaries or successors. For example, he did not regard "dogma" as having come to an end with the Reformation, as did Harnack (who restricted the term to a formal, technical meaning), but rather considered the history of dogma (understood as the history of Christian thought in all its forms) to continue without interruption into his own time. Nor did he believe that the history of Christian dogma (or theology) had been brought to an end with Hegel's philosophy. Rather theology and philosophy were now to be seen in a new and much more essential connection, one in which philosophy shares the content of theology, and theology the form of philosophy. But this is only a stage in an ongoing process, the future of which is beyond anticipation.[67]

I have already suggested that the task of dogma, according to Baur, is to effect a transition from one form of faith to another—from faith as unmediated assent to a network of objectively formulated teachings (faith as a container to be filled with objects of belief), to faith as the co-presence in consciousness of divine and human Spirit (faith as an event of spiritual, conscious, free encounter).[68] The stages in the history of dogma are to be interpreted as the progressive realization of this task. This is most clearly apparent from the way Baur defines the three major periods in the history of dogma in his *Lehrbuch der christlichen Dogmengeschichte:* the dogma of the ancient church—"the substantiality of dogma"; the dogma of the Middle Ages—"the dogma of self-

66. Cf. *LHD,* 262–65, 276–78, 280, 318.

67. *LHD,* 271, 280, 305, 333–34; cf. also *Lehrbuch der christlichen Dogmengeschichte* (3rd ed.), 355–56, and *The Formation of Historical Theology,* 95, 172, 242.

68. See *LHD,* especially 315; also 329, 343.

reflective consciousness"; and the dogma of the "recent period" (beginning with the Reformation)—"dogma and free self-consciousness." By
means of this approach, both the continuity in dogmatic development
and its genuine novelty and progression are grasped. The first period
—that of the "substantiality of dogma," or, as Baur sometimes puts it,
of "unmediated objectivity"—represents the richest and most creative
flowering of dogmatic reflection of all the eras in the church's history; in
the first six centuries the major doctrinal foundations of the Christian
faith achieve conceptual clarity and definition. But at the same time
these doctrines are given expression in abstract, objectivizing formulas
that confront the believer as something extrinsic, to be accepted on the
authority of the church rather than understood reflexively. Dogma is
"substantial" in character—a body of ecclesiastical propositions, a content to be assimilated in the assent of faith. "The determinations in which
dogma is given specific expression, the propositions of faith that give it a
fixed form, obtain an authority that binds the subject, and from which
he can no longer withhold recognition. This authority confronts him as
an objectivity within himself, which, even if it is only of his own making, increasingly wrests from him an independent power and constricts
his free movement to ever narrower limits." [69] Scholasticism (the dogma
of the Middle Ages) represents a significant attempt to alter this situation, "to remove dogma from the externality and immediacy it possessed
as an absolute given, resting on the bare authority of ecclesiastical faith,
and to place it in subjective consciousness, to mediate it with consciousness." The "moving principle" of scholasticism is the "liberation of self-
consciousness in its relation to dogma," the mediation of dogma with
consciousness, the gradual penetration of piety by dialectic. But the
efforts of scholasticism in this direction remained for the most part
"purely formal" in character—a logical clarification of terms, more
precise determination of content through distinctions, enumeration of
arguments and counter-arguments in respect to every conceivable point.
Dogma itself remained essentially unaltered, "an unmediated objectivity,
simply a thing absolutely given, a solid, impenetrable authority into
which the subject could never enter with the power of his self-
consciousness," indeed more oppressive than before by virtue of scholasticism's massive systematization of dogmatic materials.[70]

The Reformation and the period of dogmatic development beginning
with it represent the completion of the process already initiated by the

69. *LHD*, 299–300, 309–310; quotation from 299.   70. *LHD*, 300–302, 311.

scholastic theologians (hence the high significance of the latter for the history of dogma). "The basic conception by which scholasticism itself was moved—without, to be sure, being able to bring the actual task clearly into consciousness—was the quite correct supposition that an understanding of dogma was possible. An inner bond of unity must exist between the truth of dogma and the self-consciousness of Spirit." [71] This "inner bond of unity" becomes a reality in the act of faith, now understood by Protestantism as the unity in consciousness of the human subject and the divine truth of reconciliation. In faith, consciousness and truth freely cohere. The subject no longer knows the truth of the Gospel—the reconciliation between man and God—as something imposed upon him extrinsically by ecclesiastical tradition and authority, but rather as the truth of his own being. Faith in the Protestant sense "is the essential principle by which the subject frees himself from that *outward* objectivity which never lets him come to himself, and by which he raises himself to free, self-conscious subjecthood." [72] In the understanding of faith awakened by Protestantism, objectivity is fully mediated by subjectivity for the first time. For Protestantism, the divine authority of Scripture (which replaces the authority of tradition and magisterium) and the freedom of faith are essentially correlative principles. The authority of Scripture "could only rest on the assumption that the subject, in the consciousness of his subjective freedom, might acknowledge as true only what was given as true in his thinking reason. Thus through the Reformation the subject obtained for the first time the consciousness of his freedom, or the freedom of his self-consciousness, in relation to dogma. Dogma no longer confronted him in its externality and with the externally imposed authority of ecclesiastical doctrine; rather, it derived its significance only from the subject's knowing himself to be internally at one with divine truth, which he recognized as the essential content of dogma." [73]

I have said that Baur's analysis of Spirit in his *History of Dogma*, and his conception of dogma as the primary objectification of Spirit in history, serve as the hermeneutical key to his treatment of church history, the larger whole in which the history of dogma is a crucial element. When Baur turned his attention more fully to the study of church-

71. *LHD*, 303.

72. *Vorlesungen über die christliche Dogmengeschichte*, III, 5 (italics mine); cf. *Epochs*, 249.

73. *LHD*, 303–304, 311. On Baur's understanding of faith, see *The Formation of Historical Theology*, 119–21, 174–81, 255–56.

historical method and the task of writing a church history, he developed a new or at least a broader conceptuality for describing the historicity of the church—one based, however, upon his earlier analysis of Spirit and dogma. The church as a historical reality is constituted, he proposed, by an essential dialectic between "Idea" and "manifestation."

"Idea" as a category of historical interpretation was first brought into systematic usage in *The Epochs of Church Historiography*, although Baur had originally learned it from Schleiermacher and Schelling and had employed it in some of his early, pre-Hegelian writings.[74] The category is now enriched and fleshed out by the Hegelian analysis of Spirit, appropriated and refined by Baur in his "middle period" (1833–47). An "Idea" (*Idee*)[75] is the self-expression of Spirit; it is the conceptual instrument by which Spirit thinks and thus lives. Since thinking is a process that transpires concretely, historically, Idea constitutes the life, the substantial reality, of history. The *moving* Idea of history, that which constitutes its foundation and essence, is the self-expression of God as Absolute Spirit, although the Ideas of finite Spirit are also a vital part of the total matrix of history. History is the conceptual expression of God and man together. It is important to recognize that, according to Baur, Ideas do not exist as disembodied abstractions, but only as ingredients in concrete historical "forms" or "manifestations." One must immerse oneself in the materials of history in order to know the Idea not as an "abstract concept" but only as it acquires "the concreteness by which it first becomes a true universal—in the unity of the particular with the universal." The historian must not impose *a priori* and abstract theories upon the concrete data of history, for he has access to the underlying meaning and movements of history only by means of a slow and painful analysis of these data. His interpretive principles are not "read into" history but are learned from it. There is, in other words, a strongly empirical or phenomenological basis for Baur's speculative hermeneutic. But on the other hand he makes it clear that the Idea cannot *simply* be "abstracted" from the particular, even though it never can be perceived apart from the particular. The historian brings to the data at least a preliminary conception of the total historical process, representing his theological and philosophical "standpoint," which both informs and is reciprocally modified and enriched by his detailed analysis of the data. As a

74. Cf. *The Formation of Historical Theology*, 92–93.
75. To indicate the distinctive and systematic usage of *Idee*, it will be translated in the texts to follow as "Idea" with a capital *I*.

category of historical interpretation, Idea functions as the "universal" (or the "universal principle") by which the underlying unity and meaning of history can be fathomed in its individual parts.[76]

The relation between Idea and manifestation can best be understood as that of a distinction-within-unity. The Catholic view of the church tended to dissolve the distinction and simply to identify the historical forms of the church with its ideal essence, thus supernaturalizing the church and lifting it entirely out of the realm of history. The danger in the Protestant tendency was of dissolving the unity, thus treating the visible, empirical church as a purely historical phenomenon, radically separated from the invisible, ideal church. The identification of Idea and manifestation produced a dualism between a supernaturalized church and profane, pagan history—the characteristic dualism of old Catholic historiography. The dissolving of the relation between Idea and manifestation produced another form of dualism, that between the invisible and the visible church, which was characteristic in different forms of Protestant orthodoxy and rationalism. Both views need to be transcended in a conception that neither *identifies* the Idea of the church with the historical phenomena in which alone it lives and moves, nor *separates* it from them. The relation is a dialectical one. The Idea is "freely related" to the manifestations "in the same proportion that it stands above" them.[77]

The history of the Christian church is the movement of the Idea of the church; it is that continuity of historical manifestations in which the Idea of Christianity progressively embodies and thus actualizes itself. This is the basis for the internal coherence of church history.[78] The Idea of Christianity is to be understood as the Idea of reconciliation or of divine-human unity and union, the Idea of God-manhood, as perceived originally and definitively in the person of Christ, in the fullest perfection conceivable for a single individual. This unity and union of God and man is the "substantial content of the historical development of the Christian church." It is realized for Christian consciousness in various "forms" which constitute the historical life of the church, forms of the absolute Idea of Christianity. The relative primacy of these forms marks the historical development of the church and the different periods into which it is divided. It would probably be accurate to say that for Baur

76. *Epochs*, 101, 205, 241–42, 256–57.
77. See *Epochs*, 242–43, 245–53; quotation from 248.
78. *Epochs*, 241–42; cf. *Vorlesungen über die christliche Dogmengeschichte*, III, 283–84.

the church itself is the fundamental historical form of the Idea of Christianity,[79] and that in turn its life is made up of certain fundamental elements, which, by virtue of their shifting primacy relative to one another, define the several phases of church history. The two fundamental church-historical forms are dogma on the one hand and polity—the hierarchical-institutional structure of the church—on the other. The shift in primacy between these two forms marks the transition from the ancient to the medieval periods in church history. In the third major period of Christianity, that of the Reformation and post-Reformation eras, the church is split into rival understandings of the proper relation between Idea and manifestation. In Catholicism, the traditional conception of dogma and hierarchy is perpetuated, whereas in Protestantism dogma assumes a new form, that of the free self-consciousness of faith; and it could be said, although Baur does not put it quite this way, that in Protestantism the major form in which the Idea of divine-human unity is actualized is that of faith, now understood as the unity in consciousness of the human subject and the divine truth of reconciliation. Indeed, faith would seem to be the form most adequate to this content. In addition to the major forms of polity and dogma (including dogma in the form of faith), there are several subordinate manifestations of the Christian Idea that are essential to the church's life in all its periods: worship, the moral life of the community, and the dissemination and curtailment of Christianity (the situation of the church in the world).[80]

It is beyond the scope of this Introduction to show in detail how the interaction between and changes within the major forms of the Idea of Christianity provide the basis for the periodization of the church's historical development. The periods are based, not upon chronological epochs or events in political history, but upon church-historical motifs or "moments" (*Momente*). The first three moments can best be understood as together comprising the originative event of the church, since by means of them the two fundamental elements definitive of its nature are assured: on the one hand, its ideality, universality, or absoluteness—the divine truth of reconciliation, which is its "Idea"; and on the other, its historical positivity and concreteness. These three moments are as follows: the primal emergence of Christianity in the teaching and person of Jesus (in whom the two elements of ideality and positivity are normatively co-present); the assurance of the *ideality* and *universality* of

79. See *LHD*, 261; and *Epochs*, 254.
80. For this paragraph as a whole, see *Epochs*, 244–47, 254–56.

Catholic Christianity against a devolution into Jewish sectarianism, by means of the struggle between Paulinizing and Judaizing tendencies during the century following the death of Christ (up to about A.D. 150); and the assurance of the *historicity* of Catholic Christianity in the struggle against Gnosticism and Montanism during the second century. The first two centuries have, then, a unique and unrepeatable significance in the history of the church. Following this era, Baur's church history is ordered according to the relative primacy and evolving characteristics of dogma and polity, as mentioned above. The era of dogmatic primacy stretches from the New Testament writings (thus embracing chronologically the second and third "moments") to the end of the sixth century; here church history most closely corresponds to the history of dogma. The transition to hierarchical-institutional structure as the dominant form of the church reaches a climax with the papacy of Gregory VII (1073), which inaugurates the era of papal absolutism, by which all elements of church life and thought are profoundly affected. The late-medieval dissolution of the church's political structure anticipates the Reformation and the shift to a new church-historical moment, one marked by the antithesis between Protestant and Catholic forms of the Christian Idea. The implication would seem to be that the next major "moment" in the evolution of the Christian Idea will be some sort of transcendence of this antithesis, although such intimations of future direction are very rare in Baur.[81]

In conclusion, let us note the significance of Baur's approach: the structure by which the history of the Christian church is made intelligible is itself a function of the nature of the church as perceived theologically. The history of the church is not ordered according to external criteria [82] but according to the changing modes of its historicity. Baur's fundamental achievement in church historiography was to recognize the intrinsic connection between the nature of the church, theologically conceived, and its history. By means of the speculative method, he believed, the historical theologian is able to penetrate to the objective real-

81. This survey of Baur's total conception of church-historical development has been synthesized from a number of sources, which are cited in *The Formation of Historical Theology*, 207–12, 251–56. See especially *Epochs*, 244–56, and *An Herrn Dr. Karl Hase*, 82–83, 85. On the transcendence of the Catholic-Protestant antithesis, see *Der Gegensatz des Katholicismus und Protestantismus*, 422–36; *LHD*, 362–64; and *Lehrbuch der christlichen Dogmengeschichte* (3rd ed.), 55–58.

82. See Baur's criticism of Mosheim, Spittler, Planck, and Hase in this regard, *Epochs*, 144–46, 176, 194, 236, 251.

ity of the subject matter itself—the given—and elicit *from it* the criteria
and categories by which he is to order and interpret its history. Church
history is to be viewed as the process of the self-actualization of its
Sache, the Idea of Christianity, the Idea of divine-human unity as perceived in the fullest perfection possible for a single individual in the
person of the church's "founder," Jesus of Nazareth. The speculative
conception of church-historical development must show the essential
connection between this originative event and the church's subsequent
historical forms; it must (against rationalism) elucidate the comprehensive meaning and continuity of church history, while at the same time
describing its genuine novelty and development; and finally it must
transcend the dualism of supernaturalism by perceiving the church, precisely in its historicity, as the self-mediation of God in the Idea of reconciliation, the outward historical patterning of the inward dialectic of
the life of Absolute Spirit. Even if we should wish to quarrel with the
content of Baur's theology of the church and history, as most of us
probably would to a greater or lesser degree, we should still have to
grant that his church historiography as a whole is a unique and impressive attempt to satisfy these self-imposed criteria. A historical theology
of our time that did not address itself to these fundamental questions and
seek to resolve them anew would surely be inadequate to the task and
challenge laid before it.

4. *Translation and Acknowledgments*

In preparing these translations, I have attempted to follow two principles: fidelity to the meaning and style of the original, and creation of a
fluent, idiomatic English text. I am well aware of the difficulties involved. As Gadamer rightly observes, "Every translation that takes seriously its task is both clearer and flatter than the original. Even when it is
a masterful reproduction, it must lack something of the overtones that
reverberate in the original." [83] For translation requires interpretation;
and the interpreted meaning tends to be expressed more directly and
simply, and often just for that reason less subtly, than the original.
Hence it may sometimes be difficult for readers fully to appreciate the
sustained rigor and penetrating, expressive power of Baur's writing—as

83. Hans-Georg Gadamer, *Wahrheit und Methode: Grundzüge einer philosophischen Hermeneutik* (2nd ed., Tübingen, 1965), 364.

well as to discern his occasional obscurities and imprecisions—from the translations that follow. I can only hope that sufficient motivation is provided to go to Baur in the original and to uncover some of the treasures concealed there.[84]

Attention must be given to the translation of certain words with more or less systematic meaning for the author. We have already examined the important terms *Geist* and *Idee*, translated as "Spirit" and "Idea," with initial capitals.[85] *Begriff* is sometimes used in a technical sense similar to *Idee*, to refer to the conceptual expression of thinking Spirit; in these instances it is translated as "concept"; in other instances it is translated as either "concept" or "conception," depending upon the context. *Sache* has usually been translated as "subject matter," so as to distinguish it from *Subject* ("subject") and *Object* ("object"). *Das Denken* has been rendered as "thinking" rather than "thought," in order to convey its relation to the active verb *denken* ("to think") and the adjective *denkend* ("thinking"), and its distinction from the noun *Gedanke* and the past participial form *Gedachte* (both meaning "thought"). "Thinking" (*das Denken*), as used by both Hegel and Baur to describe the life of Spirit, means "the process of thinking" rather than "thoughts" in the sense of static, past, reified ideas. *Erscheinung* contains an ambiguity, inherited from its root, *scheinen*, which can mean either "to shine forth" or "to seem." An *Erscheinung* on the one hand is a fully concrete and tangible, palpable happening, but on the other hand is the visible mani-

---

84. One reason for the neglect of Baur in English has been the unusually poor translations (the only ones to be made from his entire corpus) of two of his major works, *Paulus, der Apostel Jesu Christi*, and *Das Christenthum und die christliche Kirche der drei ersten Jahrhunderte*, issued by the Theological Translation Fund in the 1870's. In fact, the translation of the first volume of *Paul* (London and Edinburgh, 1873) was so bad that the publishers, Williams & Norgate, took the unusual step of prefacing the following note: "The Publishers desire, in issuing the present volume of the Series, to express their consciousness and regret that the translations both of the first, and in some degree the present volume, are not equal to what they had reason to expect. Instead of offering any excuses, they prefer to express their disappointment, and to assure the Subscribers that steps have been taken to insure for the future not only faithful, but readable translations." The volume should never have been published. It was issued in a second edition in 1876, revised by the Rev. Allan Menzies, who also translated the second volume of *Paul* (1875) and edited the translations of *The Church History of the First Three Centuries* (2 vols., London and Edinburgh, 1878–79). The Menzies revisions and translations are an improvement, but they still remain awkward and theologically insensitive. They give the impression that Baur was a wooden thinker and writer, whereas nothing could be further from the truth.

85. See above, 23, 32.

festation of an inward, intangible reality (e.g., the "Idea" of Christianity). "Manifestation" has ordinarily been preferred as best rendering this double meaning, since it is free of the Platonic and Kantian associations that accompany the terms "appearance" and "phenomenon," although occasionally the latter words have been employed where they were more meaningful in the context. Where *Erscheinung* is used in technical association with *Idee*, it is uniformly translated as "manifestation."

Auffassung has been rendered as "comprehension," "understanding," or "interpretation," depending on the context. Its root meaning derives from *fassen*, "to grasp hold of." *Betrachtung*, when employed in such phrases as *die geschichtliche Betrachtung*, is usually translated as "reflection" or "consideration," but in some instances is rendered more loosely as "perspective." As the preceding discussion has shown, both these terms are of hermeneutical significance for Baur. The distinction between *Darstellung* and *Vorstellung* has been preserved by translating the former as "presentation" and the latter as "representation." The author sometimes uses these terms to describe contrasting modes of historical reflection—the one a striving for authentic objectivity, the other a spurious subjectivism. Where this contrast is not at stake, *Darstellung* has often been translated as "portrayal" or "description." The archaic term *Lehrbegriff* (used primarily in reference to the eighteenth-century church historians) has been translated as "doctrine" rather than as "system of doctrine" or "system." *An sich* (literally, "in itself") has often been rendered as "implicit" or "intrinsic"; *für sich* (literally, "for itself"), sometimes as "explicit." *Moment* (or more commonly the plural form, *Momente*) is a term peculiar to German idealism. It is often used to describe the phases in the process by which Spirit comes to be, not only in itself (*an sich*), or for itself (*für sich*) in the other, but in and for itself (*an-und-für-sich-Sein*)—i.e., the process by which Spirit is fully constituted in the dialectic of thinking as the concrete universal. *Moment* can describe either the temporal phases in this process, or the objective elements that constitute the being of Spirit in its own otherness. *Element* is sometimes used as a synonym for *Moment*. These terms have been variously translated as "moment," "element," "component," "phase," or even "motif," depending upon the context. *Das Positive* is also a distinctly idealistic-Hegelian category, referring to the objective, factual, historical character of the phenomena in which Spirit actualizes itself. In its few occurrences in these works, it has been translated as "positivity" (reflecting the cognate German term, *Positivität*) or as "the positive historical element"—of, e.g., Christianity. For the translation of

Bestimmung as "determination," see page 276, note 21. With *bestimmt* I have been somewhat more flexible, rendering it as "specific," "definite," or "determinate." Finally, *Wissenschaft* and *wissenschaftlich* have been translated as "science" and "scientific," intended in the broader sense of the disciplined, critical, and (for Baur) "speculative" acquisition of knowledge (*Wissen*) by a method appropriate to the subject matter at hand. In this sense, theology and the other human studies (the *Geistes-wissenschaften*) are "sciences." Baur believed that an authentically "scientific" theology must acquire the methods of speculative thinking and historical-critical research. Upon occasion I have used a looser rendering for *Wissenschaft*, such as "scholarship" or "discipline."

With a few exceptions, the quotations from Greek and Latin texts in the *Epochs* and the Introduction to the *History of Dogma* are cited by Baur in the original language. They are given here, for the most part, only in English translation. These translations are from standard English editions where they exist. When no English editions are cited in the footnotes, or when such citations are preceded by "cf.", the translations given in the text are mine. In a few instances, Baur has translated the original into German, but the English translations are from a standard English edition or from the original, as the case may be. English translations of German works cited by Baur, where they exist, have been utilized in accordance with the procedure outlined above. Individual words and short phrases in Greek and Latin have been retained in the original with a bracketed English translation immediately following, except where the English would be a mere transcription of the Latin or where the word or phrase has become familiar through repeated use. Titles of books or other writings in German, Latin, and Greek have been translated only if the work itself has been translated or if the meaning of the title is necessary to an understanding of the text.

Frequently I have found it necessary to simplify sentence structure and to break up long paragraphs into shorter segments, in the interests of English style and intelligibility. Chapter subheads for both works are found in the tables of contents but not the texts of the originals. I have introduced them into the texts as well, and have numbered them. The original footnotes in the *Epochs* are Baur's own, whereas some of the footnotes in the *Lectures on the History of Dogma* were provided by F. F. Baur, the editor of that posthumously published volume. Baur's frequent citations of page and volume numbers in the body of his text have been put into footnotes by me without special notation. Standard bibliographical data, such as place of publication and first name or initials of authors, have been added to Baur's references in both text and footnotes without special notation. Footnotes designated as "editorial" ([ED.]) are those in which additional information of any sort other than that mentioned above is provided. I have attempted to provide a brief biographical and bibliographical sketch of each of the church historians and historians of dogma to whom Baur devotes major attention in both documents, since many of these names are unknown to American readers. Here I have relied on standard reference sources, such as *The New Schaff-Herzog Encyclopedia of Religious Knowledge*, the third edition of *Die Religion in Geschichte und Gegenwart,* and the *Allgemeine deutsche Biographie.*

I am indebted to many persons in the preparation of this volume, especially to Professor Claude Welch of the University of Pennsylvania, whose favorable reaction to the initial suggestion of including a volume on Baur in A Library of Protestant Thought helped to get the project under way. Professor Welch and Professors James Hastings Nichols of Princeton Theological Seminary and Jaroslav Pelikan of Yale University constituted an editorial committee on behalf of the Library. They assisted in the selection of texts and have provided valuable guidance in the process of translation itself. They have read the manuscript at various stages and have made many suggestions for improvement. They are not, however, to be held responsible for remaining errors and inadequacies in the translation. Translations from the Greek and Latin texts cited by Baur were prepared by Messrs. James E. Shelton and W. Wayne Reinhardt, graduate students in classics and church history, respectively, at Vanderbilt University. Professor Francis L. Newton, formerly of the Department of Classical Languages and Literatures, assisted in this project. I am indebted to the editorial board of A Library of Protestant Thought, and especially its chairman, Professor John Dillenberger of the Graduate Theological Union, for generous financial assistance; to the Research Council of Vanderbilt University for three grants in aid, which supported my work in several ways; to Vanderbilt Divinity School for helping to cover secretarial costs; to the Reference Department of the Joint University Libraries for obtaining hard-to-find materials on inter-library loan; and to Mrs. Joyce Barrus for her careful typing of a difficult manuscript. I should like, finally, to thank Miss Amy Clampitt for her valuable editorial assistance in improving both the accuracy and the English idiom of the final draft.

PART ONE

❖

The Epochs of Church Historiography

PREFACE

Hitherto, the method of historiography has not sufficiently been made the object of an investigation of its own. Among the scientific endeavors of the present day, interest in historical investigations and presentations occupies no small place; but the more productive our age has been in the area of history, the less it has been thought necessary to reflect on the *how* of historiography. In regard to specialized topics, we can leave aside a general question of this sort, but it becomes all the more significant when we confront the vast extent of history as a whole. Church history has an advantage over general history in that questions concerning the method of historiography become more specific and concrete when applied to the significant and homogeneous phenomena of this more narrowly delimited field. The greater the number of prominent writers who have worked through the same field independently, the more pressing becomes the question as to how they have sought to discharge the common obligation from such different points of view.

The present book has grown out of such considerations. It is an attempt to characterize the epochs of church historiography, in so far as this can be done in a general survey. Three elements come especially into view. Above all, the essential traits of each of the church historians who are to be looked at as major representatives of church historiography must be understood and depicted. Since, however, individual church historians, when compared with one another, have much in common despite all individual differences, and since the closer they stand to one another in time, the more they have a common character, a second important task is that of dividing them into various groups. Finally, because the various major forms of church historiography emerge in the process, the third part of the task here projected is to bring these forms into relation with one another so that in them, as the epochs of church historiography, the whole course of development can be recognized in the inner continuity of its individual moments.

43

The extent to which I may have been successful in discharging this threefold task I shall leave to the expert judgment of those who share my interest in the subject. I readily admit that there will be a great deal to be added and some things even to be corrected in the details concerning the extensive materials to be worked through; and I admit even more that, in accord with the variety of theological points of view, various opinions can arise about the major idea from which I derive the general task of church historiography. But it is just this that I consider to be the major point, which must be firmly established if there is to be any talk at all of a method of church historiography. In any event, no one can deny it to be in the nature of the case that, whereas on the one hand historical research must immerse itself in the mass of details (not without the danger of losing itself in the particular), on the other hand it must also rise again to the universal, to those Ideas that must be the guiding points of view and illuminating stars on the long journey through the centuries.

Perhaps it may not be without a certain relevance in our day to direct our attention back to the venerable leaders in church historiography, both in antiquity and in more recent times. In the last few years a whole series of works in general church history has appeared; and indeed it has been mostly younger men who have undertaken this work.[1] The limitation to a reasonable selection,[2] appropriate to a general survey in concise and simple presentation, was only an exception. As a rule, this new generation of younger church historians, of whom one after another rushed to publish a church history from the standpoint of his own requirement and idea, has appeared with the lofty consciousness of being the first in the entire theological world to have taken up the task and to have grasped the significance of church history. For example, we read that "the rule . . . by which the history of our spiritual and ecclesiastical-religious life is to be treated, provided that a work claims to be scientific in character," must be defined by the momentous statement "that the law of spiritual life is development," not progress, as the modern worldview asserts.[3] Even though the authors of these textbooks themselves confessed that the occasion for their work was purely individual and

1. [ED.] Baur has in mind W. B. Lindner, G. A. Fricke, J. L. Jacobi, J. H. Kurz, and H. F. F. Schmid, all of whom published textbooks in church history between 1848 and 1851. See below, 240, n. 43.

2. [ED.] As in this work.

3. [ED.] W. Bruno Lindner, *Lehrbuch der christlichen Kirchengeschichte, mit besonderere Berücksichtigung der dogmatischen Entwicklung* (Leipzig, 1848), I, v.

subjective, at the same time they emphasized even more expressly that "individuality and subjectivity, . . . considered in themselves, have a justified claim to the endeavor of becoming objective." [4] These younger men have dismissed, some of them quite boldly, the accomplishments of the predecessors on whose shoulders they stand. As a result, Neander himself could not refrain from taking note, with good-natured irony, of the originality of the epitomizer of his church history. It should not be surprising that this course, begun rashly and confidently but without plan and without lasting intellectual equipment, began to slacken even at the first or second stage and came to a precarious standstill. We were expected to see where the true journey, or at least its major direction, ought to lead, however, in those who were sufficiently persevering to attain the happy epoch of a return to ecclesiastical confessionalism and a point in the present where "the courage of science goes hand in hand with the courage of confessionalism in the manner of a Hengstenberg" —after an age in which "destruction and downfall have engulfed even the church" because of "the emergence of unbelief." [5]

From the image of the old masters in church history—a Mosheim and a Semler, or a Spittler, a Planck, and a Henke, who now are not infrequently disdained in the self-imposed darkness of our own ecclesiastical consciousness—the younger generation can learn above all the way in which these men have earned the well-deserved reputation by which they will continue to live in the literature of church history, and indeed will outlive many still to come.

Tübingen, February 1852

4. [ED.] G. A. Fricke, *Lehrbuch der Kirchengeschichte* (Leipzig, 1850), I, v. Both Lindner and Fricke were professors of theology at Leipzig and representatives of the so-called "believing theology" or "believing scholarship" (*die gläubige Wissenschaft*) of the Mediating School.

5. [ED.] I am unable to locate this quotation. E. W. Hengstenberg was editor of the *Evangelische Kirchenzeitung,* official organ of the Evangelical Lutheran Church in Prussia and uncompromising defender of Lutheran confessionalism against modernism, rationalism, and speculative theology. The "unbelief" mentioned in the quotation is probably intended to refer to Hegelianism.

INTRODUCTION

The word *history* has both an objective and a subjective meaning. This double meaning sets up as an immediate unity that which critical analysis causes to split widely and indeterminably apart. History is both what has happened objectively and the subjective knowledge of what has happened. But just as not everything that has happened is a historical occurrence, so also not all knowledge of what has happened is historical knowledge. Historical knowledge first emerges when the event becomes important enough not merely to be known for the moment but also to be transmitted to the enduring knowledge of posterity.

Once interest in such a presentation of what has happened has been awakened, the question arises as to how knowledge concerning events is related to the events themselves. The more precisely this relation is considered, the less can it simply be assumed that historical presentation is nothing but the true, adequate reflection of what objectively has happened. The difference in time that separates the historian from the object of his presentation is often considerable. And, in general, a great deal can come between the historian and his object, so that it may appear to him in a light completely other than would accord with the actuality of the subject matter. Thus, there is no historical presentation that must not first be critically tested in order to determine the relation in which its author stands to the pure objectivity of historical truth. But even if all those questions concerning the credibility of the historian, his talent for historical presentation, the character of the sources he employs—everything that has to be drawn into the realm of historical criticism—can be answered as satisfactorily as possible, history itself, as the essence of what has happened, remains something so infinitely large that its contents can never be exhausted by historical knowledge, through which what has objectively taken place is also to become subjectively known.

The first requirement of a presentation corresponding to the idea of history would seem to be above all that the historian stand as close to the object of his presentation as possible, in order to become acquainted with all the details that can be obtained only by immediate perception. But on the other hand, after further consideration, we are aware of the opposite: the data of history appear to us in their true light only when we consider them from a greater distance, and when the causes and effects that determine the character of a given historical realm not merely are present in their first beginnings but have already developed in a wider connection. For history itself is an endless tissue of varied manifestations, interpenetrating in the most manifold of relations. The truth itself thus emerges in something like genuine objectivity only through the comparison of various possible standpoints, from each of which must be removed whatever has too subjective a character. How else could it be explained that all parts of history, especially those belonging to more or less ancient times, repeatedly become the object of historical presentation, if it were not of the nature of history itself that, from every standpoint from which we look anew back into the past, there is presented a new image, through which we obtain a truer, more vital and more significant perception of what has happened, even if only in a particular respect?

What applies to history in general applies also to the history of the Christian church. Indeed, in this more limited field, the nature of historical presentation becomes all the clearer when its task consists in setting forth the objectively given for subjective consciousness. One cannot trace an extensive period of general history, either as a whole or in one of its more significant parts, without having certain questions grow increasingly important—such as the means by which the whole series of phenomena that make up the continuity of causes and effects are joined together in unity; or how the particular is subordinated to the universal; or which Idea serves as the dynamic principle of the whole. Likewise, all this takes on a considerably higher and more definite significance as applied to the sphere within which the Christian church follows its historical course.

Here we may not simply abstract the end toward which every individual thing is striving from an indeterminate flux of manifestations. Rather, everything proceeds from a starting point in which the Idea that is to be realized through its entire temporal manifestation is clearly and definitely expressed; and once initiated, the development proceeds from one point to another in a continuity in which it should not be difficult to relate everything individual to the Idea that is the basis of the whole, or to determine the relation in which one thing stands to another. Historical presentation seems therefore to have here only the simple task of following the objectively given course, and of grasping and assembling everything so that it corresponds to the objectivity of the subject matter itself. But this is only the apparent prerogative of church historiography. The more everything in the history of the Christian church depends on the beginning from which it proceeds and by which it is conditioned through the whole continuity of its development, the more everything depends on the way one understands this beginning itself, which is so significant. The historical presentation as a whole is based on this fundamental perception. Easy as it may be, indeed, once the general point of view is established, to subordinate particular details to it, and to understand those details under the unity of this perspective, nevertheless all the difficulties to be overcome by a historical presentation are concentrated in the beginning itself. From every point of historical presentation, therefore, we are constantly referred back to the beginning, in relation to which we must orient ourselves for the purposes of a general survey.

If historical presentation follows the movement of the subject matter itself, as is its task, it will repeatedly arrive in the course of its procedure at points leading in very different directions, all reaching backward and assuming varied modes of perception with reference to the whole. Thus at the outset we cannot enter the entire course that subsequently is divided in such multiple fashion without knowing beforehand with which side we are to align ourselves throughout all differences. Just as the church, which at the beginning was at unity with itself, split asunder and divided into the great antithesis of Protestantism and Catholicism; and just as other religious parties appeared in addition to the Protestant Church, as well as views that emerged within the Protestant Church itself, deviating more or less from orthodox doctrine and claiming for themselves the same title to the Protestant principle—so also all these differences embrace equally numerous and varied points of view from which the entire development of the Christian church could be understood. Just as Protestant historiography is essentially different from Catholic, even so that of the rationalists is wholly different from that of the modern supernaturalists. And as the respective theological systems of rationalism and supernaturalism have outlived their usefulness, having each evolved to a degree that oversteps the antithesis between the two, so is it impossible for the most recent historiography of the Christian church, if it is not to remain attached to an obsolete standpoint, to be either rationalistic or supernaturalistic in the older, absolute sense.

The more highly developed a theological position is, the more a particular historiography tends to be conditioned by it, or rather to emerge from it. The first and most important task of every theological position can only be to investigate the nature of Christianity; but this can occur only through a return to the beginnings of Christianity and through the most precise investigation of the sources from which a knowledge of its origin must be derived. But once the basic point of view has been established in this way, the necessary consequence must be that the entire view of the course of development of the Christian church is also determined by it. If each of the various theological standpoints that have achieved a high degree of independence has disclosed and impressed itself in its own treatment of the history of the Christian church, then there can be no comprehensive work in church history whose view of history does not wholly manifest the theological vantage point of its author. Thus there are as many different views of history as there are different theological vantage points; and it is worth the trouble to consider them more closely in their relation to one another and to set them in the perspective of a historical process taking its own peculiar course. If the general task of raising the content of the objectively given into the clarity of subjective consciousness remains always the same, nevertheless the attempts at its solution are very different; and it can be seen at each important juncture not only how differently the same objects can be interpreted, but also how the view concerning them always changes in accord with the general conditions determining the consciousness of the time. Taken together, all these attempts, representing the various possible points of view in particular historical presentations, form the epochs of church historiography, in whose course the Spirit working in the depths and struggling toward the solution of its task has raised itself, at first gradually, to the level on which it stands in the present mode of perception.

No matter how, in accord with the general and formal requirements that are to be made of a historical presentation, we evaluate the merits and weaknesses of individual church historians—their faithfulness and credibility, the quality of their sources, the ways and means of their presentation—the first thing we need to investigate in order to obtain a more specific and concrete picture of their individuality is their entire historical perspective, including those characteristic attitudes in which it is expressed. To sketch at least the preliminary outlines in a characterization of the major church historians, from the most ancient to the most recent times, is the purpose of the following essay. It is not our task to review the entire corpus of works that make up the literature of church history,[1] but only to focus upon the main points at which church historiography has made a more specific, more deeply penetrating, and more comprehensive effort toward the completion of its task.

1. Cf. Karl Friedrich Stäudlin, *Geschichte und Litteratur der Kirchengeschichte* (Hanover, 1827). [ED. On Stäudlin, see below, 205.]

THE OLD CATHOLIC VIEW OF HISTORY:
EUSEBIUS AND HIS SUCCESSORS

If we wished to trace church historiography back to its earliest beginnings, we should have to go back not merely to the Book of Acts, which from ancient times has customarily been considered the first historical portrayal of the Christian church—the one that initiates the succession of church-historical literature—but also to the Gospels. If it is true that, as the history of the Christian community emerging in its first beginnings, Acts already has a valid claim to the title of a "history of the Christian church," so also may the Gospels, in so far as their subject is the life and work of the founder of the Christian church, be considered a part of the same beginnings of church historiography that lie before us in the writings of the New Testament. Since, however, a characterization of this first Christian historiography, or a response to the question of how far we are to regard the contents of these oldest documents of Christianity as a purely objective presentation of the original facts, is not possible without going to a large extent into questions whose investigation is the concern of New Testament criticism, we have good reason to drop the matter at this point.

1. *Hegesippus* [1]

The Jewish-Christian writer Hegesippus, who immediately followed the apostolic period and was the most important predecessor of Eusebius

1. [ED.] Very little is known of Hegesippus' life. He lived and wrote in Rome during the period from about A.D. 155 to 189. He probably was born early in the second century, since he indicates that the deification of Antinoüs, a slave of the Emperor Hadrian, took place in his own day (cf. Eusebius, *Historia ecclesiastica*, IV, VIII). His home was probably somewhere in the East, and Eusebius concludes from his writings that he was of Jewish origin. There is indication that he died during the

51

(who obtained a large portion of his oldest material from him), cannot be given closer consideration because we know him solely from the few fragments of his work in Eusebius. Eusebius says that "he collected his material [συγγράμματα, or ὑπομνήματα, "memoirs"] in five books, giving in the simplest style of writing the unerring tradition of the apostolic preaching" and "a complete record of his own opinion," [2] and that he undoubtedly made journeys for purposes of his historical description, during which, in Corinth, Rome, and other places where he talked with the bishops, "he found the same doctrine among them all," and obtained the greatly satisfying conviction that "in each list and in each city things are as the law, the prophets, and the Lord preach." [3] If so, there is evidence that at the outset church historiography was still totally colored by the particular conditions and interests from which the church itself came forth. The tendency of his historical description [4] to show how the church remained a pure and unspoiled virgin up to the beginning of the second century, although the seed of doctrines by which some tried to corrupt the sound canon of the σωτήριον δόγμα [saving dogma] was already secretly present, derived from his Jewish-Christian standpoint. He also tried to show how, after the holy chorus of apostles had come to an end in different ways, and the generation of those who had been deemed worthy to hear the ἔνθεος σοφία [inspired wisdom] with their own ears had disappeared, the σύστασις [confederation] of ἄθεος πλάνη [godless error] made its beginning by the deception of ἑτεροδιδάσκαλοι [heretical teachers], who, now that no apostles remained, brazenly dared to preach ψευδώνυμος γνῶσις [what is falsely called knowledge] against

reign of Emperor Commodus (180–92). Under the Emperors Hadrian (117–38) and Marcus Aurelius (161–80) he was known as a prominent champion of the orthodox faith against various heresies, including Gnosticism. Eusebius quotes frequently from a work by Hegesippus known as the *Hypomnēmata* or "Memoirs," composed of five books written at different times, intended as a historical apology for the authenticity of the traditions received from the apostles. It consists of a series of narratives and pictures, reaching from the Apostle James to the pontificate of Eleutherus in Rome, and it is valuable for an understanding of the development of orthodoxy and episcopacy in the second century. Its purpose is to demonstrate the unity of faith in the churches of the leading cities and their bishops, both past and present. The fragments of the *Hypomnēmata*, collected from Eusebius' citations, are found in M. J. Routh, *Reliquiae sacrae*, I (Oxford, 1846), 203–84; and in English translation in *ANF*, VIII, 762–65.

2. [ED.] Eusebius, *Historia ecclesiastica*, IV, VIII, 2; IV, XXII, 1 (*The Ecclesiastical History*, trans. Kirsopp Lake & J. E. L. Oulton [*Loeb*, 2 vols., 1926, 1932], I, 320–21, 374–75).

3. Cf. Eusebius, *H.E.*, II, XXIII; III, XXXII; IV, VIII; IV, XXII. [ED. Quotations are from IV, XXII, 1, 3 (*Loeb*, I, 374–75).]

4. As appears without doubt from the passage cited by Eusebius in *H.E.*, III, XXXII.

the κήρυγμα [proclamation] of the truth. Authentically apostolic truth and heretical falsification were thus the elements whose antithesis determined his historical perspective, and we have here already the archetype of the old Catholic historiography, which remained unchanged thereafter. Hegesippus (who lived and wrote under the Roman Bishops Soter, Anicetus, and Eleutherus) had before him, however, only a very short span of the church, which was still undergoing its first development, and for a period of nearly one and a half centuries no successor followed in his footsteps. Hence the famous Bishop Eusebius of Caesarea is the one who, on account of the ten books of his historical work, deserves to be called the father of church history, much as one would speak of a father of secular history.[5]

2. *Eusebius* [6]

Eusebius himself comes forward with a consciousness of being just that. After giving the plan of his work in the Preface to his church history, he proceeds as follows: he must at the very beginning ask forbear-

5. Cf. my programmatic essay, *Comparatur Eusebius Caesariensis, historiae ecclesiasticae parens, cum parente historiarum, Herodoto Halicarnassensi* [Eusebius of Caesarea, the Father of Church History, Compared with Herodotus of Halicarnassus, the Father of History] (Tubingae, 1834).

6. [ED.] Eusebius, Bishop of Caesarea, often referred to as Eusebius Pamphili because of his friendship with Pamphilus, was born at some time between 260 and 280, and died, probably at Caesarea, in 339 or 340. As a young man he collaborated with Pamphilus in attempting to continue the work of Origen in text criticism of both the Old and New Testaments. He became Bishop of Caesarea sometime after 313. His involvement in the Council of Nicaea and in the doctrinal struggles that both preceded and followed it are well known and need not be reviewed here at length. Eusebius' theological orientation was toward a left-wing Origenist Logos-flesh Christology, with marked affinities to Arianism and Apollinarianism, although he defended his interpretation of the Nicene formula against both the Arians and the anti-Origenist Nicene defenders. His denial of the reality of the soul of Christ, his supernaturalist conception of church history, and his Christian imperialism join together in a theological "syndrome" of marked significance for his own historical work as well as that of his successors. (Cf. Aloys Grillmeier, S.J., *Christ in Christian Tradition: From the Apostolic Age to Chalcedon*, trans. J. S. Bowden [London, 1965], 180–81.)

In addition to his early studies in text criticism, Eusebius did work in history, apologetics, dogmatics, and exegesis. His most significant contribution by far was in history; and his two major historical works were his church history (the *Historia ecclesiastica* [PG, XX; *The Ecclesiastical History*, trans. Kirsopp Lake & J. E. L. Oulton (*Loeb*, 2 vols., 1926, 1932)], which is the major subject of Baur's treatment below) and his universal history or chronicle (the *Pantodapē historia*). The latter is divided into two parts, the first purporting to give an epitome of universal history

ance and admit that it is beyond his strength to measure up in a completely satisfying way to the task he has taken upon himself. Since he is the first to undertake such an enterprise, he is venturing, as it were, upon a lonely and still untrodden path. Indeed, he prays to have God as his guide and the power of the Lord as his support. But he has been unable to find even a trace of those who traversed the same path before him, except that a few of them left behind some brief stories about the times through which they were living. "They [raise] their voices as a man holds up a torch from afar, calling to us from on high as from a distant watch-tower, and [tell] us how we must walk, and how to guide the course of our work without error or danger." [7]

The way in which Eusebius chiefly substantiates this judgment about the insignificance of all those who had begun to cultivate the field of church history before him—among whom Hegesippus at least could not have left so few traces, in light of Eusebius' own testimony and even more that of Jerome, according to whom Hegesippus recounted "a history of all ecclesiastical events from the passion of our Lord, down to his own period" [8]—is that his predecessors had all left behind them only σμικρὰς προφάσεις [short prefaces] and μαρικὰς διηγήσεις [partial narratives]. Therefore, what raises him above them and awakens in him the high consciousness of being the first church historian is chiefly the universality of the plan and purpose of his church-historical work. From this point of view he begins his history as follows:

> I have purposed to record in writing the successions of the sacred apostles, covering the period stretching from our Saviour to ourselves; the number and character of the transactions recorded in the history of the church; the number of those who were distinguished in her government and leadership in the provinces of greatest fame; the number of those who in each generation were the ambassadors of the word of God either by speech or pen; the names, the number

arranged according to nations, and the second to furnish a synchronism of the historical material in parallel columns. The work has been lost in the original but can be reconstructed from various sources. The *Historia ecclesiastica* was probably completed in A.D. 324, just before the Council of Nicaea. Other historical works include a martyrology, which may have been a preparatory study for the church history; a life of Pamphilus, of which only fragments remain; and a life of Constantine (*Vita Constantini*, PG, XX; NPNF [2], I), which was compiled after the emperor's death in 337.

7. [ED]. Eusebius, *H.E.*, I, 1, 3 (*Loeb*, I, 8–9). Quoted by Baur in German.

8. Jerome, *De scriptores ecclesiastici*, XXII. [ED. NPNF[2], III, 368. See below, 74, n. 40.]

and the age of those who, driven by the desire of innovation to an extremity of error, have heralded themselves as the introducers of knowledge, falsely so-called (ψευδωνύμον γνώσεως), ravaging the flock of Christ unsparingly, like grim wolves. To this I will add the fate which has beset the whole nation of the Jews from the moment of their plot against our Saviour; moreover, the number and nature and times of the wars waged by the heathen against the divine word and the character of those who, for its sake, passed from time to time through the contest of blood and torture; furthermore the martyrdoms of our own time, and the gracious and favoring help of our Saviour in them all.[9]

All of the topics here designated have such a general interest that they emerge as the essential contents of the historical presentation and form the major points to which everything else is connected.

Since the apostles themselves are already the successors of the Lord, and since in accord with this basic condition the whole of Christianity rests on the tradition that has come down from the apostles, the church historian must likewise not lose sight of the thread that continues unbrokenly through all ages. The διαδοχαὶ τῶν ἱερῶν Ἀποστόλων [successors of the holy apostles] represent the major conception advanced by Eusebius himself; they are the substantial form of church history, by which its entire content is sustained and held together; everything that belongs to it first obtains its historically based continuity through them, so that at every point in history one is aware of the full historical continuity in those men who are considered the successors of the apostles. All this must have been especially difficult at a time when the apostolic succession was not yet concentrated, as it was later, in a single individual, but was distributed among several different places. But since at that time a few specific episcopal sees were already elevated above others and were given preference as apostolic sees, to attach to them the apostolic succession was only a matter of course. To Eusebius, therefore, it is especially important to record by name exactly which men were bishops in Rome, Alexandria, and Antioch, men who represented in themselves the unity of the apostolic succession.[10]

Just as his church history has its formal unity in the continuing series of these bearers of the apostolic succession and tradition, so the substance of its contents is a function of the character of the times it describes. As long as Christianity had to struggle for its position in the

9. [ED.] Eusebius, *H.E.*, I, i, 1–2 (*Loeb*, I, 6–9). Paraphrased by Baur in German.
10. *H.E.*, II, XXIV; III, II, XI, XIII, XIV, XV, XXI, XXII; IV, I; etc.

world, the major object of historical presentation could only consist of the dual battle it had to wage, against both the heretics who threatened the purity of its dogma and the political opponents who threatened its existence generally. And since the historian himself had just lived through the period of the decision that turned out so happily for Christianity, his church-historical consciousness was given a new impetus by the thought that he was the first who could deliver to posterity a coherent, harmoniously contained presentation of so great an achievement, in which everything thought to be the goal of the entire historical development of Christianity now seemed to have been reached.

Although Eusebius designates the succession of the holy apostles as the real sphere within which church history moves, nevertheless he believes it possible to begin only with the first dispensation of God regarding our Lord and Redeemer, in view of the gracious and kindly assistance the Lord has accorded the church in his own time in its victory over the pagan world and the Roman State.[11] That is to say, since the person of the Redeemer has a dual aspect, a divine and a human, church history can regard only that which is supreme and highest in the person of Christ itself to be its true beginning and point of departure. To be sure, it can begin in this regard only with the confession that no word can adequately describe the lineage, the dignity, the substance, and the nature of the divine Logos existing before all things. But the fact is thereby established that in the appearance of Christianity what already existed implicitly in a supratemporal mode stepped forth under the conditions of time, revealing itself in different manifestations even in the pre-Christian era, from which it can be clearly seen that the religion proclaimed in the teaching of Jesus is not new and foreign but is rather the original and only true religion.[12] It is already noteworthy that, whereas Hegesippus (as Jerome expressly says) began his account *a passione Domini* [with the passion of the Lord], Eusebius was carried back beyond the διαδοχάς [successors] of the apostles, as though instinctively to the incarnation of Christ in order to establish in it the real beginning of his church history. But here is to be found, when it is correctly under-

---

11. *H.E.*, I, 1, 2, 8 [*Loeb*, I, 8-11]: "My starting-point is therefore no other than the first dispensation of God touching our Saviour and Lord, Jesus the Christ. . . . For he who plans to hand on in writing the history of Christian origins is forced to begin from the first dispensation concerning the Christ himself, which is more divine than it seems to most, seeing that from him we claim to derive our very name."

12. *H.E.*, I, 11 f.

stood, the first characteristic trait of his authentically Catholic historical perspective.

Even if every church history can begin only with the acknowledgment of the divine origin of Christianity and its founder, nevertheless everything depends upon the way in which this is done and upon the meaning that is assigned to it—whether the supernatural aspect of the origin is intentionally emphasized and regarded as the innermost substance of the subject matter itself, or whether it is regarded actually only as a presupposition that must be made in order to have a beginning but that for the sake of the subject matter itself will be put aside. Eusebius has taken this supernatural aspect in its highest and most definite conception, and has given it the most effusive expression. Since he immediately begins his church history with the dogma of the divinity of Christ, the history of the Christian church is in his view only the earthly continuation of the same history that, seen from the metaphysical heights of early orthodox theology, has taken its beginning from eternity in the innermost nature of God and has assumed the form of a series of transcendent facts in the generation of the Son, the procession of the Spirit, and the decree of salvation, until, with the incarnation of the Son, it shifted the theater of its further development to earth.

It is obvious that a truly basic perspective is thereby furnished for the entire field of church history. A history that is so transcendent, so supernatural, and so miraculous at its starting point cannot disown that character in its further development. Even if it must follow the natural continuity of causes and effects after its entrance into the human order of things, the supernatural is still the actual element, the substantial foundation, on which all historical manifestations are based. It is quite natural that the supernatural principle, which is the moving cause of the whole, continuously breaks through the natural continuity of events and makes itself known in its higher, overriding causality. The more important a sequence of events is, or the more likely a decision is to affect the advancement of the cause of Christianity at this or that point, then the more certainly is it to be expected in advance that there will be no lack of the most obvious evidences of the activity with which the invisible Ruler of the whole intervenes in particular instances as well. And not only does this happen at those points where we are lifted by the inner meaning of events above the ordinary course of affairs, but also, where miracle is already so essential and pervasive an element, there is no longer, generally speaking, a dividing line between the natural and the supernatural. Each flows into the other indistinguishably; and from this point of view nothing is outwardly so accidental and insignificant that it cannot be regarded as a miracle. The significance of the role played by the most varied forms of miracle in all the ancient church historians, beginning with Eusebius, is so well known as to need no further mention here. In the work of Eusebius we have the principal substantiation of this view of miracle in the care with which he has placed the dogma of the divinity of Christ at the summit of his church history. Just as the supernatural principle that entered into human history in the incarnation of the Logos continues to work through miracle at the most remote distances, so also its efficacy reaches back into the pre-Christian era. That which is implicitly and in its entire manifestation so extraordinary and miraculous cannot emerge in a single stroke, immediately and without preparation; it must rather have been announced prophetically and typologically beforehand. This is the connection between the Old and the New Testaments. Eusebius maintains this connection only in order to prove the doctrine of the divinity of Christ, and to combat the reproach concerning the novelty of the Christian religion; but here the tendency to preface the church history of the New Testament with a church history of the Old is already found.

A conception of church history such as Eusebius', which is in principle so dogmatic that it makes the dogma of the divinity of Christ its starting point, must regard dogma in general as the substantial content of the history of Christianity. If the divine Logos has become man in order to proclaim the σωτήριον δόγμα [saving dogma], then everything depends upon the pure and unfalsified preservation of the teaching delivered by Christ and the apostles; and it must therefore be the most important task of every historian of the Christian church to direct his attention to everything that attests to the pure preservation of the apostolic doctrine. Eusebius explicitly emphasizes, among the subjects he intends to describe in his historical work, the men who preached the divine Word orally or in writing; and those sections in his church history that describe not only the ecclesiastical but especially the literary activity of the most significant church teachers up to his time—Clement of Rome, Bishop Dionysius of Corinth, Irenaeus, Clement of Alexandria, Origen, and many others less well known—prove what care he bestowed upon this part of his work. To the same point of view belongs his special concern to provide exact information, so far as possible, as to which of the canonical writings have been mentioned by name from the most ancient times and may be regarded as genuinely apostolic writings according to church tradition. Church history should evaluate the authenticity of these writings, e.g., the grounds on which we may be assured that they are the authentic documents of Christian doctrine and not writings interpolated with false doctrines. Everything that refers to these writings, to the doctrines contained in them, and to the whole apostolic dogma handed down orally and in writing, quite naturally forms—in a history resting so essentially on a basic conception that is dogmatic in character—the most important part of its contents.[13]

The only difficulty is that what the object of historical study in dogma might be cannot be seen if the dogma that in dogma nothing changes, that dogma therefore has no history, is regarded as basic. Accordingly, there could only be attempts—which have in fact been made—to establish and bring to general recognition something other than what dogma contains. In contrast to the objectivity of dogma, which remains unchanged throughout all ages, the source of such endeavors could only have been the mania for innovation, the self-conceit, the subjective arbitrariness of heretics (as they are customarily called for this reason) who opposed their own self-chosen opinions to the universal tradition. Church history must, therefore, give special attention to such phenomena and show how dogma in its purity keeps them under control; it must show how everything that by origin was so lacking in all inner reality could not but disintegrate internally as soon as it emerged. From this point of view, Hegesippus had already given close consideration to the first emerging heresies. Following his example, Eusebius also left nothing belonging to the same category unnoticed. The Ebionites and Nicolaitans, the Gnostics (especially the Marcionites), the Montanists, the Quartodecimans, the Novatians, the opponents of the orthodox doctrine of the Trinity, Sabellius and Paul of Samosata, and finally the author of Manichaeanism, Manes, are listed successively as especially important figures following Simon Magus.

At a time when dogma was still in the process of ferment and formation, it must have provided abundant material for historical presentation. The oldest historiography, however, is characterized not by this material but by the notion that even the historian should consider it only from the dogmatic, not the historical, point of view. No changes in dogma touch the inner substance of dogma itself but have only an external relation to it, in so far as everything in the broad field of heresy is related

13. [ED.] *H.E.,* I, i; III, xxv.

only as truth and error are related. While dogma remains always the same and represents in its whole temporal manifestation only the pure apostolic tradition, the heresies form a self-composed sequence of continually changing phenomena, which in their continual reaction to dogma only serve to place the eternal, unshakable truth of the latter in a vivid light.

This antithesis between truth and error—between dogma remaining eternally the same, on the one hand, and heresy attaining all possible forms in its human subjectivity, on the other—is only a special form of the generally dualistic view of the world in which the inner substance of the old Catholic historical perspective is first disclosed to us more deeply. The higher the principle that has entered into world history through the incarnation of the divine Logos, the more it must have as its antithesis another, more than human principle, for the combating and overcoming of which so great and extraordinary an event is sufficiently motivated. Only the Devil, as the enemy and destroyer of the human race, can stand opposite the Son of God who became incarnate for the salvation of mankind. He is the real cause of all that takes place in opposition to Christianity, the founder of all heresies for the adulteration of the Christian faith, the originator of all persecutions by which the enemies of the Christian name attempt to suppress Christianity. A historian such as Eusebius cannot fail to recall the efficacy of this hidden principle at every point where Christianity is threatened anew. It was the Devil, already at the time of the first dissemination of the Christian faith, who used Simon Magus as his instrument in order to take away Rome beforehand by means of his magic arts. The more the Christian church prospered as time went on, the more the enemy of truth (since he had accomplished nothing by persecution) put into action new means of plunging into the abyss of destruction those believers who permitted themselves to be misled by deceitful men who only seemingly had accepted the name of Christianity. From Menander, the successor of Simon Magus, there emanated, as from a two-headed serpent, two heresies, one of which had as its leader the Antiochene Saturninus, the other, the Alexandrine Basilides. The entire phenomenon of Gnosticism, which branched out so widely, is derived from the same anti-divine principle. When persecutions break out, such as those against the Gallic Christians in Lugdunum and Vienna,[14] it is the Adversary who leaves nothing untried and who in the vehemence of his assaults intends to give

14. [ED.] I.e., the modern Lyons and Vienne in southeastern France.

a foretaste of his coming, when all restraint will be cast aside; or, if a new and peculiar heresy like that of the Montanists appears, once again it is the enemy of the church, who delights in evil, who never omits any sort of cunning against men, and who dispenses strange heresies like poisonous snakes.[15] A teaching that stood in so sharp a contrast to Christianity as that of Mani appeared, moreover, to carry even in the name of its founder (in which the acuteness of the church fathers could detect a more than accidental affinity with the Greek word μαίνεσθαι [to be mad]), the sign of its demonic origin upon its forehead.[16]

Generally speaking, the more serious and significant the struggle of Christianity against its internal and external enemies, the less, from this historical perspective, may reference to the supersensual origin of these phenomena be omitted. Accordingly, the great Diocletian persecution of Christians in particular is a major act of the Devil in his special role in the drama that Eusebius' church history performs before us. Before the persecution had yet become general and violent, it was he who sallied forth, as if awakening from a deep sleep at the end of the long peace Christians had enjoyed since the last persecutions under Decius and Valerian—but not immediately with his assembled might and open violence. Rather, he first attacked the church only secretly and in disguise; and he introduced measures that thereupon brought about, in a series of the most manifold scenes of persecution, a bloody struggle that endangered the entire existence of the Christian church.[17]

Since the entire stage on which Eusebius' church history takes place is divided into two hostile camps and depicts the scene of a great struggle in which the followers of Christ must fight not merely their visible enemies but also the invisible powers, those men on the Christian side who put up the most successful and courageous resistance against the various assaults the Christian church has had to endure, attract especial attention. While the danger that threatens the purity of Christian dogma through heresies is met by those who through Word and Scripture defend the truth of the divine teaching, similarly, the Christian martyrs

---

15. Eusebius, *H.E.*, II, XIII; IV, VII; V, I, XIV, XXI.

16. *H.E.*, VII, XXXI, 1 [*Loeb*, II, 226–27]: "The madman (ὁ μανείς), named after his devil-possessed heresy, was taking as his armor mental delusion; for the Devil, that is Satan himself, the adversary of God, had put the man forward for the destruction of many. His very speech and manners proclaimed him a barbarian in mode of life, and, being by nature devilish and insane . . . ," etc. [ED. Although similar, the words Μάνης (Mani) and μανείς have no etymological relation.]

17. *H.E.*, VIII, IV.

are the bearers of their victorious weapons for the cause of Christianity. Historical interest in them becomes the more intense the more the final verdict depends upon their courage and religious zeal, their steadfastness and persistence. Eusebius' church history is in large part a history of Christian martyrdom. Eusebius himself considers this to be a major task of his presentation. Especially in the history of the Diocletian persecutions in the eighth and ninth books, his church history seems to disintegrate almost entirely into a description of individual martyr scenes, narrated with great precision of detail, in which Christianity appears at its most splendid. The martyrs are the athletes of Christ, the champions of the great Christian army, in which, as with the heroes in a Homeric battle piece, the general struggle is individualized in direct engagements of the most varied sort that continuously bring into view a new configuration of the whole. The more significant the catastrophe in which they are involved, the more they give to Eusebius' portrayal the appeal of vividness and vitality.

Within this antithesis, the fundamental historical perspective is dualistic. But where the principles confronting each other in their hostile antithesis are by nature so thoroughly different, and where the antithesis to the divine is the demonic, the outcome cannot be in doubt. The content of history as a whole is by no means an immanent development proceeding through various phases that mutually condition one another; it is simply a conflict of hostile powers, between which no reconciliation and settlement, no fluid transition mediated by the inner nature of the subject matter itself, is possible. The two principles meet only to repel each other and maintain themselves in their constant tension, such that periodic predominance falls sometimes to the one and sometimes to the other side. The Divine, overreaching everything in its infinite power, is certain beforehand of victory; but the harsher the opposition, all the more certain must one be—in the immediate present as well—as to what in every conflict between the two principles is divine and what demonic by nature.

Just as the heresies appearing here and there have a seeming existence only until their inner nullity has been uncovered, and thus apparently have the purpose merely of disclosing by their constant alteration the truth that remains eternally identical with itself; so also the external enemies of Christianity must give testimony of its divine power. They not only succumb to it but must also not infrequently be punished for their presumption in a rather conspicuous fashion. The historiography of

Eusebius displays its essential pragmatism in the constant illustration of the truth that everything pleasing to God is rewarded and everything that resists him is punished. If, in accord with the mode of perception of the time, the higher hand ruling over everything intervenes everywhere visibly in the order of human affairs, that hand can least of all remain unattested where there is a question of placing within its bounds the human wantonness that has sinned against God, and of executing the eternal laws of divine judgment. The greater the sacrilege, the more certainly and obviously will the deserved punishment overtake its perpetrator. The fate that befell the first persecutor of Christianity, the Jewish king Herod, who died of a horrible disease immediately after his notorious deed,[18] was repeated again and again upon all who followed in his path. So great was the misfortune that befell Pilate after the death of Jesus that he laid the avenging hand upon himself and was the instrument by which he fell to divine judgment.[19] The disastrous downfall of the Jewish nation was, moreover, the self-incurred punishment for what had happened to Jesus; but it was brought about especially by the martyr's death suffered just before by James the Righteous at the hands of the Jewish people.[20]

According to this retributive justice, fortune and misfortune are distributed throughout the entire course of history. Before the final, great, devastating struggle came about, so long as the rulers still maintained a friendly and benevolent attitude toward Christians, there was nothing but blessing and abundance in the Roman Empire; men lived in peace and festive joy; everything enjoyed an unhampered progress. But as soon as the war of persecution started, everything changed. What had never before happened now took place: the Roman Empire was divided internally, and the most disgraceful ruin, worthy of their crimes, came upon the rulers who had themselves been the chief authors of the horrors of persecution.[21]

The *mortes persecutorum* [deaths of the persecutors] is the permanent category of this most ancient historical perspective, which lives in the most concrete awareness of the divine judgment. Those, however, whom divine Providence named as its favorites and destined to carry out its

18. *H.E.*, I, viii, 3 [*Loeb*, I, 66–67]: "But it is worth noticing in this connection the result of the crime of Herod against the Christ and the children of his age; for immediately, without even a short delay, the justice of God overtook him while he was still in life, showing the prelude of what awaited him when he had passed hence."

19. *H.E.*, II, vii.   20. *H.E.*, II, vi, xxiii.   21. *H.E.*, VIII, xiii, xvi; IX, viii.

intentions are distinguished most royally. They are to harvest the richest reward for their pious disposition and action, which is well pleasing to God. This is the eminence from which Constantine, at the end of Eusebius' church history, and in the panegyrical memorial Eusebius prepared in the form of a work devoted specifically to his life, outshines all other mortals. In the life of this emperor, God has given the most obvious proof of the gifts of grace with which he rewards those who honor and praise him. God has

> shown on the one hand the fearful end of those tyrants who denied and opposed him, and at the same time [has] made it manifest that even the death of his servant, as well as his life, is worthy of admiration and praise. . . . [The God] who is the common Saviour of all, having treasured up with himself, for those who love godliness, greater blessings than human thought has conceived, gives the earnest and first-fruits of future rewards even here, assuring in some sort immortal hopes to mortal eyes. The ancient oracles of the prophets, delivered to us in the Scripture, declare this; the lives of pious men, who shone in old time with every virtue, bear witness to posterity of the same; and our own days prove it to be true, wherein Constantine, who alone of all that ever wielded the Roman power was the friend of God the Sovereign of all, has appeared to all mankind so clear an example of a godly life. And God himself, whom Constantine worshiped, has confirmed this truth by the clearest manifestations of his will, being present to aid him at the commencement, during the course, and at the end of his reign, and holding him up to the human race as an instructive example of godliness. Accordingly, by the manifold blessings he has conferred on him, he has distinguished him alone of all the sovereigns of whom we have ever heard as at once a mighty luminary and most clear-voiced herald of genuine piety.[22]

The epoch-making significance of Constantine provides Eusebius' church history, in conformity with its entire structure, with a conclusion that brings everything to an end in complete unity. This unity of the whole gives Eusebius' work an aesthetic value that none other from ancient times can share with it. The struggle of Christianity against paganism, which continued through the first three centuries, ends with a catastrophe by which Christianity attains the most complete and glorious victory. In Constantine, Christianity mounts the throne of the Roman Empire and sees the entire Roman world lying at its feet; thus the his-

---

22. *H.E.*, IX, XI; Eusebius, *Vita Constantini*, I, III–IV. [ED. Quotation from latter work; *NPNF* 2, I, 482. Quoted by Baur in German.]

torian looks back on the period of time described by him with infinite satisfaction as having attained a result that one could scarcely wish to improve. But the perception of the historian, seen in his way of fixing the goal now achieved, appears no less limited than this awareness of the victorious power of Christianity over all hostile oppositions appears elevating. The historian's view is founded on the condition in which he finds Christianity at the end of his work, namely, at the peak of its temporal development—as though in that development Christianity should now have achieved at one stroke everything that the infinity of its Idea contains in itself; as though, after having struggled for so long, and having exhausted itself in the struggle with the world, instead of taking further struggles upon itself, it now had only to enjoy the fruits of victory.

In its immediate unity with the Roman Empire, Christianity indeed became the dominant state religion, but thereby the ideality of its nature had already disappeared; it became increasingly embodied in the confining, material forms of its time; in a word, the Roman state church now became the essential content of the historian's fundamental perception. The world-historical significance that Christianity had attained with its victory over paganism and the Roman state was so identified with Constantine's personal part in it that everything distinguishing this epoch was seen only in his person; similarly his government, and everything that characterized it, became the authoritative norm for the future. Besides the abolition of tyrannical power and the establishment of a true Christian regime, Eusebius knows of nothing more to be praised among Constantine's achievements in the cause of Christianity than that he repaired damaged churches and built new ones considerably larger and more imposing, made the most favorable laws for the Christian religion and church, distinguished bishops and clerics by honors and privileges of all kinds, and in general elevated the hierarchically organized church to the prevailing center of the government as a whole.[23] The interest in hierarchy, as it became ever more dominant both in dogma and in all other connections, remained thereafter the point of view to which the historian of the Christian church had chiefly to adhere.

It is of high significance for ancient church historiography that no one after Eusebius made the era first described by him the object of a new presentation. All that those who followed after him did was either to make excerpts and translate from his work or to carry that work fur-

23. Eusebius, *H.E.*, X, 11 f.

ther: this indicates the degree to which he is the classic historian of the ancient period and, as the first who undertook to write the history of the Christian church over a longer period of time, the father of church history. That this is so can be simply explained by the adequacy of his conception and presentation, by its very nature, to the views of the age, so that subsequent historians simply did not know what in it could be altered and improved. They could only repeat what he had said or take up the thread of his narrative where he had dropped it. The church, after being fused by Constantine into a total unity with the state, had so measured and uniform a course of further development that no difference could arise that was not immediately reabsorbed into the current of the general movement. Hence the progress of historiography could likewise only consist in continually adding new segments to what already existed. Since the basic perception remained always the same, there was no interest in making an era already described the object of a new treatment. The object of historiography was already exhausted, and each new historian who went further along the previously charted route took such complete possession of the new field before him that a later historian could only widen and supplement the material; he could not make a substantially different presentation.

3. *Socrates, Sozomenus, Theodoret*

Such is the relation of the three church historians immediately following Eusebius—Socrates, Sozomenus, and Theodoret[24]—to one another

24. [ED.] Socrates Scholasticus (meaning "lawyer") was born in Constantinople about 380. Nothing is known of his life other than brief autobiographical indications in his church history. His *Historia ecclesiastica* (*PG*, LXVII; *NPNF*[2], II) begins with the accession of Constantine (A.D. 306), when the persecution begun by Diocletian came to an end, and terminates with the year 439 (the seventeenth consulship of Theodosius II). Socrates probably lived a few years beyond that date but died before the end of Theodosius' reign in 450. His history in its present form is not a first edition, since it contains evidence of revision. It shows heavy reliance on sources such as Rufinus, Eusebius, Athanasius, the collections of the acts of the councils by the Macedonian Sabinus, Eutropius, lists of bishops of major cities, and others, which Socrates often copies word for word. He was not interested in strictly theological issues, and adopted a lenient attitude toward heterodoxy.

Salamanius Hermias Sozomen[us] was born in Palestine about 400 and, like Socrates, was trained as a lawyer. His first work in church history has been lost entirely; it covered in twelve books the history of the church from the ascension of Jesus down to Licinius. The second and longer work, the *Historia ecclesiastica* proper

as well as to Eusebius. Since they announce themselves to be merely continuers of the church history of Eusebius, they renounce the claim to stand on the same level with him. In the era described by them,[25] they indeed stand in uniform succession to one another, but since none seems to have known the work of the others and each goes his own way independently of the other two,[26] this parallel relation is at bottom only accidental; and the three historians who concur so unintentionally in the largely identical and analogous content of their works are, so to speak, only one. In comparison with the other two, especially with Sozomenus, Socrates can be commended in that he judges the heresies more equitably and with less prejudice, is more temperate in his interest in orthodoxy and hierarchy, is less lavish with eulogies for the heads of church and state, and in general displays a clearer awareness of his task as historian. But these individual differences have no special significance; the three works are so similar in content and form that recognizable differences subsequently disappear. Since from the very beginning everything

---

(*PG*, LXVII; *NPNF* 2, II), begins with the overthrow of Licinius by Constantine in 323 (the date with which Eusebius' church history ends) and closes with the death of Honorius in 423. Apparently about half a book is missing, since Sozomenus indicates in the Preface that the work was to continue down to 439, and both Nicephorus and Theodorus Lector appear to have read this section of it. It is clear that Sozomenus wrote after Socrates, his dependence upon whom is evident everywhere. He also made use of other sources, sometimes in an effort to improve upon Socrates, but with only partial success. Like Socrates, he is not interested in theological questions, and considers his task as historian to be only that of assembling facts without criticism or interpretation.

Theodoret, Bishop of Cyrrhus, was born at Antioch in 393 and died about 457. In addition to becoming embroiled in ecclesiastical politics, he did scholarly work in dogmatics, exegesis, and church history. He was a member of the School of Antioch in the christological controversies preceding Chalcedon, and sought to prevent the condemnation of Nestorius, although he criticized the latter's alleged doctrine of two sons and his refusal to accept the term *theotokos* (mother of God). His chief christological work, in addition to numerous polemical treatises arising out of controversy, most of which have been lost, was the *Eranistēs etoi polymorphos*. His *Historia ecclesiastica* (*PG*, LXXXII; *NPNF* 2, III), which begins with the rise of Arianism and closes with the death of Theodore of Mopsuestia in 429, is inferior to those of Socrates and Sozomenus. He made use of sources otherwise lost, but his propensity for miraculous and personal embellishment reduces the accuracy of his material. He also wrote a "Religious History" (the *Philotheos historia*, *PG*, LXXXII), which contains the biographies of thirty famous ascetics, held forth as religious models; and a "Compendium of Heretical Accounts" (*Haereticarum fabularum compendium*, *PG*, LXXIII), which includes a heresiology and a compendium of the theology of the Greek Fathers.

25. [ED.] From about 323 to 439.
26. [ED.] This judgment has been questioned by later scholarship.

concerned with dogma was regarded as the historian's major object of attention, the dogmatic controversies that occurred in this period form the main content of the presentation—above all the Arian controversy with its various ramifications, and the Nestorian and Eutychian controversies following upon it.

After the church had become a state church, state and church were most intimately interconnected; consequently the thread of church history could be carried forward only in the history of the emperors. Already, for this reason, ecclesiastical and political matters had had to go hand in hand in the works of church historians; but as these historians perceived it, nothing of political significance could occur that did not, on the whole, have to be placed under the specific view of the church. It was regarded as a general canon that the fortune and misfortune of governments is conditioned only by the piety of the rulers; [27] and the manifestations of favor enjoyed by church and hierarchy provided the criterion by which the rulers were measured. Just as the vaunted Constantine was continually held up to all his successors as a shining example, so the most forbidding example of the opposite was found in the Emperor Julian, whose death was the visible punishment for his apostasy and his persecution of Christianity.[28] In general, the ruling hand of the Deity intervenes in the same way as with Eusebius, sometimes rewarding, sometimes punishing; and the most obvious miracles of every sort occur upon every occasion where the glorification of the church and its favorites is concerned.

Since the persecutions had ceased, except in countries outside the Roman Empire such as Persia, church history indeed had little to tell about the heroic deeds of martyrs. But in lieu of these a new and rich field, one cultivated with special preference by Sozomenus and Theodoret,[29] was opened up in the manifold phenomena of the ever more widely expanding monastic life. Just as the opposition that the church

27. Cf. Sozomenus, *Historia ecclesiastica*, IX, 1: "It appears to me that it was the design of God to show by the events of this period, that piety alone suffices for the salvation of princes; and that without piety, armies, a powerful empire, and every other resource, are of no avail" [*NPNF* 2, II, 419]. Cf. VI, 11, concerning Julian: "It is very obvious that, throughout the reign of this emperor, God gave manifest tokens of his displeasure, and permitted many calamities to befall several of the provinces of the Roman Empire" [*NPNF* 2, II, 347].

28. Sozomenus, *H.E.*, VI, 11 (cf. V, viii); Socrates, *Historia ecclesiastica*, III, xxi; Theodoret, *Historia ecclesiastica*, III, xx.

29. Sozomenus, *H.E.*, I, viii, xii; Theodoret, *H.E.*, IV, xxiii f., and the *Philotheas historia* [Religious History].

has to undergo in conflict with the world, and with all the enemies whom the Devil stirs up against it, becomes especially evident in the martyrs of the ancient church, so the Christian ascetics who resist the same enemy in their own flesh belong to the struggle by means of which the history of the Christian church moves forward. The historical material grows in proportion as the church, engaged in constant struggle, gains ever wider domain by combating heretics, by converting pagan peoples, and through the endeavors of the monks. But the progress made by church history in the cultivation of its field is only quantitative. Period follows upon period, the scope and forms of church life expand, here and there something new appears; but just as the church itself always moves forward in the same direction, so the picture that we encounter in the presentations of its historians is always the same.

4. *Theodorus, Evagrius*

In this fashion, Socrates, Sozomenus, and Theodoret continued the history of the Christian church from the point at which Eusebius left off to about the end of the reign of Emperor Theodosius II.[30] They are joined in a further continuation by Theodorus and Evagrius.[31] The latter, in the six books of his church history, advanced to the twelfth year of the reign of the Emperor Mauritius in 594. In none of these historians is there the least internal distinction in historical perspective; their relation to one another is merely one of aggregation or of chronological order. Where one leaves off the other begins, and what motivates them to write is not the desire to grasp the subject matter of church history from a new, more accurate standpoint, corresponding more fully to the objec-

30. [ED.] I.e., from about 323 to 450.

31. [ED.] Theodorus Lector was a sixth-century Greek church historian who compiled four books of excerpts from Sozomenus, Socrates, and Theodoret, in a work entitled *Ekloge ek tōn ekklesiastikōn historiōn* [Selections from the Church Histories], commonly known as *Historia tripartita* [Tripartite History], which covers the period from the twentieth year of Constantine to the death of Constantius II (361). He continued this work with a *Historia ecclesiastica* of his own, beginning with the death of Theodosius II (450) and ending with the reign of Justinus I (518-27), which has been lost except for a few citations in later authors and in acts of the Seventh Ecumenical Council, collected in *PG*, LXXXVI. Evagrius Scholasticus (c. 536 to c. 594) settled in Antioch as a lawyer (hence the title "scholasticus"). His *Historia ecclesiastica* (*PG*, LXXXVI) is severely orthodox, criticizing even Eusebius, and is a major source of information on the dogmatic controversies of the period it covers (from the Council of Ephesus, 431, to 594).

tive truth, but only the simple reflection that things have happened which have not yet been told and which ought to be narrated and preserved for the knowledge of posterity. The Preface with which Evagrius begins is characteristic of this whole class of church historians.

> Both the advent of the beneficent God among men and his ascension into heaven have been treated in the best possible way by Eusebius the son of Pamphilus, Sozomenus, Theodoret, and Socrates, and also such things as were done by the holy apostles and the others, the martyrs who fought for the faith, and whatever else worthy of praise or its opposite has been done by us, up to a certain time in the reign of Theodosius. Because however the things which took place after these, although not much inferior to them, have not been treated in any orderly narrative, it seemed advisable to me, although I am not skilled in such matters, to undertake this toil and write an account of these things, trusting in the one who gave wisdom to fishermen and moved a senseless tongue to the harmonious utterance of sound both to resurrect the deeds now buried in oblivion and to give life to them by word and make them immortal in memory: so that each one of our readers may know what and when and where and how and against whom and by whom these things were done, up to our own times, and so that nothing worthy of memory may remain hidden because of careless and unbridled laziness and be hidden by the oblivion which is closely related to laziness. I will begin, trusting in the divine aid, at the point where the writers whom I have mentioned broke off their histories.[32]

So one after another joins the series and spins out the same thread of narration. If a certain diversity of views and principles seems here and there to become evident, one should not be deceived. The perceptions of all these writers are so genuinely Catholic that all differences and contradictions between them constantly dissolve into the most complete unity and harmony. In the same connection in which Sozomenus expresses the principle that the historian must pursue only the truth, he confesses to be of the conviction that the doctrine of the Catholic Church will appear in its purity only when it is shown that it has often been tested and tried through the persecutions of its enemies, but has always regained its old power and drawn all churches and peoples to its truth, since God gave it victory.[33] Thus in the presentation of these his-

---

32. [ED.] Evagrius, *Historia ecclesiastica*, I, Preface. Translated from the Greek text, *PG*, LXXXVI, 2420 A–C. Quoted by Baur in German.

33. Sozomenus, *H.E.*, I, 1.

torians, their Catholic perspective always transcends everything else.

If any of these older church historians expressed a freer view regarding the opinions of the heretics, it was the above-mentioned Evagrius.

> Let none of the pagans laugh at me [he says] on the grounds that later bishops condemn the earlier ones and are always adding something new to the faith. For we, examining the ineffable and inscrutable love of God toward men and wishing to honor and extol this love to the greatest possible extent, follow either this opinion or that one. In addition, none of those who have contrived heresies among the Christians wished in the first instance to speak blasphemously or slipped into error with a desire to slander the divine, but rather did so with the belief that he was saying something better than that which had been said before. The things which are essential and important have been agreed upon by all in common. What we worship is the Trinity, and the things that we glorify are the unity: God and Word born before all ages, becoming flesh in a second birth out of indulgence to men. If, however, any innovations have been made regarding other matters, these have come about because our Saviour God has entrusted them to the one who also has power over them, so that rather the holy Catholic and apostolic church may direct the things which have been said on this side and on that toward what is proper and holy, and may come to the one smooth and straight road.[34]

Is it possible to adjudge any more equitably and open-mindedly the relation of heretical opinions to the doctrine of the orthodox church? But lest one should believe that the assertion here advanced deviates from the predominant view of the Catholic Church, one need only compare the damning judgment made by this same Evagrius upon the heresy of Nestorius—how he sees in him only a tool of the Devil, who, as the μισόκαλος δαίμων [spirit who hates the good], could not endure knowing that shortly before Julian's godlessness had been choked in the blood of martyrs, the insanity of Arius had been placed in unshakable fetters at Nicaea, and Eunomius and Macedonius had perished at the Bosporus and the holy city of Constantine as if blown away by the Holy Spirit;[35] and who thus had no peace until he succeeded in instigating a struggle of a completely different kind.[36]

---

34. Evagrius, *H.E.*, I, II. [ED. Translated from the Greek text, *PG*, LXXXVI, 2449 A–C. Quoted by Baur in German.]

35. [ED.] This refers to the condemnation and banishment of Eunomius and Macedonius, leaders of two Arian sects in the fourth century.

36. Evagrius, *H.E.*, I, 1 f.

5. *Philostorgius*

So similar is the character of all these church historians that even the unorthodox Philostorgius,[37] who likewise belongs to their ranks, changes nothing. He describes the period from the beginning of the Arian controversy up to the reign of Valentian III in 423 from an Arian perspective. If he saw the error in the doctrine of the divinity of Christ to lie on the Catholic side, then, to be consistent, the antithesis between Catholic truth and heretical error should also have appeared to him in another light. But this consequence lay beyond the scope of his vision. During the period in which there was a balance of power between the Arian and Catholic systems, he is an opponent of the Catholic Church on this one point alone; in all other matters his mode of perception is no less Catholic than that of the other historians.

6. *Nicephorus*

The Byzantine historian Nicephorus,[38] who lived in the first part of the fourteenth century, is a unique figure. While bringing to a close the line of Greek church historians, he at the same time recapitulates the

37. [ED.] Philostorgius (c. 364 to c. 425) was a polemical writer in the Arian cause. At an early age he met Eunomius, whose works he studied. The twelve books of his *Historia ecclesiastica*, intended to justify the Arian party, are lost, except for excerpts in Photius and others (collected in *PG*, LXV), which are however unreliable; the work apparently was used by Nicephorus (see below).

38. With the surname Callistus or Callisti, i.e., son of Callistus; not Callistius, as Karl Hase calls him in his *Kirchengeschichte* (Leipzig, 1834), 103.

[ED.] Callistus Xanthopulus Nicephorus (d. 1335?) grew up in Constantinople and apparently was trained by the Patriarch George of Cyprus with a group of classical students who cultivated style and phraseology. C. de Boor in *Zeitschrift für Kirchengeschichte*, VI (1884), 478–94, argued that Nicephorus' *Historia ecclesiastica* (*PG*, CXLV–CXLVII) was nothing but the modernization and plagiarization of an anonymous church history of the tenth century. (Cf. *Schaff-Herzog*, VIII, 159.) This theory is no longer accepted, and the work is regarded as an independent accomplishment. Cf. *RGG*, IV, 1483; and G. Gentz and K. Aland, "Die Quelle der Kirchengeschichte des Nicephorus und ihre Bedeutung für die Konstituierung des Textes der älteren Kirchenhistoriker," *Zeitschrift für die neutestamentliche Wissenschaft*, XLII (1949), 104–41. Nicephorus has been severely criticized by most Roman Catholic and Protestant writers other than Baur, but has been well regarded in the East.

entire historiography of the Greek Church. Like Evagrius, Nicephorus also took up the thread of church history where it had dropped from the hands of his immediate predecessor; thus he expressed his surprise, above all, that during the long period since the end of the sixth century it had occurred to no one to describe ecclesiastical events of the ensuing eras, which surely were no less numerous and important than those preceding—this having remained undone either because of apathy of mind or because of awe before the greatness and difficulty of the task. He would therefore endeavor to add what in later times had been passed over, and bring to termination this history—which he hoped would be useful for his readers—shortly before his own time. Since Nicephorus himself mentions the completion of his work, one would expect a church history continued to the beginning of the fourteenth century. However, the major part of his work does not cover the era following his predecessors, which he had intended to describe independently of them, but rather the earlier one, in which he was obliged to hold for the most part to the works of the older church historians, even though he also used new sources. For that very reason, what gives him significance in the literature of church history is not what he accomplished in the way of continuation but rather the universality of his literary plan. He intended not merely to describe the ecclesiastical events of subsequent eras but to link them with those of earlier times and to provide a coherent work, written in one style and tone, proceeding uniformly in a well-connected chain, which, in containing the doings and destinies of the Catholic Church in a single volume, would as far surpass the works of others as the whole surpasses the part and a coherent work a fragment.

In accord with this plan, Nicephorus dealt in eighteen books with the history of the Catholic Church up to the death of Emperor Phocas in the year 610. Of five further books there exists only an outline of contents, and we do not know whether he continued his work any further than the era to which these books refer, up to the year 911. Thus the work remained far behind the original plan and design of its author; but even in its incomplete form, it is remarkable that the idea of a universal history, encompassing the entire course of the Catholic Church, is expressed and at least partly brought to realization for the first time. For now the concern is awakened in the field of church history not merely to continue the narrative piecemeal but to comprehend the whole as well, and to place it clearly before the eye in the unity of an unbroken, uniformly progressing narrative. However, this could not happen without taking pains to abbreviate as much as possible and to draw within narrower limits the narrative of predecessors (who, within the shorter period they are describing, could accord greater space to particular details); to omit whatever did not seem to belong to the subject matter itself; and in general to subordinate the particular to the unity of the whole, according to the criterion of the more general view one intended to maintain. This is related to another form of historiography that comes into view especially at this point.

7. Rufinus and Jerome; Cassiodorus

In the Greek church historians, a spark of the free, versatile spirit of the historians of ancient Greece—a spirit marked by fluency of expression and skill of presentation—continued to live on. It is otherwise in the Latin Church, where church history more and more took the form of chronicles, in so far as it was not satisfied with the mere translation of the works of the Greeks. Rufinus and Jerome had already turned to this. The former not only translated the church history of Eusebius but also shortened and altered it and continued it in two further books to the end of the reign of Emperor Theodosius I.[39] The latter planned the two of his writings that are relevant at this point, the Chronicle and the catalogue of *viri illustres,* or of *scriptores ecclesiastici* (subsequently continued by the Gallic presbyter Gennadius), entirely for the purpose of providing a compendium or survey of the most noteworthy events and persons in chronological sequence.[40] The less the value and usefulness of

39. [ED.] Tyrannius Rufinus (c. 345–c. 410) was a Latin ecclesiastical writer, translator, and ascetic. He spent many years in Egypt and Palestine before returning to his place of birth, Aquileia, where he settled for the rest of his life. At the urging of Macarius, he translated into Latin Origen's *Peri archōn (De principiis),* the first draft of which was completed in 398 or 399. Jerome sought to show the inadequacy of Rufinus' translation by engaging upon one of his own, and a sharp controversy between the two men ensued. Rufinus also translated Eusebius' *Historia ecclesiastica,* continuing it to cover the period from 324 to 395; this work was completed at Aquileia about 401. The two books of Rufinus' continuation are found in *PL,* XXI. He translated a number of other works, and wrote a *Commentarius in symbolum apostolorum* [Commentary on the Apostles' Creed], the earliest Latin exposition of the symbol. A critical edition of his Latin translation of Eusebius was prepared by T. Mommsen (Leipzig, 1903).

40. [ED.] St. Jerome (Eusebius Sophronius Hieronymus) was born about 345 and died near Bethlehem in 420. The story of his life and literary career is generally well known and need not be reviewed here. His earliest work in church history was

church history could be denied, the more the respective writings were arranged for the practical purpose of historical instruction. This was especially the intention of the twelve books of the so-called *Historia tripartita* undertaken by Cassiodorus,[41] in which the works of the three church historians Socrates, Sozomenus, and Theodoret are blended into a coherent presentation in Latin.

8. *Sulpicius Severus*

Since in the utilization of the works of the Greek church historians the endeavor had already been made to shorten them and to compress their contents, the chronicle developed—the more this soil was abandoned—as the true form of Latin historiography. It consisted of a mere summary and bare narrative of factual occurrences, but strove all the more, on the other hand, to encompass the whole and to provide a survey from the very beginning of history up to the present. The Gallic presbyter Sulpicius Serverus,[42] the first writer of the Latin Church to work in church history independently of the Greeks, transposes us completely, in the Preface with which he began his "Sacred History," into the perspective of the need from which the treatment of church history

---

the translation into Latin of the chronological tables that comprise the second part of the *Chronicon* [Chronicle] of Eusebius, with a supplement covering the period from 325 to 379. This translation, known as the *Temporum liber* [Book of Dates], is found in *PL*, XXVII. His most important work in church history, *De viris illustribus* [The Lives of Illustrious Men, or Catalogue of Ecclesiastical Writers] (*PL*, XXIII; *NPNF*[2], III), was produced after his retirement to Bethlehem in 392. The title and arrangement are borrowed from Suetonius. It contains short biographies of 135 Christian authors, from St. Peter down to Jerome himself. Gennadius of Marseilles (died about 496) continued this work, adding an additional 99 writers, up to about 480, the time his work was completed (*PL*, LVIII; *NPNF*[2], III).

41. [ED.] Flavius Magnus Aurelius Cassiodorus (c. 480–c. 570) was a Roman historian and statesman who retreated about 540 to the Benedictine monastery at Vivarium to pursue a scholarly career. His *Historia ecclesiastica tripartita* [Tripartite Church History] (*CSEL*, LXXI) filled a gap in the Western knowledge of church history and was the principal handbook used in the Middle Ages for the period it covered.

42. [ED.] Sulpicius Severus (c. 360–420) was a lawyer who later assumed the ascetic life. The two books of his *Chronicorum* [Chronicles] or *Historia sacra* [Sacred History] (*PL*, XX) appeared about 403, and have the flavor of the formal culture of southern France. He wrote two other important historical works, the "Life of St. Martin of Tours" and his "Dialogues"; the latter is an attempt to win Gallic Christianity for asceticism.

proper to the chronicle arose. He has undertaken, he says, to summarize briefly the events that are found in Holy Scripture, beginning with the creation of the world, and to continue up to the present by means of a division into periods, since many who wished to perceive the Divine in a concise instruction have earnestly requested it of him. He has acquiesced to their wishes and has endeavored to summarize in two small books what was contained in many volumes, and indeed so that despite the brevity, the facts would be deprived of little. But it has seemed to him not unsuitable, since he has already covered sacred history up to the crucifixion of Christ and the deeds and fortunes of the apostles, also to tell what happened subsequently: the destruction of Jerusalem, the persecutions of Christians, the ensuing times of peace, and after that the disturbances that again arose inside the church. Just as the church history of the New Testament later was prefaced by that of the Old Testament, so Sulpicius Severus, whose sacred history is nothing other than a church history of the Old Testament, believed that the history of the New Testament ought not to be separated from it. The broader the temporal period he described, and the more he made it his task to compress the entire content of what had happened into a summary, the more his presentation bears the predominant character of a chronicle. But the chronicle is concerned not so much with the past as with the present, and it starts from the past only so as to obtain a firm foothold in it. The further back it goes, the more it must limit itself, finally, to a narrow sphere. The intention actually is only to narrate in chronological sequence the events of the present from the immediate sources of a specific contemporary history, with special attention to details.

9. *Gregory of Tours, Bede, the Middle Ages*

The first of the more significant historical works of this kind are the Frankish church history of Bishop Gregory of Tours [43] and the Anglo-Saxon church history of Bede.[44] The first of these starts with the cre-

43. [ED.] Gregory of Tours (538 or 539 to 593 or 594) was appointed Bishop of Tours in 573. His most important work in church history is his *Historia Francorum* [History of the Franks] (*PL*, LXXXI), completed a few years before his death.

44. [ED.] Bede (known as "the Venerable") was the first great English scholar; he was born in 672 or 673 and died in 735. He was placed in the monastery at Wearmouth at the age of seven, and settled permanently at the monastery of Jarrow in 682. His most important work is his *Historia ecclesiastica gentis Anglorum* [*The Ecclesiastical History of the English Nation*, trans. Ernest Rhys (London & New York, 1910)] (*PL*, XCV), which gives in five books the ecclesiastical and political

ation of the world, proceeds through sacred history down to Gaul, with fleeting reference to secular history, and then pursues the special history of that country from the time when a new political and ecclesiastical order had been established by the conquest of the Franks. Gregory describes the history of the Frankish Empire down through the sequence of events experienced by himself (until the year 591; he died in 594) from the point of view of the church. As he himself describes his point of view in the preamble to the first book, the church had to undergo conflict with the opposing world in the conflicts of kings with hostile peoples, of martyrs with pagans, of the church with heretics. Bede does not start so far back; he begins at the landing of Julius Caesar in Britain, and describes, in a fashion similar to Gregory, the history of the Christian church among the Anglo-Saxons up to the year 731 (he died in 735), based on fresh sources of oral tradition and his own experiences. Such works, which in character are basically chronicles, have their value as immediate sources and documents of history. A higher claim they do not themselves make; and when they rise to a more general reflection concerning what has happened, their complete pragmatism (as is especially true of Gregory) can be seen in the way they gladly make use of whatever opportunity presents itself to draw attention to the Providence visible in so many phenomena of life, both rewarding and punishing. Like the ancient church historians, they especially attribute sudden illnesses and premature death to the directly revenging hand of God.[45]

The historians of the Middle Ages who follow Gregory and Bede, and who continue the historical tradition, bring nothing especially distinctive to the general task of church historiography in their merely narrative works, which do not pass beyond the limited view of the chronicle and which belong to secular history just as much as to church history. This is true up to Antoninus of Florence,[46] whose *Summa historialis* is the most comprehensive but also the most superficial collection of historical material to be passed on in this form. Hence, for our purpose, there is no need to dwell any further on these writers. In general, the Middle Ages, which were engaged in the progressive formation of their own still-emerging frame of reference, possessed a historical sense only in so far as

history of England from the time of Caesar down to 731. The first twenty-one chapters are compiled from earlier writers; but after 596 he uses documentary and oral sources. He also did considerable work in biblical exegesis.

45. Cf. J.W. Löbell, *Gregor von Tour und seine Zeit* (Leipzig, 1839), 438 f.

46. [ED.] Saint Antoninus of Florence (1389–1459) was a member of the Dominican order and Archbishop of Florence. His world chronicle, the *Summa historialis* [Historical Compendium], was published in three volumes in Venice in 1480.

it was necessary to continue the thread of the historical transmission of events. Their vision was directed only to the present and to the history continuing in it. If any one looked back into the past, he regarded what lay in it merely to be factual truth, which forever had become part of history, requiring no further investigation. As we can see from the false decretals of Isidore,[47] this lack of historical sense went so far that past and present were identified outright, and what belonged to the present was believed to exist for the first time in its true historical significance when it had been given the character of a tradition from the past.

If we think of the force with which the whole consciousness of that age was held under the sway of tradition, we can also imagine the beam of light that must have struck a dawning historical consciousness when the clear and definite insight first arose at only a single point that the objective reality of history was something quite other than what up to then had been the common belief of the time. So it was with Lorenzo Valla when, around the middle of the fifteenth century, he recognized the alleged *donatio Constantini* [donation of Constantine] as the most obvious historical deception, and made known this discovery in tones of the most intense indignation.[48] With this a beginning had already been made in tearing away the veil that lay upon the historical consciousness of the Middle Ages.

47. [ED.] The Pseudo-Isidorian Decretals were a group of forgeries produced by a churchly party in France around the middle of the ninth century, and were purported to have been collected by a certain Isidore Mercator. They consisted of decisions of Popes and councils of the first eight centuries, in which the early Popes claimed for themselves supreme jurisdiction and bishops asserted their autonomy vis-à-vis secular authorities on the one hand and archbishops on the other; all bishops had the right to appeal directly to the Pope. The so-called "Donation of Constantine" was included among the Decretals. The authenticity of these documents was not questioned until the fifteenth century.

48. *De falso credita et ementita Constantini donatione declamatio* [Declamation Concerning the Falsely Credited and Forged Donation of Constantine].

[ED.] Lorenzo Valla (1405–57) was an Italian humanist, philologist, historical critic, and priest. While under the patronage of King Alfonso V of Aragon, he published, about 1440, his famous *Declamatio*. The King protected him against ecclesiastical discipline. He also composed a *Collatio Novi Testamenti* [Collation of the New Testament] and wrote various essays in defense of free inquiry vis-à-vis the fetters of ecclesiastical tradition.

THE REFORMATION AND THE OLD PROTESTANT VIEW OF HISTORY: THE *MAGDEBURG CENTURIES*

1. *The Reformation*

The old Catholic view of history remained unchanged as long as the Catholic Church maintained an unrestricted forward movement and an undisturbed unity. But after the great schism caused by the Reformation had torn that unity apart, a completely different view of history now opposed the earlier one. Just as the Catholic Church rests on the presupposition in principle that it alone is the saving church, containing in itself the pure and absolute truth, so the Reformation is the absolute antithesis of this assumption. It denies what the Catholic Church asserts, and sees in the condition of the latter as a whole the direct opposite of what the Catholic Church considers to be its own substantial nature. In its antithesis to the Catholic Church the Reformation is a return of religious consciousness to itself, in order to establish a connection of the church in its present condition with its Idea, or with what the church is intrinsically and ought also to be in reality as the essential content of religious consciousness. Here, then, is to be found the task of looking back into the past from the present. If the church in reality is not what it ought to be intrinsically, then it must at one time have become what it is now, since it is unthinkable that its original condition should not have been adequate to its Idea; and the problem now is to explain from history how in the course of time so great a change ensued.

The Protestant view of history is thus directly opposed to the Catholic. If for Catholicism there is no historical movement by which the church could have become something essentially different from what it was originally, and if it sees in the whole course of the church only the immanent truth realizing itself to an ever greater extent and coming to a wider recognition, then in the Protestant view, on the other hand, the

79

church in its present condition is cut off by so wide a breach from what it originally was that between the two points an infinitely large series of changes must have taken place. For Catholicism, actually, there is so little sense of historical becoming that it regards what has developed temporally as something that has been from the beginning. But in Protestantism there arose for the first time a truly historical consciousness of the church, such that it cannot accept the origin and the continuation of the church as simply identical but must keep them separate in their essential difference. It sees in the history of the Christian church an ever more radical alteration—and only of such a sort by which the church has moved ever further away from what, in accord with its Idea, it ought to be. In the same proportion that, for Catholicism, divine truth shines in ever greater splendor throughout the ages of the church, Protestantism sees only an ever greater dimming of the light and the total conversion of truth into error. Even though each of these views may be as one-sided as the other when they are set against each other in direct antithesis, nevertheless it is already an essential step forward that an equally absolute denial should have confronted an absolute claim; and historical consciousness, divided between thesis and antithesis, could attend to its object only in critical fashion.

This opposition of views was of the very essence of the Reformation. Although the principle of the Reformation is considered to be its return to Scripture and its unconditional acknowledgement of the authority of the Scripture principle, nevertheless this was not its first and immediate principle. For the return to Scripture was only for the purpose of becoming aware, by that criterion, of the complete difference intervening, in the past of the church, between its present and its original condition. No matter how we may conceive and define the essence of the Reformation, it directly involves an essentially different view of history; and in the nature of the case one could not be of so different and completely opposite an opinion concerning the outcome of the whole course of development of the Christian church, without having the same antithesis between the two parties extend to everything that is the necessary presupposition of this outcome. The discussions and controversies occasioned by the Reformation everywhere afford the clearest proof of this. The basic principles of the Reformation could not be maintained, nor the objections and reproaches of opponents refuted, without returning to history and demonstrating from it the justification of the newly won point of view. It therefore lay in the interest of the Reformation itself to bring ever more clearly into consciousness the special view of history on which it rested. This could be done in two ways, both providing oneself (for one's own religious interest) with a more exact account of the new vantage point at which one stood, and for the polemical purpose of refuting opponents. However sharp the opposition to the Catholic Church, and whatever the reassurance to be found in an awareness of standing on the solid ground of Scripture, nevertheless the entire past of the church could not be so simply overlooked that there was no need of tracing, even through the times of greatest darkness, the slender thread of historical continuity. No matter how greatly, in the course of time, the light of divine truth in the church may have been obscured, still it could not have been so totally extinguished but that there were always a few witnesses by whom the consciousness of truth would have been kept alive from period to period.

2. *Matthias Flacius*

Out of the need for such a demonstration arose the *Catalogus testium veritatis* [1] of Matthias Flacius, which appeared in 1556. It was the first writing in which the view of history instituted by the Reformation was

1. They are the ones, says Flacius in his Preface, who "before our age cried out against the Roman pontiff and his errors. From these historical testimonies themselves it can be abundantly proved that there have always been at least a few of the pious, those who were more upright in their judgment than the common crowd and who joined with us in condemning the entire Papacy or certain parts of it. But the devastating passage of time has devoured many others, and the Antichrist with his followers has most zealously suppressed such writings; and finally, one teacher very often has had many pupils and followers. Wherefore most false is that sophistry of the Papists, who try to attribute to us and to our religion the hateful charge of novelty, and to attribute to themselves the dignity of great age." Cf. A. Twesten, *Matthias Flacius Illyricus, eine Vorlesung* (Berlin, 1844), 14 f.

[ED.] Matthias Flacius Illyricus (1520–75) was born and educated in Italy as a Roman Catholic. Under the influence of an uncle, he gave up intentions to become a monk, and went instead to Germany, where he studied under Melanchthon in Wittenberg, and eventually under Luther. The defense of the Protestant doctrine of justification by faith alone thenceforward became the guiding purpose of his life. Indeed, his strict defense of this doctrine against the more moderate attitude of Melanchthon, and his objections to the latter's concessions in the Leipzig Interim, brought him into a long and bitter controversy with the Melanchthonians. He settled in Magdeburg in 1549 and made that the headquarters of his struggle against the Wittenberg party, against Osiander and Schwenckfeld, against the Synergists, and against the Roman Catholics. Later he moved to Jena, to Strassburg, and to Frankfort. His *Catalogus testium veritatis, qui ante nostram aetatem reclamarunt Papae* (Basel, 1556) was a "Catalogue of Witnesses to the Truth, Who before Our Time Cried Out against the Pope."

not merely given casual expression but was set out in its historically motivated continuity, in order to demonstrate that just as during the time of the prophet Elijah God spared seven thousand who did not bow down before Baal and who represented the true Israel, so at all times there have been in the Christian church witnesses of truth who, amid the errors and corruptions of the great mass, preserved the divine fire from extinction until it was again kindled into a bright flame by the light of the Reformation. The inversion of the relation between light and darkness during various periods of the Christian church, as viewed by the two parties, can be seen from the succession of these witnesses, who, even if they are not completely lacking at any time, still comprise only a very small number. But in order to refute the opponents more thoroughly it was necessary to draw attention not merely to the sparks of divine truth that always remained even in darkest times, but also to the darkness itself—to show how it spread increasingly from century to century and finally became an all-enveloping power of obscurity, exhibited in its full capacity.

3. *The Magdeburg Centuries: Its Plan*

To this end, the same Protestant theologian who, by his catalogue of the witnesses of truth, had already acquired as great merit in church historiography as in the cause of the Reformation, took the decisive step. The great historical work undertaken by Flacius in the *Magdeburg Centuries* [2] has a significance for the literature of church history that has

2. It appeared in thirteen folio volumes during the years 1559–74. As he also expressed it in the Dedicatory Preface to the second edition of his *Catalogus testium veritatis* in 1562, three things appeared to Flacius still to be lacking for the perfection of the church: (1) "a certain concise explanation of the sacred books, or (as it is commonly called) gloss"; (2) "a separate and complete elucidation of the Hebrew language"; and (3) "a full and accurate history, which should fully and completely unfold and illustrate the nature of the church and of religion from the birth of Christ onward, so that no one might be able to impose on us either the Papacy or other errors and abuses under the pretended authority of remote antiquity." The extent to which Flacius lived in this genuinely Protestant view of history is remarkable.

[ED.] Flacius began planning the work in 1553, while he was still at Magdeburg. He secured the support of patrons, commissioned assistants to search libraries throughout Europe for sources and documents, and, together with Johann Wigand and Matthäus Judex, stood at the head of the entire project and worked out the details of the plan. In 1557 he was called to Jena, but he continued to direct the project from there. The work was published in Basel between 1559 and 1574 under the title, *Ecclesiastica historia, integram Ecclesiae Christi ideam, . . . secundum singulas Cen-*

still not been sufficiently appreciated, even though its great historical value could scarcely be denied. The more closely one is acquainted with it, the more one compares it with all earlier achievements in the field of church history, the more one is convinced of the truth of the assertion that with this work, for the first time, the church has risen to a truly historical consciousness of its entire past. No other church-historical work was to have been initiated, and carried through as far as it went, with such a clear awareness of the task that church history in general must perform, and in accord with so definite and methodical a plan. The work's high merit is not merely in the great material enrichment of the contents of church history by the investigation of so many sources, in part disclosed for the first time, and by the care and exactitude with which the many aspects of church life were investigated and presented. No, it is epoch-making above all by virtue of the idea at the foundation of the whole, the inclusive conception of church history from which it proceeds. The authors of the work express this more fully even in the Preface to their work, and, although briefly censuring the major deficiencies of the older church historians beginning with Eusebius, they justly note that from those who stand on a higher level of religious understanding a more thoroughgoing insight into the course of the Christian church is to have been expected.

In accord with the plan of the work,[3] first the character and contents of the history of each century are described in general, then [in the second chapter] a survey of the scope of the Christian church and the dis-

---

turias . . . per aliquot studiosos et pios viros in urbe Magdeburgica [A Church History Embracing the Whole Form of the Church of Christ, . . . by Individual Centuries . . . by Several Zealous and Pious Men in the City of Magdeburg]; hence it was called the *Magdeburg Centuries.* Separate volumes treated each of the first thirteen centuries. The work was never completed. Wigand and after him Stangewald worked on the fourteenth through sixteenth centuries without completing the chronicle; a manuscript dealing with the sixteenth century, compiled by Wigand, is in Wolfenbüttel. In the Catholic Church the *Centuries* became known as the *pestilentissimum opus,* and a worthy opponent was found in Caesar Baronius (see below, chap. III). For a recent study, see Heinz Scheible, *Die Entstehung der Magdeburger Zenturien: Ein Beitrag zur Geschichte der historiographischen Methode* (Gütersloh, 1966). Scheible has also published brief selections from the *Centuries* and from Flacius in *Die Anfänge der reformatorischen Geschichtschreibung* (Gütersloh, 1966).

3. [ED.] What follows is a description of the contents of each volume. Each century was treated in a separate volume, and the topics or chapter subjects taken up in each were identical—hence Baur's criticism that each century was forced into a rigid pattern of treatment. This plan is summarized in the *Methodus historici operis, ac singulorum capitum metae generales* [Method of the Historical Work, and the General Goals of the Individual Chapters], following the *Praefatio in historia ecclesiastica* in the first volume (see below, 95, n. 23).

semination of Christianity is provided; to which is added [in the third chapter] a further description of the external situation of the church, i.e., whether it suffered persecutions or lived in quiet and peace. The fourth chapter is especially important; here the doctrines of the church existing in each age are analyzed and set forth as exactly as possible in the order of individual articles. The fifth chapter then treats the heresies and errors by which the pure doctrine of the church was distorted; the sixth, the ceremonies or rites of the church; the seventh, the polity and government of the church (here in particular the unification of individual churches into a whole, the relation of church and state, and the question of the primacy of the Roman Church are discussed). The eighth chapter treats the schisms and less important controversies; the ninth, the councils; the tenth, the life and personal conditions of bishops and church teachers; the eleventh, heretics; the twelfth, martyrs; the thirteenth, miracles and prodigies; the fourteenth, the outer or political circumstances of the Jews; and at the end, in the last two chapters, the most important developments in the field of non-Christian religions and political history are also listed. The work is laid out, as this survey shows, according to so comprehensive a plan that nothing essential and important in the content of church history is omitted; and the sphere it describes is traced rather too broadly than too narrowly.

If we take a closer look at the internal aspects of the work, it is not difficult, to be sure, to discover deficiencies of various kinds. We can criticize the merely external division according to centuries; the uncertainty of much information on which the work is based; the use of writings that should not be counted as sources of history at all; and even more, the great dispersion and parceling out of the material, which has not only produced many repetitions but has also kept separate what in the nature of the case belonged together. For example, heresies are treated in one place and heretics in another, and the discussions of persecutions and of martyrs are found in different chapters. We can further criticize the lack of a necessary assimilation of the historical material, which so often is given only in its raw and naked form, as though the work were not a historical presentation but only a compilation of documents and notes. Further deficiencies are the inclusion of so much biographical, literary, and highly specialized information, which has no particular interest for the general purpose of church history, and in general, an inadequate consideration of all the requirements in such a work for an artistic form of presentation. Since it is not for us to provide

here a detailed criticism of the work, however, but only to characterize
the general view of history on which it is based, we shall limit ourselves
to what has been indicated above and shall rather emphasize the features
characteristic of the historical standpoint of its authors.

4. *The Criticism and Polemicism of the Centuries*

The *Magdeburg Centuries* is the best representative of the old Protestant mode of perception, which in turn derived from the principal tendency of the Reformation. In the view of its authors, the whole development of the Christian church takes an increasingly darker and more sinister course. The center of the ever-widening darkness is the Papacy.
Just as it was the most decisive conviction of the Reformers that the
Pope is the Antichrist, so also the Centuriators saw in the church, in so
far as it was controlled by the Bishop of Rome, only the realm of the
Antichrist; and their most urgent effort is now directed to the rigorous
tracking of this "Antichristianity" from its very beginnings through its
gradual growth up to the point at which it found in Protestantism the
opponent by whose resistance its power was broken.

In its antithesis to Catholicism, Protestantism is implicitly critical. Since
it contests the claims of the Catholic Church, refutes its false contentions,
and in general takes a position to which the authority of tradition in itself
gives no validity, it must first of all raise questions about the grounds on
which whatever is traditional rests. Doubts and suspicions are often justified even concerning what is generally accepted. In all these aspects,
Protestantism has an authentically critical tendency, which in the field of
church history automatically had to become a historical criticism, one
which everywhere has penetrated more deeply the more it has been
sharpened by polemical interest. In no part of their comprehensive work
did the Centuriators prove better critics than in the many chapters investigating the history of the Papacy. They tried to disclose the ground-
lessness of the presumptions on which the Papacy was based at the very
beginnings of the Roman Church; and thereafter in the history of each
century their attention and research were directed to nothing more than
to all the attempts made either by the Roman bishops to expand their
power or by their opponents to restrain and limit them and to refute
their pretensions. It is a laudable proof of their historical criticism and of
the independence of their judgment that the authority of the old legend

of the Apostle Peter's Roman episcopate did not deter them from confronting the principle of the claims of the Roman bishops on the grounds of the Gospel history itself. Even if Peter seems to have had a certain pre-eminence among the apostles, they asserted, be it because of his superior gifts or his age, nonetheless it is proved by a series of arguments (which admit of no exceptions on account of Matthew 16:18, since here Peter is addressed only in the name of all the apostles) that Peter had no primacy among the apostles as a result of which he could have become universal bishop of the church. That Peter came to Rome cannot, indeed, be denied outright, in view of the clear testimonies of the church fathers that we have; but since difficulties not easily dismissed are encountered at every one of the periods in which he could have come to Rome, the truth of the matter can only be left undecided. In any event, if Peter was in Rome, it can only have been for a very short time and not in the capacity attributed to him.[4]

Since history has been falsified by so many forged documents in the interests of the Papacy and the hierarchy, it must be regarded as a very significant merit of the Centuriators that so many frauds of this kind were uncovered by them. The inauthenticity of the decretals that speak of the Roman bishops of the second and third centuries as though they were Popes of the eleventh and twelfth was proved on grounds that not only do honor to the Centuriators' critical acumen but also refute the fraud so convincingly that this question was in essence settled for all who did not intentionally remain blind. The chapters dedicated to the investigation of the papal decretals had been worked out with special care; they belong, in fact, to the ranks of investigations by which a new path was broken for historical truth.[5] Just as they conceded no historical justification to the origin of the Papacy, so also they remained firm in the conviction that the Roman bishops from the beginning had intended nothing less than to strive for the power that they later actually executed as Popes. Nothing related to this, rightly or wrongly, is left unnoticed.

4. In the Baumgarten-Semler edition (1757), I/2, 944 ff.

[ED.] Siegmund Jakob Baumgarten and Johann Salomo Semler (eds.), *Centuriae Magdeburgenses seu historiae ecclesiastica Novi Testamenti cum variorum theologorum continuationibus ad haec nostra tempora* . . . (4 vols.; Nuremberg, 1757–65). Baumgarten died after the publication of the first part of Vol. I, and the work was continued by Semler. Hence it is usually referred to as the "Semler edition." A complete set of this edition is not available in the United States, and for citations from later *Centuries* I have made use of the Basel edition, 1559–74.

5. Cf. *Cent.* II, VII (Semler ed., II/I, 133–62); *Cent.* III, VII (Semler ed., II/2, 457–92).

With all the keen-sightedness of their Protestant mistrust, they trace the endeavors by which this or that bishop sought to seize the power that was so damaging for the church, and always to extend it further in all directions. Already by the third *Century*, the *mysterium iniquitatis* [mystery of iniquity], which partly *agere coepit* [begins to work] and partly is *ab aliis repressum* [restrained by others], has become the permanent formula for reference to the primacy in the church.[6] In the fourth *Century*, the transition to the history of the primacy is made in the following words: "As in previous centuries the Roman bishops began, given the opportunity, gradually preparing for themselves an approach to the primacy; and thus in this century the mystery of iniquity has not been idle, but has gradually advanced more and more, seizing opportunities, even the slightest opportunities, on all sides." [7] This is completely true of the fifth *Century*, as is stated in the general survey:

> In the first place it is most worthy of observation that in this century the spirit of the Antichrist, working through certain Roman bishops, has quite shamelessly scattered the first seeds of its primacy and pre-eminence over all the other bishops of the church of Christ. For although certain sharp and vigorous watchmen had in the case of a certain foul and deceitful deed (because, to be sure, the Roman prelates wickedly tampered with the Nicene decrees) caught a wolf by the ears, so to speak, and had offered a certain amount of opposition by which they were repressing that vain and wicked claim, nevertheless more than too much has been conceded, so that indeed in this century the Antichrist, who was brought forth for the following century as a mature offspring, seems to have been conceived in the womb.[8]

Then in the sixth century "the mystery of iniquity, now for a long time active among the Roman bishops, repeatedly made progress in increasing its power, both by exalting itself above all the churches and by establishing a universal episcopate." [9] Finally it came about, as is reported in the seventh *Century*, that the "mystery of iniquity . . . finally made manifest in this century" what it "thus far had done with great effort . . . among the Roman bishops." [10] After many years of controversy between the bishops of Constantinople and the Roman pontiffs, Boniface III, "having obtained an emperor very like himself in crimes," with great

6. [ED.] *Cent.* III, vii (Semler ed., II/2, 478).
7. [ED.] *Cent.* IV, vii (Semler ed., III/1, 444).
8. [ED.] *Cent.* V, 1 (Basel ed., V, 2).
9. [ED.] *Cent.* VI, vii (Basel ed., VI, 425).
10. [ED.] *Cent.* VII, vii (Basel ed., VII, 228).

effort got the "assassin Phocas" to decree that the Roman Church should be the head of all the churches, and that its pontiff should have the title and dignity of an ecumenical bishop.[11] Besides, it seemed especially significant (*non carere mysterio* [not free of (the) mystery (of iniquity)]) that, with the permission of Emperor Phocas, Boniface IV allowed the Pantheon—a temple in which all the pagan gods had been venerated—to be consecrated to the honor of the Virgin Mary and all the holy martyrs. "For the Antichrist, after rejecting the true God, ought to worship the foreign god of the Maozim,[12] and to increase the frenzies for idol worship of every sort, and scatter them far and wide for the purpose of leading people astray."[13] The harmful influence of the Roman Church had already previously manifested itself chiefly in matters of the cultus. Hence, already in the third *Century*, in the chapter on ceremonies and usages, those of the Roman Church are especially mentioned; for in this Church superstitious representations and practices proliferated most of all, since the *mysterium iniquitatis* had to disclose itself in its activity above all at the place accorded it (Rev. 17).[14] Following the point at which the Papacy now already stands before the eye in its nakedness, the succeeding *Centuries* had only to depict "the way in which the Antichrist, sitting in the temple of God, displayed himself as God, and indeed played the role of the son of perdition and exalted himself above those who are called gods, that is, [above] the magistracy, and mounted the beast, that is, the Roman Empire."[15]

Even these few passages can show the preponderance of the dark side in a history of the Christian church for which the Bishop of Rome is the

---

11. [ED.] *Cent.* VII, vii (Basel ed., VII, 228). Boniface III (elected Pope 607) established friendly relations with the usurper to the Roman throne, the Emperor Phocas (d. 610). Boniface had been commissioned by his predecessor, Gregory the Great, to settle the strife over the title of "universal bishop," which was claimed by the patriarch of Constantinople, John the Faster. In this, Phocas apparently acquiesced and according to early accounts (the *Liber pontificalis*, Paulus, Diaconus, and Bede), he recognized Rome as *caput omnium ecclesiarum*. Boniface IV (Pope 608-15) maintained the same friendly relations with Phocas, from whom he acquired the Pantheon in Rome, which he transformed from a pagan temple into a Christian church. (Cf. *Schaff-Herzog*, II, 222-23.)

12. [ED.] This is apparently an illusion to the Vulgate text of Daniel 11:38. *Maozim* is merely the transliteration of a Hebrew word whose meaning apparently was unclear to the Vulgate translators, who supposed it to be the name of a place or people. In the Revised Standard Version, the word is translated "fortresses."

13. [ED.] *Cent.* VII, vii (Basel ed., VII, 229).

14. [ED.] *Cent.* III, vi (Semler ed., II/2, 451).

15. [ED.] *Cent.* VIII, vii (Basel ed., VIII, 477).

Antichrist incarnate. Despite the propriety of the Centuriators' having brought to view the arrogance of the Roman bishops and the many falsifications of history, nevertheless their entire historical consideration of the Papacy is one-sided and directed solely by polemical interests. Once the presupposition is established that the Bishop of Rome is the Antichrist, it is merely consistent that the entire history of the Papacy should be construed from this idea.

If the history of the Papacy, even on the most unprejudiced and equitable assessment, offers very abundant material for the purposes of such a presentation, which in the hands of such editors must obtain a very decisive influence on the character of the whole, it was just as natural, at a time when historical criticism was still so weak and uncertain, that information should have found the most willing acceptance that could make only a very slight claim to historical credibility, both in the quality of its sources and in its unmistakable tendency. It is to be expected that for such historians there could not be a more desirable finding than a story such as that of the female Pope Joan.[16] To the Centuriators it seemed, by virtue of its very contents, to bear in itself the most obvious stamp of historical truth and to provide unmistakable proof of the fact that the Papacy was a Babylonian whore. They even ascribe to her a genuinely teleological character and therefore placed her in the section in which those are listed "who made opposition to the tyranny of the Roman Antichrist," with the following introductory words: "In this century God has revealed by a marvelous and conspicuous deed the baseness of the pontifical see and has exposed that Babylonian harlot to the eyes and gaze of all, so that the pious might recognize that holy pontifical dignity, which was held in reverence by the whole world, to be the mother of all fornication, spiritual and corporeal,

16. [ED.] The legend concerning Pope Joan dates from the middle of the thirteenth century. It occurs for the first time in the chronicle of Jean de Mailly, who dated her about 1100. The legend was chiefly disseminated, however, by the chronicle of Martinus Polonus (d. 1278). According to him, she was born either in Mainz or in England, disguised herself as a man while studying in Athens, was deeply admired in Rome for her learning, and was finally elected Pope in 855, ruling two and a half years under the name of Johannes Angelicus. She died in childbirth during a street procession and was buried on the spot. The legend is now believed to be traceable to a local Roman tradition concerning a lost statue allegedly bearing the epitaph of the female Pope, and for a while it was circulated by Catholic historians. The name Joan (Johanna, Johannes) is probably intended to imply a connection with the numerous Popes John, some of whom had notorious reputations. The two dates of 855 and 1100 reflect an effort to fill alleged lacunae in the list of Popes at those times.

and learn to curse and detest her." [17] Indeed, subsequent Popes seem to
have expressed a condemning judgment on this infamous deed, so that
they avoided the street in which it occurred and struck the name of the
whore from the list of the Popes; "but nonetheless such ones indeed
remained, patrons to be sure of all idol worship and fornication, slaves of
the Devil." [18]

If the Papacy is conceived from this point of view, then in fact it is
not surprising that one has no understanding, either of anything that is
to be judged above all by the results of the hierarchical system, or of
such acts as do make a claim to moral attention, or of the love of justice
on the part of some Popes, their sense of order, right, and legality, and
the courage with which they opposed the tyranny and wickedness of
princes and the brutality of the people. The recognition due them must
be refused. Everything the Popes have ever thought and done only
forms an endless web of the most diabolical intentions and endeavors. In
all the quarrels of the Popes with emperors and kings, bishops and
clergy, the Centuriators take the side of the opponents. Whoever defied
the Popes and withstood them boldly and steadfastly has won the game
beforehand; he stands in the ranks of the champions of right and truth.
For example, the Archbishops of Trier and Cologne, so notoriously ill-
famed in the marriage affair of the Carolingian Lothar, are placed on this
side against Nicholas I. One is even forced to believe that the praise
accorded the opponents was measured above all by the degree of their
resistance to the Pope. The German emperor Henry IV was praised by
the Centuriators as one of the most excellent princes, although they
could not complain enough about the deplorable conditions of the
church under his reign and his responsibility for it; whereas in Gregory
VII they discern, from the very sound of his name, "Hildebrand," the
villain fallen into hell, "the most monstrous monster of all those that this
earth has borne." [19]

Their view of history emerges most clearly with this chief architect
of the Papacy. They come with deepest regret to the "utterly pitiful and
doleful history, which no wise person can read without tears, recording
how Hildebrand treated the Roman Emperor with unheard-of arro-

17. [ED.] *Cent.* IX, VII (Basel ed., IX, 337).
18. [ED.] *Cent.* IX, VII (Basel ed., IX, 337).
19. In the Preface to the eleventh *Century* it is even said of him that he is a
"notable necromancer"—"that is, *he had covenants directly with the Devil himself,*
by whose aid he aspired oftentimes to higher honors." [ED. *Cent.* XI, *Epistola
Dedicatoria* (Basel ed., XI, 8).]

gance, impudence, and spite, hissed him off the stage, and indeed placed him before angels and men as a spectacle and a laughing stock." They depict him as a "shameless monk," who, "boiling with incredible ambition, shameless audacity, and remarkable cleverness, continually strove by means of money and necromancy to climb by hand and foot to major orders in the Roman Church, until finally he had made his way up to the very peak of the pontifical office, contrary to the canonical ordinances." It is easy to conclude, "with such a head raging rather than ruling in the Lord's church, of what sort are the rest of the members who depend on this monstrous and insane head." In the series of "crimes" committed by this "Roman monster," the "trampling under foot of political magistracy" and the "forbidding of marriage" take first place as the "two distinguishing marks—stigmata, as it were, branded on the Antichrist." [20] The Centuriators themselves cannot avoid the objection that, though Hildebrand is like this, all the Popes need not be, and that the entire Papacy should not be condemned because of the personal failure of one Pope. But their brief answer is that if one knows one Pope, one knows them all; and the fact remains that the Antichrist is condemned in all his forms by God himself by the clear content of his Word.

5. The Dualism of the Centuries

The tenuous claim to historical truth made by such an understanding and portrayal can now be seen. Where the general view is not drawn from what is factually given, but rather, as here, a previously conceived idea is simply made the criterion for the assessment of all details, objectivity of historical judgment must be abrogated in advance. A merely partisan view is expressed in such a portrayal, and polemical interest defines the guiding criterion.

However sharp the antithesis between the Protestant and the Catholic views of history, the two points of view coincide in that the one is as biased as the other. The difference is only that the two members of the antithesis have traded places. Where for Catholicism the luminous aspect of history is to be found, Protestantism sees only darkness, and vice versa. But when light and darkness, truth and error, confront each other once and for all in such sharp antithesis, fundamentally it makes no

20. [ED.] *Cent.* XI, VII (Basel ed., XI, 370 ff.).

difference for historical reflection whether the two parts of the antithesis are related in one manner or another. This whole way of viewing things is dualistic, and in the final analysis it has its roots in a basic conception that is purely dogmatic, either on the one side or on the other. The difference is so infinitely great that in all the centuries dominated by papal history, beginning with the most ancient period, the one side sees only the kingdom of the Antichrist and the ever expanding power of darkness, whereas the other side sees in the same period the Vicar of God and Christ exercising his blessed rule. Hence, simply by prescinding from this one point of difference, we can discover in the Protestant view of history all the characteristics of the Catholic.

The dualism of the Catholic view is given concrete form by the significance ascribed to the Devil. But the Devil plays the same role in the *Centuries* of the Protestant historians. The Preface to this great work starts off with a complaint about the disastrous eclipse suffered by true history because of the Devil. Thereby, this enemy of the human race intends nothing other than that he "might propagate and instill in miserable men horrible errors directed toward the dishonor of God and the ruin of men, in accord with his hatred and rage against God and men and his removal of heavenly truth. So that God might repress these attempts and spread the light of his truth among at least some men, preserving it and not allowing all men to be drowned in a certain sea of lies, illusions, and darkness, he willed, therefore, that histories be written; and he snatched them from the common fire, so to speak, and saved them." [21] This great kindness of God is justly given the highest praise. For human life would be truly bestial if one knew nothing about all that had happened previously, if everything lay buried in great oblivion and in hideous disorder and darkness.

Inasmuch as the whole undertaking of the Centuriators proceeded from the standpoint of a struggle, which, according to the precedent and example of the scriptural historians, must be directed against the Devil and the powers darkening the spiritual conscience of mankind, they must also perceive everywhere in the realm of church history the influences of the same diabolical power. Already in the second *Century* special attention is drawn to the fact that in a very short time after the apostles the Devil openly spread in the Christian church the most harmful and abominable heresies, by means of Saturninus, Basilides, Carpocrates, and a whole series of Gnostics. "In this matter the fury of the

21. [ED.] *Cent.* I, *Epistola Dedicatoria* (Semler ed., I/1, unnumbered pages 13–14).

Devil is clearly seen—the fury of him who wished to defile the church of Christ by his blasphemies, to contaminate it and to overturn it from its foundations, so that he might cause trouble for God and alienate many from the true doctrine. For just as good and beneficial teachers in the church are gifts of God, so in turn are heretics instruments of the Devil and foul monsters." [22] Even if the second century is somewhat purer than the first, one can still see how horribly the enemy of the human race, the father of all lies, desecrated the church of God after the demise of the apostles, not merely by the most inhuman persecutions but also by abominable heresies. Some who were not last in the company of the teachers of truth already had been contaminated by less than sound opinions; indeed, even the fundamental article of the justification of man before God had already begun to be obscured.

In general, this is the normal course of history. Scarcely has the saving truth appeared in a new and vivid light through divine Providence than the Devil makes even greater efforts—once the witnesses to truth called forth by God had again withdrawn from the scene of their activities, as did the apostles in the second century—to burst into the vacuum as into an abandoned house. It was no different in the age of the Reformation: after the death of the German prophet Luther, by whom the light of the Gospel was brought forth from its Egyptian darkness, various erroneous opinions immediately spread again in a fashion analogous to that of the second century—opinions that necessitate the redoubled vigilance and efforts of all pious servants of the Gospel. What the Devil thus attempts through heresies in the realm of dogma is accomplished by him with the same devastating effect in the form of the Antichrist through everything that belongs to the history of ceremonies and the hierarchical organization of the church.

Hence the same antithesis of light and darkness, of a good and an evil principle, runs through all periods and realms of the Christian church. According to the Catholic view, the enemy of the Christian church actually harasses and disturbs only its borders and succeeds in obtaining a firmer foothold upon the center of the church itself only at isolated moments now and then; but the Protestant view comes close to the extreme of a Manichaean dualism. The Devil, like the Manichaean Prince of the World, has erected his throne in the midst of Christendom; he has poured the poison of his destructive influence into all the veins of eccle-

22. [ED.] *Cent.* II, *Praefatio* (Semler ed., II/1, unnumbered page 46). Cf. also *Cent.* II, XI (Semler ed., II/1, 243–50).

siastical life; the church is essentially and substantially diabolic, anti-Christian. One is very vividly reminded here that the chief author of the *Centuries* is the same Protestant theologian who declared original sin to be the substance of human nature. As he intended, however, simply to surrender man to the Devil as a substance, but not as a spiritual subject, the energy of his Protestant self-consciousness expresses itself in the Manichaean dualism of his view of history. The Devil may hold sway or rule as he likes; but the more mightily he gains ground, the more unshakably the Protestant stands fast in the conviction, based on the certainty of his consciousness, that he will nevertheless hold the field through the One by whom he knows himself justified. This is the divine ray of light that shines through the Manichaean darkness of church history, even if only in the small number of individually diffused sparks of the faithful, shining forth everywhere.

Since in the struggle between the two principles, whose antithesis is the moving principle of the church, there is merely a question of driving back and warding off the invading enemy, church history does not proceed in its development from a principle and move forward from moment to moment; rather, it only represents the preservation of what existed from the beginning and remains identical with itself, even if periodically obscured. The same trait is also characteristic of this view of history. Where two wholly antithetical principles confront one another, neither can become something that it originally was not. Since no internal mediation of one with the other is possible, there is only an external contact between them; they quarrel continually, and even when one of them achieves a periodic supremacy over the other, the endeavor of each is to return to a pure identity with itself and to appear outwardly as it always had been intrinsically. Generally speaking, therefore, in a dualistic world view there is no immanent development but only a struggle for self-preservation.

But the less a thing is able to become what it originally was not, the more it smacks of dualism to place both of the principles, in the full extent of their essential reality, at the apex of the entire historical movement. The *Centuries*, too, gives evidence of its dualistic world view by assuming that the absolute perfection of Christianity and of the church was achieved at the very beginning of its history. At no other period was the condition of the church as a whole so entirely adequate to its Idea as the first, at the time of Jesus and the apostles. In it, not only was the divine truth that constitutes the substance of Christian doctrine perfectly revealed from the very beginning, and brought to light for the universal consciousness of mankind, but also everything having to do with the constitution and government, the entire organization of the church, was so ordered and established by the apostles that the church in all subsequent periods can only attempt to embody the original form of the apostolic church. Therefore church history can only have the task of awakening and keeping alive the consciousness of primitive Christianity and the apostolic church, and in all ages of showing how the condition of the church at each time compares with the original apostolic age.

The following were set forward by the Centuriators as the chief benefits of church history: (1) it places before the eye the Idea of the Christian church as in a single scene; (2) it shows the constant agreement of all ages in the teaching of the individual articles of faith; (3) it shows the origin and growth of errors and depravities, especially the beginnings and progress of the Antichrist; (4) it gives the proper and unquestionable norm for the assessment of heresies ("for oftentimes the same deceits of the most shameless Devil reappear"); (5) it shows how the government of the church was established, enabling one clearly to know how much of the first and most ancient form has been retained and where there has been deviation from it; (6) we can learn from it the marks of the true and the false church, and can see how the latter for the most part held sway and exercised its brutal power over the pious; (7) we can also learn how from time to time God awakens heroes, through whose service he again brings to light true doctrine and the true worship of God from the thick darkness in which the Devil has enveloped everything; (8) we can also learn from it the examples of those who did not avoid a struggle against corruptions of every kind, and who, under the most horrible persecutions, "did not become indifferent by accommodating themselves to the age or by placating the enemies of the Gospel through dissimulation and other unlawful and wicked means; rather they made their confessions steadfastly, fearlessly, and openly, by which they accomplished much more than by ill-timed surrender and bribery"; and so on.[23]

23. Cf. the *Praefatio in historia ecclesiastica causas contexendae historiae et commemorationem utilitatum et denique quandam ipsius scriptionis formam atque rationem sue methodum continens.*

[ED.] "Preface to Church History, Containing the Reasons for Compiling the History and a Mention of Its Usefulness, and Finally a Certain Plan of the Work Itself and the Scheme or Method of Procedure," Semler ed., I/1, unnumbered pages 18–27. A total of fourteen "benefits" are enumerated by the Centuriators, unnumbered pages 22–24. This Preface is followed by a *Methodus historici operis, ac*

If these and other, analogous factors are brought together, they blend into the picture of a struggle in which everything is aimed at maintaining the predominance of the good over the evil principle, in so far as it has this predominance from the beginning and must have it in the nature of the case; everything is aimed at preserving the position it originally had, and at pushing back the evil that has invaded the arena of the good to the limits it can only periodically transgress. The historical course of the church does not, therefore, proceed in a single direction such that every particular thing would be a moment in a self-developing continuity; rather, two parallel courses run side by side, which do not merge into a single, unified outcome, but meet and interlock only to repulse each other again and again in the antithesis of principle. Thus there is here, as in the Catholic view, an absolute presupposition that in the entire historical sequence of the church everything remains as it was from the beginning, and no change can take place by which the substantial forms of the church might be essentially altered. In the Protestant as in the Catholic view, since nothing can subsequently become what it originally was not, so everything belonging to the full reality of the church is supposed to have existed from the beginning; the two views differ only in the much sharper and stronger dualism of the Protestant view, so that the struggle to preserve the continuing self-identity of the church is also much more serious and goes all the deeper.

6. *Dogma as the Substance of History*

Since dualism is implicitly dogmatic and rests on an idea that can only be dogmatically based, it is characteristic of a church history resting on a dualistic world view that, among the various forms of ecclesiastical life in which the Idea of the church is actualized, dogma should occupy first place. The struggle between the two principles of good and evil, light and darkness, truth and error, is essentially conditioned by the fact that doctrine, which is regarded as the absolute essence of truth, is given to the consciousness of humanity in its pure objectivity, and that everyone can recognize it clearly and definitely for what it is. One must above all know what one is fighting for in order to be aware of the absolute necessity of the struggle.

---

singulorum capitum metae generales [Method of the Historical Work, and the General Goals of the Individual Chapters], unnumbered pages 28–55.

In this aspect as well, the Centuriators differ from the historians of the Catholic Church only in so far as they must, from their Protestant point of view, give the history of dogma an even higher and greater significance for the general history of the Christian church. Dogma is the substantive focal point around which ecclesiastical life revolves; it is the absolute norm according to which everything must be defined and tested, and on which—in its rigorously Lutheran form—everything belonging to the concept of justification depends. In each of the *Centuries*, as soon as the outer shape and situation of the church has been described, a weighty fourth chapter *de doctrina ecclesiae* [on church doctrine] presents "the inner and more proximate form and plan of the church," and the history of dogma as "a clear and well arranged recitation of the articles of doctrine, just as might have been set forth by teachers in any century. This the minds of the pious require most particularly, and it is, so to speak, the light and the very sun of sacred history." [24] But here we can see most clearly how, on the basis of this view, there could be no change that would represent true and real progress in history. The historical course of dogma is only a progressive obscuring of light by darkness,[25] at the culmination of which light will be restored to purity from its temporary night. Therefore, the entire positive significance of dogma in history is concentrated in the contents of the first *Century*, in which the teaching of Jesus and the apostles is expounded. Here we find ourselves wholly translated into the realm of New Testament theology to the broadest extent, and still what is given here as the teaching of Jesus and the apostles is nothing other than the system of Lutheran dogmatics, with all definitions and distinctions advanced only as they could be from the standpoint of the Reformation period. Yet how could it be otherwise? If the Reformation is the restoration of the pure teaching of the Gospel, then nothing can be established and renewed that did not previously exist. The content of the one period corresponds completely to that of the other, and the intervening *Centuries* have only to determine the extent to which, from century to century, men have strayed from the dogmatics of the primitive period, and the extent to which light and darkness have entered into an inverse

24. [ED.] *Cent.* I, *Praefatio* (Semler ed., I/1, unnumbered page 20).

25. Or, more specifically, a progressive obscuring of the doctrine of justification. In the final analysis, all are guilty of the *obscuratio doctrinae de justificatione* [obscuring of the doctrine of justification]; specifically, the great increase in monastic life is explicable by this (cf. *Cent.* IV, v [Semler ed., IV, 609]). Likewise, the Papacy itself can be derived from this. [ED. I am unable to confirm this citation.]

relation. When the substance of absolute truth as a perfected whole is as pat and ready-made as is here supposed, and subjective consciousness can only be passive toward the objectively given, then truth on the one hand and error on the other stand face to face without any mediation.

Following the chapter *de doctrina ecclesiae* comes the one *de haeresibus et erroribus manifestis* [on heresies and manifest errors]; and the concept of heresy has the same significance for the Protestant historians as for the Catholic. Indeed, without it the Devil would have lacked a major element in his diabolical struggle against the church. Just as the church has in the Devil its principal enemy and adversary, so also everything that does not agree with the teaching of the church, but more or less deviates from it, in its ultimate root and source derives only from the principle of darkness. As little as the two principles can ever become one, so little can there be any mediation between the truth of godly doctrine and the pernicious error of heresies.

Regardless of this, at just this point the Centuriators found themselves compelled somewhat to soften the sharpness of the antithesis. If the truth that ought to be regarded as the substantial content of Christian dogma has been so exactly formulated from the very beginning that the system of Lutheran dogmatics, with its specific attributes, is merely a true reflection of the teaching of Jesus and the apostles, then it follows that church teachers of subsequent centuries remained loyal to pure doctrine only in so far as they were acquainted with the Lutheran formulas. But the number of such church teachers is terribly small! Is there even one of whom this could be unconditionally true? How disproportionately vast would be the field of heresy if all who were discovered not to be true Lutherans were relegated to the class of heretics! Even to the Centuriators this seemed a peremptory order, incompatible with their historical conscience. Therefore they inserted between the teaching of the church and the heresies a remarkable intermediary link, by which the connection with the church could be preserved even for those whose orthodoxy did not appear to be pure and spotless in every respect. Specifically, there are also deviations from ecclesiastical doctrine not to be regarded exactly as heresies; one can distinguish from the *doctrina ecclesiae* "a tendency of doctrine embracing peculiar and unsuitable opinions, chaff, and errors of teachers." Even the most distinguished church teachers are not free of certain *naevi* [blemishes], which, surely, do not invalidate their ecclesiastical orthodoxy, but nonetheless cast a sullying shadow upon it. Even of Augustine, the Centuriators could not forbear saying that he "retained not a few blemishes from teachers of the previous century, although in certain cases he was of better judgment." For every century, a series of opinions is appended to the history of church doctrine which, because of the men who have advanced them, cannot absolutely be declared heretical, but which still may not be sanctioned in themselves. The historical view forced itself upon the Centuriators as a whole "that the greatest men have clung not only to ordinary weaknesses but also to the most base opinions, and sometimes even to the stains of corruptions, so that it becomes clear that the plan of the teaching of the prophets and apostles is far different from that even of the outstanding men in the church." [26]

The teaching of the prophets and apostles is supposed to be above any doubt, but the teaching of the most distinguished church teachers is to be tested only in accord with the former, and if it does not coincide, it is to be rejected. But if they are so objectionable, why should they not also be regarded as heretical? Evidently, the Centuriators here permit themselves an inconsistency and allow a little personal consideration to prevail. They do not regard it as just and reasonable that church teachers who otherwise generally are regarded as the chief props of orthodoxy should be declared heretical only on account of some false and inappropriate expressions. It is no longer so universally and unconditionally true that a teacher can only be either orthodox or heretical. There is also a middle position: he can be neither absolutely orthodox nor absolutely heretical. Since he is both at the same time (but only as the one is delimited by the other) there arises from both a third category; but the precariousness and ambiguity of this new category becomes immediately evident. For how is a secure boundary line to be drawn between the two? If even in the most significant church teachers there are greater or smaller *naevi* of this sort, how is the extent to which each individual is orthodox, and where he ceases to be orthodox, to be so exactly determined? In the second *Century* it is already "worthy at once of being wondered at and deplored that a great obscuring of the great articles of faith gradually occurred so soon, that some most distinguished teachers in the church held certain unsuitable opinions of their own—certain blemishes, as it were, by which in later centuries the church was shaken and disturbed even more." [27] Already in the second century men began to falsify the doctrine of *liberum arbitrium* [free will] and to ascribe too

26. Cf. the *Praefatio in historia ecclesiastica*, mentioned above [95, n. 23].
27. [ED.] *Cent.* II, *Praefatio* (Semler ed., II/1, unnumbered page 46).

much to human power. If the church teachers of this period themselves did not teach clearly enough the article of justification, and if they ascribed more to the works of the justified than was warranted, how can it be otherwise than that such *naevi* have given a false direction to all the doctrines added by the church teachers? The more precisely one investigates the doctrines of the various church teachers and becomes acquainted with them in detail, the more one is convinced that their presentations of dogma are in no way the monotonous repetition of a doctrine formulated from the very beginning, as should have been expected from the standpoint of the Centuriators. One is rather convinced that their dogmatic discussions, even where no definite reproach can be made against their orthodoxy, at least bear the color of their individuality, and that it is therefore fruitless simply to apply only the standard of the Lutheran formulas to their dogmatic ideas and assertions.

If, however, one cannot condemn the orthodox church teachers on account of such differences—if they are mere *naevi*, blemishes, which do not harm the purity of the whole—then on the other hand the heretics could likewise claim a more equitable judgment. If the former are not as pure and spotless as they ought to be, then neither is everything concerning the latter so black as is ordinarily supposed. The error that makes them heretics concerns at most only one specific teaching, and we are not entitled to suppose that they have deviated from church doctrine in everything else as well. If the same mixture of orthodoxy and heterodoxy is found in them as in most of the church teachers, and if the difference between the two is not explicit but only one of degree, why then should one wish to refuse extenuating circumstances on the side of the heretics, but rather to pass an absolutely condemning judgment upon them? The Centuriators themselves write in the Preface to the second *Century*:

> This matter ought to warn men of all times, lest they be too shocked or hold the Christian religion in suspicion, because even in this present age they see the most outstanding men in the church occasionally clinging to some blemishes and improper opinions. For often there was a mixture of this sort in the church, so that some men with greater sincerity, almost without any Pharisaic leaven, handed down the heavenly doctrine, whereas others, not only equal to them in gifts but even superior, held certain opinions that certainly were not good, indeed were base and pernicious. Moreover, just as no one ought to approve of blemishes, so in turn it is not right

to repudiate or condemn the sound form of doctrine that has been properly and skillfully set forth.[28]

But even if only so much is conceded, how can the antithesis between church doctrine and heresy still be fully maintained?

The result of all this can be stated in brief: the abstract dualism from which the Centuriators proceed, and by which they discover the conflict in church history between two mutually exclusive tendencies, is shown to be completely untenable as one draws closer to historical reality and looks more deeply into the concrete manifestations of individual life. The rigid and unvarying antithesis of the abstract theory is dissolved into the infinite multiplicity of purely relative antitheses by those subjects whose individuality fits neither the one nor the other category. There is no rift in history that absolutely separates the one from the other; the whole movement of history is a fluid transition, a continual mediation of the one with the other; and thus every individual thing first comes into its own as a historical reality when it is allowed to be considered for what it is in the immediacy of its particular existence.

7. *Further Characteristics of the Centuries*

We have already said what still needs to be added to our characterization of the *Centuries*—that everything tends to be forced into the categories of an abstract, external formalism. A notable peculiarity of the *Centuries* is the strictness and precision with which the content of church history is classified and systematized according to specific points of view. Thus, for example, the highly specialized divisions of the *loci* of the Lutheran dogmatics serve as the basis of the history of dogma in each century; and however little is known of the teaching of a heretic, wherever there is a question of dogma the same schematism is employed as repeatedly as possible. If, however—once the general outlines are traced and the antitheses established that divide the whole into right and left—all the requirements of historiography seem to have been satisfied, the details themselves within the various divisions come far less clearly into view historically. The propositions of individual church teachers are listed next to one another quite externally and disconnectedly in the history of dogma and in the section on church teachers, which are repeti-

28. [ED.] *Cent.* II, *Praefatio* (Semler ed., II/I, unnumbered pages 46–47).

tious for the most part; moreover, generally one detail merely follows another, and we have in the end only an arbitrarily connected aggregate. There is no proper sense of historical concreteness, no interest in pursuing the continuity of the details so that they can be perceived in the unity of an organic development. Since the whole mode of perception proceeds not from the particular to the universal but from the universal to the particular, the particular is already so predetermined by the universal that what it is in and for itself cannot come historically into its own.

In a presentation such as is offered by the *Centuries*, the Papacy never appears in the grandeur of its historical development. Everything that might lead to an objective conception of the subject, when perceived in its continuity, is dismembered and isolated. Instead of a description of the Papacy as it gradually came into being through the inner continuity of mutually conditioning factors, there is only a series of individual actions, *opera Antichristi* [works of Antichrist], in which the Popes actualize their papal existence while their adversaries oppose them. But the main thing remains insusceptible of being grasped, namely the continuity of the whole and the inner principle of movement throughout. The superficiality of this whole mode of consideration is to be seen in the identification of the fortuitous act of favor supposedly granted by the Greek Emperor Phocas to the Pope of his time as the major factor in the historical process by which the Papacy becomes what it is. The most important events are not given a place corresponding to their historical significance; for in the history of the Papacy during the eleventh century, the decisive struggle between Gregory VII and Henry IV is recounted not in the major section *de romanorum Pontificum principatu et tyrannide* [on the sovereignty and tyranny of the Roman pontiffs] but in the subordinate chapter, *de schismatibus ac dissidiis multiplicibus* [on manifold schisms and disagreements]. There can be no interest in pursuing the often complex sequence of historical occurrences, so as to understand events in their true continuity and to grasp what mediating factors are crucial to their historical development, if so important a part of church history as the Papacy—conceived from the beginning in the plans and assaults of the Antichrist—is already so complete an entity that there is total indifference to the outward occasion by which the Papacy as pre-existent ideal is fully unveiled and takes on historical reality.[29]

29. Compare with the above the following passage in the Preface to the eighth *Century*, in which the history of the Papacy is characteristically summarized:

Obviously, a historical perspective that penetrates so little into the objective continuity of events, that sees in them only an atomistic aggregate of random occurrences, and that is so little able to bring the particular and the universal, the sensible and the supersensible, into an inner relation, is essentially supernaturalistic. Abstract dualism, whose antitheses are the general categories for the analysis of the particular, is implicitly so transcendent that it is related to the natural order of things as a supernatural principle; and the distinction between the natural and the supernatural becomes thoroughly fluid. Just as on the one hand the divine in its relation to the human is the principle of a supernatural revelation, so on the other hand the Devil enters no less directly and supernaturally into the course of human affairs. On the basis of either principle, the natural continuity of history is so disrupted and torn apart that the same phenomena can be regarded as both natural and supernatural. In this the Centuriators completely share the point of view of the ancient historians; they are so much the prisoners of their supernaturalistic world view that in each *Century* they devote a separate chapter to the *miracula* and *prodigia*. If, as they say, they wish to recount only such miracles and prodigies as "appear in tested authorities, or contain significant teaching," then no further proof is needed, with miracle an established category, of the wide latitude given here to the most ill-defined belief in miracles.

Since miracle is part of the teleological way of viewing things, the Centuriators share with the ancient historians an especial interest (which is intimately connected with their historical pragmatism) in demonstrating most visibly how the hand of God intervenes directly in the phenomena of history, to punish and to warn. They could not describe any persecution of Christians without indulging in an observation of their own about the punishments the divine justice has inflicted upon their persecutors through sickness, sudden and painful death, and mishaps of

---

"Although . . . in earlier centuries too the Antichrist, as though burrowing underground, oftentimes aspired to his eminent position over all the churches and empires of the world, nevertheless he was in some way pushed back down into his darkness by the vigilance of the teachers and the severity of the governors—until by parricides and many other foul crimes the infamous Phocas, who was indeed the property of the Devil himself . . . , a huge and horrible monster, lifted him into that great seat of pestilence (which we were obliged to call the supreme pre-eminence in the whole world). Later however, he raised his head higher, and (as John describes him) he touched the very stars of heaven with his tail, undertaking to cast them down." [ED. *Cent.* VIII, *Epistola Dedicatoria* (Basel ed., VIII, unnumbered pages 4–5).]

various sorts. This theory of punishment has indeed been developed into the further notion that God punishes not merely with bodily but also with spiritual evils. As is indicated in the Preface to the fifth *Century*, three things generally follow one upon another in a short span of time. After the great blessings of God there come great sins by men, and after these come great punishments. There are no greater blessings of God for this present life than the revelation of the divine Word, its establishment and dissemination. There are no greater sins of man than contempt for the divine Word and all that belongs to it; and no greater punishment occurs in this life than when the Word of God is obscured by philosophy or human custom and the arts of persuasion, or when free play is given to corruptions, deceivers are rewarded, all doors are closed to the confession of truth, and men are carried away by their perverted senses, and are blinded and seduced by fraud. Idolatry, superstitious worship, fanaticism, pagan ravings, come in the wake of these punishments; in step with them is the punishment that consists of political misfortune. Rome became the seat of the Antichrist when the triple conquest and plunder of that city in the fifth century proved fruitless. That was the time of divine wrath, and it was necessary that the Antichrist should flourish at the holy place, so that the unthankful world should receive the deserved punishment for its foolishness, its contempt and malice against the revealed will of God and his religion. Since even the Antichrist is only the subservient tool of divine justice, the monarchy of God is indeed maintained; but the realm of church history is transformed into a theater of the most horrible chastisements when in all parts of the Christian world, wherever Lutheran dogma is not confessed in its purity, the wrath of God inflicts spiritual punishments of this sort!

The agreement between the old Protestant and the old Catholic views of history, despite the sharpness of their antitheses, is thus quite extensive. Both views consider the entire development of the Christian church from a purely dogmatic standpoint. Dogma is the substantial content of church history. Just as the Catholic in his doctrine of tradition denies any real change in dogma, declaring it to be impossible, the Protestant sees in the historical course of the church only a continuous struggle to maintain in its pure self-identity the truth of Christian dogma, which was expressed at the beginning in its full reality for the universal consciousness of mankind. In the course of time they become further separated in their view of the relation of the church as it is in historical reality to what it was originally. Yet for the Protestant the church of the early centuries is, in its essential character, still so pure and uncorrupted that he at least looks back, with great longing and admiration, through the darkness of subsequent ages to the "most flourishing ages such as existed under Constantine the Great and also for a while during the following century, when the heavenly voice of Augustine resounded in the church of Christ." [30] And for him also, the dogmatic conclusions of the ecumenical councils of the fourth and fifth centuries are valid, the unshakable pillars of the truth of the Christian faith.

30. [ED.] I am unable to locate this citation.

III

CATHOLIC AND PROTESTANT OPPOSITION TO THE *CENTURIES:* CAESAR BARONIUS AND GOTTFRIED ARNOLD

1. *Caesar Baronius*

PLAN AND ANTITHESIS OF THE ANNALS

The direct antithesis to the *Magdeburg Centuries* is the *Annales ecclesiastici* of Cardinal Caesar Baronius.[1] The occasion and circumstances under which this famous work was undertaken are well known; but the actual cause of its origin was the inner necessity of the circumstances themselves. A work [such as the *Magdeburg Centuries*] whose innermost motive was so polemical in nature, and which transferred to the broad

1. [ED.] Caesar Baronius (Cesare de Barono) was born in the Kingdom of Naples in 1538 and died in Rome in 1607. In 1557, after studying theology and law, he went to Rome, where he assumed a scholarly life as a member of the newly founded Congregation of the Oratory. He became interested in church history, and for thirty years worked amidst the vast amount of unpublished materials in the Vatican archives. Friends prevailed upon him to utilize this study in defense of the church against the *Magdeburg Centuries,* a task he agreed to undertake and which occupied him the rest of his life. In 1596 he was made a cardinal, as well as librarian of the Vatican, by Clement VIII. At the papal elections of 1605 he was a candidate against his will and came near to being chosen. He died two years later. The *Annales ecclesiastici* [Ecclesiastical Annals] begin with the birth of Christ and come down to 1198; in form they resemble the ordinary medieval chronicle. As Baur explains, the work does not take the direct form of a polemic against the *Centuries.* The opposition appears rather in the simple, fundamental conception that true history can only be written by the aid of the documents to which he had access, guaranteed by the authority of the Roman Church, and that it is only necessary for these documents to be known in order to secure recognition of the validity of Roman claims. The first edition of the *Annales* appeared in twelve volumes at Rome, 1588–1607. Other early editions were published at Mainz (1601–1605), Antwerp (1597–1609), and Venice (1600–1607); the Venice edition is cited in the editorial footnotes. The *Annales* were continued down to the end of the sixteenth century by various later authors.

field of church history the conflict that separates the two parties in such sharp antithesis, in order to seize church history in its entirety and enlist it on behalf of the Protestant principle—such a work could not remain unanswered from the Catholic side. Even though the author's Catholic self-consciousness did not permit him to declare outright the antithetical purpose that was the true and original intention of the *Annals*, it is clear as day that he has the work of his Protestant opponents in mind from the beginning, and wishes to confront the church's entire past from his own point of view just as they did from theirs.

The religious and ecclesiastical antithesis brought about by the Reformation also suggested to him the necessity of answering the question of how the antithetical standpoint from which each of the two parties confronted the other, and from which each believed itself to be fully and absolutely in the right, could be historically justified. In this matter the Protestants, who had above all an interest in showing the justification for their standpoint, had already taken the lead. It was in them that a more vital interest in the history of the church and an authentic historical consciousness was first awakened by this question. Following their precedent, the Catholic now became conscious for the first time of the more real and specific importance of the history of the church for his ecclesiastical consciousness. If the Protestants projected their work on a scale so grandiose as to encompass the entire content of church history and to bring it as precisely as possible into the light of historical knowledge, then the Catholic historian, aware both of the close and direct connection of his church with the entire past of the Christian church and of the abundant resources offered him by the papal archives and libraries, wished least of all to lag behind in this matter. The Protestants had measured the historical course of the church by centuries; now it should be traced much more precisely, year by year.

As Baronius says in the Preface, he meant to choose the word *Annals* only in the sense by which the ancients "distinguished annals from history, because history properly treated the events of its own times, which the author either saw or was able to see, and pointed out not only what was done but also in what way and with which intention it was done. On the other hand, the writer of annals set down ancient affairs, which for the most part his own age did not know, and he treated these by individual years." [2] For the church historian, the strictest love of truth must be a far more sacred duty than for other historians. Therefore,

2. [ED.] *Annales ecclesiastici,* I, *Praefatio,* unnumbered page 2.

in order not to give ground to the slightest suspicion of a distortion of truth, he would relinquish to the pagan historians "those speeches prolonged through excessive and bombastic circumlocution, and orations put together with the greatest artistry, invented, composed in accord with the opinion of each person and arranged at will," and would write *annales* rather than a *historia*.[3] Since in the main this also applies to the distinction between the *Annals* and the *Centuries*, it is evident that he intended to indicate, by means even of the title, the great superiority that his work, in accord with its entire design, claimed to have over the *Magdeburg Centuries* in respect of its historical precision and credibility.

Among the particular subjects of church history, nothing can be more important for the Catholic historian than the history of the Papacy, with respect to which he made it his task "to demonstrate through successive periods that the visible monarchy of the Catholic Church was established by Christ the Lord, was founded upon Peter, and, through his legitimate and true successors, the Roman pontiffs, was preserved inviolate, was guarded scrupulously, and was never broken or interrupted but perpetually maintained; and that there has always been recognized one visible head of this mystical body of Christ, the church, whom all members obey." [4] Here, above all, on the new path he intended to open he was confronted by those adversaries who, "having been banished from the Catholic Church and professing that they were going to gather together the deeds of the ancients, attempted nothing other than to obstruct this means of access open to us by heaping up lies and blocking the wide open, royal highway. As though they had joined arms and sworn a war against the truth, they heaped up all sorts of false things and, in brief, turned everything upside down, attempting nothing other than the building of a new tower of confusion reaching to the sky, if indeed this could be done, whereby they might fight against God and his saints." [5] Of the representation of the Pope as Antichrist, he says that it is not otherwise "than as if someone should tear apart a picture of some king composed of gems of admirable beauty, and with these same gems should try to devise an utterly deformed representation of some monster, and yet impudently dare to assert that this very picture, the work that was put together from the same gems, was the original, most noble picture of the king. To be sure, these same men, making use of the same Scriptures in which the church is portrayed most beautifully, have in

3. [ED.] *Ibid.*   4. [ED.] *Ibid.*, unnumbered page 3.
5. [ED.] *Ibid.*, unnumbered page 1.

this way made of the church a synagogue of Satan, of Jerusalem a Babylon, in order to weaken and destroy her countenance, which has no stain or blemish; and finally (a thing most horrible to say) they have made of Christ the Antichrist." [6]

Concerning this part of the work and the results attained in it for the refutation of opponents, the praise heaped upon its author by admirers of the *Annals* is largely justified. They praise him as the "most valiant champion of Christ, who—just as another Scipio—had hurled the mightiest thunderbolts thus far into the camp of the heretics, and, after wreaking measureless destruction and gloriously overthrowing and trampling underfoot the hosts of Satan [*ac centuriis Satanae*], which had been brought forth from the gates of hell for the destruction of the church, had filled all places everywhere with fear of his name." [7]

Following the same tactic as in the Introduction, where he ignores his Protestant opponents as far as possible and refuses to dignify them by direct mention, in the work itself Baronius enters into special consideration of the *Centuries* and its assertions much less frequently than one might have expected. It seems that for him polemic is merely secondary; what is of importance is only the objectivity of the facts, the authenticity of the sources, the comprehensiveness and richness of the presentation, in which history as it were lifts its veil before us, and apparently wishes to have us look with all candor at its innermost nature. The whole measure of what is given should provide direct proof that things are in each and every detail as they are recounted here.

In a Church such as the Roman, how could there be anything other than a history attested by documents! As the *pontifices* [high priests] were charged by the ancient Romans with the composition of annals from the very beginning of the city, so the Christian church could even

6. [ED.] *Ibid.*

7. Cf. the *Parentalia Justi Baronii Vetera Castrensis Theologi, . . . in obitum Caesaris Baronii* [Memorial of Justus Baronius, Theologian of Vetera Castro, . . . upon the Death of Caesar Baronius], at the beginning of the first volume.

[ED.] Justus (Baronius) Calvinus was born a German Calvinist c. 1570 in Xanten on the Upper Rhine north of Düsseldorf. Following theological studies at Heidelberg, he went to Rome, where he was warmly received by Cardinals Bellarmine and Baronius and by Pope Clement VIII. He converted to Catholicism in 1601, after returning to Germany, and took for himself the name of Baronius. In Roman times, Xanten was called Vetera Castro (Old Camp). By employing the ancient Latin name of his native city, Calvinus may have intended to indicate not only his birthplace but also that he was a "theologian of the old camp" (as distinguished from "the camp of the heretics"). This Memorial is not contained in the Venice edition of the *Annals*.

less permit any lack of the same conscientiousness. Almost simultaneously with the origin of the Roman Church, as Baronius asserts in the dedication to the Pope preceding the second volume, St. Clement, as the "highest priest of the Christian religion," chose for the same task seven notaries, to whom were later added the same number of subdeacons. "All of [these] things were most carefully written and reviewed by the Roman pontiff, who in like manner inquired into them with the greatest precision, and they were stored away in the public records of the church." [8] Even though these carefully collected and preserved documents were to perish in the great fire that also destroyed the Holy Scriptures under Diocletian, there were to remain some remnants that might be brought to light by the industry of the historical investigator.

How could one not believe a historian who on the basis of such sources is able to recount so exactly what happened from year to year! The Catholic historian seems to provide only a purely documentary account; and the more impartial and free he is from the polemical interest so openly and bluntly exhibited by the Protestant historian, the more he gains the advantage of being able to count on the faith of his readers even where his history serves only the interest of the Roman bishops and rests on sources whose credibility has become more than doubtful through Protestant criticism. Where he speaks or where he is silent, he wishes only to permit history to be its own witness; and the more exactly all details are recorded by years, the less is the correctness of the data to be placed in doubt. It is simply factually true to report for the year 44 that Peter, after having been bishop of Antioch for seven years, came to Rome, transferred his bishopic there, and administered it for twenty-five years in the Roman Church. The decretals of the earliest Popes, rejected by the Centuriators, are nevertheless listed in the proper place: it is precisely the chief basis for the Protestant rejection of their authenticity that speaks for their antiquity; the Roman bishop was indeed from the beginning the *episcopus universalis ecclesiae* [bishop of the universal church].

Still there are also, according to Baronius, documents that, though favorable to the Roman Church, cannot be regarded as authentic and unforged. This is especially true of the famous *donatio Constantini*, to which Baronius gives no credence, but surely for a totally different reason than the Protestants. Although Constantine's generosity and fidelity to the Roman Church, which he recognized as the center of the

8. [ED.] *Annales ecclesiastici*, II, unnumbered page 1.

whole Christian religion, left nothing to be desired, and although the Frankish kings merely returned to the Roman Church what it had already possessed, nevertheless it would be beneath the dignity of the Roman Church if it were to have *humano jure* [by human right] what it has *divino* [by divine right], and should owe to one man what had already been bestowed upon it by God and Christ in Peter. Baronius therefore suspects the Greeks, envious as always of the privileges of the Roman Church, of having here perpetrated a deception. The well-known saying, *timeo Danaos et dona ferentes* [I fear the Greeks even when bearing gifts] finds application here. John the Deacon,[9] in holding to the edict of donation forged by the Greeks, made the legitimate possession more doubtful than assured.

The principles of historical criticism are always taken, in the final analysis, from the dogmatics of the Roman Church. Either the Greeks or the heretics are to be blamed for whatever in the documents speaks against the interest of the Roman Church. It is *a priori* impossible that a Pope could ever have been condemned as a heretic. How, then, in the acts of the sixth ecumenical council, can the name of Pope Honorius stand among those who were condemned at that time as adherents of the Monothelete heresy? How can the Roman Bishop Leo II have testified to the condemnation of his predecessor in a letter to the Emperor? There is nothing more certain than that deceivers have simply added the name of Pope Honorius wherever he is mentioned in such a connection.

Baronius could advance such claims with all the more confidence the more often he was able to show by striking examples how little historical truth there was on the side of the opponents. In such instances, he did not neglect to assert with cutting sarcasm his historical correctness against the innovators, as specifically in regard to the Emperor Phocas and Pope Joan. "Those shrewd innovators," he said in discussing the year 606, "who made that outstanding attempt to gather together from all sides devices for the destruction of the primacy of the Roman Church, as soon as they discovered that the primacy was granted to the Roman Church by the Emperor Phocas—you can imagine how they received that opinion with applause and made it known by their acclamations and amplified it in their declamations, saying of course that its prerogative over all churches was usurped in a tyrannical way, was granted by a tyrant, and indeed was imparted in the first place to Boniface III, the pontiff of the Roman Church, by the Emperor Pho-

9. [ED.] Antipope to Sergius II, elected in 844.

cas!" [10] What Phocas has bestowed upon the Roman Church is only the explanation that the Bishop of Constantinople usurped the title "ecumenical," which belonged to the Roman Church.[11] Everyone knows how ludicrous the assertion is that "[the innovators] have reviewed one by one in 'Annals' the years that have elapsed from the coming of the Lord down to the time of Phocas and have seen that scarcely a year elapses in which the primacy of the Roman Church is made manifest. It is easier to deny that the sun shines or that fire produces heat than to darken the rays of shining truth of this sort which are scattered everywhere." [12] In the same fashion, he is most vividly aware that the truth belongs wholly to his side when he explains that the story about Pope Joan is merely a fable. It seems to him only deplorable when the quarrelsome innovators make the vain effort to exploit the story to the detriment of the Roman Church, for even if it were true, it would only follow that the Roman See had been vacant for a couple of years, as has often happened. No one can be so foolish as to assert, in contradiction to all church laws, "that it had been possible for a woman actually . . . to be *pontifex maximus*." [13]

Visibly aware of his good cause, and with deep contempt for the anonymous defense that had recently appeared of Henry IV—this *perditissimus homo* [utterly corrupt man], who ought "to have been buried already by oblivion in the sewer of filth"—he intends solely to refute, and only with the authority of factually attested history, all the lies and slanders brought against Gregory VII. He therefore regards it as completely superfluous to add anything further about the notorious scene at Canossa, which offends the national and religious consciousness of the Protestants in the same manner, other than the simple remark that it would be a lie to assert that Henry did not seek confession and absolution freely but was only forced to do so by the Pope.[14]

Hence there is no important point at all in history at which the antithesis of the two views that runs through the whole does not find specific expression. In this regard, the contrast in experiences, as difficult and demanding as they were divinely glorious and providential, which the Papacy had to endure just as much as Protestantism, is quite remarkable.

10. [ED.] *Annales ecclesiastici*, VIII, 149 (Year 606, Sec. IV).

11. [ED.] See above, 88, n. 11.

12. [ED.] *Annales ecclesiastici*, VIII, 149 (Year 606, Sec. V.)

13. [ED.] *Ibid.*, X, 74–78 (Year 853, Secs. LXIX–XCV); quotation from 76 (Year 853, Sec. LXXXVI).

14. [ED.] *Ibid.*, XI, 292–310 (Year 1073).

The latter extols as a special proof of the grace watching over the Christian church that there were always some in the darkest times who preserved the Word of the Gospel in its purity and did not permit the true faith completely to be extinguished. These witnesses to the truth are the pillars of support by which God always rescues his church. But the Papacy also had to endure such dangers, which it could survive only by the special favor of divine Providence. "What was it like," Baronius recalls in the dedication of the sixth volume to Clement VIII, in those "most deplorable times, during which, among other unfortunate things, there was in the entire Christian world not a single Catholic prince, when all kings and emperors together were entangled by heresies, and when, together with Italy, Rome herself and the Roman Church were beginning to groan under the Gothic and Arian sword? Quite without expectation, God then awakened a second David, a true servant after his own heart, a confessor and zealous champion of the Catholic religion—the most Christian Clovis, king of the Franks, who not only established Catholic Christianity among the Franks but also before his death acknowledged in outstandingly pious fashion, by means of the golden crown he sent to the Apostolic Prince, that he knew of no other visible head of the whole church." [15] So here and there a new star of salvation appears when things are at their worst.

The same signs in which the Protestant sees coming to light all the infamy and depravity of the Papacy, only provide the Catholic with a greater witness of its godliness. In the Introduction to the history of the tenth century, Baronius says that one ought not to be shocked at encountering the horror of destruction in the holy place. That the church is the work of God now becomes all the more apparent when, as so often before,

> it might have seemed that the ship of Peter, which is the type of the universal church, bereft of almost all oars, was being overturned entirely as that deluge of crimes grew to immense proportions—had it not been protected by the highest power of the promise of Christ. . . . Although from time to time a very deformed and ugly head happened to be placed upon the church, it had to be tolerated none the less, because the head was found to be not altogether mad but rather to remain firm in the Catholic faith. It was advanced, to be sure, above the other members of the body by the promise of God, not without cause or plan but by his great balance of judgment. So that God might show that this same church was by no means the

15. [ED.] *Ibid.,* VI, unnumbered page 2. Last sentence quoted by Baur in German.

invention of men but clearly a divine institution, it was necessary to demonstrate that it could in no way be destroyed by the work of depraved bishops and be reduced to utterly nothing, just as it is agreed that this was also done in the case of various kingdoms and well-constituted states. . . .

The solace always remains for the pious that if Christ was asleep, he slept in the same ship. The godless innovators, who know nothing of the evangelical faith they confess, fall into the blasphemy that Christ is not in the little ship of Peter that they see inundated by the waves.[16]

THE TWO EXTREMES

With an exertion and persistence rare in the history of literature, and with an equally great expenditure of erudition and penetration, the two works [the *Centuries* and the *Annals*], which are so similar in outward scope, accomplished their antithetical views in grandiose style. Since, however, the one is only the antithesis to the other, and since one indulges in optimism and the other in pessimism, the judgment can be reached only that each displays an equally one-sided partisan spirit and dogmatizing polemicism. If in this there is any difference between them, then it could scarcely be denied that the reproach of partisanship and of a view of history based upon it falls more heavily on the Protestant historians than on the Catholic. The latter has on his behalf the advantage that, against the innovating efforts by his opponents, he makes it his task to defend and maintain a position that rests on the entire tradition of the past and is acknowledged by the overwhelming majority. On the other hand, little as the justification in principle for their standpoint is to be doubted, the Protestants seem to have in mind only the most thoroughgoing application of their principle, and the intention of entering into the whole realm of history in so revolutionary and radical a fashion that in many places their presentation cannot fail to give the impression of the most extreme claims.

We need only to consider how much, for anyone who is not so overcome by the bias of partisan interest that freer reflection in him is stifled, the natural sense of truth should already have resisted the demand that he see in the entire historical course of the Christian church only the

---

16. *Ibid.*, X, 674; cf. 641 679. [ED. The first sentence of the preceding quotation is found in the Venice edition, X, 439 (Year 900, Sec. II). The balance of it was apparently added in a later edition, to which the author refers in this footnote.]

most complete perversion into Antichristianity.[17] And yet, if one has only this choice—either to maintain with the Catholics the absolutely unchanging identity from the beginning of all substantial forms of the church, and thus not to accept any essential change, or else to subscribe to what must have taken place according to the Protestant view—one can at the very least only take the side of the latter and agree that, if in general there is a historical movement, the church also must become in its temporal course something essentially other than what it was at the very beginning. Therefore, the question is simply whether, between the two opposing and extreme assertions, a mediation is possible such that the one-sidedness of each is transcended, and both are led beyond themselves by means of their mutual negation; whether, therefore, there exists a historical becoming that neither on the one hand gives merely the outward appearance of such, nor on the other consists in the absolute negation of being-in-itself—i.e., a historical development that is indeed also immanent to the concept of the subject matter, but only one by which the concept is mediated with itself in the various moments contained in it intrinsically, in order to be in the concrete reality of its existence what it is intrinsically. But if there is such a development, then it is self-evident that things cannot assume from the beginning the forms they acquire only subsequently. But it is equally clear that the mediation of the two opposing views at issue here cannot be sought on that side whose basic view is essentially that everything has existed from the beginning just as it appears in the course of subsequent development.

Just as certainly as the Catholic Church can relinquish nothing of its dogma of tradition, no less certainly can it have no other view of the history of the Christian church than the one for which Baronius is the classical authority. In his own Church he has found not only continuers but also critics of his historical work; but their criticism was directed only upon subordinate questions, especially chronological ones, which, though they might have become more important, at any rate were not pursued further. On the whole, his standpoint was never questioned; and even if a few, such as the historians of the Gallican Church, took a more or less divergent direction in accord with the principles of their Church, the most recent Catholic historiography on the other hand—different in

17. Here the same argument finds its place that Bellarmine so often employs against his dogmatic opponents, as when, for example, he argues in *De missa,* I, xxiii, that if the Catholic sacrifice of the Mass were an error, then the church would have ceased to exist, and Christ would have lost his bride and inheritance, for a church that served idolatry for so many centuries cannot be the church of Christ.

other respects though its whole method of treatment may be—provides all the more proof that Catholic consistency must always lead back to the point at which Baronius already stood, and at which alone it can persevere in its opposition to Protestant historiography. Therefore, if it is possible to break through the original antithesis between Catholic and Protestant views of history and to obtain a freer and broader scope, this can happen only from the Protestant side; and indeed this possibility is so real that sooner or later it must necessarily occur. To give this question its most concrete expression: is it really essential to the principle of Protestantism to see in the history of the Papacy only an ever wider expansion of the kingdom of the Devil and the Antichrist? If this view is obviously partisan, one-sided, and false, then there must also be a progression that leads beyond this original Protestant view of history, and it is a question, then, of how that progression has come about. This alone is the point from which we can further pursue the above question.

2. *Gottfried Arnold*

His Point of View

The old Protestant view of history was the natural result of the principles on which the system of the old Protestant dogmatics rested; it had, therefore, to remain dominant for as long as this system maintained its undiminished rule and authority. At first a rather long period followed the *Magdeburg Centuries,* during which there was no important development in church historiography as a whole and in general, although in particular aspects of church history conspicuous and successful accomplishments were not lacking. A work such as the *Centuries* was too significant a literary accomplishment for another with equal claim to be placed alongside it in the same Church in so short a time. For the time being, there could only be the intent of absorbing the rich material contained in it, of elaborating it further and making it generally more accessible and useful for historical instruction by means of selections and compendia. This was all the more sufficient in that the theological activity of that period was chiefly concerned with consolidating the dogmatic system internally and providing it on all sides with the bulwarks its defense against so many opposing parties seemed to demand. In the long series of controversies that continued unbroken from the middle of the sixteenth century to the end of the seventeenth, and that repeatedly were ignited anew, all other aspirations had finally to be swallowed up by the dogmatic-polemical concern.

However, the more the dogmatic system headed persistently toward its own disintegration in this most vigorous period of polemics, the more visibly the bonds loosened that joined religious consciousness to the orthodox dogmatics and the authority of the symbols; for men were disgusted and wearied by this endless and inexhaustible controversy. And for that matter, the smaller the success with which the orthodox party already combated Calixtine syncretism and the freer view on which it was founded, the more a changed view in the field of church history was also prepared. If the rigidity of the old dogmatics was broken against the more vital Christianity of Spener's pietism, in order to make room for a freer form of dogmatic consciousness, which returned to the inner center of religious life, then the significance of Spener's epoch is also evident in that it was strong enough to call forth a new and original work in the field of church history as well. All the reflections and conclusions resulting from Spener's stimulus in church history were gathered by Gottfried Arnold into a new total view, whose character is already indicated by the title of his work, which he called a history of the church and of heretics.[18] It should be, he expressly added, an "un-

18. *Unpartheiische Kirchen- und Ketzerhistorien vom Anfang des Neuen Testaments bis auf das Jahr Christi 1688* [Unpartisan History of the Church and of Heretics from the Beginning of the New Testament to A.D. 1688] (Zürich, 1699).

[ED.] Gottfried Arnold (1666–1714) began the study of theology at Wittenberg in 1685, but soon gave it up for independent reading in early church history. Through the influence of Philipp Spener, then court preacher in Dresden, he came into contact with mystic and separatist circles in Dresden and Quedlinburg. In 1696 he published *Die erste Liebe*, a eulogy of the early church in which his hostility to dogma and ecclesiasticism first became apparent. For his church history, he insisted on studying the writings of the heretics themselves rather than the polemics of their hostile contemporaries. In 1697 he spent an unsuccessful year as professor of history at Giessen. Later in life he became reconciled to established theology, and in 1704 he entered the pastorate. In his extreme pessimism and dualism, his idealization of the earliest church and his theory of a "fall" that ensued shortly after the end of the first century, his hostility toward dogma and all forms of ecclesiasticism, his criticism of the dogmas of the Reformation as well as those of the Catholic Church, and his theory that only the monks and a few other inwardly pious Christians have preserved a "true and vital Christianity" in the midst of a fallen anti-Christian church, he anticipates in remarkable fashion the ideas of the nineteenth-century Basel church historian Franz Overbeck. In light of Overbeck's polemic against Baur in his *Christentum und Kultur* (Basel, 1919), 180–82, it is valuable to note Baur's careful treatment and criticism of Arnold in the following pages, in order to obtain some idea of how Baur might have responded to the sort of attack that was brought against his work in church history by critics such as Overbeck.

partisan" history. The less the author regarded this word as superfluous, the more it proves afresh how difficult it still was at that time to regard the past as other than a reflection of the present. This fact stands out so strikingly that we can only start with it in order to find a correct basis for characterizing and evaluating the work.

It was the same with Arnold as with the Centuriators. The latter transferred to the history of the Christian church as a whole the impression made upon them by the Catholic Church at the time of the Reformation, and above all by the Papacy as the source of all abuses and depravities; and they were so imbued with this impression throughout all the centuries (to a lesser degree the further they moved from their point of departure) that they were able to divest themselves of it completely for the first time only on the soil of the apostolic church, with whose teaching they thought their own to be identical. For Arnold as well, it was not an immediate, objective interest in the history of the Christian church that led him to it and guided his presentation, but rather the repulsive aversion he felt toward the ecclesiastical conditions of his time and of his closest surroundings. The controversies and charges of heresy that were the vital element of the orthodox church, the religious coercion exercised by its dogmatic formalism, and many unhappy events that seemed to him to be the consequence of the latter—all this occasioned in him the conviction, as it did in Spener and his followers, that true Christianity, generally speaking, does not consist in dogmas and symbols, but only in repentance and confession, in faith and love, and in everything that shows its practical efficacy in the inner life of man as a whole. The more there are quarrels and disputes, the greater the weight placed upon dogmatic formulas and definitions and upon the authority of symbols; and the more it is believed that everything must be judged according to this standard, the more the chief thing is abandoned—the vital Christianity of the reborn.

This perverse tendency very quickly gained the upper hand in the evangelical church, and even Luther is not to be absolved from the guilt of having cooperated with it. It is indeed true, says Arnold,[19] that in the first years of the Reformation a great movement and change of heart took place among countless men in Saxony and other places, as well as in

19. In the Schaffhausen edition (1740), I, 665. [ED. The *Unpartheiische Kirchen-und Ketzerhistorien* comprises the first two volumes of the Schaffhausen edition of Arnold's works, published in three volumes, 1740–42. All of Baur's citations are from the first volume.]

Switzerland, where Zwingli taught. With many it was, to be sure, still a first love, which not only was strong and ardent in itself but also was splendidly fanned and maintained by the fires of distress. But after the arrival of peace and security, things soon changed, in a way not unlike what happened in the early church. Since at that time all—Luther, Zwingli, and the others—still stood as one man against the Pope, they had purer intentions, and the scandal of quarrels and other evil passions was still left aside, and a great many more blessings were experienced. But there was a dark side even to Luther: the noble modesty and humility with which he appeared at the beginning, as he stressed true salvation flowing from grace and union with Christ, were increasingly subdued by the natural vehemence of his fiery temperament. In words and deeds he transgressed the proper limit and thus gave his adversaries frequent cause for unfavorable judgments. What was even worse, many of his followers were inclined to emulate him in this rather than in his virtues or in the gentleness and love of Christ. Hence that unfortunate quarrelsomeness that brought such great harm to the evangelical church had its beginning even with Luther; and instead of making the re-orientation of life the main thing, men were satisfied with mere knowledge, with confession by rote and idle talk, or with the mere upbraiding of the papists.

Arnold ascribes to Melanchthon an even greater share in the deplorable turn of events that in so short a time were taken by the Reformation. He brought more darkness and error into theology than light and strength, Arnold maintains,[20] since he prepared an open way for corrupted reason to suppress the simplicity of Christian doctrine and to pervert the truth by pompous, quarrelsome speculation. If, as Melanchthon believed, one might not be an interpreter of Christian doctrine without literary erudition, which is not merely an embellishment of the Christian church but also sheds light on doctrine itself, then the apostles must themselves have lacked this light. One could also thank Melanchthon and his needle-like reasoning for the institution of systematic theology among Lutherans and Reformed. In this connection, Melanchthon referred specifically to the example of John of Damascus and the prattler Peter Lombard, who inaugurated the school-theology in a period of the greatest corruption and the most abominable darkness. By a preference for Aristotle and his methods, he introduced human propositions, his own opinions, and rational conclusions; and in a few years he again

20. *Ibid.*, 702 f.

brought into prominence at Wittenberg that school-theology whose decline men had only recently ceased to applaud. This unjustly famous art was first commended to the people with the pretexts used by Melanchthon; thereafter, it was recommended by the authorities and imposed by their command. So men not only were inclined but also were forced to follow human doctrines and to accept them as criteria, as the history of the symbolical books shows. The superstitious esteem of men went so far with many that they downright made an idol of Philippus and his clever theology; and the harm done to the church by this idolatrous and more than papist intention cannot be sufficiently deplored.

The same evil deplored by Arnold in Luther and Melanchthon is seen to be gaining ground in the times that followed to an ever greater extent and in infinitely manifold forms, increasing beyond measure. His depiction as a whole of the two centuries following the Reformation, which his church history also encompasses, only gives evidence of the constantly reiterated complaint of the church's increasingly serious and deplorable condition. The more detailed his history becomes, and the more it approaches his own time, the more repellent and dispiriting becomes the impression that is imposed from all sides in such a mass of details. And yet even for him, the divine ray of light in the midst of gross darkness, without which the Christian church cannot exist, cannot be completely extinguished. Bad as things may be with the Christian church, there must still always be a few men in whom a true and vital Christianity lives on. All those evils and corruptions from which he traces such a gloomy picture constitute only the dark side of a more hopeful perspective that is at the same time not lacking in him. The question is only where we are to look for that perspective; but wherever it may be, all that belongs to it is merely a light shining in darkness. We have here, therefore, the same antithesis, the same dualistic world view, into which the Centuriators cast the history of the Christian church as a whole.

The Difference between Arnold and the Centuriators

We must above all understand Arnold's view of the church of the time in which he lived in order rightly to comprehend his view of history in general. It rests on the supposition that the church has always remained identical with what it originally was. He himself expressed this general view only now and then, to be sure, but very characteristically, in these words: "There are new actors but still a single pageant." [21] A closer examination of his historical work shows clearly enough the extent to which he lived by this thought. Just as the ecclesiastical conditions of the present, in which he must have found such fruits as the Reformation should have borne for practical Christianity to be lacking in so high a degree, filled him with the bleakest impressions, so the church of the past could likewise appear to him in no other light. The same connection of cause and effect is to be found everywhere. The causes so inhibiting the vital activity of the divine Word in his time have worked in the same fashion from the beginning and have increasingly aggravated the condition of the church. Therefore he can perceive in the history of the Christian church only an increasing darkness, and here he agrees with the view of the Centuriators.

He differs from them, however, in that for him the Pope as Antichrist was not in the same fashion the personal manifestation of the sinister principle ruling the church. To be sure, for him also the satanic and anti-Christian Papacy is the greatest outrage in Christendom. It has become increasingly worse since that tyrant and bloodhound Phocas declared Boniface III, reckoned as the most obvious Antichrist, to be the head of all congregations.[22] But the Pope does not have for Arnold the same concrete and particular significance as he does for the Centuriators. The same guilt attributable to the Pope affects the papal clergy in principle as well. Pope and clergy belong together. If, therefore, one regards everything by which the church has been perverted as the Antichrist ever more visibly emerging, then this anti-Christianity is not to be dated from the beginnings of the Papacy but from the first hierarchical formation of the church and everything connected with that.[23] This is a not unimportant point of difference between the two works.

In the *Centuries* we find no description of the period of the Reformation and after, as we do in Arnold, since they do not go this far. But, as their occasional remarks leave no doubt, the Centuriators, too, depicted the moral-religious condition of the evangelical church of their time in

---

21. *Unpartheiische Kirchen- und Ketzerhistorien*, 359. [ED. "Es sind andere Personen und doch einerlei Aufzüge."]

22. [ED.] See above, 88, n. 11.

23. Cf. *Unpartheiische Kirchen- und Ketzerhistorien*, 323: "In considering the decay of Christendom, one must not always place all the blame on the Pope alone, since the narratives on the whole . . . sufficiently confirm that the rest of the clergy was not worth much either."

just as unfavorable a light as Arnold and other Protestants, whose testimonies Arnold has collected in great numbers. In this connection, we need only to compare the Preface with which, in the year 1562, Flacius, Wigand, and Judex opened their fifth *Century*. Concerning the evangelical church of their time, they break forth with the lament: "Oh shame! With what dreadful ingratitude do we mortal men receive these great benefits of almighty God! What foul sins, crimes, and disgraceful deeds abound in the Christian world! Indeed, we shudder to mention these things." They intend to mention briefly only a few. Even if there are still a few scattered teachers of the church who hold to the pure Word of God, they are ridiculed and persecuted by their own colleagues. These abominable sins committed during the time of the Interim by leaning toward the Antichrist still do not cease. Most have yielded in favor of the papists on the article on free will; they have yielded on the position that we are justified *principaliter* by faith (no one would wish to quarrel over the particle *sola* before the comrades of Antichrist); they have yielded to the position that good works are necessary for blessedness or righteousness, or that in the ceremonies the bodily mask of the Antichrist is to be accepted, etc. Thus the Centuriators also deeply bemoan the condition of the church at their time. But the main object of their complaint is simply that men have not held fast enough to the pure Lutheran system and have turned again to the dogma of the Catholic Church, whereas Arnold discerns the cause of the evil to lie much deeper, not in this or that dogmatic direction but in the prevailing dogmatism in general and in the hierarchical interest so closely bound to it. Incontestably, the latter view is more correct and consistent. If the Papacy itself is merely the consequence of Catholicism, the culminating point of the self-developing hierarchical system, then it is shallow and superficial simply to remain with the Papacy in investigating the causes of the decay of the church, and to make the Popes responsible for everything in the church that is to be censured. If in the church before the Reformation everything depends so exclusively on the Papacy as the Centuriators represent it, then there cannot be a satisfactory explanation of how the evangelical church, after it had freed itself from the Papacy, could nevertheless so quickly have sunk back into a condition wholly similar to what had existed before. If the same phenomena direct us to the same causes, then the historical continuity must be investigated more deeply; and it is to be acknowledged as Arnold's merit that from this point of view he was able to go back beyond the Popes to the more general foundation of such phenomena of ecclesiastical life.

Here it is not without interest to note from some examples the influence of this method on his presentation in comparison with that of the *Centuries*. For the centuries immediately preceding the Reformation, as well as those somewhat earlier, his conception of the major elements of history agrees in essentials with that of the Centuriators. Yet his judgment is modified in many respects, indeed always in such a way that it rings more sharply and critically than that of his predecessors. How completely different the intention of his criticism of scholasticism had to be from that of theologians who themselves were already in the process of introducing the same scholastic formalism into their own system, and of "drawing from the stinking well out of which most of their terms and opinions gushed"![24] Every word he said about scholasticism shows the deep hatred and wrath he harbored against it as the source of school-theology.

Concerning Henry IV and Gregory VII, he too sides with the former. But he is much more annoyed by the insolence with which the priests have accused the good king of the most horrible misdeeds than he is by the humiliation caused him by the Pope. He is certain for just this reason that there must have been something good in him and that since the infamous priests and hypocrites could not tolerate him, he must have had an unhypocritical, upright soul.[25] For him the matter of Pope Joan is not at all doubtful because there are so many witnesses, and also because one could not imagine anything more foolish, godless, and absurd than the situation at that time; indeed, one might all but wonder that it was not worse.[26] With respect to Boniface, the apostle of the Germans, whom the Centuriators also call the greatest sycophant of the Popes, and whose business it therefore was to enlarge the kingdom of the Antichrist and to transplant the popish superstition to Germany, his final judgment is even more emphatic: any rational person could only regard him as a true anti-Christian priest and as a member of the beastly tribe described in the Revelation of John.[27] It can already be seen from these examples how the distinctiveness of his point of view is expressed all the more in the sharpest and most thoroughgoing of his historical judgments. He is more bitter and caustic even than the Centuriators because he saw, in everything that happened under the authorities of the church, whatever titles they might have—"under the Pope and his following, or, as we call them, the *ministerium* [ministry]"[28]—the same hierarchical power and

24. *Unpartheiische Kirchen- und Ketzerhistorien*, 372, 389, 401.   25. *Ibid.*, 345.
26. *Ibid.*, 324.   27. *Ibid.*, 308.   28. *Ibid.*, 309.

authority that aroused for him the greatest horror and loathing in his immediate environment.

Just as a difference between Arnold and the Centuriators is already to be found in this connection, he is increasingly distinguished from them the further back we go with him into the apostolic period. Church teachers for whom recognition and high admiration by the Centuriators are still wholly in accord with the Catholic Church receive from him only very limited and ambiguous praise. Even Athanasius, in his opinion, was free neither from gross errors nor from other shortcomings; he serves rather as proof of how the fame of purity of doctrine, to say nothing of the purity and holiness of life, is so often questionable even on the part of the most highly praised teachers. A period in which there is so much controversy and debate over dogmas is not at all to his liking. He takes great offense at the Council of Nicaea and its doctrine of the *homoousia*. That Council introduced a newly invented and unscriptural creedal formula simply the better to distinguish the heretics; and it tied Christianity, right belief, and the work of salvation to the external repetition of such formulas, indeed to a single word. This is already the time in which the clergy asserts itself in all its power, its pretensions and arrogance, its perverse and godless nature. Just as affairs are altogether bad with Christians outwardly, so everything internally connected with faith and love is also corrupted. The more value is attached to outer, seeming virtues and works, the less one can distinguish hypocrites from true Christians; already Christians have almost all fallen into the very opposite of what earlier periods had regarded as laudable.[29]

The chief blame for the corruption that broke out so violently in that period is borne by Constantine, from whose wreath of honor, once so gloriously embellished with virtues and merits, Arnold mercilessly tears away the last twigs still left him even by the Centuriators. For Arnold, Constantine's Christianity is a highly ambiguous matter; he doubts, indeed, whether he had even been baptized. On the whole, there is still a great deal about him that is pagan; for whatever good is imputed to him, he has only to thank his weak submission to a flattering and hypocritical clergy. Christianity's situation at the beginning of the fourth century is already so miserable that it could not become much worse until later on, with the complete invasion of worldly vanities. The most knowledgeable scribes admit that the church has never since the age of the apostles been plagued more heavily and fiercely by quarrels, disputes, disunity, slander,

29. *Ibid.*, 187 f.

and abuse. Satan would seem, then, to be completely at large and in no way fettered. The majority of the clergy, including the most eminent, seem already to be immersed in all sorts of outrages, and have everywhere and unabashedly shown their ambition and greediness and their sumptuous, opulent life. The flourishing state of the church would seem to result simply from the clergy's ruling over the poor people at will, accusing all who stood in their way of heresy, and suppressing them. "In the midst of this, true and active faith no longer had a place, and religion consisted of certain concepts and terms invented by reason, as well as of outward oral confessions and other *operibus operatis* [works performed]. Whoever could adapt himself properly to the accepted way, and not doubt the already firmly established authority and power of the bishops, was called orthodox; he might or might not have been an upright Christian. But whoever could not find all their sentences, opinions, and artificial words in the Bible, or otherwise could not regard them as acceptable with conviction of conscience, must be called a heretic. Thus the majority of the people fell into the most outward security and wickedness, such that there was often little to distinguish them from pagans." [30]

His Ideal

From one century to the next, the same forbidding picture confronts the penetrating gaze of the historian, and forces him to seek what he would find at an ever greater distance; thus his pious disposition can be satisfied only with the apostolic age and with the period immediately following. Then everything was completely different, because nothing yet existed of what has so tarnished and darkened the history of later ages. Arnold cannot picture ideally enough the moral and religious life of the Christians of the first and second centuries. At that time, nothing was done for the sake of appearance; there was no religious intolerance, no clerical power and authority, no false Christianity of any kind, but only faith and love, active Christianity, unity and peace. Everything that belongs to a godly life is no mere fiction, but is actually found in the still extant written documents of that time.

As proof of the mystical life in God, which he also cannot fail to see in the piety of the oldest Christians because of the mystical bent of his spirit, he is much inclined to regard the writings of Dionysius Areopagite as an authentic product of the apostolic age. The grounds on which Dalläus

---

30. *Ibid.*, 138, 159 ff. [ED. Quotation from 161.]

had already demonstrated the inauthenticity of these writings could not have been unknown to him; but the whole expression and style seemed to him so excellent and so full of divine testimonies of love and divine secrets that he could not doubt the deep communion with God of such a man (who was taken up, as it were, into heaven and ravished with divine love), and thus also his apostolic antiquity.

In regard to the teaching of the earliest Christians, remarks Arnold, one ought not to seek anything systematic in the writings of their teachers, because the first teachers could not have imagined such limitations of spirit and faith. He therefore desires, in his portrayal of doctrine, to restrict himself to the apostolic writings, without any use of conventional terminology, since it would not be a pure and unpartisan description of the first and oldest theology if it were perversely judged according to the more recent theology. He thus distinguishes himself from the Centuriators, who systematize everything and above all record even the system of Jesus and the apostles according to the framework of their theological *loci* and articles. Dogma in general has for him so little importance that he believed himself permitted to accord it so much attention only in the first two centuries, when it was still at its best.

His Patronage of Heretics

But why, we must still ask, did Arnold want his church history to be regarded expressly as a history of heretics? In answering this question, a glimpse into the innermost concept of his work is for the first time opened up to us completely. It was a part of his original plan to devote his work especially to the history of heretics. The same forbidding impression, which forced him to escape from the quarreling and wrangling, the hypocrisy and godlessness of the orthodox church to the quiet peace and pure simplicity of the primitive apostolic period, also drove him to the opposite side, where, according to the customary view, there were only heretics. He was guided by the simple reflection that if the convictions about the orthodox church that served as the basis of his historical presentation were correct, then its judgment of those whom it condemned as heretics could no more be true than that on the whole true Christianity could be found in it. If this is the untrue church, perverse in its antithesis, then it must follow that one is to regard as true Christians precisely those whom that church considers to be untrue.

It is generally true that, if one's whole standpoint is essentially different, then all the details within the sphere of one's consideration must appear in a different light. Hence it is certainly a fundamental deficiency in Arnold's work that his view of the heretics is merely constructed *a priori*. The negative judgment, in itself justified, that the heretics could not be what the orthodox church regards them to be, because the latter proceeds upon a false assumption, was far too quickly changed by him into the positive judgment that they must be good Christians to the same extent that the orthodox are not. Though he was correct in calling his history of heretics "unpartisan" in so far as he did not share the customary prejudice against the heretics, and did not intend to take the side of the orthodox party against them in advance, nevertheless his "unpartisan history of heretics" was made just as partisan by his deciding in advance to take the side of the heretics against the orthodox as a basic principle, and to find in them as much that is good and praiseworthy as the orthodox saw in them to condemn. In order to justify the heretics and put them in a more or less favorable light, it is enough for him merely to say that they are heretics—for they would not have been heretical had they not been the exact opposite of what the orthodox church regarded as true Christianity.

In the general remarks found at the beginning of Arnold's history of heretics, this *a priori* procedure can be clearly recognized as his guiding point of view. He gives there a long series of questions about possible cases of heresy, which are answered in the following major propositions. Not only in ancient times, but also among Protestants and Lutherans, many, indeed most, have been branded heretics and condemned on emotional grounds. Incompetent zealots have made the name "heretic" so common and despicable that indeed most have come to regard it as an honor. The degenerate clergy have raved most frequently and violently of all against true, interior Christianity, whose confession and practice is described as heretical. In this perverse world, nothing can happen more easily and quickly than that an innocent person should come under the suspicion and actual charge of heresy. One need only speak a single word not in accord with the clergy, and the mantle of heresy would be ready; and so on. Little as one can object to the truth of these statements in general, it is also clear that their application to individual cases may be quite different. Arnold wants, to be sure, as he asserts, to base his judgment of individual cases only on an unpartisan investigation of the sources; but the general view from which he proceeds has too visibly preponderant an influence for us to be able to regard his judgment as unprejudiced. Far too often, he is the solicitor and eulogist of heretics for no other reason than his hatred and mistrust of the orthodox church. He is always inclined to excuse as much as possible whatever the heretics were accused of, and when this is not possible, at least to turn to their favor for the sake of Christian love. Indeed, it is certain that in all times, as now, the best men have been heretics; and one was already a heretic if he tried to investigate the truth according to his own insight, free from common errors.

But, one must ask, if truth and error each confronted the other to the degree that the orthodox church had come into power, then were there not already heretics in the earliest church? And, valid though the grounds may be for defending heretics against unjust accusations, did they not also very often teach notorious falsehoods, which are rightly rejected? Arnold cannot deny either of these assertions. But concerning the latter he is aided by his dogmatic indifferentism; and concerning the first, one can ask on the other hand what at that time was regarded as the major issue. To be sure, heretics are already mentioned in the earliest periods. But what was found objectionable in them is not so much the deviation of their teaching as the immorality of their lives; and one must be very cautious in regarding as historically true everything that is told of the oldest heretics, since so much of their guilt has been fabricated by later writers. Concerning this, there are found in Arnold many striking remarks concerning the earliest history of heretics. He distinguishes the earliest sources from later ones, draws attention to the deficiencies, contradictions, and suspicious character of their statements, and knows in particular how to evaluate properly Epiphanius' reports of heretics. By such exaggerations, Simon Magus, the Nicolaitans, and others first became the arch heretics they are customarily supposed to be. Concerning heretics such as Valentinus, Marcion, and others, he not only is reasonable enough not to think them as vicious and wicked as they have been pictured, but also admits that by reflection upon divine things they have arrived at their peculiar opinions, and have expressed in them only their well-intentioned conviction. He even defends the Manichaeans against much of what they are reputed to have taught by their opponents, who have not rightly understood their meaning and sought to make their heresy as black as possible.

In the history of the great controversies during the fourth and fifth centuries, Arnold finds himself reminded, to be sure, that the praises given to heretics applied only to their piety, not to their doctrine, and he would not want in any way to interfere thereby with the divine truth. But all the more, after this reservation, he believed himself compelled to find the guilt of all those whom he condemned only on the side of the orthodox, in their seeking of quarrels and persecution and in the evil means they were accustomed to use against their opponents. When they happened also to defend doctrine that in itself was true, then these controversies were a mere wrangling over words; and no heretic has had the luck to be spared lies. The only heretics who do not deserve a mild judgment of this sort are those who condemned others to heresy and who thus bear in their own fate the just judgment of God, such as Nestorius and Eutyches. On the other hand, a favorable light falls on Pelagius, precisely in connection with dogma, since he was only moved to elevate the powers of free will, as others had also done before him, and because, in his first enthusiasm for true Christianity, he disapproved of the public scandal caused by the open evil, certitude, and hypocrisy of the so-called orthodox, especially the teachers, who appealed to God's grace and to their own natural weaknesses in order to clothe their sins. The result would have been completely different, had there been any basis in a morally pure life, and if instead of having his words distorted, Pelagius had been rightly understood, and not treated with such hostility.

It is unnecessary to add further examples of this sort, or to show how the course of history itself confronted the historian all the more obligingly, permitting him to carry on his assumed role as a general patron of heretics up to the most recent figures, who had to suffer under the weight of the current *ministerium*, just as the earlier ones had to suffer under the *ministerium* of their time.

His Mystical-Pietistic Bias

In a word, this is a mystical-pietistic view of history. Like the old Protestant view, it sees in history only light and darkness. But though for the orthodox Protestant the light shining in darkness is not extinguished so long as there are a number of witnesses to the truth who hold fast to the article of justification *sola fide*, this is not sufficient for the pietist and mystic, in order to satisfy his religious consciousness by the examination of history. The doctrine of justification is also merely a dogmatic proposition, a part of the orthodox system on which the dominance of the church rests. True Christianity is in better condition anywhere but in the orthodox church, which has desecrated the ground of its existence by all the horrors of its delight in controversy and persecution, its hypocritical Pharisaism, its immorality and godlessness. One would prefer to associate with the ascetics and monks in solitude, in order to lead a quiet, contemplative life far from the clamor of the ruling church. So long as the monks remain in their solitude and have nothing to do with anything concerning the church as a whole, they are for the mystic a beautiful manifestation of the Christian life, with whom he can be on friendly terms far more easily than can the strict Protestant, who must fear from their endeavors an impairment of his doctrine of justification. Therefore, precisely where one ought above all to see true Christianity in its full bloom, nothing is to be found. It exists only outside the limits of the orthodox church, among those who have withdrawn into themselves, or among those whom it has cast out—among the silent and hidden, the misunderstood and the oppressed.

In contrast to the predominant attitude, it is certainly bold and original to take the directly opposite point of view, and to test on a large scale whether in so many cases, indeed in all periods, the historical verdict should not have been wholly different from what it has been up to now, whether it should not be flatly reversed; or, to put the matter more specifically, to focus the entire history of the Christian church on the question whether those who according to the customary view are true and proper Christians are not much rather untrue and false Christians, and whether those who hitherto have not been considered Christians at all, and indeed have been regarded as the very worst sort of men, are not in fact the very best Christians.

This is the question Arnold put to himself. But we have now to consider what must become of history when the question is answered in Arnold's sense, or in general when the task incumbent upon the historian of the Christian church is reduced solely to this question. Is it the task of historical study above all to ask which members of the Christian church in its several periods are good or bad Christians, or to examine the Christian piety of all those who enter the theater of history as actors, and of the parties confronting one another here and there? If history must ask only this, then its special object would be just what it can know and evaluate least of all. If one locates true and vital Christianity, as Arnold rightly does, in the inner life of man rather than in his external behavior, and if one does not make it depend upon whether one confesses this or that form of dogma, as Arnold also does quite rightly, then how can it be known historically who in this sense is a good or bad Christian? It is obvious that here a confusion of objective and subjective Christianity occurs, which confounds and destroys the conception of history. The object of history can only be the objectively given—not what Christianity is subjectively in the inner life of men, but rather how it stands before us as a historical phenomenon, as a power in history, independent of individual subjects. In general, history ought only to present, not to judge—not even morally, except as the judgment itself emerges from the objective course of the subject matter. If, nevertheless, Christianity in the subjective sense is regarded as the proper content of history, and if the latter is required to give account of good or bad Christians in the various periods, then a demand is made of it here to which it can correspond either not at all or only in such a way that what is regarded as true Christianity is defined according to a standard whose relation to the subject matter it ought to define is totally inadequate.

This obviously applies to Arnold. He looks everywhere for true and vital Christianity, and for him everything depends on distinguishing true and upright Christians from those who are false and merely apparent. But who are the true Christians and who are the false? The latter are the orthodox; the former are those who either are completely indifferent to the orthodox church or have been persecuted and suppressed by it. Therefore, the standard of judgment is still orthodoxy—not in the positive sense, which for Catholics and Protestants makes ecclesiastical orthodoxy the first condition of a good Christian, but in the negative sense that a man can be regarded as a true Christian only if he has no contact with the orthodox church. That this is as arbitrary as it is inconsistent may not at first be evident. Not to mention anything else, what right has Arnold only to suppose that the rulers of the church have had no motive for their behavior other than malice, hypocrisy, godlessness, and the greatest moral perversity, as he so often maintains? Just as this point of view is quite unjustified even with respect to the moral issues involved, so it leads also to a treatment of history in which history loses its real content, and interest in it must be weakened to the most extreme degree. One peruses Arnold's history of the church and of heretics and asks oneself whether the total impression is of anything other than the most tedious monotony. One repeatedly hears the same complaint from one century to the next, from the beginning of the downfall of the church in the third century onward—namely, that the situation is the same in every period, or that the condition of the church both internally and externally has become increasingly worse and more miserable, or that

the power and malice of the clergy have risen to an ever higher degree, or
that the wrath of the clergy toward everything not conforming to their
intention and will, even against the slightest glimpse of truth, has blazed
forth from the deception of their lies. The same theme is repeated with
endless variations, and one always knows in advance where everything is
heading. "There are new actors but still a single pageant."

Instead of becoming richer in content and more full of life, history
increasingly shrivels up in the centuries before the Reformation; it only
becomes more empty and paltry, duller and more spiritless. What could it
recount as new that had not already happened often enough? If this is
true of the church as a whole, as is here supposed, then there is nothing in
any part of its history—either in the area of dogma or in that of polity or
of cultus—in which one could have any interest, for the sake of the
subject matter itself, in pursuing the course of historical development.
Rather, everything is such that one can only observe the same melancholy
condition of the whole from a new perspective and complain about it
with a new expression of dismay. If the same depravities are forever
repeated in stronger measure, how can one be surprised when the historian collects all these impressions into a common judgment? In such evil
times there would be almost nothing good to find amongst either the
clergy or the laity.[31] Everything appears to him in the same dark and
gloomy aspect. Even phenomena in regard to which a more general consideration would seem to be called for cannot dislodge him from his
limited sphere of vision: e.g., he regards the universities as having been
founded, one after the other, only to afford great assistance to the anti-
Christian clergy in realizing their schemes; and as for the art of printing,
there was no great reason to laud its invention when the state of its
corruption and misuse was recognized.[32]

For him this is always the predominant consideration, and it is especially characteristic that even the Reformation cannot interrupt the
monotony of his presentation, or emerge as an epoch-making event. Even
here, nothing essentially new takes place. Even though the light whose
weak glow has always previously illuminated the darkness of the ages has
now begun to shine more brightly, the old scene is nevertheless re-
enacted. The light shines now, only to be dimmed again as quickly as
possible. The situation becomes all the worse and more hopeless the more
the historian—the closer he comes to the present—is directly related to
the phenomena of history, has a far greater wealth of materials before

31. *Unpartheiische Kirchen- und Ketzerhistorien*, 361.   32. *Ibid.*, 401, 414.

him, and receives from all sides the same discouraging impressions that have hitherto so darkened and clouded his view of history.

Here, in fact, we stand for the first time at the point where we hold the key to his entire view of history: it is nothing but a reflection of the total impression made upon him by the present day, and of his sympathies and antipathies toward the ecclesiastical life of his time. Arnold's history of the church and of heretics undoubtedly gives the general impression that there could scarcely be a portrayal more thoroughly stamped by the subjectivity of its author. It is therefore a very graphic example of the sort of church historiography in which the subject cannot yet tear himself loose from his immediate environment and from himself, from the views and interests that link him with the present—in order to transpose himself entirely into the subject matter itself and to pursue the objective course of that subject matter alone, by virtue of a pure devotion to the object. Such historiography still depends too much on the present not to have to carry its image into the past as well. And since the present is split by an antithesis in which one is attracted to the one side as much as he is repulsed by the other, one subject wholly to the impressions of the present, when he looks back into the past, only sees, running through all periods, the same antithesis by which he himself is affected. In this respect, therefore, Arnold, the patron of the heretics, still wholly belongs with the Centuriators, the deadly enemies of the Papacy. He shares with them the same passions of hatred and love. The only difference is that for him the clergy, the priesthood, or "as we call it, the *ministerium*," is to be hated much more than the Papacy; and for him the alternative is not the objectivity of dogma—e.g., the basic article of *justificari sola fide* confessed by the witnesses to truth in all periods—but rather, subjectively, the series of individuals who carry true and vital Christianity in their hearts in faith and love, without dogma and school theology.

IV

THE GRADUAL TRANSITION FROM A DUALISTIC WORLD VIEW TO A CONCEPTION OF HISTORICAL DEVELOPMENT: WEISMANN, MOSHEIM, SEMLER, WALCH

1. *The Impact of Arnold's Work*

A work such as Arnold's, which not only attacked so unsparingly the customary prejudices of the orthodox church, but even threatened to overthrow the basic principles on which it stood; a work that expressed itself in the tone of bitter personal irritation against all who considered themselves the special representatives and authorities of the church, and that seemed to have the sole purpose of uncovering their errors and shortcomings and placing them in the most odious light; a work that, besides containing so much that was damaging and derogatory, spoke out so forthrightly in the German language, which is likewise characteristic of it—such a work must of necessity have called forth the liveliest opposition. The writings that appeared on both sides, to challenge and to defend Arnold's history of the church and heretics, comprise a not inconsiderable part of the theological literature of the time.[1] It was easy enough for

1. The most important are found in the third volume of the Schaffhausen edition of Arnold's works. Cf. also J. G. Walch, *Einleitung in die Religionsstreitigkeiten der lutherischen Kirche* (Jena, 1733–36), II, 687 f. One of the major opponents was E. S. Cyprian. The tendency of these polemical writings can be seen most clearly from the title of a work by Pastor Corvinus in 1701: *Gründliche Untersuchung der sogenannten unparteiischen Kirchen- und Ketzerhistorie, und einiger andern Schriften G. Arnold's, in welcher klar und deutlich gezeigt wird, dass er in derselben nichts weniger als unparteiisch sich erwiesen, sondern vielmehr nach allen Kräften, wiewohl ganz vergeblich sich bearbeitet, die historische Wahrheit unverantwortlich zu verfälschen, alle, auch die ärgsten Ketzer unl Ketzereien, von Anbeginn, zusammt einigen Verfolgern der Kirchen, zu vertheidigen, die Kirche Gottes auf das Äusserste zu schmähen, auch gar zu läugnen, dero rechtschaffenste Lehrer und die ersten christlichen Kayser zu verunglimpsen, die in Gottes Wort fest gegründete*

opponents not simply to point out many mistakes and errors in matters of detail, but above all to show the author's whole position to be extremely one-sided and erroneous and the claim to impartiality to be completely unjustified. However, the violence of the controversy over Arnold's work only showed the force of the impact it made and the importance that even its opponents had to ascribe to it. His bias, though extreme, was the necessary antithesis to the no less extreme bias of the previous view; and Arnold had only done what sooner or later was bound to be done: he had placed himself on the opposite side and asked, from this standpoint, whether those who hitherto had been so quickly dismissed with an adverse judgment did not also have the right to be evaluated according to another, more equitable criterion. It could not be denied that Arnold's work had broken a new path; his presentation contained, in its praise as well as in its censure, too much that was true for it to remain unused in future treatments.

Hence the most immediate consequence was a conviction that the extreme of the two views, which here confront each other in sharp antithesis, had to be avoided on both sides. The first step was to move from the abstract transcendence of the mutually exclusive antitheses to the firm ground of concrete historical truth. To the same extent that the phenomena of history were no longer approached from a particular presupposition, which placed them in advance on either one side or the other of an antithesis permeating all individual events, it first became possible to see more deeply into the natural continuity of events, so that it might be grasped through the inner course of its development, according to the various moments determining its historical existence.

At the same time, the polemical spirit that had had so large a place in previous church historiography, and that in fact had been its inner motive and moving principle, must of itself disappear. If hitherto there had been no scruples about giving free rein to polemical zeal against the Catholic Church even in the realm of history, it was now seen from Arnold how the same weapon could also be turned against one's own church. And if the virtue of impartiality that he himself claimed for his history of the church and of heretics could not be conceded to him, the nature of the true impartiality demanded by history was to be gathered on the basis of

---

und der Kirche Gottes anvertraute theure Beilage der heilsamen Glaubenslehre, theils ungewiss und zweifelhaftig zu machen, theils gar über einen Hausen zu werfen, hingegen allen falschen Lehren und Irrthümern wiederum einen freien Gang zu öffnen. . . .

everything that one lacked in his impartiality. Here Arnold's work provided a not unfruitful lesson. In place of that passionate, polemical excitement evident upon every occasion and often given such unbridled expression in the Centuriators, in Baronius, and in Arnold, there now appeared more and more frequently a quieter, gentler tone, more in accord with the dignity of history.

2. *Weismann*

Among the immediate successors of Arnold in whom this influence of his work is noticeable, the Tübingen theologian C. E. Weismann is the most prominent. His work encompassing the whole of church history [2] is very favorably distinguished from earlier works of this kind in its entire tone and character. To be sure, he still advances a dualistic mode of perception, expressing it even in the title of his work, but the conception and presentation of the details show that it already has become foreign to him. He sees the dark anti-Christian principle neither in the clergy, as Arnold does, nor in the Papacy, as do the Centuriators. In general, the activity of this principle is not to be represented in the history of the Christian church in so direct and personal a fashion. He regards the Papacy as a natural development of the hierarchy as it is given aristocratic shape by the power and consequence of a few bishops; and he therefore locates its fundamental beginnings in the fourth century, after which the prestige of the Roman See had so grown, thanks to auspicious temporal circumstances, that even if at the time there was no thought of papal

2. It appeared in 1718–19 in two quarto volumes, and in 1745 in a second revised and enlarged edition. The title of the first edition was: *Introductio in memorabilia ecclesiastica historiae sacrae Novi Testamenti maxime vero seculorum primorum et novissimorum ad juvandam notitiam regni Dei et Satanae cordisque humani salutarem* [Introduction to Ecclesiastical Memorabilia of the Sacred History of the New Testament, Particularly of the First Centuries and of the Most Recent Ones, Written for the Advancement of the Saving Knowledge of the Kingdom of God and of Satan and of the Human Heart] (2 vols.; Stuttgart, 1718–19). The second edition (2 vols.; Halle, 1745) no longer found the apposition, *maxime . . . novissimorum* [Particularly of the First Centuries and of the Most Recent Ones] to be necessary.

[ED.] Christian Eberhard Weismann was born and died in Württemberg (1677–1747). He was educated in Tübingen, to which he returned in 1721 as professor of theology. He was strongly pietistic and known as a distinguished preacher. In addition to the work mentioned above, he wrote *Orationes academicae de causis cur tot eximia Dei dona, nostra maxime aetate, ut plurimum sine fructu pereant* (Tübingen, 1729), and *Institutiones theologicae exegetico-dogmaticae* (Tübingen, 1739).

monarchy and infallibility, nevertheless the Papacy emerged as a natural result. The same absolute power was divided into the two branches of Papocaesarism and Caesaropapism, by which all spiritual, divine, evangelical power in the church was devoured. However, the church did not thereby become satanic and anti-Christian but only worldly and carnal; and the absolute presupposition of a supernatural principle is not to deter an investigation of the natural causes of the emergence and development of ecclesiastical monarchy in its historical circumstances.[3]

He characterizes the century in which, in the person of Gregory VII, the Papacy obtained the highest level of omnicompetence as the "venerable century of the Roman Curia, blessed, golden, and full of rejoicing, but hateful to all men of prudence because it demonstrated by an amazing experiment what deceitful, clever, and sanctimonious ambition, which is especially fatal and deadly to our own Germany, can do among the multitude, who are blind and simple as regards the flesh."[4] Vividly though the historian sides with the right of the Emperor and with German honor against Gregory VII, his depiction of this struggle still remains entirely within the limits of historical laws; and of Gregory, nothing other than psychological and natural motives is presupposed. "The pontifical arrogance of Gregory VII and his dream of papal omnipotence were alone responsible for those most unfortunate and most wicked attempts by which he conceived the notion to wrest for the Roman pontiff by whatever means he could, with or without the consent of Henry, this ancient and legitimate right of the Emperor, and to wrest for the minor orders all the remaining rights as well."[5] Similarly, evidence of a disposition freer from partisan interest, as well as of a more accurate estimation of the historical facts, is to be found in the willing repudiation, concerning Pope Joan and Emperor Phocas, of the use of those weapons to which the Protestants hitherto had been accustomed.[6]

Since Weismann generally tried as far as possible to avoid the extremes of the previous historical understanding, he could not, for this reason alone, simply agree with Arnold concerning the heretics. Since in advance he neither had the good opinion Arnold had, nor could agree with the customary harsh judgment, he was brought concerning them all the more to a correct historical procedure. He tries to explain the striking phenomena of the great number of heresies arising in the second century on the basis of natural causes. He draws attention to the great spiritual unrest

---

3. Weismann, *Introductio in memorabilia ecclesiastica* (2nd ed.), I, 433.
4. [ED.] *Ibid.*, I, 869.   5. *Ibid.*, I, 902.   6. *Ibid.*, I, 665, 778.

and the crises that generally occurred at that time, as well as to the after-effects of Judaism and paganism, the influence of philosophy, and the natural inclination of the human heart to prefer an imagined higher wisdom to the simple truth of Christianity and to justify its moral aberrations by a patently contrived theory. Besides, he is quite inclined to regard the often flamboyant reports of the ancient heretics as exaggerated and fictitious.[7] He judges the heretics more mildly and equitably, and deplores the proceedings against them in which so often even insignificant errors, such as ought to have been passed over in silence, have led to such great agitation because of a delight in controversy and a desire to magnify things out of proportion. Even the actual teachings of Eutyches and Nestorius were probably not so dangerous and objectionable.[8]

On this and similar points, a considerable forward progress is generally undeniable. However, the essential deficiencies, because of which Weismann still remains on the same level with his predecessors, must not be overlooked. Among these in particular is the overemphasis on the original perfection of the apostolic age—the purity of its teaching and its life. The first century is, according to Weismann, "apostolic, primitive, and glorious in its divine simplicity, humility, and virtue; to be sure not altogether free from the blemishes and convulsions of its own age; nonetheless an archetype for the following centuries, although very dissimilar from them." [9] To be sure, the teachings of Jesus and the apostles possess this archetypal, normative character quite uniquely, but how can that be regarded as a special advantage of the first century? And if it cannot be denied that even this first period was not wholly spotless, how is a precise line to be drawn? The absolute distinction between the first century and all those following therefore becomes relative. This overestimation of the first century is also detrimental to the portrayal of subsequent centuries, for the more highly the first period is esteemed, the more deeply those that follow must be overshadowed by it. Not only must there be an immeasurably wide gap between the first and second centuries, but also in the ensuing period an ever greater downfall [10] must be assumed—so

---

7. *Ibid.*, I, 123, 162 f.   8. *Ibid.*, I, 557.   9. [ED.] *Ibid.*, I, 1.

10. [ED.] This criticism of the theory of a "fall" by the church subsequent to the apostolic period, at the end of the first century, is relevant to a similar theory propounded by Baur's student, Albrecht Ritschl, in the second edition of his *Die Entstehung der altkatholischen Kirche* (Bonn, 1857), and adopted as one of the great leitmotifs in Adolf Harnack's *Dogmengeschichte*. Cf. Philip Hefner, *Faith and the Vitalities of History: A Theological Study Based on the Work of Albrecht Ritschl* (New York, 1966), chaps. I, II. Such theories are not original with Ritschl

much so that, even when for once a brighter light does break forth, the condition of the church subsequently becomes much worse than before, as happened in the time of the Reformation. To be sure, God unveiled a new epoch of his grace for souls thirsting after salvation, but at the same time "the subsequent fortunes of men of all classes—who are wicked, ungrateful, obstinate, stubborn, dissolute, and defiant, because of their own fault, not God's, and the intolerable abuse of divine gifts—have become worse than their former ones, because of the vengeance of God and at the instigation of the Devil." [11] But why, one must ask, does God bestow such grace when it only has such consequences? Perhaps only to have all the more opportunity to punish, or to reward all the more gloriously the few who persevere as faithful souls in such times?

The concept of a development immanent to the nature of the church is still lacking here. Another, related deficiency is that the treatment, without having the whole course of events in view, is too preoccupied with details and consists in large part only of biographical notes about teachers and leaders of the church. Arnold at least made a permanent distinction between the internal and external conditions of the church. Finally, Weismann has not yet shed the superficial form of narration according to centuries, although by that time Adam Rechenberg, in his manual of church history,[12] had already made the transition to a division according to periods. Since periods can be distinguished only where a definite sequence of occurrences comes to an end and a new turning point appears, the division according to periods already presupposes a view that penetrates more deeply into the objective continuity of events and is in a

---

and Harnack. As Baur makes clear, they already are anticipated by the Centuriators, Gottfried Arnold, and Weismann, and seem to be a characteristic ingredient of Lutheran church historiography, in orthodox, pietistic, or liberal dress.

11. [ED.] *Introductio in memorabilia ecclesiastica* (2nd ed.), I, 1280.

12. *Summarium historiae ecclesiasticae in usum studiosae juventutis* (Leipzig, 1697). He adopted the following periods, accommodated as much as possible to centuries, but on the whole correctly worked out: (1) "period of the planting and propagating the church," the first three centuries; (2) "period of the church rejoicing in freedom under the Roman and Byzantine Empires," from Constantine to Phocas; (3) "period of the suppression and hiding of the church," especially because of the growing predominance of the Bishop of Rome, the menacing relations with Muhammadanism, and the deep decline of scholarship and theology—from the beginning of the seventh to the end of the tenth century; (4) "period of the church groaning and wailing under the tyranny of the Roman pontiff and the Saracen-Turkish yoke," from the beginning of the eleventh to the end of the fifteenth century; (5) "period of the purgation and liberation of the church," from the time of the Reformation to the eighteenth century.

position to distinguish more precisely the various moments contained in it. The greater concentration of the whole for purposes of a general survey necessitates broader sections, to be placed under precise general headings, as Rechenberg did. There remains only the task of grasping the different moments in the unity of the total concept.

GENERAL PROGRESS

The treatment of church history as a whole in a single work such as Weismann's, which is rather like some others in the same period,[13] shows the general progress that the spirit of the times has already made in the area of church history. Concerning the church-historical works of this period it can already be outwardly perceived how Spirit, as it struggles with the vast materials, succeeds more and more in gaining mastery over them. The older works—the *Magdeburg Centuries*, the *Annals* of Baronius, even Arnold's history of the church and of heretics—are impressive by virtue of their considerable volume; one is astonished by the diligence that has gathered and deposited so much in these works, as in plentiful storehouses, for the use of posterity. But the content of these works still consists in large part of raw materials, a mere collection that must first be critically sifted and worked through for the purpose of a coherent historical treatment. Volume still has a considerable preponderance over form.

13. Next to Weismann, the Reformed church historian Friedrich Spanheim [1632–1701] deserves to be mentioned with special distinction. His *Historia ecclesiastica a nato Christo ad coeptam superiore seculorum reformationem* (in the first volume of Spanheim's *Opera, quatenus complectuntur geogr. chronol. et hist. . . .* [Leyden, 1701], 486–1918) provides in a moderately sized volume a content rich in special data and for the most part appropriately selected. But it still breathes the polemical spirit of the *Centuries* against the anti-Christian Papacy, in connection with which Spanheim does not intend to omit the fable *de papa femina* [concerning the female Pope]. As a historical critic, he follows more successfully in the footsteps of his Reformed predecessors when he expresses doubts, in an essay of his own, concerning the journey of Peter to Rome, and when he sharply denounces Baronius, as he often does in his church history; cf. the "isagogical and critical rules for distinguishing the genuine sources of Christian antiquity from illegitimate and spurious ones," at its beginning. Christoph Matthaeus Pfaff [1686–1760] provided only a brief compendium—overcrowded with names and details, yet of liberal conception and independent judgment—in his *Institutiones historiae ecclesiasticae* (Tübingen, 1721). Like Spanheim and Weismann, he too followed the sequence of centuries; but he at least called attention to the following four epochs: from Caesar Augustus to Constantine, from Constantine to Charlemagne and the schism between the Latin and Greek Churches, from the schism to the Reformation, and from the Reformation to the present.

As the field of church history was further cultivated, however, the extent of the material was abbreviated, essentials were more sharply distinguished from non-essentials, details were placed under precise headings in accord with their heterogeneous nature, and the whole was brought into a more easily manageable and attractive form. Already with Weismann's work we move from the long series of ponderous folios, as from the halls of an ancient edifice, into the more comfortable residence of quartos occupying only a moderate amount of space. Compendia, summaries, and breviaries, which after the beginning of the eighteenth century become a not unimportant part of church-historical literature, especially show the increasing effort to delve into the available materials and to arrange them as clearly as possible for more general use. The further we advance into the course of the eighteenth century, the more we come upon a period in which the previously dominant religious and dogmatic ecclesiastical interests must yield to a freer, more manifold, and more universal aspiration. The restrictive bonds of ecclesiastical authority grow weaker. The more independent one becomes of them, the more does Spirit, returning into itself, not only become conscious of its freedom and autonomy, but also occupy a standpoint from which what previously was of very limited and particular interest for it now appears in a wholly different light, opening up a new area of spiritual endeavor.

In the field of church history, this gradually unfolding general evolution is recognizable in the fact that church-historical studies hitherto primarily in the service of polemics and partisan interests are now more and more emancipated from this heteronomy, and have value and fascination in themselves. Whereas up to now it was believed possible to use church history in its entire scope only for particular purposes, the more genuine historical interest now awakening—the interest in history as such—turns chiefly to special investigations. Already several works of this kind from the middle and second half of the seventeenth century—such as the historical monographs of G. Calixt, and the writings of historians in the Reformed Church such as J. Daillé, D. Blondel, J. and S. Basnage, and others, which are very laudably distinguished for their historical criticism—prove how completely different and how much more objective a content and value church history can have when built on such foundations. If we compare the church-historical works from the first decades of the eighteenth century with earlier such works, it is easy to see what progress has already been made; how the general view has been altered; how much has already been stirred up; what important critical questions have come to expression; how a judgment vacillating between opposite assertions must first be established; and how frequently the territory covered has already been worked over and enriched with new investigations and ideas, and its further cultivation prepared as to content and form. But all this is scarcely initiated, and the right laborers must first appear, to pursue further in grander style the work now begun.

The next historians to engage in this work are Mosheim and Semler, to whom can also be added the younger Walch.

3. Mosheim

His Methodological Procedure

Among church historians of ancient and modern times, scarcely a name has greater repute than that of the noted chancellor of the thriving Georgia Augusta [the University of Göttingen].[14] It is generally agreed

14. Cf. G. C. F. Lücke's *Programm zum Jubelfest der Göttinger Universitat im Jahr 1837* (Göttingen, 1837), which includes the "Narratio de Ioanne Laurentio Moshemio," 37 ff. Mosheim first published his *Institutiones historiae ecclesiasticae Novi Testamenti* in Helmstädt, 1726. He divided it into four books, or periods, but completed only three. In 1737 it appeared in a new edition as *Institutiones historiae antiquioris*, to which in 1741 he added *Institutiones historiae recentioris* as a special work. By 1739, he had already begun to rework ancient church history anew in *Institutiones historiae ecclesiasticae saeculi primi majores*. In addition to the above, he wrote *Versuch einer gründlichen und unparteiischen Kirchen- und Ketzergeschichte* (Helmstädt, 1746), on the Ophites and the Brothers of the Apostles; *Anderweitiger Versuch einer vollständigen und unpartheiischen Ketzergeschichte* (Helmstädt, 1748), on Servetus; and two major works, *Commentarii de rebus Christianorum ante Constantinum Magnum* (Helmstadt, 1753), and *Institutionum historiae ecclesiasticae antiquae et recentioris* (4 vols.; Helmstädt, 1755); the latter, in German translation, is the real church history of Mosheim.

[ED.] Johann Lorentz von Mosheim was born in Lübeck in 1694/95 and died in Göttingen in 1755. In 1716 he entered the University of Kiel, where he attracted the attention of Leibnitz. In 1719 he joined the faculty of philosophy, and in 1723 accepted a call as professor to Helmstädt, where in 1729 he assumed leadership of the entire university. The influence of Helmstädt waned rapidly after the establishment of Göttingen, where Mosheim was active in the organization of the theological faculty. In 1747 he accepted a call to Göttingen as its first and only chancellor. In addition to the wide range of his scholarship, he was an outstanding stylist in both German and Latin, and was well acquainted with the literature of England, France, and Italy. In addition to church history, he did work in systematic theology, the most important being his *Sittenlehre der heiligen Schrift* (5 vols.; Helmstädt, 1735-53). As a theologian, he occupied a middle position between pietism and rationalism. On the one hand, he was opposed to confessional orthodoxy since it prevented theology from being scientific; but on the other, he was among the first in

that he not only possessed the most fortunate combination of the usual qualities in a church historian, but also especially excelled in his brilliant and stylish treatment. Even the errors from which he cannot be absolved are to his credit, since in general they had their source in the gift of combination peculiar to him in so high a degree. If recent church historiography is correctly dated from him, he already shows very definitely its characteristic traits; for this historiography can be recognized only in the fact that by now church history had divested itself of the ceremonious attire of the church fathers—in which Arnold, the earnest preacher of virtues and repentance, still presented it, at least—and had clothed itself more and more in the less ponderous modern dress of political history. This, variously modified, is the essence of its fundamental view.

What in Mosheim must be stressed above all is his methodological procedure. Hitherto, it had not been sufficiently asked what church history is and how it is conceived. For the most part the older church historians (of whom only the Centuriators set forth the idea of their work more specifically) proceed without digression to the completion of their task. The more ardently their immediate interest is directed toward either attacking the Papacy or defending it, or toward depicting the heretics as the oppressed and the orthodox as their oppressors, the more their conception of church history as a whole is consumed by this particular purpose, and they do not reflect upon it further. Weismann, to be sure, put a *dissertatio praeliminaris* at the beginning of his church history, but in it he discusses only "certain major hindrances to the profitable writing or reading of ecclesiastical history, which deserve to be noted before many others." These hindrances he finds to be one-sided reporting, exaggerated scepticism, imprudent delight in legend, violent partisan spirit, the servile mind of men, the superficial knowledge of the learned, etc.

Mosheim, proceeding from the concept of what church history is in itself, defines it as the clear narration of what has happened in the society of Christians, outwardly and within, in such a fashion that from the continuity of cause and effect we can recognize divine Providence as it establishes and sustains, and thus becomes wiser and more pious. He compares this society with a state, whose condition is variously altered by what it encounters externally as well as internally, and thus he makes the

Germany to attack the deists. In church history, he is best known for his combination of broad perspective and minuteness of detail.

distinction between the external and the internal the basic division of his church history. The external is to give account of what, auspiciously or otherwise, befalls the Christian society; the internal has to do with Christianity as a religion and with the changes that have occurred in that aspect of it. Here, once again, the analogy with the state is of value, in order to divide and arrange everything that pertains to church history in a fashion corresponding to the concept of the subject matter. The church also has its regents in its teachers, among whom are those who play a major role in history, having distinguished themselves partly as the overseers of individual congregations and partly by their writings. In addition, the church has its laws, divine as well as human; the former are the teachings concerning faith and morals contained in Holy Scripture; the latter concern primarily the cultus and what is connected with it. Everything that has changed in the church among all these matters during the course of time is therefore the object of church history. Here again, the analogy of the church with the state is at the basis. Just as wars and disturbances arise from time to time in the secular state, so it is in the church, where frequent controversies have arisen over doctrines and usages, the authors of which are called heretics in ecclesiastical language. Mosheim does not align himself in advance, with the partisanship and partiality of an Arnold, on the side of the heretics, but he at least assists their cause in that he removes everything odious from the concept and from their name. He adheres only to the most general aspects and would have considered heretics in a pure and formal sense only those who through their own or others' fault have occasioned disturbances and controversies in the Christian society, irrespective of the content of their teachings and opinions.

The Objective, Yet Political and Pragmatic Character of His Historiography

These definitions, by which at first only the concept of the church is to be marked out and its limits marked off, in themselves clearly show that we are confronted here by an essentially different standpoint. The narrowly ecclesiastical and particularistic interests that inspired earlier historians are removed from church history. The church, like the state, is only an association of men. If neither the content of the teaching that lies at the basis of the church nor the specific form of government given it by the Papacy is considered, there remain only the most general characteristics, shared in common by church and state: like every other organically connected society, it is in general a society of men constituting a unified whole. If the historian considers church history from this general point of view, then he is already in the situation of establishing himself in a purely objective relation to it. Thus it is merely his task to know in general what has happened in the Christian church and to recount the changes that make up the content of its history. All the motives by which others were so often led to transfer the interests of the present into the past must remain foreign to him. Mosheim himself is aware of the objectivity of his standpoint, and expressly posits as the most important principle of church historiography an independence from everything subjective that can have an influence on historical comprehension. He speaks of a threefold condition of dependence, upon time, men, and opinion, in which one may easily find oneself. The time in which we live has such great power over us that we judge all times according to it and believe that what can or cannot happen now, could have happened or not have happened in previous times as well. Men on whose testimony we place great value, especially those who stand in high repute for their holiness and virtue, deceive us by their reputation. The predilection for the doctrines and opinions to which we are attached so dominates us that we put events into a false light, often without knowing it. Far too often, we argue thus: because we think thus and so, the early Christians also must have thought so; because we regard this as an authentic Christian principle, they also must have followed it; because this does not now happen, it could not have happened once.

If we consider how infrequently hitherto church historians have confronted the object of their treatment in such a way that it could not be influenced by their own subjectivity, then we must find it entirely natural that Mosheim, with his articulate awareness that it is the task of the historian to distinguish himself as much as possible from his object, was himself aware of the higher level of historiography on which he stood. It cannot be denied that his historical presentations are characterized by an objectivity not previously found anywhere in the area of church history. The quiet, sedate tone, free of agitation, which is typical of him throughout, in itself testifies to the superiority that must in this regard be conceded to him. It could only appear that this objectivity of presentation should occasionally pass into sheer indifference. Mosheim passes with cool detachment over such scenes as the one at Canossa, about which none of the previous German church historians were able to conquer their national self-esteem. It is wholly different with Mosheim, for whom the few words he devotes to the mere recital of the affair already appear far too great a display.

To this is related what we must now emphasize as the chief character-istic of Mosheim's historiography. His view of history is essentially that for him the church becomes a state. But since he can thereby gain access only to what the church has outwardly in common with the state, the conception of the church itself becomes for him a very superficial and lifeless one. He does not succeed, therefore, in understanding the organic continuity of the various components of church history. The previous ordering of historical materials within each period was, to be sure, also very deficient. How illogical is the schematism of the *Centuries*! How little it suffices to distinguish, as Arnold does, between the external and internal condition of the church, when there is still so much that lies altogether beyond this basic division! Mosheim tries to derive his division of the contents from the conception of the church. But the distinction between the external and the internal is terribly vague. And the division of the whole is quite unequal when the external history deals only with the conversions that have led to the expansion of Christianity and with persecutions at the hands of external enemies, whereas everything else falls to the internal! The latter contains, therefore, everything concerned not only with doctrine but also with the cultus and constitution of the church. But this combination is superficial, for the justification is merely that the overseers of the church were originally teachers! And, as the state must have not merely rulers but also laws according to which it is ruled, so the church also has its laws, in the doctrine that forms the content of the Christian religion—as though doctrine were divinely re-vealed only so that the church might be governed by it, and thus only for the sake of the church, not that the church should contribute to the practical efficacy of doctrine! We thus obtain a division that is neither logical nor fundamental.

But still more important is the question: if church history is to recount what has happened in the church, and it is thus to be assumed that all has not been the same from the beginning but has changed to some degree, then what is the cause of the change, what is the moving principle of development in the Christian church? Here again, Mosheim's concept of the church shows itself to be so superficial and empty that one cannot understand why, after all, the church has a history. That history exists, surely, because so much in it has changed; but if the changes are only fortuitous and arbitrary, so that no one can understand where they come from and where they are bound, then the concept of history is not satisfied. But how can there be changes of any sort other than these when everything definite and concrete is eliminated from the concept of the church, and is placed so much in alignment with the state that only the most general truth about the church can be expressed—namely, that it is a society of men analogous to a state? Accordingly, if this society is to have a history, one is left, in this connection as well, with only the most general truth—that it has gone through a series of changes because history in general is movement and change. But what the moving inner principle of these changes is, and where its goal and final purpose lie, must remain undecided. Yet Mosheim himself speaks of a continuity of cause and effect, from which the divinity by which the church is established and preserved may be recognized. But how is this possible if it is not known why there is a history of the church? The older dualistic view of history was much better able to account for this in making the Devil the inciting principle of historical movement in the church; once it was established, all the more important elements of its history were understood as reactions from one side or the other.

That Mosheim's conception of the church is so lifeless can be attributed to his identification of the church with the state. If the church is regarded as analogous to the state, then it is only consistent if the epoch-making factors in its history are determined chiefly according to a political point of view. But the more vitally the concept of the church is understood, the more readily its historical articulation can be determined from the epochs of its history. In this connection, then, very little is to be expected of Mosheim. He has, indeed, retained the old division into centuries; but he has made them mere subdivisions, since at the same time he has seen fit to superimpose a division into larger periods. Four periods, marked off by major changes, have been adopted; the first ends with Constantine, the second with Charlemagne, the third with Luther, and the fourth with the most recent times. It is conspicuous in this division that the extended period lasting from Constantine to the Reformation, in which the hierarchical system of the church was so greatly developed, is cut in half at Charlemagne; thus once again political history has been made determinative for the history of the church. On the whole, these sections have indeed been established, but they have no further justification. We are given no further explanation of what at these points in time is epoch-making, or of how they are related to one another and to the concept of the church itself. As though all this were self-evident, the historian turns immediately to a narration of particulars. As for the history of doctrine, the only clue is the general remark that there should be an examination of what the value of Holy Scripture has been conceived to be in the various periods of the church, and of the ways it has been interpreted, since the condition of religion as a whole is dependent on it.

His Merits

The general deficiency of Mosheim's view of history is the externalization and secularization, or generalization, of the concept of the church. That concept is reduced to a highly abstract generality when Mosheim's conception is compared with what the older church historians understood by the church. Whereas for them the church was the visible kingdom of God in its antithesis to the kingdom of Satan, what we have here is only a society of men. For them, the substantial content of the church was the revealed Word of God, of which the vessel, so to speak, was the church alone; now, the concern is with laws by which the church is governed. For them, the heretics were those who sinned against the essence of the divine doctrine; now, they are only disturbers of the peace—as though, merely to guard against strife and unrest, nothing whereby the original condition of the church might be altered were permitted to occur.

Yet though the concept of the church seems thus to have lost so much of its specific significance, nevertheless it can only be regarded as an essential step forward that a freer and more universal view of the nature of the church now appears in place of a limited dualism. A new form of perception is, at least, now available, and the question is simply whether it is also to acquire a fitting content. The empty form must first incorporate the spirit by which the concept of the church becomes more vital, and embraces the principle of its historical movement. That Mosheim did not fail to do this is evidenced by his own peculiar aspiration toward a pragmatic treatment of history. The historical pragmatism [15] of the older church historians consisted in a general discernment, whenever a major change took place in the condition of the church, of a reaction by one or the other of the two principles whose mutual antagonism constituted the history of the church. In a political view of history such as Mosheim's,

15. [ED.] On the meaning of Baur's use of the term "historical pragmatism," see below, 168, n. 1.

historical pragmatism must assume a political character. Instead of returning to the intentions and schemes of a supersensible causality, its efforts
must be directed toward discovering in the participants the motives and
mainsprings from which changes in the history of the church proceed.
Since according to Mosheim history first obtains its true value and usefulness when it shows not merely what has happened but also how and
why it happened, or when it traces the occurrences to their causes, he
especially demands of the historian a precise knowledge of human nature,
as well as of the testimonies of the author and of the history of the times;
for whoever is acquainted with the spiritual capacities, the character, the
tastes, and the desires of men, and with the force of their passions, will be
all the more capable of explaining events.

Mosheim regards as especially necessary a more exact knowledge of the
history of philosophy, in order to probe more deeply into the inner life
of the Christian church; and though he speaks only with regret of the
influence that human science and philosophy have had on the divine
doctrine of Christianity, which differs so greatly from them, it is nevertheless precisely here that he excels as a historian of the Christian church.
No one understood so well as he—possessing as he did so penetrating a
sagacity, such skill in combination, and, for such a task, a spirit so able
and richly endowed—how to reconstruct the various systems in which
the spiritual movement of the earliest period chiefly consisted. The major
work that most particularly sets forth the results of his many years of
research—his *Commentarii de rebus Christianorum ante Constantinum
Magnum* (1753)—is in this respect an epoch-making work of church
history. It shed new light on an important aspect of ancient church
history by its investigations of Gnosticism in general and of the various
branches into which it was divided; of the Neoplatonic philosophy and its
relation to Christianity; of Origen's system, the relation he established
between philosophy and theology, and the principles and rules for his
allegorical interpretation of Scripture; of the doctrines of the anti-
trinitarian heretics; and of the Manichaean system of religion.

Even if his accomplishments are judged only according to the standard
of his own time, and even though it is not hard from our present-day
standpoint to uncover their deficiencies, nevertheless their positive value
remains preponderant. On the whole, Mosheim was at least on the right
track; and it must be acknowledged as a special merit that he not only set
forth very precisely the content of doctrines and systems by thorough
investigation of the sources, but also always grasped the particular from

the continuity of the whole and always sought to return to the fundamental perception from which that continuity had emerged. In regard to Gnosticism, for example, the so-called oriental philosophy that he took to be its source is a vague conception, a mere abstraction; and it is a weakness of his presentation of the Gnostic systems that he was unable to enter into the Gnostic predilection for personification, which treats ideas in the form of symbols and myths; and indeed the old inclination to regard the Gnostics as enthusiasts and madmen still appears strongly.[16] On the other hand, he has perceived quite correctly the dualistic character of Gnosticism, the antithesis of the two principles, spirit and matter, into which the general world view of antiquity is divided, and by reason of which Gnosticism represents the same point of view as Manichaeanism.[17] His talent for such investigations is brilliantly displayed in his portrayal of Manichaeanism, which constitutes a very significant part of his *Commentarii;*[18] and in spite of its failures and errors,[19] it far surpasses anything accomplished in the field of ancient church history either previously or for a long time afterward. He had a special interest in the ancient heretics, as is demonstrated by his attention to Gnosticism and Manichaeanism in particular and by the great care and precision with which he examined their doctrinal systems. But his predilection for them did not, as with Arnold, have its foundation in a belief that he must protect them as persecuted and suppressed in the face of the injustice and hatred of the orthodox church. He was strongly attracted, rather, only by the originality, sublimity, and spirituality that he discerned in their doctrines and systems.

16. Cf. my *Die christliche Gnosis* (Tübingen, 1835), 5. Also, Mosheim says of the Valentinian system in his *Commentarii de rebus Christianorum ante Constantinum Magnum* (Helmstädt, 1753), 375: "It is difficult to believe that there is any shrewdness and wisdom in this long story, and those who have thought to call these stubborn, sick-minded jesters back to reason and truth have thus far accomplished nothing." For further comment, see 377 f.

17. Cf. Mosheim, *Commentarii*, 387: "The entire system of the Orientals, Gnostics, and Manichaeans tends in the direction of teaching that, when the world was formed from corrupt and formless matter, without the will of the supreme power, no small part of the divine and heavenly substance, whether by chance or by plan, was mixed in, and that indeed God was doing this so that . . . ," etc. "There are various forms of this teaching, some more subtle, some more crude, some more simple, some more cleverly and ingeniously devised, but in every case the major point is the same."

18. Cf. *ibid.*, 728–910.

19. Cf. my *Das manichäische Religionssystem nach den Quellen neu untersucht und entwikelt* (Tübingen, 1831), 105, 120, 163, 168.

It can be clearly seen from his portrayal of Manichaeanism how Mosheim first had to overcome in himself the after-effects of ancient prejudice against such heretics in order finally to arrive at a more lenient and equitable total judgment than could hitherto have been expected. Manichaeanism is for him too "a new pestilence, more deadly than all that came before," breaking into Christianity; and he pictures Mani as a "singular man" who "was rich in talent, eloquence, rashness, and all those things by which people can easily be stirred up and inflamed. Whether because he was deluded by a certain sickness of the mind or was burning with a desire for glory, he devised a new form of religion, concocted in amazing fashion from the philosophy of the Persians and the Christian teaching; and he dared to thrust it on the people as something handed down from a divine source." His doctrine of salvation, "although full of fictions and childish trifles—no wiser than the Gnostic fables and more absurd than many of them—spread over a broader area than all the great sects of former times." And yet it must finally be said of Mani's teaching, concerning which so many different and opposing judgments have been made: "He who wishes to be fair will acknowledge that the teaching, if viewed as a whole, is by no means the work of a man devoid of talent, for the whole series of teachings proceeds from a few principles, which seem to present the appearance of great clarity, and all the parts of the system are consistent." Of the details, surely a great many are absurd and fabulous. Since Mani could not have explained all the phenomena and changes of nature from his few principles, he was forced to make a false use of his sagacity in inventing fables, and, where reason did not serve, in obtaining assistance from fantasy.[20] Here at least the consistency of the system and the rational character of the whole are acknowledged.

Mosheim derived Gnosticism and Manichaeanism from an oriental philosophy, whose connection with Christianity could only give birth to systems more or less alien to the latter. Hence he saw in philosophy generally the most dangerous enemy of Christianity. The church teachers of the second century had already gone too far in their application of philosophy to Christian religious teachings. In such founders of sects as Theodotus and Artemon the fruit of the acceptance of Greek philosophy among Christians can first be seen. But Mosheim especially reproaches the Alexandrines, and in particular Origen, that by their philosophical treatment Christianity more and more loses its original simplicity and dignity. Furthermore, "the cleverness of human ingenuity was joined with divine

20. Mosheim, *Commentarii*, 885.

intentions, and then troublesome disputes and quarrels concerning the understanding of certain mysteries arose." Since almost all the evils by which in the second century Christianity was polluted and falsified are supposed to have come out of Egypt, Mosheim also reckons among them especially the Platonism of the Alexandrines, their allegorical interpretation of Scripture, and the so-called *disciplina arcani* [secret discipline] introduced by them.[21]

Moreover, he sees a continuing struggle within the Christian church against a heterogeneous hostile principle. But the place of the old malicious and treacherous enemy, who here and there breaks out of his hidden ambush in different forms, is now taken by the thinking and searching spirit of men, with which there must repeatedly be a reconciliation in acknowledgment of its natural rights—so grave appears to be the conflict of man's philosophical thoughts and eccentric speculations with the simple truth of Christianity. And the greater the effort Mosheim made, with such notable success, to comprehend and present in their rational continuity the doctrines, opinions, and systems that for him were the product of philosophy in the period of the ancient church, the more evidence he provided of a spiritual content not yet exhibited by church history in this realm, as well as of the extent to which, as a result, its concept as a whole might still be spiritualized through learning to penetrate more deeply thence to the inner continuity of the powers that move the church.

On the whole, it is Mosheim's acknowledged merit that he brought church history out of the polemical and pietistic confines to which it still clung into the vantage point of a freer and broader circle of vision. Just as he opens his history with a very comprehensive survey of world conditions at the time of the appearance of Christianity, he endeavors throughout to present church history in the light of world history, the history of religions, and the history of philosophy, and especially to endow it with new spiritual content by a more exact investigation of those elements concerned with the development of dogma and the inner nature of Christianity.

21. *Ibid.*, 272, 299, 302, 430, 604.

4. *Semler*

His Relation to Arnold

When, with this impression of his church-historical writings, we move from Mosheim to Semler,[22] the latter seems to do everything he can to retract the higher conception of church history awakened by Mosheim, and considerably to moderate our opinion of the impetus he gave to church historiography. As though from a second Arnold, we hear from Semler the same complaint, which runs through all his church-historical writings, that there is still no true and real church history, that nothing hitherto accomplished, either by Catholics or by Protestants, even merits

22. [ED.] Johann Salomo Semler was born in Saalfeld in 1725 and died in Halle in 1791. At an early age, under the guidance of his father, he came under the influence of pietism, but gradually freed himself from it. At the University of Halle, he was attracted to Siegmund Jakob Baumgarten, whose teaching served as a bridge between pietism and rationalism and at whose insistence he returned to Halle in 1752 as professor of theology. Semler's critical investigations were first directed to Scripture, where he concerned himself with matters of text and canon. His recognition that the canons of Old and New Testament underwent historical development and were formed only by degrees, and that consequently they could not be regarded as "inspired" in the traditional sense—as was made clear in his work, *Abhandlung von der freien Untersuchung des Kanons, nebst Antwort auf die Tübingische Vertheidigung der Apokalypsis* (4 parts; Halle, 1771–76)—had a revolutionary impact on the theology of his day. At the same time, however, he believed that the Old and New Testaments represented two distinct stages of religion, one inferior and nationalistic, the other universal and spiritual. He also tended to be more conservative in his own theological orientation than might otherwise have been expected, especially in his labors as a critic; for example, he engaged in a keen polemic against the Wolfenbüttel Fragments.

In church history, he worked both as an editor (of Tertullian and the Lutheran symbolical writings) and as a critical researcher; cf. the *Historiae ecclesiasticae selecta capita* (3 vols.; Halle, 1767–69), his *Commentarii historici de antiquo Christianorum statu* (2 vols.; Halle, 1771–72), and *Versuch eines fruchtbaren Auszugs der Kirchengeschichte des Neuen Testaments* (3 vols.; Halle, 1773–78). He stressed the importance of working with the original sources, the relevance of purely natural factors and of development in the history of the church, and the place of psychological considerations in historical study. He also de-emphasized the importance of dogma and theology as compared with religious experience, and believed that all doctrinal systems and indeed all religions were merely attempts to comprehend the one divine truth. In later years he became interested in the natural sciences, alchemy, mystical theosophy, and freemasonry. For a recent discussion, see Gottfried Horning, *Die Anfänge der historisch-kritischen Theologie: Johann Salomo Semlers Schriftverständnis und seine Stellung zu Luther* (Göttingen, 1961).

the name. He also nourishes the same suspicion and mistrust toward the ruling church. In his view, only the heretics can be accorded moral respect; it is merited by no others. Like Arnold, he speaks with extreme disdain even of the most distinguished teachers of the church. Everywhere he sees only a terrible increase of ignorance and superstition, as a result of which the dominance of the bishops could easily have been strengthened. Confusion and corruption have increasingly gained the upper hand under the mask of an arcane Christian religion. The simple and practical power, comprehensible and convincing, of the teachings of Jesus, is completely lost sight of in the intellectual vagaries of some unspiritual minds, and is put aside as a trifling matter in which nothing astonishing or peculiar was to be found. Well-intentioned Christians have long enough recognized their good and pious notions to be the core of those gleaming shells which unimproved and for the most part unworthy Christians have in fact still failed to make their own.[23] All this in fact has frequently enough been heard from Arnold. Now, since it is not to be supposed that Semler owes his church-historical reputation to the mere repetition of Arnold's complaints and assertions, we must also recognize in evaluating him that everything he has in common with Arnold at the same time essentially distinguishes the two. However characteristically his general view of history appears in all his church-historical writings, it is nevertheless far from easy to elucidate his conceptions, which suffer in part from unclarity and insufficiently grounded assertions.

His Difference from Arnold

To Mosheim's definition of church history—that it is the clear narration of events concerning the Christian society—Semler raises the objection that any history is a narration of events regarded by its author as noteworthy, useful, or true. The same object is perceived differently by different subjects. This difference does not lie merely in the malicious or partisan intention of the historian but in the nature of the case; it is a consequence of the most sublime management of God in the human world, but it has hitherto been considered far too little. If an author intends by his presentation to obtain a specific end, then the reason for the differences in narration lies clearly before the eye. Whatever an author regards as noteworthy, useful, or even true for himself, he narrates

23. Cf. Semler, *Versuch eines fruchtbaren Auszugs der Kirchengeschichte*, I, 99, 105, 115, 117, etc.

with lively participation. But not everything he narrates is real history; the historian himself, deliberately or consciously, has attributed much to history for the first time; he gives the account a direction not objectively grounded in the occurrences themselves.[24]

True as this is, and justifiable therefore the demand that we distinguish our own standpoint from that of the historian, Semler takes no less great a leap when he draws the conclusion that follows: because we can recognize as the true nature of Christianity only that which makes it a moral religion [he argues], then those who do not possess this insight, and who are as little concerned with the free growth of moral knowledge as they are with the unceasing final purpose of the whole Christian religion, can only be immoral men. Having introduced a static formula with a fixed and unchanging content, they do not regard as valid any moral knowledge or any moral welfare outside the church, which they declare alone to be competent in morality. These are the lengths to which Semler goes to substantiate his view of history as not merely objectively true and authentically Christian, but also as the only moral view, in distinction from the subjective standpoint by which it is customary to understand the history of the Christian church. He could himself, he says, explain the open opposition against the universal spirit of the completely free religion Christ has established through the apostles by the fact that rulers of the new and higher states have not known or loved the spiritual, morally free religion at all, but rather have disdained and neglected it for a very immoral attitude, so as to be in the position of providing an interpretation of the Gospels, the epistles, and all the writings that the church must select and introduce for its confederation, and of asserting how they conformed to the totally unspiritual principles taken from political tradition.

In order to understand all this, we must not overlook the subjectivity, for Semler, of everything related to the nature of religion. No Christian can occupy the same level of moral belief as any other Christian, for the degrees of moral welfare in which men come to share through the blessing of Christ are infinitely various; and these degrees cannot all be bound up in the same standard of knowledge as would be defined by the doctrinal formula of any one church. This was the very first new knowledge Christians should have acquired from the teaching of Christ; the further they remove themselves from it, the poorer, the more ignorant, and the

24. Semler, *Neue Versuche, die Kirchenhistorie der ersten Jahrhunderte mehr aufzuklären* (Halle, 1788), 3 f.

more imperfect they become as Christians. Semler concludes from this that if we wish to search out the true and actual history of the church, we in our own time are not to put ourselves once again in the place of the Christians of the first centuries. The differences between men, ages, and all incessantly changing conditions are so decisive and, according to God's ordination, so incontrovertible, that one can easily uncover the intention of those who have made an unalterable ecclesiastical system the goal of their endeavors; for what could they have intended other than an unalterable ecclesiastical regime?

> To say that the salvation of Christians is bound by God, by Christ, by any of the apostles, to a single, much more recently established sum of ideas and judgments, and that the Catholic Church has this single sum in its own hands alone to secure the salvation of all its members by virtue of its immutability, is the most despicable contention that could be brought forth and maintained by evil or wholly ignorant men. For thereby the whole morality of the new spiritual or perfect religion is unceremoniously abrogated, and there can be no greater sin against all of historical truth or against the true and actual history of the Christian religion. The free spirit of history is quite deliberately smothered, and a comedy written in advance—an ecclesiastical drama completely outlined beforehand—is performed; this is called a true and actual history of the Christian religion. We are still lacking, therefore, in a true history of the first centuries. The very first error—which has transformed all true history into a totally unhistorical chaos of untruth—consists in the elevation and extension of local and singular notions into universal, firm, and unalterable prescriptions for all Christians, who would be guided into a false religion. This was done only in order to establish a single great society that let itself be ruled by the intentions of superiors.[25]

From such exposition, repeated in endless variation through all of Semler's church-historical writings, we can now see more specifically how he differs from Arnold. The main thing at which Semler takes offense in the history of the Christian church is not, as for Arnold, the steadily increasing depravity and wickedness brought on by the guilt of the rulers, but the immutability of the system dominant in the church, which contradicts the moral nature and infinity of Christianity. Consequently, a true conception of church history is obtained only by one who proceeds from the view that the church has fallen into the condition of being untrue, false, and unworthy of Christianity—a condition in which

25. *Ibid.*, 28 f., 68 f., 102. Cf. the Prefaces to the *Historiae ecclesiasticae selecta capita*, I, and to the *Versuch eines fruchtbaren Auszugs*, I.

everything has obtained an inflexible form, closed once and for all. The individual has had to submit to the pressure of ecclesiastical authority, instead of retaining his own freedom in faith. In a word, the church had become Catholic. Since the principle of immutability applicable in the church is nearly as old as the Christian church itself, and since everything belonging to the immutable character of the Catholic Church is only tradition going back to the earliest times, all the force of Semler's polemic is directed against the untrue conception of church history in its first period. The main object of his complaints and criticisms is not so much that there is no impartial history of the Christian church as that a real history of the first centuries is still lacking.

Arnold's disposition, though dismayed by the sorry and ever more prevailing downfall of the church, was always brightened and cheered from the moment he could look back upon the lovely era of the apostolic church, an age of pure innocence hovering before him as the ideal realized at that time for the future of the church. But it was Semler's express intention to destroy this image likewise as false and empty. He cannot adequately stress the necessity of dealing with the earliest period of the church as precisely as possible, not regarding the standpoint of the first Christians as our own, nor implying that their actual situation was what has usually been supposed. It is a great and ancient prejudice, he tells us, that the first church, the apostolic church, at once contains the perfect pattern of divine instruction and represents the correct understanding and application of the Christian religion. Contained in this prejudice is the bitter and unhealthy source of all the unceasing depravity and moral imperfection that we constantly encounter in the Catholic Church when we put together its history and destroy its lying masks—that is, if we really know ourselves in our position as free, independent, contemporary Christians, and consequently place the history of our Christian knowledge, experience, and practice alongside the history of those Christians; and if we thus firmly and correctly distinguish, from the true and honest description of that still very modest Christian religion (i.e., the Christian religion of that age, as we must understand it in its true condition), our contemporary Christian religious knowledge which (in a wholly different representation) we have in fact up to now so patriotically foisted upon those first centuries, as though it were our obligation and a homage required of us—or which we have so readily found in it because of constant prejudice. As contemporary observers of the whole previous history of the Catholic Church, we must first go behind the historical truth in order to know and rightly to judge a true history of this church, which first becomes such a church only after the apostles and their writings.[26]

The views and assertions that reveal Semler's peculiarities in the field of church history chiefly concern the first period; and in order to be sure of focussing on his main preoccupation, he has allowed to slip from view nothing in the whole period of the first three centuries that might serve to strip from it, in so far as possible, the glories of martyrdom with which it customarily shines. There is a great deal in this period which, the more favorable it appears for Christians, only increased his own suspicion. To him the *paucitas martyrum* [scarcity of martyrs] maintained by Dodwell [27] seemed equally evident. He was willing to place the responsibility for the Diocletian persecution on the Christians themselves. Despite their undeniably wicked life, they proved their religion by not visiting pagan temples and offering sacrifice; but if they had already not done so for thirty years without being persecuted, the reason that from this time onward the degenerating religion was regarded as an enemy of the civil state and the general welfare must have been due in part to fanatical principles and in part to worldly political intentions.[28] Nearly all literary products of the second century are ill regarded by Semler so far as their value is concerned, and some are openly declared suspect and falsely attributed. Semler himself raises a whole train of doubts concerning the letter of Pliny, governor of Bithynia, to the Emperor Trajan concerning the Christians in that province. Despite the acuteness in detail of this criticism, still basically it consisted only of the argument that Christians were far too insignificant to have been able to attract such a high degree of attention from a Pliny or a Trajan. A letter containing so much praise of Christians could only have been invented by a panegyrist of their cause, such as Tertullian.[29]

Thanks to his restless scepticism, which led him to transgress all limits of the probable, it was easy for Semler, as soon as the question was raised, to destroy the false semblance of those virtues and superiorities which the apostolic and post-apostolic ages had hitherto been thought still to possess in such measure. The more the customary view was reassured by finding in the Christianity of the most ancient period at least a firm, substantial kernel, which remained untouched by all worldly influences, and which was assimilated by the church of later ages, the more Semler was aroused

26. Semler, *Neue Versuche*, 113 f.
27. [ED.] Henry Dodwell (1641–1711); English theologian, professor of history at Oxford.
28. Semler, *Versuch eines fruchtbaren Auszugs*, I, 55 f.
29. Semler, *Neue Versuche*, 119 f.

to investigate it with the destructive acumen of his criticism, and to dissolve previous conceptions of it into empty illusion. Even those teachings of Jesus and the apostles found in the writings of the New Testament did not seem to him so firm and self-contained that one could look back on them as the secure norm at the basis of the whole development of the Christian church.

The Claim of Subjectivity and Individuality as the Principle of His View of History

From the essentially moral content of the Christian church Semler distinguished the temporal or local content, or what he was accustomed to call the Judaizing conceptions, which were assimilated by Jesus and the disciples into their teaching merely as a practical accommodation, but which on this account must again be separated as the unessential from the essential. Moreover, there was for him on the whole no objective conception of religion and Christianity. "I in fact begin," he himself admitted in a work dated 1783,[30] "by holding it to be untrue that such a firm, determinate description of Christian truths or concepts is contained in the Bible that only a single conception must and ought to be the true conception forever, as has been taught so long. I must regard it as a theological theory that was authoritative for a certain period of time, and that is also valid for the purpose of an outwardly united religious society, and for the sake of common outward aims; at any one time there can be only one dominant public language in a society. But for authentic inner religion it is not valid, it is not possible." Why? Because of the infinite variation among single individuals, to which Semler in the last analysis always returned in everything related to the essence of religion. In its true nature, Christianity was for him only the right of the individual, expressed by Christ for the consciousness of mankind, to have his own private religion in opposition to everything claiming recognition as public religion. From this purely subjective conception of religion, Semler as a church historian could only be interested in seeing how, in the history of the Christian church, the inalienable subjective claim of the individual is related to all the power of public religion that confronted it. The history of the Christian church as a whole is the unremitting conflict of moral, private religion with public religion. On the one hand, Semler can only see in the great mass of historical phenomena the attempt, annihilating

30. *Johann Kiddels Abhandlung von der Eingebung der heiligen Schrift, mit vielen freiern Zusätzen von D. Johann Salomo Semler* (Halle, 1783), 150 f.

itself by its own contradiction, to impose the character of unchangeability on that which by nature is most free and changeable. On the other hand, all objective content of religion dissolves for him into the infinite variation of individuals in the endless multiplicity of subjective feelings and representations.

No view of history makes the self-existing individual the substantial content of history to the same degree as that of Semler. Whereas Mosheim reduced the church in the old sense to the conception of a society analogous to the state, according to Semler it is an aggregate of individuals, who are bound to one another by no other bond than the purely formal claim of the individual existing for himself. What can the history of such individuals have as its content but a constant succession of changes, whose moving principle is only the subjective tendency of individuals to react with all the power of their subjectivity against whatever may strive to impose the pressure of uniformity and unalterability on the infinite multiplicity of single individuals? All of history is regarded in this way—as a totally fluctuating element, in which nothing remains the same, nothing in itself has objective consistency and stability, and everything that asserts itself with the power of objectivity exists only to be absorbed by the stream of reacting, subjective emotions of feeling and will, which repeatedly break forth with fresh power. Just as he traced everything in religion back to the right of individuality and subjectivity, he entreated the same right in the area of history, seeking to preserve in its full distinctiveness everything that had already been separated by differences of time, persons, and circumstances. Thus he felt obliged repeatedly to remind us that others do not share our standpoint, and that those so far removed from us in time cannot make the same claim to education and enlightenment.[31]

31. "That we are now in a far different world . . . ," he immediately impresses upon us in the Preface to the first volume of his *Historiae ecclesiasticae selecta capita* (1767), 35. Thus we should have no unnecessary respect for such authorities. It is remarkable how excited Semler becomes as soon as he believes the right of his individuality to be threatened by something even in the distant past. I add here the following as characteristic evidence of his view of history: it was a crude deviation from the already established moral, spiritual religion, which God has so clearly revealed through Christ, when the church introduced the law that all Christians of all times must have and retain the same measure and the same content and extent of Christian religion in knowledge, judgment, and proper application—a measure possessed perhaps by bishops of the first, second, third, and fourth centuries. This is, on the contrary, a wholly un-Christian and merely political prescription; it pushes Christians back into the ancient moral darkness and imperfection, and the same unworthiness in which all subjects of the Jewish Sanhedrin and the high priests in all

His Investigation of Sources

The more Semler became confirmed in this fundamental view of history, the more he lived with it in his innermost thoughts, the more he was the man who had energy and persistence enough to work through the entire field of church history from every side. What especially distinguishes Semler is his inexhaustible diligence in the investigation of sources; here he has been surpassed by few church historians. Since like Arnold he was thoroughly convinced that we still have no true and actual church history, at least for the first century, he believed it all the more necessary fundamentally to examine the whole basis of the subject matter, and so he turned mainly to the original sources. Several of his church-historical writings concern themselves directly with these sources—for example, the attempt to facilitate using the sources of the history of state and church of the Middle Ages, with which he embellished his continuation of Baumgarten's church history in 1761,[32] and the Prefaces with which he introduced Baumgarten's *Untersuchung theologischer Streitigkeiten* (Halle, 1762–64) and *Evangelische Glaubenslehre* (Halle, 1759–60). He so regarded church history as a mere narration from the sources that he believed it necessary to express this opinion even in the titles of his major church-historical works, one of which he called *Historiae ecclesiasticae selecta capita* [Chapters Selected from Church History],[33]

---

pagan states found themselves, who likewise all endured an iron outer order and prescription of thought, and who left the veneration of the deity to persons acting in their place. . . . All these orders and prescriptions of bishops are above all simply the political bond of members who belong together in a public, local religious society; . . . but the moral religion ought to exist in many thousand degrees as an inherent, internal condition of all individual Christians alongside this external religious society. . . . Thus all the pretensions and assertions of the Roman Church are vain and completely ridiculous; the irrefutable history of the church shames all those flatterers of church and Pope. . . . All this is completely intolerable, disgusting, or childishly foolish and wholly contemptible, and must, with sublime indignation, be increasingly disdained and rejected as old clerical machinations. The infinite blessing of Christ, the great moral (not physical) merit of Christ, encompasses an unceasing, inexhaustible treasure of moral concepts and judgments, which in countless degrees are endlessly developed and practically applied in the faith of individual Christians. Cf. *Neue Versuche*, 69 f.

32. [ED.] Siegmund Jakob Baumgarten (1706–57), Halle theologian and church historian. The work referred to is his *Auszug der Kirchengeschichte* (4 vols.; Halle, 1743–62). See above, 153, n. 22.

33. I.e., as he says in the Preface, "from the ancient writers themselves, not neglecting, however, assistance from more recent writers" (I, 34).

another, *Versuch eines fruchtbaren Auszugs aus der Kirchengeschichte* [Endeavor at a Fruitful Excerpt from Church History]. The first, in three volumes (1767–69), goes to the end of the fifteenth century; the second (in three volumes, 1773–78) brings church history down to the seventeenth century. Never did he shrink from undertaking the same work afresh and from working through the same period even more fundamentally and comprehensively with a new investigation of the sources. The *Commentarii historici de antiquo Christianorum statu* (2 vols., 1771–72), which appeared between these two works, was written only because, as he says in the Preface, he had already convinced himself that "many books and ancient writers were to be examined, and that the authoritativeness claimed by these authors should be diligently re-examined." And scarcely had his *Novae observationes, quibus studiosius illustrantur potiora capita historiae et religionis christianae usque ad Constantinum Magnus*, appeared in 1784, than he permitted the *Neue Versuche, die Kirchenhistorie der ersten Jahrhunderte mehr aufzuklären*, to follow in 1788.

But however often he entered on the same path, he never succeeded—by mastery and compression of the material, by the unification of details into a more general point of view and an inclusive unity—in giving his church-historical works even the form of presentation that is Mosheim's excellence, at least in his *Commentarii*. So little did he care to do so that he clung more tenaciously than anyone else to the traditional arrangement by centuries. In general, his work consists simply of bringing to light a mass of raw and more or less undigested details extracted from the sources. He also considered it a prerogative of his individuality to present everything as though it were the direct result of his scholarly investigations, indeed as though each of his writings were only a new expression of the same basic, endlessly varied and recurrent thought in which his whole life and spiritual being had been spent. This is to be found especially in his Prefaces, which invariably became treatises. With this one thought, for him, the entire field of higher ideas was exhausted; and he remained, in so far as his sceptical criticism did not make him suspicious, with a very matter-of-fact and popular way of viewing things.

5. *Walch*

Beside Mosheim and Semler, C. W. F. Walch has a subordinate position; yet his *Entwurf einer vollständigen Historie der Ketzereien,*

Spaltungen und Religionsstreitigkeiten[34] is too significant a work, and penetrates too deeply into church history, to go completely unmentioned here. The interest of his time in church-historical studies is expressed in him, as it is in Semler, chiefly through his diligent and zealous study of the sources of church history in order to bring all the materials to light as completely and exactly as possible. In all these respects, the work mentioned above is among the richest of which the literature of church history can boast. It represents Walch's individuality in a very characteristic way. Whereas Semler was repeatedly driven back to the same point by the restlessness of his moving spirit in order to undertake the same work once again with new rigor, the ponderous Walch remained tenaciously devoted to the same object, and did not move on until he had elucidated everything as thoroughly as possible.

Both, however, show the same lack of aesthetic sense for the form of presentation; both typify a rather philistine tastelessness. Yet it is more agreeable to follow the fluent eloquence of Semler—who at least is excited by his pet themes—than the formalism of Walch, which drags along with the most painstaking monotony, and is dry, rigid, and emptied of all flesh and blood. However, the greatest contrast is of Semler's neology[35] and dogmatic indifference with the antiquated orthodoxy and solemnity

---

34. In eleven volumes (Leipzig, 1762–85), which however continue only to the end of the iconoclastic controversy.

[ED.] Christian Wilhelm Franz Walch (1726–84), son of the Jena theologian J.G. Walch (1693–1775), was educated at the University of Jena, where in 1750 he was appointed associate professor of philosophy. He then accepted a call to Göttingen, where from 1754 until his death he was a member of the theological faculty. He was a collector of data rather than an original thinker, as evidenced by the many textbooks he wrote. Although declaring that there are no necessary truths in history, and that events occur fortuitously, as maintained in his *Gedanken von der Geschichte der Glaubenslehre* (Göttingen, 1765), and *Kritische Nachricht von der Quellen der Kirchenhistorie* (Leipzig, 1770), he nevertheless believed the Lutheran Reformation to have been strictly guided by divine Providence; cf. his *Geschichte der evangelisch-lutherischen Religion als ein Beweis, dass sie die wahre sei* (Jena, 1753). In theology he was a moderate Lutheran. He engaged in a polemic against Semler and Lessing in his *Kritische Untersuchung von Gebrauch der heiligen Schrift in den vier ersten Jahrhunderten* (Leipzig, 1774). Walch was a prolific writer; the works mentioned above represent only a fraction of his total output.

35. [ED.] The term *Neologen* or "innovators" customarily refers to a group of theologians who introduced the Enlightenment in Germany. They embrace approximately two theological generations, and exercised their greatest influence from 1740 to 1786. In addition to Semler himself, the following are usually regarded as *Neologen*: J.A. Ernesti, J.J. Spalding, J.D. Michaelis, and J.G. Töllner. They are forerunners of the Enlightenment theologians proper, beginning with G.E. Lessing. Cf. Emanuel Hirsch, *Geschichte der neuern evangelischen Theologie*, IV (2nd ed., Gütersloh, 1960), 9.

of countenance with which Walch confronts the various figures in his history of heretics. But even here, no great malice is intended; he does not wish to regard the figures in his history of heretics as malicious; they are for him the object on which he can display the full wealth of his scholarship; they are too much beloved, too valuable to be treated so rigorously. He does not intend simply to support either the old and unduly harsh judgments that for the most part have been taken by Protestant authors from the writings of the Roman Catholic party, or the more lenient opinions of an Arnold or a Beausobre.[36]

Love of truth and an upright scrupulosity are his inviolable precepts; but he intends besides and in particular to apply a pragmatic method and to search for the causes and sources of occurrences—partly in the persons themselves, in the extent of their spiritual capacities, in their qualities of mind, their passions, etc., and partly in their external circumstances. The conception we are to form of this pragmatism can be seen from certain questions, on the response to which (provided it can be given) a great deal depends. It is to be asked specifically whether the heretic was a scholar; whether he had studied philosophy; to which philosophical party he had adhered; whether before his conversion to Christianity he was a Jew or a Greek; whether he occupied a religious teaching office in the church; and with what people he associated.[37] Indeed, we might think we were dealing here with a police officer or examining magistrate, rather than with a church historian! In fact, upon examination of the entire apparatus that is constructed here—in order first to give a general personal description of the defendant and to bring him forward and interrogate him, then to set in motion the calling of witnesses, to ascertain the facts, to enter the results of the investigation in the proper place, and finally to pass sentence with the necessary practical recommendations—such a procedure can be compared only with a police or judicial undertaking, in accord with the most stringent rules of a bureaucratic machine. And now let us imagine what it would mean to adhere to the same procedure with all its rubrics through the entire eleven-volume work, covering all heretics up to the

---

36. Walch, *Entwurf einer vollständigen Historie der Ketzereien, Spaltungen und Religionsstreitigkeiten*, I, Preface.

[ED.] Isaac de Beausobre (1659–1738), a distinguished French Protestant preacher, was superintendent of the French churches in Berlin, and privy councilor of the king of Prussia. Cf. his *Histoire critique de Manichée et du Manichéisme* (Berlin, 1739), and *Défense de la doctrine des Réformés sur la Providence, la prédestination, la grâce, et l'Eucharistie* (Magdeburg, 1693).

37. Walch, *Entwurf einer vollständigen Historie*, I, 15.

ninth century! Walch, in managing to do so, has given proof of a strength and perseverance that certainly merit recognition; but what reader will have the patience to follow him uninterruptedly? Nothing is more lifeless, spiritless, and intolerably dull than Walch's history of heretics.

If we compare his method with a well-instructed court procedure, at least the methodology is deserving of appreciation. But Walch's treatment of history has also been compared with the record of an illness, in which the elements under consideration are classified under the three rubrics of diagnosis, pathogenesis, and therapeutics.[38] Walch's historical pragmatism actually consists in treating heretics as patients; one must first of all come to terms with the symptoms of their illness, but at the same time maintain the hope of keeping them alive. But if we look closer, every heretic whom he subjects to really detailed analysis is for him at bottom already a *caput mortum* [dead man], fallen into the history of the dead; and, when we see how he is dissected and dismembered, and how one by one the pieces are taken up for the purpose of demonstration, we cannot but compare Walch's historical presentation with an anatomical dissection. The importance he himself assigns to medical and anatomical criteria in his history of heretics becomes clear from his pragmatic judgment concerning the well-known way in which the unfortunate Arius [39] met his death; he regards it as most certain that we can be content with the general theory that Arius was found dead, having suffered a sudden end, since we have reason to place a certain mistrust in the medical and anatomical erudition of historians. If daily experience also shows that cases of sudden death can occur within a few minutes without either the deceased or others having previously noticed the slightest signs of indisposition, the actual situation cannot be discovered in any other way than by an exact medical description of the corpse; but since this is completely lacking, no grounds exist for maintaining with certainty that it had been a natural death.[40] The latter remark, which concedes so much to a belief in

38. Friedrich Carl Albert Schwegler, *Der Montanismus und die christliche Kirche des zweiten Jahrhunderts* (Tübingen, 1841), 11. [ED. Schwegler was a student of Baur.]

39. [ED.] Under the influence of the Eusebians, Arius was recalled from banishment; but the day before he was to be welcomed back into the church at Constantinople, he died suddenly, at over eighty years of age. His enemies interpreted the manner and timing of his death as a direct interposition of Providence and a condemnation of his doctrine, whereas his friends attributed it to poison.

40. Walch, *op. cit.*, II, 505 f.

miracles, shows his pragmatism in another, rather unflattering light, and indicates another great difference between him and Semler.

In what respect, then, can everything mentioned here as characteristic of Walch be connected with the view of history represented above all by Semler? Put briefly, it is the absence of all higher ideas. Where these are lacking, there can be no insight into the objective continuity of history, and purely subjective and individual elements are all the more dominant. Everything of concern in history becomes totally subjective if history exists only so that the subject who regards it can become aware of his claims to individuality. Likewise, if the subjects appearing in history have their substantial significance only in their claim to individuality and their individual self-existence, each confronts the other only as a monad; the objective continuity joining them together is lacking; history is only the free play of subjective freedom and subjective caprice. That which joins individuals together in unity and subordinates them to a power and authority limiting their subjective freedom is unjustified and reprehensible; it ought not to exist. From this, Semler's view of history, that of Walch differs only in that historical subjects are not so much monads, of which each asserts its claim to individuality, as rather a fortuitous aggregate of particularities, whose relations to one another are based on a purely atomistic mode of apprehension. It is a simple matter of being adjacent; and when we ask why one is so and another is different, this view never takes us beyond the sphere in which individual existence is isolated as a being-for-itself. If in this fashion the center of gravity of history is at the locus of individual self-existence, then it is not history that carries and holds individuals with its objective power; rather, individuals are the power ruling history, to such a degree that history exists, so to speak, only for the sake of individuals. Hence it is only a natural consequence of this view of history to be concerned above all about the subjective utility of history. When Semler called his major work "a fruitful excerpt from church history," what did he intend to say but that church history, by its conception, tends to be essentially practical? Its greatest fruit ought to be that one learns from it how to act in order to safeguard one's private, moral religion against the encroachments to which it is exposed.[41]

41. Cf. what Semler says in the Preface to the third volume of his *Versuch eines fruchtbaren Auszugs der Kirchengeschichte* about the utility of church history, in accord with his treatment of the same. The custom of exhaustively and specifically pointing out the utility of church history dates largely from this period. Cf. Mosheim's Introduction to his church history. And Weismann had written his

But generally once church history is viewed according to the utility of its substantial content, its value and utility will always be identified with very subjective interests and particular purposes. How trivial of Walch to praise the utility of his history of heretics largely because it gives such very fruitful examples of the rules of prudent behavior in the face of emerging dissensions! The behavior of those who deviate from the truth or who otherwise have shared guilt for the dissension teach us what caution is to be exercised in dealing with such people in similar cases. We see Satan's cleverness in sowing tares among the wheat, sometimes under the appearance of zeal for the truth, sometimes under the mask of piety. The deception is dispersed, and the true sources of pride, lust for power, and debauchery aroused by numerous objects, are uncovered before our eyes; and all this gives rules of thumb that an upright servant of Christ ought to obey in similar situations; and so on.

Thus we are reminded very vividly of the period in which the whole of theology became a mere theory of utility. And therefore we should not believe that for the church historians of this period intentions such as those mentioned above were merely secondary; they were the primary thing for them, without which history was not to be thought of. This shows how much we have descended from the transcendent heights of the dualistic antithesis in which church history was perceived to move by the old church historians. History exists only for the sake of the subject examining it—so that he can know, in accord with his subjective purposes, needs, and interests, how he must behave in future situations so as not to be outwitted by Satan, who thus far still plays his role. If the stream of church historiography is not to run dry in the sands of subjectivistic particularism, the direction in which a new path must be broken is clear.

Introductio in memorabilia ecclesiastica historiae only *ad juvandam notitiam regni Dei et Satanae cordisque humani* [for the Advancement of the Knowledge of the Kingdom of God and of Satan and of the Human Heart]. [ED. From the title of the work.]

THE PRAGMATIC[1] METHOD OF HISTORIOGRAPHY: SCHRÖCKH, SPITTLER, PLANCK, HENKE

The church historians to be considered here form a distinct group who belong together, and who, in spite of their individual differences, have a common character. They proceed further in the direction discussed in the last chapter, systematically constructing a form of historiography conditioned by that direction, indeed in such a fashion that their bias emerge all the more clearly.

1. *Schröckh*

THE SUBJECTIVITY OF HIS VIEW OF HISTORY

To continue what was said at the end of the previous chapter: the endlessly trivial talk with which J. M. Schröckh opens his many-volumed work[2] already reveals to us the sort of historical subjectivity with which

1. [ED.] By "pragmatic," Baur means rationalistic, subjectivistic, and, above all, utilitarian. The "pragmatic" study of history represents its utilization for purposes of moral and/or religious edification, or the demonstration or proof of a conviction believed to be true by the historian. Historical pragmatism is the characteristic church historiography of the period of the Enlightenment.

2. *Christliche Kirchengeschichte* (35 vols.; Leipzig, 1768–1803); the period since the Reformation is covered in eight volumes (Leipzig, 1804–1808); two more volumes, the ninth and the tenth, were edited by H. G. Tzschirner after Schröckh's death (1810–12).

[ED.] Johann Matthias Schröckh was born in Vienna in 1773 and died in Wittenberg in 1808. He was educated at Göttingen and taught at Leipzig before being called to Wittenberg in 1767 as professor of poetry, exchanging this chair in 1775 for that of history. In addition to his most important work, mentioned above by Baur, he wrote *Lebensbeschreibungen berühmter Gelehrter* (Leipzig, 1764–69), *Allgemeine Biographien* (Berlin, 1767–91), *Lehrbuch der allgemeinen Weltgeschichte* (1774), the fourth part of the *Unparteiische Kirchengeschichte Alten und Neuen Testaments* (Jena, 1766), *Historia religionis et ecclesiae Christianae adum-*

168

we are confronted. Although, as can already be seen from the outward volume of his work, he has very little to say about the conception of church history, he is inexhaustible when it comes to its practical utility, with respect to which, as he himself says, one can never be too detailed and extensive. The number of things for which church history is practical and useful can scarcely be imagined. The nourishment it extends to the mind and heart of man is so inexhaustible that all other knowledge of events must recede before it, and without it one can be neither a servant and teacher of religion, nor a scholar, nor even a good Christian. There is no theological magnitude but in the field of church history or in the exegesis of Holy Scripture, or in both together. All the monuments built by many famous men merely from singular and ingenious thoughts, or from bravely conducted controversies, or from a quantity of repetitious writings, collapse into a heap at the least breath of posterity so long as they are lacking in this nobler knowledge.[3] From the pathos of such declamations we can best see how at that time all that has to do with the concept and task of church history dissolved into the single concern of its utility.

But we can look for the first time more deeply into the spirit of this historiography when we become acquainted with its method, on which Schröckh has expressed himself in detail.[4] It is in a word, as he himself says, the pragmatic method; and it consists in narrating events not merely as something accidentally occurring, but rather in an investigation of their causes and motives. The more precisely Schröckh describes the peculiarities of this pragmatic method, the clearer it becomes how superficially it is related to the true, inner nature of history. If the pragmatic historian is to investigate as much as possible the inner motives and intentions of those who act—which is his most important task—he must immediately be reminded on the other hand how essential it is to observe necessary caution, since one still cannot see into the inner nature of men, and nothing would be more erroneous than to base intentions and motives on mere surmise. If, furthermore, the pragmatic method is to explain the continuity in which occurrences mesh together like links in a chain, and if it is to pursue their proximate as well as their more distant conse-

---

brata in usum lectionum (Berlin, 1777), and *Allgemeine Weltgeschichte für Kinder* (4 vols.; Leipzig, 1779–84). The theological position of Schröckh was a modified supernaturalism.

3. Schröckh, *Christliche Kirchengeschichte*, I, 56 f., 96, 129.
4. "Methode der Untersuchung und des Vortrags der christlichen Kirchengeschichte," *ibid.*, I, 251–318.

quences, it must not be forgotten at the same time how little we can follow precisely the deeper threads of such a continuity. We must therefore confess once again that this method is not able to accomplish what is demanded of it.

With respect to a third factor, there emerges an even larger consideration. The application of occurrences to the terms in which we live is intended above all to be the true touchstone for the utility of history. What we cannot use, says the pragmatic historian, we do not need to know. If we know how to select events well, we should be able to use ancient church history for our instruction as well as we do the fortunes of religion in recent times. We must compare centuries and persons, similar situations and incidents, goals and results; we must generalize them and know how to rejuvenate them. Then we shall discover that men are the same in almost all ages, and have on the whole always conducted themselves in the same way in religious matters; contingent circumstances make little or no difference; the inclinations and intentions of men never change.

But if this is indeed the situation, we must ask in what way history generally is still of service to us. What interest can we have in seeking in the past what we already have close at hand and in the present? The culmination of this subjective view of history is that, although it asks everywhere only for subjective utility, in the final analysis it has no subject other than the mere subjective ego, to which everything ought to be related. But if the subject sees only himself in the entire content of history, why does he need a history? For surely everything is always the same, the same reflection of the present, in which the subject lives with his subjective interests and endeavors. So considered, the pragmatic method annuls itself in its subjectivity; it points beyond itself, the further it is pursued, to an objectivity confronting the subject. In order to investigate motives and intentions, we must not only return to the deeper, unifying foundation in the character of those who act, but also take into close consideration the spirit of the times and the character of peoples. But what is it that gives to a time its spirit and to peoples their character, when the moving power of history consists only of individual subjects in their individual self-existence?

A peculiar relation between the acting subjects of history and the period of their historical emergence must be imagined when Schröckh illustrates his pragmatic method by the ease with which, in the three major periods of its history, the Christian religion was accepted, altered, and improved in the world, as follows: "Christianity could not have appeared in a more suitable century, and, when one considers only human means of advancement, would have found in no other either so quick or so glorious an entrance. Similarly, it is quite apparent that the Reformation could have begun neither earlier nor later if it was not to have failed; so many factors coalesced in the first half of the sixteenth century to prepare its way. Likewise the Popes happened upon the idea of becoming unlimited rulers of the world at just the right time, namely, at a time when men, blinded by ignorance and superstition, had their eyes only half open and scarcely noticed the net that was thrown over their heads." [5]

But what is it, we must now ask, that made the first century so suitable for Christianity, that permitted the Reformers to succeed precisely according to their plan, that inspired the Popes at just the right time to exploit the ignorance of the world to their advantage? What secret agreement, what peculiar conspiracy here takes place between the acting subjects of history and the spirit of their time? How clever must we suppose the heroes of history to be, if as soon as the spirit of the times shows only a slight inclination, they immediately watch for the opportunity to bring their plans to completion, seemingly behind its back? What made the world so feeble-witted and short-sighted that the Popes could so easily outwit it? And how completely different would world affairs have been if at the right moment the spirit of the times had noticed the malicious deception perpetrated by the Popes, and had opened the eyes of a world only half-awake? It is a totally peculiar representation of the course of affairs in the world if, as soon as anything good and wholesome occurs, the spirit of the times is indeed of assistance and congenial to the intentions of those who act, but only in so far as it is clearly seen that if the opportunity is not seized quickly and at the right moment, then everything intended for the improvement of the world will be jeopardized for a long time, perhaps for ever; and if on the other hand everything of an opposite sort that is of a great disadvantage to humanity, such as the Papacy, is to be explained only by the failure of the spirit of the times to be watchful and alert enough to prevent such a disaster.

If this is an authentic historical pragmatism, then we must admit that according to this view the moving power of history is only shrewdness and circumspection, or cunning and craftiness, by means of which individual subjects appearing here and there know how to exploit the more or less favorable conditions of the time for the execution of their subjective

5. *Christliche Kirchengeschichte*, I, 284.

intentions and interests. Thus there is nothing in history that is so objective as not ultimately to have its origin and point of departure in the subjectivity of an individual who excels others in spiritual capacity; and the subjectivity of a treatment of church history following this pragmatic method can therefore be calculated in advance. If this one-sided tendency toward the subjective does not appear as conspicuously in Schröckh's history as we might have expected from his fundamental perspective, it is only because in general it has too material a character, and because its author has been accustomed to proceed in the evaluation of details with too great a sobriety and prudence and too exact a consideration of the various elements confronting and balancing one another, to have been able to sustain a general standpoint with greater consistency.

His Division and Arrangement

As a part of the method of historiography Schröckh is especially concerned with the division of history into periods and the purposeful arrangement of the material within each of them. Concerning the first period, Schröckh has provided an admirable proof of his capacity to follow the obective course of history and its various turnings as it surpasses the subjectivity of single individuals; for he was the first to do what even Mosheim had not yet done, namely, to drop altogether the division according to centuries and to adopt larger periods. Schröckh quite rightly observed that a new pattern of the world does not begin precisely with a new century; many things develop for the first time only later, often long after the beginning of a century. In the arrangement of periods, he followed Mosheim and assigned four, the second of which he permitted to run up to Charlemagne. Since he proceeded from the correct view that periods can be assigned only where a series of similar developments comes to an end and a new and different series begins, he tried to determine more exactly the character of the various periods and their relation to one another.

Since Semler's ideas were still little known at that time, for Schröckh the guiding point of view was the high idealization of the first period, which extended through the first three centuries. Here everything appeared to him in the most glorious light; it was the period when religion appeared upon earth in its purest form; teachers were only servants of religion and the church; and the life of Christians was so rich in virtues and so exclusively directed to the divine that one could see in it only a preparation for eternity. With Constantine, however, everything was totally changed, and with Charlemagne began the iron age of the Christian religion and church, which lasted until the beginning of the sixteenth century. With the fourth period a thoroughgoing change again occurred. In the first period everything came from religion itself; in the second, everything came from the inclinations of its confessors, who were left to their own devices; in the third, from the lust for power and the self-interest of its teachers; and in the fourth, from freedom of opinion and practice in religious matters, which causes Christians to quarrel with one another.[6] To be sure, each of the four periods has its peculiar character, and it is self-evident that if in the first period the Christian religion had already reached the highest level of perfection, the changes introduced subsequently could only take an opposite direction. What, then, is the principle of historical movement as a whole? And the conception of the fourth period is extremely indefinite if it is designated only as the period of religious freedom and controversy.

Schröckh is just as unsatisfactory on the second point, concerning the arrangement of the material. He describes his method as a combination of topical and chronological organization, but for a long time he could not make up his mind about this arrangement. Only later in the course of his work did the following permanent categories emerge as the books or sections into which the periods themselves are further divided: (1) summary of the civil history of the period; (2) history of the arts and sciences; (3) history of the dissemination of Christianity; (4) history of the Roman Popes, the clergy, and church law; (5) history of monastic life; (6) general history of religion; (7) general history of theology; (8) history of religious controversies. The major elements in the division, then, would be the dissemination of Christianity, the constitution of the church, and doctrine. but if these three elements are derived from the concept of the church, as they must be, what happens to the history of monastic life and the history of worship? As constituent parts of every church history, are they to be joined to one or another of the three major elements, or do they stand alongside those elements as equally autonomous determinations of the concept of the church? Schröckh includes the history of worship under the general history of religion, but this is a very vague designation, in which ecclesiastical usages and dogmatic representations are not adequately separated from one another.

Schröckh is distinguished from Mosheim in that, while the latter held

6. *Christliche Kirchengeschichte*, I, 307.

fast to a concept of the church as such, or of the church as an outward society, the former intended to write a history of the Christian *religion* rather than of the Christian church. His work was to be, as he himself said,[7]

> . . . first and foremost a history of the Christian religion itself, i.e., not merely of its dissemination, not of its outward confession or of errors introduced into it by certain parties, but rather much more the history of all the less notable changes, additions, embellishments, adaptations, degenerations, and re-establishments, by means of which it has come to us through those Christians who believed themselves constantly to possess it in its unalterable purity. To this, however, the history of theological doctrine, which so often has made of religion something totally different from what it was originally, has been inseparably joined in its emergence and gradual formation, its manifold forms and variations. Also it could not be satisfactorily explained without a complete presentation of the laws and writings by which that doctrine has grown and has been strengthened or transformed. Again, this led to the history of theological scholarship among Christians, upon whose flourishing or deplorable condition the state of Christianity and of church doctrine has in all times depended so heavily. Here it was not enough simply to enumerate the exegetes, dogmaticians, and other writers who have appeared in each age, the titles of their books, and approximately what their contents are. Rather, the theological methods, discoveries, and prejudices, the entire course of the science, the gains or losses experienced in every age, had to be faithfully traced by a more precise analysis. But proper clarity in this could not be obtained without a careful history of the Christian teachers during the first centuries, when they had Christianity and the system and science of religion almost completely under their control—men who for more than a thousand years determined what is and is not to be regarded as the Christian faith.

In fact, the tendency of the work is still not precisely enough described by saying that it is a history less of the Christian church than of the Christian religion; rather, we can only characterize it as a history less of the Christian religion than of Christian teachers of religion. In the final analysis, everything depends on the teachers; around them the entire history of Christianity revolves; only when we know who they were in their personal circumstances do we begin to see more deeply into the inner development of the Christian church. Schröckh gave the concept of the teacher so broad a scope that he even assigned a place to the Papacy and monasticism in the history of Christian teachers. He responded to an objection raised against him by asking: "Where can the history of the

7. *Christliche Kirchengeschichte*, XIII, Preface.

papal monarchy and all its props be drawn, to be sure in highly degenerate form, except in the history of Christian teaching? What can I do, what can history itself do, if the highest teacher of the church has become a monarch who has usurped rights to himself through the Inquisition, or if monks, who at the beginning were only laity, have transformed themselves into teachers?" [8]

No matter how much Schröckh subsequently amended this error, the character of his work remained predominantly biographical. The chief reason for its immense size is that often a whole series of volumes consists of biographies of church teachers, including a large quantity of related literary notices. For this reason above all, the work's entire structure is formless, lacking in any sort of purpose or symmetry of arrangement. If Mosheim's church history is too meager in regard to doctrine, and remains too completely in generalities, Schröckh sought to fill this gap; but he presented the history of doctrine only as the history of the doctrines and opinions deposited by church teachers, one after another, in their writings. Thus we have only excerpts; a development of doctrine—as the expression of a common consciousness within the church—is completely lacking in him. But this only leads us back to what has already been emphasized, the general characteristic of his fundamental historical perspective. The substance of his history is made up of the individual, the personal, and the subjective, preferably in the form of biography. His whole conception of history bears a thoroughly subjective stamp. To provide the highest notion of what it is able to accomplish, a historiography of this sort endeavors to present the motives and intentions of the participants as precisely as possible. Through them it believes itself able to look into the soul of history and to discern its innermost thoughts. But who can know whether this is not merely introducing one's own conjectures into history, and lending one's own thoughts to the participants? The true objectivity of history still remains foreign and closed to it. But the real masters of this historical pragmatism are two men yet to follow: Spittler and Planck.

2. Spittler

His Conception of Church History

We see in Schröckh's multi-volume work the extent to which church history can expand so long as it does not weary of following every well-

8. *Ibid.*, XII, Preface.

known personality step by step, or listing and making excerpts from the works of every author. It was, on the other hand, the chosen task of L. T. Spittler, in his *Grundriss der Geschichte der christlichen Kirche*,[9] to condense his material into the smallest space, to show what could be accomplished by means of a compressed presentation and an ingenious conception, which in general reveals only the high points of events and personalities. Even though Schröckh also intended to be a pragmatic historian, Spittler was the first to show how attractive and impressive the pragmatic method could be. It coincided beautifully with his entire manner of treating church history, which in his hands seemed to take on a thoroughly modern, political, and secular character.

That it did so can be seen even from the outward construction and arrangement, in which he sees the following major divisions to emerge as though from the nature of the subject matter itself: (1) the history of expansion (one can note the varied ebb and flow of the stream without any attention to what is in the water); (2) the history of the church considered purely as a society—its inner constitution and its external conditions, and the way both were shaped by the most various fortunes; (3) the history of this society as a religious institution, in which various doctrinal opinions, changing from time to time, are current.[10] The religious and ecclesiastical element here so recedes that it is taken up only in the third section as an unessential and merely secondary matter; as though

9. It first appeared in 1782, published in Göttingen. It is Vol. II in the *Sämmtliche Werke*, ed. K. Wächter (Stuttgart and Tübingen, 1827).

[ED.] Ludwig Timotheus Spittler (1752–1810) was born and died in Stuttgart. He studied philosophy and church history at Tübingen, and published several early works while a *Privatdozent*. In 1779 he was called to Göttingen as professor of church history and the history of dogma; his lectures there formed the basis of the work Baur mentions above. Among his other church-historical works are the following: *Vorlesungen über die Geschichte des Kirchenrechts*, and *Über die Geschichte des Monchtums* (both in *Sämmtliche Werke*, X); *Vorlesungen über die Geschichte des Papsttums*, ed. H. E. G. Paulus (Heidelberg, 1826); *Geschichte der Kreuzzuge*, ed. C. Müller (Hamburg, 1827); and *Geschichte der Hierarchie von Gregor VII. bis auf die Zeiten der Reformation*, ed. C. Müller (Hamburg, 1828). In 1782 Spittler began to lecture on general history, and in 1784 he ceased all courses in church history, so that henceforth his writings were virtually restricted to secular history, political economy, and statistics. In 1797 he returned to Stuttgart as a privy councilor; but the sudden death of his patron, Duke Frederick Eugene of Württemberg, meant the decline of his influence, although he was given many ceremonial posts; among other appointments, he was made minister of state and curator of the University of Tübingen.

10. Spittler, *Grundriss der Geschichte der christlichen Kirche*, in *Sämmtliche Werke*, II, 14.

from the most superficial consideration it could be deduced that Christians as confessors of Christianity cannot but form a religious and ecclesiastical society, and that the basic principles constituting that society have their origin elsewhere than the doctrine which is the focal point of their common religious consciousness. The Christian point of view is lost even in the establishment of periods, since the second period is delimited by Muhammad. On the other hand, Spittler correctly established the epoch of Gregory VII, bypassing Charlemagne; [11] and when he designated the founding of the University of Halle [12] as the beginning of the present period, he at least indicated one of the developments that mark a distinct change.

His View of Christianity

For Spittler, the major task of Christian church history is to find a historical explanation for the present state of the Christian church in the revolutions of the preceding eighteen centuries. In no other history is there so connected a sequence as in this one; it moves without a halt through intermittent revolutions, maintaining a unity even when the narrative shifts from one part of the world to another. For whoever intends not only to learn from history but also to become wise, particular periods contain a most splendid spectacle for observing the development of human Spirit—how, in its most important concern, it has been given shape by the mightiest endeavors and the most unbelievable aberrations. Nowhere else can the progress of human Spirit, with all its retrogressions and aberrations, be so well verified; nowhere else can the color it has assumed from the climate, from the particular conditions in which it must develop, and from other factors, be better observed. Besides, where have the most various shades and mixtures of error and vice, and the most manifold tests of the changing influence of mind and heart, been more clearly shown than in the history of the Christian church? One could indeed in many respects rightly say that church history is nothing other than a long lamentation for the weakness and depravity of human Spirit. But an unbelieving and superstitious person of the seventeenth century

11. [ED.] Charlemagne was Emperor from 800 to 814; Gregory VII (Hildebrand) was Pope from 1073 to 1085. Baur is referring to the question as to when the beginning of the medieval period in the history of the church ought to be dated. To date it from the reign of Charlemagne is to make the divisions of church history dependent on external, political factors.

12. [ED.] 1693.

acts quite differently from one in the twelfth or thirteenth; and it would be highly ungrateful not to want to take note of the great progress mankind has really made here.[13] Thus, the progress of human Spirit presents itself in the history of the Christian church; but where is this shown in Spittler's presentation? It could be detected in Christianity only if—to the same extent that the Idea of Christianity was realized—human Spirit progressed from stage to stage in order to become in reality what implicitly it is and ought to be.

But what, then, is Christianity, according to its Idea? Where is the point from which everything proceeds, the goal toward which everything strives? No other historian tells less than Spittler about what Christianity objectively is. He has very little notion that a historian of the Christian church who would depict the progress of human Spirit in Christianity, and who would relate the present condition of the Christian church to its past, must surely know above all what Christianity is in itself. But instead of defining it, in highly naive fashion he states that we do not know what Christianity is. As he says at the beginning of his history, after eighteen centuries men are still quarreling over the content of the teaching proclaimed by the disciples to the world upon the command of Jesus; and this quarreling makes up an important part of the subsequent story. Thus, even at the conclusion, he describes Christianity simply as an object of controversy. To defend positive doctrines abstracted from a book written seventeen centuries before against the objections of a philosophy that cajoles by argumentation, must really be far more difficult than our robust theological authors suppose. A large number of German Protestant theologians are not even in agreement concerning what ought actually to be defended; and the important domestic controversy over the merits of external or internal proofs of the truth of Christianity is based too much on original differences in the rational capacities of men to be susceptible of a speedy settlement.[14]

Thus not only do we not know what Christianity is, but also we do not need to know, because everyone surely takes Christianity only as it appears to him in his subjective way of thinking. As Spittler says, not even the historian may state his convictions as historical fact, since the book on whose information the whole affair must be judged ought to be in everyone's hands, and since it demands, from each individual, who ought not to remain completely indifferent to the most important concerns of humanity, an investigation of his own.[15] To this extent, then, everything con-

13. Spittler, *Grundriss*, 2 f.   14. *Ibid.*, 21, 433.   15. *Ibid.*, 22.

cerned with Christianity is left to the discretion of individual subjectivity; but little though Spittler intends to know what Christianity is
objectively, he cannot avoid allowing a specific view of Christianity to
permeate his presentation; and he only indulges in subjectivity when he
aligns himself with the contemporary Enlightenment, which takes a negative attitude toward the positive, historical elements [*das Positive*] of
religion and of Christianity.

Although he expresses himself equivocally concerning the fruits of this
Enlightenment, and although he appears to remain only a troubled specta-
tor of the immense damage a generally spreading unbelief must necessarily cause, nevertheless he cannot but betray his own partiality toward
certain men and movements. These include the Arminians, who, since
they are largely responsible for our improved theological knowledge, are
also to be credited with the increasingly dominant aversion against everything positive in religion, which has been chiefly disseminated among us
through their writings. It was P. Bayle, an adept in following this crafty
course, who first illuminated philosophy's relation to history and to sound
historical criticism.[16] Concerning many others we must be more cautious
in our sympathy, while not withholding it completely. If we cannot too
openly admit our affinity with the English and French naturalists and
with the German fragmentists, on the other hand we can console ourselves all the more over the sorry prospect of a downfall of religion with
the concluding remark "that the morality of many men in our age is
based much less than previously on the Christian religion *alone;* that the
most enlightened men, even if their private opinion is not fully and decisively that of the Christian religion, still know the great extent to which
every open declaration of such a private opinion causes harm; that within
twenty or thirty years the entire theological generation now being educated by the writings of Spalding, Herder, and Döderlein will sit in
consistories and by their wise administration will finally bring about in
general practice what has hitherto often been only the wish of diffident
sages or the rather bold undertaking of individual, resolute, enlightened
men." [17]

But if this is what the revolutions of eighteen centuries have provided,

16. *Ibid.*, 333, 369. [ED. Pierre Bayle (1647–1706), French Protestant encyclopedist
and man of letters.]

17. [ED.] Spittler, *Grundriss*, 434. With these words the work ends. J. J. Spalding
(1714–1804), J. G. Herder (1744–1803), and C. A. Döderlein (1714–89) were leaders
of the German Enlightenment and proponents of a rationalistic interpretation of
Christianity.

why be so secretive about it? The purely subjective character of such a view is betrayed by the requirement of whoever holds it that he should keep it to himself rather than to communicate it openly. We may ourselves indeed be unbelievers, so long as we do not openly and loudly declare our unbelief. Because the same view we commend as enlightened individuals produces so much harm when it takes the form of unbelief, it does not matter that we deny our true opinion and accommodate ourselves to the dominant opinion when circumstances so dictate. The equivocation and instability of a view that locates everything in the realm of subjective discretion must explain how a church history such as Spittler's, which at the zenith of its reflection is so naturalistic, so adverse to the positive, historical element [das Positive], and that speaks so glibly of fabricated miracles, nevertheless refers to the miracles by which the assertions of Jesus concerning his divine mission were made legitimate, and to the final miracle of his resurrection, as though an ingenuous belief in miracle, which elsewhere finds no place in this view, here at least is to be taken for granted.

Where it is impossible to make out an objective principle of historical development, there remains as a highest causality only chance, the contingency of outward circumstances, and the equally contingent situation of single individuals. From this point of view it makes no difference whether or not we call chance Providence. There is between Providence and the individuals confronting it a peculiar relationship, in which we do not know whether Providence has more reason to thank the individuals, or the individuals Providence.

On such a view of history, we can only be astonished that a Jew by the name of Jesus [18] should in his short lifetime have brought about a revolution which in its beginnings was so insignificant and in its ultimate consequences so highly remarkable; or that, next to his personal virtues, the conditions under which he appeared should also have been so suitable that an important change was to be expected at that time. If it was Providence that carried out, by his death, intentions that meant the greatest happiness for the human race, nevertheless on the other hand it can only be ascribed to his personality that, as a man of great tenderness, he made friends who

18. Spittler's church history begins [Ibid., 19–20] in approximately the same manner as his history of Württemberg, about which he says at the outset: "May this old story begin like so many old stories: 'Once upon a time there was a count . . . .'" This is the Christianity, thrown into the world by Providence, of which Spittler's contemporary, Planck, himself spoke in the Preface to his last work in 1831. [ED. See below, 191, n. 38.]

skillfully completed the grand design of a general improvement in religion, for which he had only sketched the outline during his life on earth.

At every important juncture in the entire course of history, there is always a similar concurrence of fortunate circumstances and of individuals who fit the conditions of the time. Fortunately, a remedy is found at the height of crisis in a decisive point of time, whereby the dominant inclination of an age may be used to the advantage of one cause or another. As a gift from heaven there appears in the midst of the degenerate race not merely an M. Luther but also a G. Calixtus.[19] Because contingent tendencies usually converge as though prearranged, so as to present the world with a gift when Providence has so decreed, luck must have it that by either the energy or the lethargy of men precisely the thing occurs which, once it has happened, is regarded as especially providential.[20] Such a view of history seems to be fully justified when so prominent a personality as Luther determines the direction of an entire age; nevertheless, Spittler's portrayal of the Reformation period shows clearly enough how one-sided it is to detect the moving principle of history simply in individuals, and to conceive of the power ruling over individuals only under the vague category of Providence. So regarded, Christianity is only the fortuitous point of contact, and the Christian church only the outer framework, of the most manifold changes, whose only unity is in the play of chance—a chance which here and there brings about a progressive or retrogressive motion by a new and unexpected turn.

His Historical Pragmatism

On the basis of this view of history, in which the subjectivity of individuals is given so free a latitude, the pragmatism peculiar to it can consist only in the art of detecting the causes of historical phenomena and the motives of participants in the subjective characteristics of individuals. The better the historian is acquainted psychologically with this subjective area, the more thoroughly he investigates it, the more pragmatic his presentation will become. This pragmatic method is especially applicable to

19. [ED.] Georg Calixtus (1586–1656), heir of Melanchthon's theological position in seventeenth-century Germany. Irenic in temper, he believed that theology should be primarily concerned not with pure doctrine but with the principles of Christian life.

20. Spittler, *Grundriss*, 19 f., 245, 350, 420.

the history of doctrine. Since from this standpoint the phenomena related to dogma cannot be grasped in terms of an Idea immanent in dogma, such phenomena are all the more subjectively grounded; the major reason for the diversity of religious opinion lies in the diversity of human temperament and powers of mind, as is already noticeable in the apostles. The less our modern way of thinking is capable of grasping so many peculiar and strange ideas, however, the more we are inclined to regard such phenomena as aberrations of fantasy and products of an eccentric fanaticism. When it comes to the Gnostics, Spittler finds the excessive imagination of these fanatics not worth the trouble of exploring; and as for the Manichaeans, he can scarcely believe that hypotheses so totally opposed to all human reason should have found many adherents. His judgment of dogmatic controversies is hardly more favorable; e.g., those in regard to the person of Christ and the Trinity represent mere bickering over arbitrarily chosen questions. The manner in which these controversies were conducted produced certain theological fashions, distinguishable from other fashions only in that they unfortunately do not possess the same adaptability, but have impressed themselves ineradicably on the human Spirit. The significance of temperament as a factor in the history of theology can be seen especially from Calvin, who is a cautionary example of the temperamental theologian, as well as from many others. That so enlightened a man, in spite of his otherwise excellent exegesis, and in spite of everything that the mind and heart of every man knows of God's kindness, could have happened upon the notion of an arbitrary divine predestination of certain men to eternal depravity is a sad proof of how very often our convictions are determined by fortuitous external circumstances; but it is even sadder that such a notion as that merciless hypothesis concerning divine grace could obtain a certain general momentum.[21]

It is no different in other areas of history. How often the most important and consequential matters arise out of an inspiration of some sort that this or that person once had! The pragmatic historian particularly reveals his sagacity in making combinations when he glimpses in the smallest and most contingent of things the greatest and most significant of possibilities. But since he brings everything under close scrutiny and penetrates into the inner character of persons and events, he knows too exactly the rational capacities and the directions of men's wills not to have, very often, in one respect or another, only the lowest opinion of them. It is self-evident that, where the noble fires of inspiration [*Begeisterung*] are cus-

21. Spittler, *Grundriss*, 32, 49, 51, 116, 326, 357.

tomarily seen blazing, he can speak only of fanaticism [*Schwärmerei*] and frenzy, as for example in the Crusades. But there are not only fanatics and madmen; there are also many fools and impostors, whom we first learn to recognize in their true shape by the perspicacity of the pragmatic historian. Even the pious Ansgar [22] escapes the suspicion of being an impostor only by some of the miracles he performed; and St. Francis ought to be happy to be regarded as such, for he is accorded honor when we believe him to have been mentally deficient. In St. Ignatius of Loyola, who didn't have the strongest of heads in any case, stupidity and madness maintain a balance; but the Deacon of Mainz, so notoriously connected with the history of the pseudo-decretals,[23] is an impostor and a fool simultaneously. It could easily have come about that the weak glimmer of the newly dawning sciences, which Charlemagne sought with every effort to make more generally effective, could at last have expressed its full power if a single fool and impostor had not ruined everything, and if the world, with ineffable simplicity of heart, had not repeated for many centuries afterward what the impostor had recited! [24]

In this latter regard we also see how the pragmatist only too happily casts a glance at the broad field of the so-called *scientia media*, since indeed everything depends upon chance and the whim of a moment. In addition, at important points in history he ponders the notion of how completely different things would have been in the world had only one thing taken place, as it could so easily have done. The world could easily have been spared the whole hierarchy, since if only Otto III had succeeded in completing his project of making Rome the future residence of his kingdom, a Gregory VII would never have been.[25] Considerations of this sort could also be associated with St. Ignatius' broken leg, which so accidentally aroused in him the decision to become a pious Don Quixote!

Since, in accord with his subjective mode of consideration, the pragmatist bears in himself the well-being and disaster of the world, his feelings are also sensitive enough to share, according to the measure of what happens, the joys and sorrows of the persons concerned. Even Leo I is

22. [ED.] Ansgar (c. 801–865), missionary to Scandinavia, first archbishop of Hamburg.

23. [ED.] At about the same time as the Pseudo-Isidorian Decretals there appeared what purported to be a supplement to the collection of capitularies of Ansegis of Fontanella made by "Benedict Levita" at the request of the late Archbishop Otgar of Mainz (826–47). It is now recognized that "Benedict Levita"—the Deacon of Mainz—is a pseudonym, having no reference to any real person.

24. Spittler, *Grundriss,* 147, 256, 339, 165.　　　　25. *Ibid.,* 177.

not too distant for the question to be asked whether, in the year 451, the news of the Battle of Châlons or of Chalcedon would have pleased him more.[26] But even more often, as is the case with such delicate considerations, the enlightened historian, who above all stands for reason, gives way in his innermost being to a noble outburst concerning a race that seems to have been intentionally blinded, yet whose sight is good; or because entire ages as well as individual men should give proof simultaneously of an educated mind and a wholly unaccountable lack of sense. He cannot vigorously enough express his wrath and anger that the Papacy never flourished more than in precisely the age when the human mind was cultivated by the finest scholastic investigations—an age when with hypercritical philosophical acumen men began to doubt everything; when trade and the arts, following the Crusades, flourished ever more greatly; when even more accelerated communications between nations should have inured men against the supposition that a man in Rome, the story of whose youth was known, whose elevation to the See was known, and whose daily machinations were visible, should be infallible, a demigod! [27] And we cannot but ask ourselves, just here, what Spittler would only say if he could see the same man more than ever playing that role of demigod in an age when communications have been accelerated by steamships and railroads? Now if we add to this how vigorously such expressions of various emotions, of anger and displeasure, or of joy and regret, and so many well-intentioned desires, are often mixed into the narration,[28] or further, how a pragmatic historian like Spittler is able to enliven the up-to-date mood of his presentation by piquant expressions, striking images, and well-placed hints, and to give it further interest by means of psychological reflections, practical truths, and common sayings —then we have more or less covered everything needed to depict this form of church historiography.

3. Planck

Nevertheless, at Spittler's side stands G. J. Planck, who is so close to him and who in many respects is an even greater master of pragmatic

26. *Ibid.*, 136. [ED. In the Battle of Châlons, June 451, Aëtius, aided by the Visigothic king, Theodoric I, defeated the Huns on the Mauriac plain, near Troyes.]
27. *Ibid.*, 278.
28. "The historian ought always to remain cold-blooded, but who is capable of doing so?" *Ibid.*, 336.

historiography. He has, at any rate, applied the pragmatic method to a far greater extent. Though Planck did not treat church history as a whole in a single cohesive work, nevertheless the two major works [29] that have made his name so famous in more recent church-historical literature are so closely related to each other as sufficiently to characterize his work as a church historian.

SUBJECTIVE PRAGMATISM AT ITS PEAK

Like Spittler, he has every justification for being designated a pragmatic historian. He himself introduced his first major work as follows: Its ultimate purpose (why should this not be mentioned at the outset?) is to write a pragmatic history of the emergence of our Protestant doctrine; to bring the whole work of the Reformation within this one point of view; to show, first in retrospect over the whole and then in regard to each

---

29. *Geschichte der Entstehung, der Veränderungen und der Bildung unsers protestantischen Lehrbegriffs vom Anfang der Reformation bis zu der Einführung der Concordienformel* (6 vols.; Leipzig, 1781–1800); and *Geschichte der christlich-kirchlichen Gesellschaftsverfassung* (5 vols.; Hanover, 1803–1809).

[ED.] Gottlieb Jakob Planck was born in Württemberg in 1751 and died at Göttingen in 1833. He was educated at Tübingen (1769–74), where he lectured as a *Privatdozent* for five years before going to Stuttgart as a vicar and associate professor in the Karlsschule. Here he completed the first two volumes of the first of the works mentioned above by Baur. This occasioned his call in 1784 to Göttingen to succeed Walch as professor of church history, a position he held to the end of his life. The first two volumes of his *Geschichte der christlich-kirchlichen Gesellschaftsverfassung* are his masterpiece; they mark a new epoch in Protestant church historiography, since they were the first attempt at a nonpartisan account of the Reformation and the rise of Lutheranism. He described his theological position as that of "rational supernaturalism," a position Baur criticized both in his former teacher at Tübingen, Ernst Gottlieb Bengel (1769–1826), and in the founder and leader of the old Tübingen School, Gottlob Christian Storr (1746–1805). Storr finished his studies at Tübingen just one year before Planck arrived, and returned in 1772 as a *Privatdozent*, first in philosophy, then in theology. Planck's theological position was undoubtedly shaped by Storr and the old Tübingen School. Among Planck's other writings are the following: a continuation of Walch's *Neueste Religions-Geschichte* (3 vols.; Lemgo, 1787–93); a new edition of Spittler's *Grundriss der Kirchengeschichte* (Göttingen, 1812); *Einleitung in die theologischen Wissenschaften* (2 parts; Leipzig, 1794–95); *Worte des Friedens mit der katholischen Kirche* (Göttingen, 1809); *Grundriss der theologischen Encyklopädie* (Göttingen, 1813); *Geschichte des Christenhums in der Periode seiner ersten Einführung in die Welt durch Jesum und die Apostel* (2 vols.; Göttingen, 1818); *Über die Behandlung, die Haltbarkeit und den Werth des historischen Beweises für die Göttlichkeit des Christenthums* (Göttingen, 1821); and *Geschichte der protestantischen Theologie von der Concordienformel an bis in die Mitte des achtzehnten Jahrhunderts* (Göttingen, 1831).

individual proposition, how, when, and where change first appeared in the representation of doctrines of faith—how it was prepared, brought to maturity, defined, changed again, and then again corrected; to show by what means truth was brought to light, by what occasions and round-about ways the spirit of those who first found it was set on its way, by what obstacles its currency was hindered or accelerated, and by which contradictions its influence was increased or weakened; to show how all outer circumstances, established partly by intention and partly by chance, have cooperated; to show what was contributed by the character of leading persons, their training, their passions, their prejudices, their hidden motivations, as well as by the political system, the plots, the circumstances, the errors of the court, and by a hundred other in part seemingly insignificant and often scarcely noticeable circumstances of place, time, and opportunity; and to some extent to explain from all of this why the whole system of our doctrine was from the beginning assembled thus and not otherwise, why it was changed here and there, why it was reshaped first in this part and then in that, and then in the end was defined just so and not otherwise in the Formula of Concord. By these characterizations Planck delineates the ideal of history that hovers before him and is reflected in his writings. The more grandiose the object, and the more the presentation is calculated to penetrate into the particularities of events and circumstances, and to give a vivid picture of the course of the Reformation period in so far as is possible, the more Planck had the opportunity to display fully the artistry of his pragmatic treatment.

This is the acknowledged superiority of Planck's writings; but whoever is only partially familiar with them also knows their less favorable aspect. The characteristic mark of this pragmatism is a deliberateness, a systematic arrangement of events, which often gives the impression that it has been imposed on history by the historian rather than that it is contained in the occurrences themselves.[30] All details are here analyzed, often with

---

30. Cf. what G. C. F. Lücke says in his biography of Planck [*Dr. G. J. Planck: Ein biographischer Versuch* (Göttingen, 1835)], 25, about Planck's pragmatism, which is shown in its full strength in his major work, *Geschichte des protestantischen Lehrbegriffs:* the subjective, personal side of development, the shadows of passions and vagaries, are exposed too starkly, and one often misses the objective pragmatism of the Idea of the subject matter itself. Planck does not sufficiently recognize that personalities, with their virtues and errors, their passions, dispositions, and expediencies, should always be subordinated and treated as individual elements in the temporal development of the historical Idea. It is remarkable, as Lücke himself mentions, that even in that period, so imprisoned by its pragmatism, the reviewer of the first volume of the *Geschichte des protestantischen Lehrbegriffs* in the *Göttinger Gelehrten Anzeigen* (1781), 758 (perhaps Spittler himself), could not refrain from

a petty exactitude, in order to detect the innermost thoughts and motives of historical agents, to consider carefully all their motives and counter-motives, and to trace them in all the subterfuges of a cleverly conceived politics. But since in the final analysis everything still depends on possible combinations and purely personal situations, the result of this rationaliz-ing and pragmatizing is often that we still do not know where we stand; and the true, actual course of the subject matter is still concealed more than it is revealed. In this regard, we need only to compare Planck's presentation with that of Ranke covering the same period.[31] How strik-ing the difference is between a thoroughly subjective pragmatism and an objectively maintained historiography—which is therefore far simpler and more lucid! If we chose to pursue this comparison further, abundant material for a not uninteresting parallel would be provided by the essen-tially different way the two historians portray Charles V, and the whole period from the Diet at Augsburg in the year 1530 to the outbreak of the Schmalkaldic War. Precisely because the decision was for so long protracted,[32] the pragmatist had before him all the more latitude to make a clever guess, on the basis not only of what really happened but some-times even of what did not happen, what under different circumstances might have happened or ought to have happened, in accord with the intention of the participants.[33]

---

asking the reader whether he does not sometimes, with the reviewer, have the ob-scure feeling that in certain places too much has been read into the souls of the an-cients. It is also remarkable that the review of the second volume in the *Göttinger Gelehrten Anzeigen* (1784), 477, is troubled by the thought, in consideration of the most excellently developed motives of historical agents, whether certain surreptitious elements must not, unavoidably, have priority here, which in the end cast a totally false glimmer and shadow on the occurrences themselves. Every psychologically reasoned history most probably loses grasp of the truth the more it goes fully into detail.

31. [ED.] Leopold von Ranke, *Deutsche Geschichte im Zeitalter der Reformation* (3 vols.; Berlin, 1839).

32. [ED.] Following the Treaty of Crespy (1544), Charles V sought to crush the independence of the Protestant states of the Empire in Germany, and to restore the unity of the Catholic Church. He was urged on by the Pope, who concluded an alliance with him and promised money and troops. The Schmalkaldic League (formed of an alliance in 1530 between the Protestant princes and the imperial cities) was defeated in the War of 1546–47. The religious issue was finally settled at the Peace of Augsburg in 1555.

33. In this fashion Planck describes the most difficult part of his task for the period mentioned in the Preface to the first part of Vol. III of his *Geschichte des protestantischen Lehrbegriffs*. Here, in fact, he reaches one of the high points of his pragmatism.

[ED.] Cf. Dilthey's criticism of the attempt made by pragmatic historiography to

One who has to weigh so many possibilities, and to consider the positive and negative aspects of the probable from so many angles, cannot be very brief. An inconclusive long-windedness, and far too familiar and colloquial a volubility, are very dominant characteristics of Planck, so that he is especially distinguished from Spittler, who loved compactness of presentation and sharp, measured expressions. The characteristic of their pragmatism is equally evident for both of them all the more in that they cannot forego mentioning the subjective impressions the events narrated make upon them, as well as in the open expression of their sympathies and antipathies. Even Planck frequently mentions his regret and surprise over the passion and moral perversity of men, and especially over their stupidity, shortsightedness, and feebleness of wit. To this is happily added the final, teleological consideration that nonetheless all has gone better and more tolerably than might have been supposed, since the divine wisdom, or the mind of God—which fortunately surpasses that of men—directs the work he accomplishes through men, who often do not know that they are working for him, or at least do not often know that they are working for him for the specific purpose to which he is able to direct their plans. The highest fruit of this pragmatism is thus the conviction that the eternal mode of God's action, observed from the beginning of the world, is to work through men, even through evil men, to elicit his own ends from the most intricate designs of human folly or human covetousness, and to use their most interested schemes, as it were, to his own advantage.[34] The whole of world history is, strictly speaking, of this

reconstruct psychological motives, which, he believes, can only lead to historical scepticism. "Historical scepticism can be overcome only if historical method does not have to count on ascertaining motives, . . . and if the understanding of products of Spirit (*geistiges Gebilde*) takes the place of psychological subtleties (*psychologische Raffinement*). The former lie before us as something externally objectified and can be made the object of skillful understanding." (*Gesammelte Schriften*, VII [4th ed., Stuttgart, 1958], 259–60.)

34. Cf. the Preface to the first volume of the *Geschichte des protestantischen Lehrbegriffs*, which in general is to be seen as the programmatic statement of Planck's mode of historiography. Notice how vividly the subjective pathos, without which there can be no subjective pragmatism, is expressed in the following passage: "It is a labor consuming body and soul to have to wend one's way through so many acts of human evil, falsehood, revenge, and bloodthirstiness, in general only to see better persons, the gentler and more enlightened, persecuted and oppressed, or the innocent visionary condemned by the guilty fanatic. It is a business that scandalizes one's feelings to have to study only the events of the controversies connected with Osiander and Hardenberg, or the Calvinist persecutions, with the patience and precision required of an investigator. And in moments of resentment, or bitterness, or the most deeply felt sympathy, it is indeed not always possible to avoid too severe or

nature, because God cannot perform and carry out everything at once. But men also belong to this history, and they are engaged in the contest between God and man to see which of them can obtain the greatest advantage over the other, although naturally he finally gains the victory who with his superior mind can best unravel the confusion wrought by men.

His Indifference Toward Dogma

The indifference of Spittler's pragmatism toward dogma is quite conspicuous. He will have almost nothing to do with it, and disdainfully dismisses and rejects all phenomena related to it. Planck appears to have wanted to correct this error, since he made it his major task to write a history of Protestant doctrine. But this is only an appearance; and it is all the more remarkable how insensitive Planck's subjective pragmatism is precisely toward what is the very kernel and substance of the objectivity of history. Planck himself must have regarded dogma as the kernel of Protestantism; otherwise, why should he have called his work a *Geschichte des Lehrbegriffs* [History of Doctrine] when, considering its purpose and content, he could just as well have called it *Deutsche Geschichte im Zeitalter der Reformation* [German History in the Age of the Reformation], as Ranke did his history? Doctrine indeed stood before him at the outset, but since he believed he must above all be comprehensive in dealing with external political history, doctrine was thrust back and set aside.[35] It is only in the middle of the work, after the completion of what can only improperly be called a history of the emergence of doctrine—since it is much more a history of the Reformation and of Protestantism itself—that space is found for doctrine. Hence we are quite surprised by the author's confession that he is tempted not to carry the work further, since he knows only too well how little interest the theo-

---

too hasty judgments, from which the mind withdraws most reluctantly. No wonder that Arnold makes this study!" [ED. In the 2nd ed., I (1791), xvi–xvii.] Also, it belongs to the characteristic manner of that period of subjectivity in German literature of which Planck is the chief representative, that in all his Prefaces the author seems to be obliged to converse and coquette with the reader, and cannot urge on him commendingly and ingratiatingly enough the purposeful, useful, interesting, and pleasing aspects of the work lying before him, and exactly in the form of presentation as given. In this respect Planck remains, from his first Preface in 1781 to his last in 1831, very much the same.

35. Cf. what Planck himself says about this in the Preface to the first part of Vol. III of his *Geschichte des protestantischen Lehrbegriffs*.

logical public now has in it, after the almost universal change that has taken place in their way of thinking during the past ten years. Not only have most of the special forms into which the individual parts of our theological system were shaped during the period up to the Formula of Concord completely lost, in our present-day dogmatics, what formerly was attributed to them, but also, for the spirit of our time, the history of their formation has lost even that negative interest that for a while could have grown out of a gradually forming and developing aversion. Only ten years ago, all this would have been different. But since then a completely new dogmatics has been formed. Men have almost universally turned away not only from those forms, but even from the more fundamental older ideas; and they are aware of having thus turned away. They no longer fear that the spirit of our theology can ever again, of itself, return to that point, or be forced to do so; and for this reason they consider it to be a wholly indifferent antiquity.[36]

It is clear proof of the extent to which Planck himself shared this revolution in modes of thinking, that he now no longer called the subject of his work Protestant doctrine but only Protestant theology. The peculiar thing is that once doctrine has arisen, it no longer exists as doctrine but only as theology. We should not believe that theology, which for Planck himself in this way becomes antiquated, has been discarded thereby only in the connection required for the objective consideration of the historian; it is stated clearly enough in the subsequent presentation that for the historian it has not only no personal interest, but also no factual interest. Little though Planck ever tires of recounting, in great thoroughness and minuteness of detail, the whole series of theological controversies and negotiations that follow one upon the other in such great number, he does not conceal his own inability to see in it anything but a history of human follies, passions, and perversities, concerning which it is futile to ask what use it has served. What interests him as a pragmatic historian is simply the art of diplomacy, seen in its full glory in the history of the Formula of Concord, with which he is able to display the intricate texture of interests, passions, and intrigues of the various quarreling parties. But concerning the matter itself—the religious and dogmatic interest—he can, in the final analysis, only turn from such a scene with loathing and disgust. His judgment, at the end of the entire work, on what has been gained for Lutheran theology by the Formula of Concord is very characteristic:

36. *Ibid.*, IV (1796), Preface, vi f.

It obtained through the Formula a determinateness previously lacking in it; and this could all the more be considered as gain since as
a consequence the change that otherwise would have taken place in
this theology approximately one and a half centuries earlier was
very probably delayed. But was anyone entitled to delay this change
—to which the spirit of the times was in so many places already in-
clining—in part forcibly, by the Formula of Concord? Can the
answer be adequately determined from what is explained of the
single articles of the Formula? Is what one receives from it really a
gain? This can be determined by the consequences that sprang directly from the Formula of Concord, and by the condition in which
our theology has been retained until now, for one and a half centuries, by the after-effects of the Formula.[37]

If the Formula has only delayed what could have occurred a century
and a half earlier, and has delayed it only forcibly and in contradiction to
the spirit of the times, then one can but wish to remove it from history.
Then what Planck describes in his last work [38] as the good fortune of the
period he believes, according to all the signs of the times, to be near at
hand, and what he regards as a turning point in the history of Christianity,
could have occurred much earlier—namely, that a knowledge satisfying
mind and heart in the same degree, answering the demands of the one at
the same time it fulfills the needs of the other, is to become more widespread; and that all are to experience in the same measure the improving,
purifying, and vitalizing power of the teaching of Jesus, and to receive it
into their hearts with equal strength and love. Once such a period is
reached, we can surely overlook everything preceding it as standing far
beneath the goal obtained and being unable in the least to provide us with
a similar satisfaction. But the question is simply whether this goal could
have been obtained without the period preceding it. The peculiarity of
the subjective mode of consideration that represents the standpoint of
these pragmatic historians is in fact that they are concerned only with the
result, without thinking of the means by which it must first be mediated,
or of the work and effort, the struggle and controversy, that were necessary in order finally to arrive at the secure possession of what they regard
as the true essence of Christianity. Since they think only of themselves,
and consider themselves fortunate, in view of their enlightenment, to
have come so far, they believe they can look back only with regret or

37. *Ibid.*, VI, 817 f.
38. *Geschichte der protestantischen Theologie von der Concordienformel an bis
in die Mitte des achtzehnten Jahrhunderts* (Göttingen, 1831), Preface, vii.

indignation upon earlier periods, in which this brighter and better knowledge had not yet emerged.

But the better we learn to see that this knowledge was not such an easy affair, that men could attain to it only by degrees, and that every age has its own peculiar form of consciousness, through which it first must work, the more moderately will we pass judgment on past ages, and the more we shall be motivated to enter into their struggles and aspirations and to participate in the same spiritual work. If every age has its own mode of perception and form of consciousness, which is not arbitrary, self-constituted, and individual, but rather something common, based on a higher necessity, then where, in the final analysis, does this fact have its basis other than that on the whole the Idea immanent to dogma contains in itself different elements, each of which has its justification and is intended to mediate the Idea for subjective consciousness? The greatest deficiency in Planck's writings is that this higher standpoint of consideration is far too remote from them. Skillfully though Planck is able to develop the causes, connections, and practical elements of the theological questions moving an age, he is inclined to see in them only fortuitous opinions, arbitrary assertions, sudden ideas, aberrations of mind, or even something worse. He cannot give sufficiently low esteem to the religious and scientific interest of such questions; he is far too ready in declaring them mere misunderstandings, and expresses in the strongest language his consternation that men have been able to quarrel so long and so stubbornly over such things. But those he treats worst of all are men whose opinions we cannot understand without transposing ourselves into their peculiar way of thinking and perceiving—men such as Schwenkfeld and A. Osiander.[39]

What would come of history if we should think away everything that did not please us and did not harmonize with our conceptions, or regard them as something whose coming to the fore has been a detriment to the church? Worthy of note in this respect is Planck's judgment on the scholastics—the strangest sort of men who have ever lived. He is of the opinion that in the handiwork with which they were in reality preoccupied—the unraveling of theological concepts—truth surely has lost ten times more than it has gained. It is undeniable that they dull the feeling of their age, since they veil its natural form under the most monstrous disguises, in which no human eye, not even their own, could

39. Cf. my *Die christliche Lehre von der Dreieinigkeit und Menschwerdung Gottes in ihrer geschichtlichen Entwicklung*, III (Tübingen, 1843), 252 f.

seek and find it. In addition, they elevate a hundred insignificant follies to the rank of articles of faith, thus often totally weakening the influence of the authentic doctrines; but this was harmful only for their own age. Veiled truth still remains truth, and it was good that it was veiled in those centuries when the power of inordinate ambition and superstition would have suppressed it completely.[40] What a totally subjective and egotistic interest is given expression here! Let scholasticism damage its own age in any way it likes, so long as it is useful to us! But how can it have damaged its own age if it is of use to us? And if it veiled the truth, when is there an age that has not likewise veiled the truth, only in some other fashion?

His Externality and Propensity for Construction

In his first major work, which in the first part contained the political history of the Reformation, and in the second the history of theological controversies from the death of Luther to the Formula of Concord, Planck was already restricting himself chiefly to the outer history of doctrine. The sequel, the *Geschichte der protestantischen Theologie von der Concordienformel an bis in die Mitte des achtzehnten Jahrhunderts*, also proceeds very externally.[41] Planck of course vividly depicts, with the pragmatic art peculiar to him, the tiresome and annoying acts and controversies produced by the passionate polemics of that age, but he does not make possible a deeper glimpse into its total spiritual consciousness and the general theological interest motivating it. He always lingers upon details alone, without joining them to an inner unity. He scarcely comprehends the point around which the history of that period chiefly moves—Calixtine syncretism, in its general character and in its theological significance. With this tendency toward the external even in the area of doctrine, Planck follows the inner tendency of his historical pragmatism only when in a special work he demarcates an area that ought to belong exclusively to external church history in the narrowest sense. His intention was to provide a genuine history of the Christian church as an exterior social institution, in which only that which belongs to the history of this society most properly speaking—its emergence, its formation, its successive expansion, its periodically changing organization, its policing and form of government, and its relation to other societies, especially to

40. Planck, *Geschichte der protestantischen Lehrbegriffs*, I, 18 f.
41. It first appeared in 1831, and was Planck's last work.

the great society of nations and its influence on that—is to be singled out and seen in its proper light. That which belongs to the history of Christianity or Christian doctrine is to be touched hardly at all, and all else is to be treated only in so far as is necessary to the history of the constitution of the church.[42]

In accord with this plan, Planck treats the history of the polity of the church, which in the ninth century becomes the history of the Papacy, from the earliest period up to the Reformation. He does so, undoubtedly, in a very instructive and attractive fashion, but also with all the externalization and secularization of the concept of the church toward which his historical pragmatism implicitly tended from the beginning. We here read the history of the Papacy with the same sort of interest that we read any history of a state or of rulers, and can completely forget that we stand not on political but on ecclesiastical soil. If the result was already to separate this part of church history from its ecclesiastical aspect, it was even more true that Planck's historical pragmatism found the greatest freedom to develop a talent for dealing with diplomacy in the area staked out as primarily political. An artificially arranged and very skillfully executed "plan of operation" here constitutes the history of the reign of a Gregory VII, or an Innocent III, or a Boniface VIII, and of many other Popes. Everything happens with methodical deliberation and consistency, and with such astute calculation and circumspect utilization of all circumstances, even of the most thoroughly contingent factors, that we marvel less at the Popes' mastery of politics than at the historian who is able to peer so deeply into their innermost thoughts and to pursue with acute and skillful penetration the artificially interwoven threads of such a web. Just as though nothing could happen except consciously and arbitrarily, every change is scrutinized with inquisitorial rigor—not merely in later history but from the very beginnings of the church; for example, the intention that might or in fact did lie at the basis of change, whether and to what extent men were conscious of that intention, the gain anticipated if this or that idea were put into circulation. There is a question of the means that were so quickly put into action, of the ingenuities that were employed to establish the new rule more firmly and to accustom the people to it, and of a pervasive spirit of speculation that sharply eyed the desired goal and superbly calculated the ways that could most surely lead to it. The only problem is that the sharp-witted historian has not sufficiently considered

42. Planck, *Geschichte der christlich-kirchlichen Gesellschaftsverfassung*, I, Preface.

the extent of the temptation to presuppose, as the conscious intention of the participants, thoughts that have merely been abstracted from the events. In the earliest history of polity especially, Planck's pragmatizing is in large part an *a priori* construction from an abstract presupposition. More recent investigations, which have been concerned only with the concrete reality of the facts, without making the constant question about intention the major issue, have led in many respects to different results.

Finally, Planck also treated the history of primitive Christianity in a special work,[43] which however is far inferior to his two major works, and has historical value now only in that it represents the same historical pragmatism in its purest form. We can see most clearly how far we have moved beyond that mode of perception by the limited significance this writing still has. In a historical field where questions of a wholly different sort now become the object of the most serious investigation, it makes a peculiar impression to see the same obsolete theme discussed repeatedly, in length and breadth—that Jesus and his apostles went about their work according to a carefully deliberated plan. The pragmatist, instead of simply devoting himself to the historical object, cannot refrain from repeatedly anticipating, from his position at the beginning of a series of phenomena, his own standpoint in the present, or from inquiring about the continuity of causes and effects, of intentions and results, of plans and their accomplishment, in terms of his own customary categories. Therefore, he cannot be sufficiently astonished that eighteen centuries ago a Jewish sage appeared as the founder of Christianity, among the circumstances and surroundings in which he found himself, with the design and plan for becoming the founder of a new religion; that, with the clearest and most vivid knowledge of all the obstacles, he nevertheless reached the decision and sketched the plans; that he made all his moves in accord with the most careful deliberation by a wisdom that took all circumstances into account; that he chose the most unlikely means for their realization and yet was entirely confident of their effectiveness; and that really everything worked out as he had foreseen it. This is a series of miracles at which the mind can only be astonished, because its course of development can be watched from a specific point. But what is astonishing about this if the Divinity guiding the whole affair stands ever ready to do his share, as soon as circumstances permit, in the achievement of its aims?

43. *Geschichte des Christenthums in der Periode seiner ersten Einführung in die Welt durch Jesum und die Apostel* (2 vols.; Göttingen, 1818).

His Concern with Reason

The historical pragmatism that Planck developed so completely and on the broadest of foundations belongs in the same category with a petty teleological mode of consideration, which, completely permeated by the idea of expediency, generally admires the prudent apparatus of aims and means, without having any notion that it is merely its own wisdom it reads into and admires in things. That pragmatism is not interested simply in sticking to events and facts but intends to go back to motives, to the intentions of the participants, from which everything proceeds. Who would not agree that such a pragmatism is right in wanting not merely to recount what has occurred but also to grasp occurrences in their continuity? But it is a major error that in the final analysis everything depends simply on the intentions and aspirations of individual persons appearing in history, who themselves were only the children of their time and were subject to the influence of ruling ideas and traditions, by which they themselves were borne and upheld in the most important steps of their public activity.

It is precisely the major factor that rarely appears in Planck's history—namely, the absolute Idea of the Papacy in its objective power, which dominated the general consciousness of the time and was the necessary consequence of an entire theological-ecclesiastical system, whose history on that very account is not to be so easily separated from the history of the constitution of the society. It is as though every Pope should always have had to begin anew to sketch for himself his papal ideal and system and the plan of operations for his papal activity, or as though the Papacy has had only the shrewdness, skill, and energy of individual Popes to thank for everything it has become; whereas at least as often the reverse is true: the mightiest lever of everything that furnished each Pope his personal significance was only the Idea of the papacy, already existing in itself, developing and coming to consciousness in individuals. We can always ask what part, for a Gregory VII, the intention to obtain more splendor and power for the pontificate has had in his plan to achieve the independence of the church, whether the one or the other is the more probable, or whether he had his new papal ideal in mind with a greater or lesser degree of clarity and definiteness.[44] The major factor is still that the Idea of the Church itself, with the whole power of its objectivity,

44. Planck, *Geschichte der Gesellschafts-Verfassung*, IV/1, 109 f.; IV/2, 618.

pressed toward the goal Gregory aspired to reach. But if merely subjective intentions, plans, interests, and aspirations are put in place of this objective power, how can it be otherwise than that where everything becomes so subjective it is only the subjectivity of the pragmatizing historian that in the final analysis is reflected in the participants? How this or that Pope really acted is not to be known, but only how he intended to act—or rather how the historian would have thought and acted had he been in the same place. What is more natural than that we should find satisfaction in this objectivizing of our own subjectivity, or that we should submerge ourselves with all the greater interest in the designs, plans, and systems of the participants the more we set forth in them to our own satisfaction the products of our own spirit?

This pragmatism has now gone so far that where previously there was a shrinking back in terror and horror from the calamitous schemes and the diabolical policy of the Antichrist, now only the most artificial plans of operation, systems of the finest political sagacity, and masterpieces of diplomatic skill are to be marveled at; it is not by accident that the historian becomes the eulogist and apologist of the Popes. Since everything in the final analysis comes down to a concern for reason, it is always the Popes alone who stand at the pinnacle of their times, surveying everything with their superior mentality, ruling everything, and knowing how to obtain advantage from everything. Planck is happy that he can acquit his Pope, Urban II, of the madness of the First Crusade, of the design of an undertaking whose enormous size could conceal its enormous absurdity only from that age. This whim first matured in the head of a monk, and the Pope participated in the general fraud only in so far as he could utilize it for his own interest. Since we may assume with certainty that he immediately thought of the possible advantages that he might be able to obtain for himself, or for the pontificate and for the church, he already had calculated several advantages that the general upheaval occasioned by the senselessness of the Crusades could bring him for the controversy over investiture.[45]

Such is the innermost soul of the pragmatic view of history—this concern with reason and its speculation as to profit and advantage. From this point of view, the same holds with respect to the supreme director of all history, divine Providence. In all the major changes that have taken place in our theology since the Reformation, and in the effect they had on the whole, in the arrangement of all the occurrences in which those changes

45. *Ibid.*, II/1, 231 f.

appeared, and in the choice of tools used by Providence to this end, the pragmatist always sees only the means to an end, which is to be missed even the less because it runs through eighteen centuries. Beginning with the first century, when Providence thrust Christianity into the world to become an eternal pursuit for the mind and heart of man, it is disclosed from time to time that the dissemination of a brighter and purer—or only a more generally effective and fruitful—knowledge of its teaching is one of the major purposes of all events in the history of mankind. But Providence can achieve such purposes only if the condition of the world provides the right time and the favorable moment.[46] Therefore, Providence also depends on the favor of the moment, and it must first scrutinize everything to see what it can obtain in its own interest from the circumstances of the time!

Since this is the highest and most universal view to which such pragmatism can be elevated, one can easily understand why it needs repeated encouragement if it is not to become doubtful about the continued existence of Christianity and the Christian church. The latter is, for the pragmatic view, an institution established by Deity by means of the introduction of Jesus' teachings into the world; despite everything men have made of it, it has remained inexpressibly beneficial for mankind as an institution for education, salvation, preservation, and security; but even so only an institution formed and deformed by men, in regard to which one can only hope and wish that, since it has thus far sufficiently proved itself, it will not perish in the nineteenth century.[47]

4. *Henke*

Although the narrow range of these subjective views and interests seems already too much protracted, to the same group of pragmatic historians must be added yet another name, that of H. P. K. Henke.[43] Or

46. Planck, *Geschichte der protestantischen Theologie von der Concordienformel an*, Preface, iv f.

47. Cf. the conclusion to the last volume of the *Geschichte der Gesellschafts-Verfassung*, and the Preface to the same.

48. *Allgemeine Geschichte der christlichen Kirche nach der Zeitfolge 1788–1804* (4th ed.; 6 vols.; Brunswick, 1804–1806).

[ED.] Heinrich Philipp Konrad Henke (1752–1809) was educated at the University of Helmstädt, where in 1777 he became professor of philosophy, lecturing in classics, history of literature and philosophy, logic, and aesthetics. In 1780 he became professor of theology, having been led in that direction by his humanistic, philological, and philosophical studies. In addition to his church history, he wrote a work of

should he any longer be strictly reckoned among them? At any rate, he also demands of history that it be pragmatic, and if he differs from Spittler and Planck in his stricter and more exact composure, the stamp of his subjectivity has been equally impressed on church history.

His Pragmatism

As we move from Planck to Henke, from the uncertain realm of intentions, plans, hypotheses, combinations, and unhurried argument to the firmer ground of facts and a compact presentation, we cannot but be favorably impressed. Henke's pragmatism consists chiefly in the art of joining individual events into a chain of occurrences, connecting one event to another in an unbroken series. For this purpose Henke, rejecting the so-called topical method, keeps as closely as possible to the purely chronological order, summarizing the traits that characterize a person or an age, and endeavoring to base historical judgment on the precise evaluation of details no less than on circumspect attention to the condition of the time. Much though Henke is concerned with the factual aspect of history, he by no means merely relates facts. His church history is rich in general views and reflections, which are abstracted from the course of events themselves and from a broader continuity that is often maintained by a nearly invisible thread. Such reflections serve as guidelines for a more adequate and many-sided evaluation of events, and for a comprehensive orientation and practical instruction either preceding the historical presentation or interwoven with it.

His Rationalistic Tendency

It cannot be denied that this pragmatism has a greater authenticity, corresponding to the objectivity of history. But the historian's subjectivity is expressed all the more in the consistency with which Henke made a rationalistic way of thinking the foundation of his view of history. The same rationalistic tendency can generally be recognized clearly enough in Spittler and Planck; but these two historians, for whatever reason, left miracles, which had been banned everywhere else, undisputed on the soil of primitive Christianity at least. But Henke had no scruples

---

dogmatics, *Lineamenta institutionum fidei Christianae historico-criticarum* (Helmstädt, 1793), in which he tried to show that the entire later development of doctrine was a perversion of the primitive Christian faith.

about asserting his point of view here too, and claimed for a purely historical comprehension even the beginning of the history of the Christian church. He reduced the Gospel stories of the birth and miracles of Jesus to the value of mere legends, and even spoke of the resurrection and ascension in such a way that we can clearly see his basic rationalistic view. Even though he ascribed a very high dignity to the person of Jesus, he nevertheless depicted the tendency of his teaching and activity as purely moral. The generally intelligible and universally applicable rational religion and ethics of the Old Testament was to be disseminated among all peoples, and the whole of humanity was to be united into a single moral state. According to this view, Henke could only regard the rational and the moral as the true kernel and center of the history of the Christian church; and therefore the chief task, for him, was to place before the eye in cautionary examples the manifold harm caused at all times by blind devotion to human authority, by sluggish, untested repetition and irrational imposition of sacred and traditional precepts and usages, by partisanship, sectarianism, moral pressure, and well-intentioned but unwise zeal, by spiritual pride and overhasty enlightenment, and by separatism and fanaticism of every sort.[49]

In the history of each century, Christianity and the Christian church appear almost totally unlike what their original design and the more accurate representations of their purpose and value intended them to be. Church history appears as hardly more than a long series of depictions of sad aberrations of the human mind, of clumsy, ridiculous, bitter, and bloody quarrels, of low deceits and knavish tricks, of hypocritical schemes and cruel acts of violence. All this refers, of course, only to the manifold deformities and masks that have been foisted upon Christianity. However, from a very early date—i.e., since the fourth century—cultic forms have mixed with it, forms previously to be found in the nations through which Christianity spread. Under the name of the Catholic Church, this new cultus assumed an exclusive validity. Christianity was further and further removed from its archetype by rulers who furthered the new cultus in every way, the more easily to dominate uneducated and credulous peoples, and by the priests who as its guardians organized their own body politic and transformed Christianity into a ponderous mass of irrevocably valid dogmas. The Reformation, in regard to which Henke quite correctly emphasizes the elements that occasioned a general revolution in world view, brought about an incurable rift and also a great,

49. Henke, *Allgemeine Geschichte der christlichen Kirche*, I, 6.

continuing struggle—the natural consequence of such dissimilar forms of religious thinking. Since the beginning of the eighteenth century, however, Henke sees, at least in the Protestant Church, everything developing more and more in such a way that only gentleness and tolerance, simplification of the articles of faith and recognition of a general moral religion, can ensue as the enduring fruit of the efforts already made by the Arminians, Syncretists, Unionists, Pietists, and Indifferentists.[50]

Henke's fundamental standpoint is that of a rationalism whose rigorous moral tendency brusquely opposes everything not of a rational and moral nature. The many judgments—sharp and cutting, even upon first impression—that Henke brings to bear on prominent personalities in history show how negatively he regards everything that does not square with his rationalism or that indeed is in direct opposition to it. Tertullian, for him, is a licentious thinker with wild, quasi-hostile ideas, whose boastfulness was a needed cover for his weakness; Athanasius is a proud and stubborn person; Augustine, an ingenious dialectical prattler; Gregory I, a base flatterer, who learned from the Devil to disguise himself as an angel of light, but with the difference that whereas the Devil fell through blatant pride, he elevated himself through a pretense of humility; and to top it off, Gregory VII, a bold daredevil, but nevertheless a man of the world of the most refined cleverness, a hero of the most determined and steadfast courage, wily and cunning, with all the pretensions of a noble pride, a self-conceited saint idolized by his successors, but a man without religion, without loyalty and faith, who made holy Satan his intimate friend, a hero in crime, though his crimes were largely virtues for his age and position.[51]

Few modern church historians are so little able to find their way into other ages and personalities as Henke. He is especially deficient in any predilection or concern for the history of the development of dogma, which in general is the weak side of his church history. How little in this connection can he be compared even with a Mosheim! It can easily be seen that Henke's presentation becomes much more attractive, internally coherent, and objective following the period of the Reformation, and that he moves in an element more congenial to his own personality as he approaches the more recent period. The sharper the antithesis between Catholic and Protestant, and the more un-Protestant tendencies come to the fore in the Protestant Church itself, the more Henke's way of considering things finds a justification.

50. Ibid., V/1, 1 f.   51. Ibid., I, 140 f., 267, 317, 425; II, 138 f.

Transition

When we look only at the consistency with which the guiding view is maintained, at the art of the presentation, at the circumspect mastery of the abundant materials, at the attention to detail, Henke's church history is one of the pre-eminent works in church-historical literature. But what can be the condition of church historiography when the choice is between a pragmatist like Planck, who injects his own subjective thoughts and his own political understanding into history, and a historian like Henke, who permits the wanton scorn of a rationalist to be heaped upon it? Is there not once again a dualism incapable of arriving at an objective historical development, when on the one hand there stands the historian with his harsh and exclusive subjectivity, receptive to nothing in which he does not recognize his own ego, and when on the other hand there lies before him a vast region in which, as he supposes, the powers of irrationality and immorality are dominant? How can history come into its own when its scope is limited to as narrow a space as possible? If, therefore, historiography is not to remain trapped in this antithesis, there must also be a view of history in which its objective reality is freely related to the subjectivity of the historian. The objective content of history indeed confronts the historian as distinct from himself, but it is not so foreign and external to him that he is not in a position to understand it on its own terms and from its own movement.

VI

THE QUEST FOR AN OBJECTIVE VIEW OF HISTORY
THE MOST RECENT CHURCH HISTORIANS:
MARHEINECKE, NEANDER, GIESELER, HASE

When the whole conception of history has been placed at the furthest extreme of the historian's subjectivity, as in the church-historical works just discussed, it is in the nature of things that a reversal must necessarily ensue. Generally speaking, the period to which we now turn saw a decisive turning point in the consciousness of the times. The age in which Planck and Henke were still the great authorities in church-historical literature—the first decade of the nineteenth century—was the period of transition from the subjectivity of Kantian-Fichtean idealism to the objectivity of Schelling's philosophies of nature and of identity. Church history, like the historical field in general, could not remain untouched by the influence of the latter on the general view of the age.

1. *Marheinecke*

In the more recent literature of church history, the most notable monument to that influence is the church-historical compendium of Marheinecke.[1] It emerged from the endeavor to provide a counterweight

---

1. *Universalkirchenhistorie des Christenthums. Grundzüge zu akademischen Vorlesungen* (Pt. I, Erlangen, 1806).

[ED.] Philipp Konrad Marheinecke was born at Hildesheim in 1780 and died at Berlin in 1846. He was educated at Göttingen and taught at Erlangen and Heidelberg before being called to Berlin as professor of theology in 1811. His early writings were devoted primarily to church history. Following his earliest work, the *Universalkirchenhistorie*, he published a study of medieval church government and law (1807) and a *Geschichte der deutschen Reformation* (2 vols.; Berlin, 1817). He was also the first to undertake a scientific study of symbolics, publishing three works on this subject. His early orientation in the philosophy of Schelling was

to the then still thoroughly dominant subjective tendency by means of a more objective form of understanding based on the new philosophical intuition of the age. Marheinecke already indicates a standpoint essentially different from what had been customary when he says, of those of his contemporaries who are accustomed to find only themselves and their opinions everywhere, that he has sought to speak out of the spirit of the age through which history has passed, and has not made a norm and criterion of his own age—which, like every other, imagining itself alone to be wise, is only a part of an infinite whole.[2]

Marheinecke has clarified his position more specifically in the essay on church history with which he opens his compendium. His standpoint, in a single word, is the Idea—the Idea of religion. Just as the Idea of world history generally cannot be understood without religion, and just as all the necessities, entanglements, and fortunes of the encompassing drama can be satisfactorily resolved only through religion, world history and especially church history must remain forever enigmatic when not regarded from the standpoint of what is beyond sensation, for there everything stands more or less closely related to the Holy itself. Still, only the conditioned is to be found within its sphere; but even pragmatism is not sufficient to understand the conditioned in its relation to anything else, for pragmatism and its law of causality are still bound up in the occurrences themselves. But there speaks and calls to us out of history, loud and clear, a high and holy Spirit, which guides the universe with the reins

-----

modified by the influence of Hegel, which became dominant after his move to Berlin in 1811. In his earliest works in dogmatics, his *Christliche Dogmatik* (Berlin, 1819) and his *Lehrbuch des christlichen Glaubens und Lebens* (Berlin, 1823), he sought to develop dogmatics as a speculative science and to argue that religion develops through three stages, of which Christianity, as the religion of revelation, is the highest. The basal mystery of all religions, even of nature itself, is the Trinity. After the cleavage in the Hegelian school, Marheinecke belonged to the right wing; in 1842 he published *Vorlesungen über die Bedeutung der hegelschen Philosophie in der christlichen Theologie* (Berlin). His dogmatics reached its fullest development in his *System der theologischen Moral* and his *System der christlichen Dogmatik* (both published posthumously in Berlin in 1847). In the latter work, he replied to Strauss's *Das Leben Jesu*, arguing that the historical Christ was the central figure in the history of the world. He also became an opponent of Schelling's later philosophy; cf. his *Zur Kritik der schellingschen Offenbarungsphilosophie* (Berlin, 1843). Baur discusses Marheinecke's theological position in his *Kirchengeschichte des neunzehnten Jahrhunderts*, ed. Eduard Zeller (Tübingen, 1862), and in his *Vorlesungen über die christliche Dogmengeschichte*, III, ed. F. F. Baur (Leipzig, 1867).

2. Marheinecke, *Universalkirchenhistorie*, Preface.

of eternal necessity behind the curtain of appearances, independent of the world and events, and which weighs right and justice and moves everything toward a single goal—God's eternal plan for the world, clearly reflected in history as in a mirror. Religion is the undertone in the soul of historiography. The highest aspiration of the observer should be to put himself in tune with it, for only in it does the sacred epic find its disclosure, order, clarity, and unity, by means of which alone the highest life and interest are introduced into history.[3]

The vision of the historian, therefore, is now indeed directed toward the Idea, toward a universal, a higher unity, to which the individual is subordinated. But the extent to which the Idea of religion is for church history a vague and abstract generality immediately strikes the eye. Its content is, to be sure, as above all in the life of Jesus, "the original construction of religion and morality," regarded as the representation of the Idea of religion; and the attempt is made, for the purposes of arranging the material and for the explanation and judgment of various phenomena, to derive guidance from it. But no vital movement of the Idea is attained when it only soars above the sphere of phenomena with which it ought to be connected, not entering into an inner, immanent relation with those phenomena; and there thus remains an unfilled void between it and the life of history whose moving principle it ought to be. Marheinecke's presentation moves in an abstract, external formalism, whose rigid stance and philosophical-sounding terminology no doubt contrast greatly with the relaxed popularity of the pragmatist. The deeper, more objective understanding intended by him is most lacking precisely where we ought most to expect it, namely in the history of the development of dogma, where Marheinecke also permits far too many of the customary external causes and motives to predominate.

Marheinecke called his compendium a "universal history"; Stäudlin, in his textbook, *Universalgeschichte der christlichen Kirche*,[4] which appeared at exactly the same time, and had a similar title, also declared that

3. *Ibid.*, 13 f.
4. [ED.] Hanover, 1806. Karl Friedrich Stäudlin (1761–1826) studied philosophy and theology at Tübingen and was professor of theology at Göttingen from 1790 to 1826. He published several works in philosophy and ethics as well as in church history. In the latter field, in addition to the work mentioned above, he wrote *Geschichte der theologischen Wissenschaften* (2 vols.; Göttingen, 1810–11); *Geschichte des Rationalismus und Supranaturalismus* (Göttingen, 1826); and *Geschichte und Litteratur der Kirchengeschichte* (Hanover, 1827). In regard to the latter, see above, 50.

church history must henceforth have universal history chiefly in view. But so long as its universality consists merely in the attempt to show that the Christian religion and church are revealed not in a single ecclesiastical society of any sort, but only in all such societies simultaneously, in its full power, scope, glory, and versatility,[5] then that universality is an empty abstraction, of which nothing can be made in church history, and which, instead of entering into the depths of historical life, only produces a leveling of its content.

2. *The Most Recent Epoch*

Important though it was that attention had now been directed to the universal, to the Idea that should permeate and control the content, nevertheless everything still depended above all on the necessity for becoming immersed in the content so that the still unattained universal would not be merely an abstract concept but would also acquire the concreteness by which it first becomes a true universal—in the unity of the particular with the universal. Every new and specific view of history can only rest on a new, deeper, and more substantial investigation of the sources, by which historical life discloses itself to us in its inner richness and in the vividness of its outer manifestation. The most recent epoch of church historiography is therefore rightly dated from the two church historians whose chief merit is not only to be acquainted far more precisely and fundamentally with the sources of church history, but also to have a completely new conception of the task of source study itself—its importance, its extent, and everything that belongs to a more faithful and authentically historical utilization of the sources. We have in mind here, of course, none other than Neander and Gieseler. And concerning these two famous church historians we need only trace the path taken by Neander in his church-historical writings in order to see immediately the means by which this view of history, which we must regard as new and essentially different from previous views, is substantiated.

5. Cf. Stäudlin, *Geschichte und Litteratur der Kirchengeschichte*, 181 f.

3. Neander [6]

THE MONOGRAPH AND HIS LOVE FOR THE INDIVIDUAL

6. [ED.] Johann August Wilhelm Neander (1789–1850) was of Jewish descent, bearing the name of David Mendel before his conversion to Christianity; through his mother he was related to the philosopher Mendelssohn. In the Gymnasium at Hamburg, which he later regarded as his home, he became especially interested in the study of Plato, which prepared him for his acceptance of Christianity. But the work that had the strongest influence on him was Schleiermacher's *Reden über die Religion*. On February 15, 1806, he was baptized under the name of Neander (New-man). Until that time, he had been intending to study law; instead, he went to the University of Halle, where he fell under the influence of Schleiermacher. Because of the war against Napoleon, he was compelled to transfer to Göttingen, where Gottlieb Jakob Planck was then teaching. Planck helped to arouse his interest in church history, a profession to which in 1807 he bound himself by a vow. In his continued studies at Göttingen, he became acquainted with the thought of Schelling and Fichte. He began teaching in 1812 at Heidelberg, and in 1813 was called to Berlin, where he lectured as a colleague of Schleiermacher, Marheinecke, and Wilhelm de Wette, in church history and New Testament exegesis, and where he remained until the end of his life. As an adherent of the Mediating School, he strongly opposed both the confessionalism of the Lutheran church party and the speculative theology of the Hegelians. His romantic theory of history is made clear in the following discussion by Baur—a discussion of considerable value for understanding by contrast the latter's position as well. See also below, 289–91.

Baur describes Neander's early monographs, published during the period between 1812 and 1826, which were intended as preparation for his major work, *Allgemeine Geschichte der christlichen Religion und Kirche* (6 vols, in 11 pts.; Hamburg, 1825–52). For more complete bibliographical data on this work, see below, n. 11. An English translation of the revised edition by J. Torrey was published under the title, *General History of the Christian Religion and Church* (5 vols.; Boston, 1871–72). Neander's other works include: (1) *Denkwürdigkeiten aus der Geschichte des Christenthums und des christlichen Lebens* (Berlin, 1822–24). (2) *Die Geschichte der Pflanzung und Leitung der christlichen Kirche durch die Apostel* (Berlin, 1832). Baur discusses this work at several places in his *Paulus, der Apostel Jesu Christi: Sein Leben und Werken, seine Briefe und seine Lehre*, 2nd ed., ed. Eduard Zeller (2 vols.; Leipzig, 1866). An English translation by J.E. Ryland was published under the title, *History of the Planting and Training of the Christian Church by the Apostles*, together with *Antignostikus, or the Spirit of Tertullian, and an Introduction to His Writings*, trans. from the 2nd German ed., Berlin, 1849 (2 vols.; London, 1887–88). (3) *Das Leben Jesu Christi in seinem geschichtlichen Zusammenhang* (Berlin, 1837). This work, written in response to Strauss, was translated into English from the fourth German edition as *The Life of Jesus Christ in Its Historical Connection and Historical Development* (New York, 1848). (4) His lectures in systematic theology and ethics were published posthumously as *Dogmengeschichte* (Berlin, 1857), *Katholizismus und Protestismus* (Berlin, 1863), and *Geschichte der christlichen Ethik* (Berlin, 1864).

Neander is the originator of the church-historical monograph.[7] All the writings that precede his great work [8] are monographic in character. The significance of the monograph for him can already be seen in the selection and sequence of subjects with which he occupied himself. First he sketched a historical portrait, *Über den Kaiser Julian und sein Zeitalter* (Hamburg, 1812); [9] next he portrayed *Der heilige Bernhard und sein Zeitalter* (Berlin, 1813); [10] then he set forth *Die genetische Entwickelung der vornehmsten gnostischen Systeme* (Berlin, 1818), and, further still, depicted *Der heilige Johann Chrysostomus und die Kirche besonders des Orients in dessen Zeitalter* (Berlin, 1821), and *Antignostikus, Geist des Tertullianus und Einleitung in dessen Schriften* (Berlin, 1825).[11]

In the last-mentioned work he explained himself more precisely, as follows:

7. He was stimulated by the monographic source studies of Planck. Cf. G. C. F. Lücke, *Dr. G. J. Planck: Ein biographischer Versuch* (Göttingen, 1835), 69.

8. [ED.] The *Allgemeine Geschichte der christlichen Religion und Kirche*.

9. [ED.] On Julian, see below, 226–28.

10. In the Preface to the second edition (1848) of this work (page 11), Neander pictures very exquisitely and attractively the happy period of his first literary activity: "The first edition of this monograph was distributed to the German public in the time of the dawn of our liberated, rejuvenated Fatherland, which was also the time of the beginning of a new life in the church. . . . It is the time to which all those who have lived through it will look back, not without a deep melancholy, from the many profane, un-German activities of the present. That was a favorable moment for such a monograph. A new life of faith was awakened, and had begun also to inspire science anew. One was thereby forced to investigate the stream of Christian life in previous centuries, to embrace everything Christian with love. A shallow, spiritless, and heartless Enlightenment, whose motto was, 'How gloriously far we have come!', which in the darkness of a sprawling poverty despised the greatest and most glorious aspects of previous centuries, was doomed by this life and this science. . . . After an unhistorical period there followed a new feeling for history, a new desire to deepen oneself in history, a new endeavor to comprehend fundamentally and deeply the individual character of historical manifestations."

11. In the same year, 1825, the first volume of the *Allgemeine Geschichte der christlichen Religion und Kirche* appeared as three part-volumes, covering the first three centuries. A second edition of Vol. I was published in two part-volumes, 1842–43. The second edition of Vol. II (312 to 590) was published in two part-volumes, 1846. Subsequent volumes appeared only in original editions. Vol. III (590 to 814) was published in 1834; Vol. IV (814 to 1073), in 1836. Vol. V, published in two part-volumes, 1845, continued to the end of the flowering of the Middle Ages, up to Boniface VIII (1073 to 1294). A sixth volume, the most recent (1852), contains church history from Boniface VIII to the Council of Basel (1294 to 1431), though only fragmentarily, edited by K. F. T. Schneider from Neander's manuscripts.

[ED.] I have freely expanded and modified this footnote to complete the bibliographical information only partially provided by Baur.

It appears that a fruitful history of theological development can proceed only from an exact characterization of individual tendencies, religious, theological, and spiritual, in the various periods, in their influence on dogmatics, morals, hermeneutics, and exegesis. And in this regard, it is especially important to portray the representatives of these individual tendencies of Spirit for every age. In those representatives we recognize at the same time the essential and characteristic tendencies of human nature, which again and again appear in the church under a changed form. It is possible for all these tendencies to find their place in the many-sidedness of Christianity, which is meant to apply to the whole of human nature; in its own way, it is appropriately permeated and elucidated by them. But any one of these tendencies could impair the essence of Christianity by onesidedness and therefore by narrow-mindedness, by a selfish exclusion and rejection of every other tendency, any one of which could also be purely human and capable of being formed into a Christian tendency. Therefore, the course of human nature's development in Christianity, guided by a wisdom other than human, is revealed in such fashion that one tendency in the church must always serve as a counterweight to another. If only the so often clumsy human hand, which never will be able to guide the free development of Spirit, had not intervened forcefully and awkwardly in the advancement of the antitheses, and had not set delimiting death in place of the development of life proceeding from within! To God what is God's! What would have become of the development of Christian doctrine and theology in the first centuries if there had been nothing but Tertullians and Origens! The voice of the whole of church history warns us above all how great minds would like to compress things into a single dogmatic form and restrict the freedom and multiplicity of the spiritual development of life.[12]

This passage expresses so clearly and definitely the peculiar character of Neander's historiography that it justly deserves to be brought to attention here. If the necessity of that period was to treat church history with a new spirit and to build it on a new foundation, this could happen only through monographs such as Neander's in which an especially prominent personality, or a smaller circle of connected phenomena such as the Gnostic systems, was given a special presentation and set into as bright a light as possible. These monographs, therefore, have the value of the most fundamental and specialized source research. To the particular, however, something universal is added. Since such individuals are considered not merely in relation to the age in which they belong, but also in their

12. Neander, *Antignostikus*, Preface, iv f. [ED. The Preface to the first edition is not included in the English translation.]

difference from other no less prominent men, equally representative of an age, there is presented in his monographs not merely a historical portrait of the time but also a picture of a definite tendency in human nature. Thus one personality stands next to another, and the more a general type of human nature is expressed in such an individual, the greater is the justification for his individual self-existence. If we think of a series of such individuals, they appear as focal points and upholders of the whole of history; it is transformed, so to speak, into a gallery of free individualities with equal rights.

The most characteristic trait of Neander's historiography is here revealed as a preference for the individual aspects of history, a joy in everything that allows us to look deeper within its spiritual organism, a pleasure and affection with which it traces now this and now that personality not merely in monographic presentations but also on the broad stage of general church history—especially in the area of missions and in the history of the moral phenomena of life—in order to observe and depict more precisely the effects of those individuals' religious zeal for the Kingdom of God, or their religious feelings and speculative reflections, their aberrations and wrong turnings, and their inner struggles together with the final victory of their better selves. The claim of individuality upon history is asserted here to its greatest extent. Since in its substantial content history consists of individuals, they must also have the right to appear in history as they are individually, and to stand each in his due place. But this is not simply the formal and abstract right of individual self-existence, as Semler asserted without asking further what the claim of individuality in itself comprises, and reserving the right to deal curtly with anyone who was not constituted as Semler's conception of a moral private religion required. Rather, he to whom Neander once accorded the right of individuality was also to have it completely; and Neander therefore regarded it as his first duty to transpose himself with self-effacing fidelity into the full circle of that individual life, in order to understand it in itself, in its peculiar nature and circumstances.

The greatest excellence of Neander's historiography is the capacity that is his in such high degree—of stepping out of his own person, and of transposing himself into the particularity of the most diverse times and persons, instead of viewing everything as a deceiving reflection of his own subjectivity. From the standpoint of the pragmatic historian, historical persons and phenomena are still so intertwined with the subjectivity of the historian that they can be freed of it only in so far as it pleases the historian to let them go, or only in so far as he may happen to agree with them; but now they are for the first time truly free. With all the claims of their individuality, they confront the historian, who rejoices in their freedom. And since in this connection it must be acknowledged as a general principle for the whole field of history that every age and every individual belonging to a particular age has its own form of consciousness, with which we must above all familiarize ourselves if we wish to understand such individuals correctly, history thereby obtains for the first time that objectivity which according to its very conception it must have.

But if the claim of individuality is of such importance then it must presuppose something else on which to rest. What could be the power of attraction even of a Julian for such a historian of the Christian church as Neander? The interest he had in precisely such a personality could only rest on the assumption that Julian's enthusiasm for the old [pagan] religion, which indeed made him an apostate and opponent of Christianity, itself had a religious basis and origin. But this assumption was not possible without returning to the general view that religion on the whole is a matter of feeling, in the final analysis something merely subjective, from which it follows that all religious manifestations can be judged only according to the immediacy of the religious consciousness from which they proceed. Schleiermacher's view of the nature of religion is also the basic principle of Neander's historiography, and in the historical area the significance of this view is as great as it is epoch-making in the area of dogmatics. The claim of individuality is first preserved when religion itself takes that claim into its custody, when religion itself declares that it has its innermost seat and home in the immediacy of consciousness, where the subject possesses only himself. Only on this view is it possible for the historian to recognize something in the strangest and most repulsive phenomena of history, and to preserve that which joins him to it; he must ward off whatever would let history fall into dualistic antitheses. Rather, he can perceive in history only a beautiful multiplicity of freely working powers, which, despite the diversity of their tendencies, do not become so completely separated from one another that they do not still have a common bond of unity.

Here we reach a point where the important question arises as to whether Neander's view of history does not afford too much freedom to the individual. Even if every dualistic consideration of history is excluded, and if on the broad stage of history the freest space is provided for the free movement of individuals, history nevertheless cannot be

merely a variegated play of freely working powers, to the degree that it is
not itself subordinated to an overriding unity. Neander considers it a
divine ordinance that one tendency should serve as a counterweight to
the other; and everything that interferes restrictively in the freedom and
multiplicity of a life's spiritual development appears to him as human
arbitrariness. But what, here, is divine ordinance? What is human arbitrariness? Once every individual has the claim to his individuality, then it
also belongs to the diversity of individuals that the spiritual powers with
which each is endowed differ greatly. Therefore, if there are higher as
well as lower powers, why should it be against the divine ordinance that
the lower are subordinated to the higher, and that superior individuals
over long periods of time wield determinatively and commandingly the
spiritual power bestowed upon them?

To this it is to be added that individuals themselves are under the
influence of their age, and the greater their significance, the more they
are to be seen as representatives of that age. Hence, the various spiritual
tendencies of individuals are to be seen rather as tendencies of various
ages. If it is required by the divine ordinance guiding the development of
human nature that one tendency should serve as a counterbalance to
another, why should not the counterbalance be established in a higher
connection, as a relation in which the tendencies of longer temporal
periods stand to one another? It is therefore not possible in general simply
to leave off with the freedom and variety of individual spiritual tendencies. Of themselves, the individual and the particular press toward the
universal. We must therefore ask whether a view of history that affords
such claims to individuality as Neander's is able to the same extent to
establish the unity of the particular and universal. On the response to this
question depends the answer to another—whether history, despite all the
variety of its spiritual tendencies, is something other than a mere aggregate, a variegated play of powers in which there is no unity and therefore
no single moving principle determining the course of development.

His View of Christianity

This brings us to Neander's view of the nature of Christianity. In order
to provide a clear representation of the course of its historical development, it is above all necessary to know what Christianity in general is.
Neander expressly elucidated his view of Christianity, as earlier he had
not even thought it necessary to do, at the very beginning of the second

edition of his church history, as follows: "Now Christianity we regard not as a power that has sprung up out of the hidden depths of man's nature, but as one which descended from above, because heaven opened itself for the rescue of fallen humanity; a power which, as it is exalted above all that human nature can create out of its own resources, must impart to that nature a new life, and change it from its inmost center." [13] How this is to be understood can be sufficiently seen from the two writings that served to complement Neander's church history, his *Das Leben Jesu Christi in seinem geschichtlichen Zusammenhang* and *Die Geschichte der Pflanzung und Leitung der christlichen Kirche durch die Apostel*. In a single word, Neander adheres to a strictly supernaturalistic conception of the origin and nature of Christianity. If Christianity is an absolutely supernatural miracle, shattering the continuity of history, then history has nothing further to do with it, it can only stand before the miracle and see in it the end of its research and understanding. As miracle, the origin of Christianity is an absolutely incomprehensible beginning.

The question, however, is simply whether the goal thus set for historical research is not an arbitrary one. If all the attempts made with such great effort in more recent times to illuminate critically the origin of Christianity could have no other result than the firmer establishment of a supernaturalistic view such as Neander's, we must in fact despair of any possible progress in church historiography. Yet the uncritical procedure of Neander in the area of New Testament criticism and in all church-historical questions connected with it, and the obvious endeavor to make belief in miracles acceptable and convincing with reasons that could serve only for apologetic interests, lie too clearly before the eye to admit of any doubt, at least for those in a condition to test the matter themselves. Once miracle is given free rein in the history of primitive Christianity, where are its limits to be set? Neander himself permits the belief in miracles, which in his view is well justified, to continue into the third century. Yet after the middle of that century the effects of the power of Christianity would seem to be just as truly and actually miraculous as the miracles of apostolic times. What is there to prevent us from allowing such miraculous effects to proceed further, indeed through the whole of church history? How can it be otherwise imagined than that, if Christianity is so supernatural in its principle and essence, it worked in the same

---

13. [ED.] Neander, *Geschichte der christlichen Religion und Kirche*, I/1 (2nd ed.), 2 (translation adapted from *General History of the Christian Religion and Church*, I, 1). This passage is not found in the first edition of the volume.

way subsequently as well? Neander himself surely intends to be able to limit this supernaturalism when he assumes that the supernatural, immediate, and creative elements predominated only in the first part of the process of development of the church; whereas in the second, the same divine principle shows itself to be effective in the form of natural continuity. But when he himself immediately joins to this the remark that we are neither justified in drawing, nor in a condition to draw, such sharply defined boundaries between the supernatural and the natural in the effects proceeding from the power of Christianity—a power which human nature at one time appropriated—he only surrenders to confusion in representing the natural and the supernatural as permeating each other in such a fashion. How can the same principle work first supernaturally, then naturally? And how meaningless it is to talk, nevertheless, of a process of development! [14]

This view is as dualistic as it is supernaturalistic. If Christianity is so different in principle from human nature that its origin cannot even be explained from the depths of human nature, then Christianity and human nature are two essentially different principles, opposites, which as such are related only externally. They work on each other externally, jostle each other, affect each other this way or that, but can never become internally one with each other. Very significant in this connection is the metaphor, used by Neander at the very beginning and so often later, comparing Christianity with leaven, which, when cast into the dough of humanity, raises it gradually. This is precisely the duality of two principles which indeed are correlative but which merely affect each other, in part progressively and in part retrogressively. Since human nature functions not only receptively and passively, but also spontaneously and responsively, and since it always represents Christianity only as one way or another modified in itself, this constantly indefinable concurrence of the two factors indeed produces an infinite variety of phenomena; but a unity of the whole and a principle of progressive development is here nowhere to be seen.

The Christian church indeed is always taking a new form, but the change of scene is only in external circumstances. There are new localities, new peoples and states, new individuals; but since in all these individuals human nature remains always the same, we always have the same relationship before us: Christianity as the yeast and humanity as the dough more or less leavened by it. Thus the situation really is as Neander

14. Neander, *Geschichte der christlichen Religion und Kirche*, I/1 (2nd ed.), 122.

clearly and simply expressed it in the opening sentence of the first edition of his church history: "On the whole, human nature, which remains unchanged in its essence, is always related to Christianity in the same way. Its fundamental tendencies are essentially the same in evil as in good, even though at the same time there are various forms, corresponding to the diversity in ages, in which it shows itself effectively." Here again, the age makes all the difference! If only these two factors, Christianity and human nature, encounter each other at precisely the right time, they can readily come to an understanding. But who gives an age its specific character? Is it not clear that as long as this mystery has not been solved, the situation of Christianity and humanity in the world cannot be understood at all?

The Principle of Movement, the Categories of Historical Reflection, the Opposition of Tendencies

Here is to be found another characteristic of Neander's kind of historiography. Where the beginning and point of departure are so unclear, a clear and definite conception of the further course cannot be obtained. The unity of a principle is lacking—the principle of movement and progressive development. Neander's church history is without any division into periods. Just as Neander on the whole passes over the general questions that one would otherwise expect to be treated in the Introduction, he also leaves out of account the demand rightly made of a historian: that by means of an intentional determination of the periods of history, which should be not mere points of repose for the outer course of the story but essential moments in the course of the subject matter itself, he should at least explain more precisely how the entire course of history presents itself to him in its unity as a continuing process of development, determined by the inner continuity of its moments.

With Neander this is not an accidental deficiency. He indeed adopts the following periods: (1) the first three centuries; (2) from Constantine the Great to Gregory the Great; (3) from Gregory the Great to the death of Charlemagne; (4) from the death of Charlemagne to Gregory VII; (5) from Gregory VII to Boniface VIII. But the divisions seem to be made according to a very superficial point of view. The undivided rule of Constantine [A.D. 324] or the Council of Nicaea [325] could with good reason be made the terminus of the first period from the subject matter itself; but why Neander should establish as this terminus the religious edict of 311, not even issued by Constantine but by Galerius in connection with Constantine and Licinius, is not explained.[15] The development of the crisis in the Roman Empire at that time was so swift that history finds a resting point for the first time only in the undivided rule of Constantine and Christianity.

Neander prefaced the history of the third period, beginning with Gregory the Great, with introductory remarks in which he says merely that Christianity now made the transition from the old world of Greek and Roman culture to that of a totally rude people, and developed according to their peculiar character. But the extent to which this peculiar character establishes a new period is not shown. Rather, there is only the question of an already existing mixture of Christianity with foreign elements, which can be attributed to the fact that the idea of the Kingdom of God declines from the spiritual and the internal to the sensuous and external, and that in place of the universal, spiritual priesthood a special, external priesthood is established as the necessary intermediate link in the connection with the Kingdom of God. This had as a consequence the transfer of the Old Testament form of theocracy to the church and in general a multiform mixture of Jewish and Christian standpoints; but for those rude peoples this Old Testament form was a healthy point of transition. It could therefore be concluded that this mixture of Christianity with foreign elements and the bringing down of the spiritual into the sensuous, as the pre-condition of the transition into the form of Old Testament theocracy, was not so bad but rather had a very good aspect; but how can this be directly asserted in a church history such as Neander's?

In regard to the general point of view, the fifth period is still more conspicuous in its vacillating unsteadiness and indecision. At least it stands out as such, whereas the fourth period does not. At the beginning of this period Neander recognizes an event of world-historical significance,[16] but immediately shows a biased point of view in the assertion that there

---

15. [ED.] In April 311, the dying Galerius revoked the anti-Christian laws in the East as an admission of failure, not of guilt. The affairs of state were going badly, and he needed the favor of the Christian God as well as of others. This edict brought to an end the Diocletian age and the period of Christian persecutions. With it Eusebius closed the first edition of his church history. (Cf. Hermann Doerries, *Konstantin der Grosse* [Stuttgart, 1958], 25–26.) The precedent may help to explain why Neander adopted this date as the terminus of the first period in church history.

16. [ED.] The claim of Gregory VII (Pope 1073–85) to temporal power.

was a question whether the system of ecclesiastical theocracy, the spiritual universal monarchy, should win or be defeated in the struggle with a rude worldly power. Menaced by complete secularization, the destruction of the church had reached its climax, and for this reason a reformatory reaction was called forth on the part of the church that could only have proceeded from the ecclesiastical, theocratic standpoint. What is incorrect about this view is Neander's designation of that part of the Christian world that forms the opposition to Gregory simply as a rude worldly power. But the latter was also a Christian church, which had its legitimate constitution under the sovereign, and which in moral respects was, without doubt, no worse than the Church of Rome. How can it be asserted that the destruction of the church controlled by Gregory VII reached its climax at a time shortly before which the Roman Church itself had had a reformer from the allegedly secularized church in the person of "Emperor Henry III, who, as all had to admit, was truly inspired by zeal for the good of the church"? [17] How can Neander speak so simply of a destruction of this church when he himself must also acknowledge that the German spirit at that time already recognized the conflict between original Christianity and the law against the marriage of priests; that it knew how to hold to the sayings of Christ and the apostles against papal arbitrariness, and showed itself to be a Germanic spirit in opposing this inhuman ambition? [18] What was called rude worldly power was in fact merely the defect that the church so designated was not yet suppressed by the absolute power of the Papacy. But how can this be made a reproach if the Papacy itself for the first time approached the actualization of its Idea in the period of Gregory VII?

For this very reason, that period in the history of the Papacy cannot be understood as a reaction to the secularization of the church. What made it epoch-making was that the Idea of the church fully actualized itself in the absolute power of the Papacy—since at this time the consequences were now simply to be sharply drawn from premises already in existence. However clearly this is to be seen, it can be correctly understood only if the Idea of the church is traced from the beginning step by step, through its historical development. But if this point of view is not correctly established from the start, at every significant point only greater confusion can be expected.

Neander's judgment of Gregory VII is only half complete. Supposedly

17. Neander, *Geschichte der christlichen Religion und Kirche*, IV, 218.
18. *Ibid.*, V/1, 176.

the Pope is inspired by the idea of an independent church, and of the religious and moral domination of the world by the Papacy, after a pattern totally foreign to Christianity—a blend of the Old Testament with the idea of the political hegemony of Rome. But this idea was not the work of Gregory; rather, it proceeded from the known course of the church's development, and the reforming reaction since Leo IX had given it a new impetus.[19] The previous brief remark about the decline of the spiritual into the sensuous can be understood only upon demonstration of the course of the development of the church to which Neander refers. That course is, however, much too vague and general for anything to be built upon it. We can thus only regard the idea as partly the work of Gregory, partly the consequence of the reaction. But what was its nature? Was it Christian or un-Christian, if intrinsically it was Christian and moral-religious, yet in form was so un-Christian? How is Gregory himself to be judged if he surrendered so completely to a distorted idea that it swallowed up all other human interests, and if all his natural human instincts were obliged to give way? How is he to be judged if he allowed himself to be guided by an idiosyncratic conscience that contradicted true conscience and the divine law? Can we then remain satisfied with the superficial judgment that papal absolutism was Gregory's moral responsibility, and that the harm he caused would have been spared the world had he only been more conscientious, a man who under the best of circumstances would not have acted merely in accord with an erring conscience? If on the other hand Gregory really was as he was said to be, namely the representative of an epoch in the world's history, then it must be demonstrated how there merely emerged in him and came to clear consciousness what had to be realized, in accord with the entire course of the church's history, as a necessary moment of its development at some point or other—realized, moreover, in one who pressed toward its realization, and in whom this general tendency of the age had, as it were, only been individualized. But for all this the vague and oblique concepts of secularization and reaction are not adequate; with Neander they nearly always recur as fixed categories, and frequently replace a more deeply penetrating and objective understanding.

In Neander's church history we find ourselves moving rapidly ahead into new times and circumstances, the more readily we follow its lavish contents. But we do not know what makes that forward movement possible, what is the driving and moving principle of history. Why do events

19. *Ibid.*, V/1, 152 f. [ED. Leo IX was Pope, 1048-54.]

always move forward? Why does history not come to a halt once it has reached the point where, so it seems, a permanent refuge has been found? Neander himself speaks of the destruction of the ancient religions in such a way that we are not sure but that we should mourn their dissolution no less than we rejoice at having reached a new level of religious development. Often, with Neander, we do not know whether to be sad or to rejoice, to blame or to praise, to look backward or forward. In such instances, the categories of secularization and reaction figure prominently. Secularization and reaction already existed in the time of Socrates. As the first great reaction of a one-sided secularization of reason against religious and moral faith emerged, it was his high calling to testify to the reality of that wherein Spirit alone can find its true life in a struggle against those secular tendencies that suppress all higher interests, and against a senseless dialectical arbitrariness.[20] Here secularization itself is the reaction; but in other instances it is precisely secularization that causes the reaction, as in the age of Gregory VII. But if only once there is a reaction, we can be certain that a new reaction will always occur. For example, if the Papacy under Gregory was a reaction, how can we regard anything that is subsequently opposed to the Papacy as otherwise than a reaction? Thus, since one thing will always react against another, reaction becomes a very powerful lever in Neander's church history. So change and movement, if not progress, come into history, which is so often a repetition. In Neander's historiography the same forms, spiritual tendencies, and antitheses appear again and again.

This is especially true of the history of dogma. But if the Papacy itself, as a universal spiritual monarchy, was the recasting of a Christian Idea into an Old Testament form thoroughly foreign to Christianity, then it is also highly important in the history of polity. Here we can see most clearly how Neander's view of history clings to the superficial and the external precisely where it ought to probe into the inner course of development and get at the essence of things. If the Papacy, in the form of Old Testament theocracy, was so thoroughly foreign to Christianity, how was this form able, nevertheless, to impose itself on Christianity to so great an extent and with such overwhelming power? How, indeed, could it have done so in the interest of Christianity itself, if the same Papacy is to be thought of as a reform, a reaction against a secularization that was a total menace to the church? Here what ought to be explained is not explained, and the one thing merely nullifies the other. Hence we can only conclude

20. *Ibid.*, I (2nd ed.), 30.

that the whole conception of the Papacy as a form of Old Testament theocracy fails essentially to explain anything, and is at any rate very superficial. How could Christianity have become so intimately bound up with the Papacy if from the beginning there had not been in it something congenial to the Papacy? The Protestant may look down on Catholicism and declare it an untrue form of Christianity—nevertheless it remains one of the forms of manifestation of Christianity and can be understood only from the essence of Christianity. Therefore, nothing is accomplished either by invoking the category of a repetition of old and antiquated forms, or by assuming a transplantation from the Old Testament onto the soil of Christianity—as Neander all too readily does in other places as well (e.g., with the episcopacy and Montanism). What has been in the past is never repeated in the same form; where we think we see merely a repetition of the old, there is nevertheless always something new, which the old cannot explain.

Various spiritual tendencies with which Neander is frequently concerned serve him further as a lever of historical movement. Neander reaches the summit of historical reflection when he is able to speak of spiritual tendencies and their antitheses—of an idealistic and a realistic tendency, a rationalistic and a supernaturalistic, a conceptual and a mystical, a dialectical and a contemplative. These tendencies and their various combinations—rationalistic-idealistic rigidity, supernaturalistic-mystical effusiveness, etc.—are the permanent categories of Neander's view of history. In the first edition of the church history, idealistic and realistic spiritual tendencies formed the major antithesis; in the second, they were replaced by rationalistic and supernaturalistic tendencies. Two tendencies of the theological spirit are distinguished, of which the one feels itself compelled to recognize and depict the supernatural aspect of Christianity in its antithesis to the natural, and the other, in its continuity with the natural. The goal of the one is to understand the supernatural and suprarational as such; the goal of the other is to understand the supernatural realm in its harmony with reason and nature—i.e., to bring the supernatural and suprarational to consciousness as rational and natural. Hence there is a predominance of either supernaturalistic or rationalistic elements, which must coalesce if the Christian church is to undergo a healthy process of development; but opposite dangers emerge from the predominance of either the one or the other.[21] Thus, the rationalistic spiritual tendency is acknowledged to be justified. But how is this pos-

21. *Ibid.*, II (2nd ed.), 874 f.

sible if Christianity is supernatural and suprarational, as in Neander's definition? No one has the right to declare that what by nature is supernatural is also natural!

This contradiction makes it already quite impossible to enter into Neander's train of thought; but the contradiction becomes even greater when the justified rationalism is placed over against an equally justified supernaturalism. The two equally justified factors of historical development are thus a rationalism and a supernaturalism of which the one vindicates reason with the same right that the other denies it. The essential element of history is therefore this contradiction; the whole of history moves forward in antitheses whose final resolution is absolutely impossible, since each member of the constantly renewed antithesis is justified, and so is the contradiction of the one by the other. This continuing contradiction, this encounter of two tendencies in Christian doctrine, of which the one is the negation of the other, is nevertheless supposed to belong to the healthy process of its development. In fact, the life of history immediately proves to be not healthy but sick. Neither of the two elements can emerge at any point of historical significance without having Neander immediately declare it to be a domination out of which antithetical dangers arise on either side. The whole of history thus consists only of dominating, one-sided elements, of aberrations, of phenomena belonging not to a healthy but to a diseased life, of total contradictions, of antitheses that are justified in themselves but unjustified in any particular case.

Historical consideration as a whole thus becomes entirely dualistic, and we simply return to the dualism Neander put at the summit of his church history, namely the antithesis between Christianity and human nature. Christianity is cut off from reason, yet it can be comprehended by human nature and reason only naturally and rationally. The two can never attain unity, since Christianity can no more surrender its supernatural character than reason can acknowledge a determination of its own limits by Christianity. Thus the whole of history comes to resemble the movement of a ball being sent back and forth between the natural force of human reason and the supernatural force of Christianity. Reason forever seeks to enter into Christianity but is in continual rebound from its suprarational and supernatural aspects. Blow follows upon repeated blow; the one principle reacts against the other; and thus again we have reaction as the main lever of historical movement. Where there is no unity of principle, but only a duality of principles, there can be no immanent development, no progression; history is only a continual oscillation of antitheses as it emerges from the reaction of the one side or the other. And yet one would not think it so difficult to escape from this dualism. Where there are spiritual tendencies, there must also in principle be a unity; and where could this unity be found but in the common religious Spirit of humanity? That Spirit alone is the true, living and concrete mediation between a Christianity that is not absolutely supernatural but natural as well, and a human nature embodied in the multiplicity of individuals.

The Nature of Subjectivity and the Theory of Feeling

When the universal principle is so far removed as it is here from a clear and specific conception, this lack must constitute a detriment at all points where there is a question of establishing the general point of view. It has already been shown many times how frequently Neander lacks a more precise understanding, one emphasizing the characteristic elements, of many important phenomena, notably Ebionitism, Gnosticism, and Montanism, and of the history of the development of dogma generally.[22] The same applies to his treatment of scholastic theology. Neander proceeds far too readily to the individual and the special, without dealing in general considerations or the necessary definition of concepts. The special and individual are far too prevalent and are given too much power over the universal, which ought to establish a stance and a unity for the whole. The predilection for the monograph, which continues to make itself felt, is revealed by a special penetration into the life and work of single, even though prominent, personalities.[23]

22. On such special points as well as the main perspective, cf. my "Kritische Beiträge zur Kirchengeschichte der ersten Jahrhunderte, mit besonderer Rücksicht auf die Werke von Neander und Gieseler," *ThJ*, IV (1845), 207–14, and my essay, "Das Wesen des Montanismus nach den neuesten Forschungen," *ThJ*, X (1851), 538 f.

23. This is especially striking in the sixth and final volume [of the *Geschichte der christlichen Religion und Kirche*], which indeed was not completely worked out, but was planned wholly in accord with the earlier procedure. In large part, it merely contains selections from the writings of the men of the period, whose content is not always very significant. What would come of church history if it were to be continued into the most recent period in the same detail as for Huss and his predecessors! How must the universal disappear into the mass of particulars! Furthermore, two remarks by Neander in this final volume concerning the relation between the universal and the particular are noteworthy. If, as is stated on page 525, the driving principles and ideas that constitute history have a greater power than the intentions of men, why has this view not been maintained for history as a

In addition, there is a practical tendency in Neander's historiography. He explained in the Preface to the first edition that he wished to present the history of the church of Christ as an eloquent proof of the divine power of Christianity, as a school of Christian experience, as a voice of edification, of instruction, and of warning, resounding throughout the centuries for all who wish to hear. In this voice of the centuries, it is very often his own voice that is heard; and Neander's church history, for all its merits as an objective presentation, is also a true image of the subjectivity of its author—as is already shown by the minutely detailed treatment of so many parties and by the preference for those (Raymond Lull, in the fifth volume, is an example) who approach most nearly to his view of the relation between faith and knowledge. Whenever it is in his own religious interest to do so, Neander does not find it difficult to reconcile with the demands of criticism the credibility of the virtues and miraculous deeds of a pious missionary, the soul-struggles and confessions of a sinner in the process of conversion, the visions and ecstasies of a mystical enthusiast, and other such manifestations of the interior religious life! [24] But on the other hand, those who have once come under the suspicion of unfaith are judged all the more severely. For example, it is considered a serious

---

whole? Similarly, on page 296 Neander blames Wyclif for having contested with too great a dogmatic zeal the doctrine of transubstantiation. "We recognize here that one-sided dogmatic tendency of Protestantism, which is inclined to lay an undue stress on formal conceptions. But at the same time we should carefully keep in mind, that before men were in a condition to understand the real historical process of development of the religious life and its relation to doctrine, they must have been quite incapable of understanding the relative necessity of certain doctrinal modes of expression for certain times, in a certain spiritual atmosphere, though such modes of expression objectively considered, may be incorrect." [ED. Translation from *General History of the Christian Religion and Church*, V, 157.] Thus there is also a relative necessity for certain ages, which we recognize only when we understand the true process of historical development. But how can this process of development be rightly understood if for the history of the Christian church in general the concept of the church in itself is not distinguished from that which is merely a phase of the concept? That which has a merely relative or temporary justification is not the concept itself but only a phase of the concept; but the relative necessity and truth of such a phase can only be understood from the universality of the concept, from the essence of the subject matter itself. Thus, generally speaking, it is not possible to consider history as a process of development when this distinction between the universal and the particular is not theoretically substantiated.

24. In one such case Neander far too readily believes he has made allowance for criticism by subtracting this or that from what sounds miraculous, by reducing contradictory reports on both sides as much as possible, and simply by not proceeding so as to trivialize everything too much. Cf. *ibid.*, VI, 170, 746.

charge against Emperor Frederick II that by his own admission he did not believe in the miracle of the Host! That could only be, Neander maintains, a naturalistic denial of the revealed religion.[25]

As he particularly remarked in connection with Tertullian, Neander considered it the task of the historian, as it was of the painter, to permit the soul of a man, the Idea that animates him, to stand out in his physiognomy. Only thus is the key provided for a correct understanding of the caricature into which the manifestation of soul and Idea is distorted. Emphasis upon that caricature ought always to be merely subordinate. The only worthy task of the historian is to recognize the divine imprint in phenomena and to bring it to consciousness out of temporal obscurity; for this reason alone is history worth the trouble.[26] The question is simply whether what appears to the historian as no more than a caricature, a strange protuberance, is not in itself the specific and characteristic aspect of history, and whether, moreover, such a principle does not afford too great an influence to the historian's subjectivity.

We must now look somewhat more carefully at Neander's timidity before the baroque, the monstrous, and what he calls the caricatural, as it is expressed, with apparent ingenuousness, in relation to Tertullian. What is behind this timidity? Neander fears that the divine imprint in such a phenomenon might thereby be obscured for him. But if just such characteristics give the stamp of truth to the phenomenon, why should they not be included in the depiction, even at the risk of thereby obscuring the divine imprint? Neander's concern, therefore, is with Divinity within the imprint of phenomena. He considers it the worthy task of the historian to bring it to consciousness out of its temporal obscurity—a task that is justified because it is certain that only the divine character of Christianity can reveal itself in the history of the Christian church. But what, for Neander, is the Divine in the history of Christianity? Since he remains within a dualism that he cannot restore to a unity of principle, there is no objective progress in the development of Christianity. One of the two principles, the supernatural aspect of Christianity, remains of necessity always the same. Historical change thus can occur only on the other, the subjective side, the side of human nature, as it shows itself, in various individuals, more or less receptive to the supernatural aspect of Christianity. Since not only is the relation of these various [subjective] forms to one another merely contingent, but since each is also merely relative,

25. *Ibid.*, V/1, 347 f.
26. Preface to the second edition of *Antignostikus*, xi.

none can be regarded as absolutely normative, and the divine imprint must be abstracted from these phenomena in order to be described objectively. That imprint can be located only in the subjective—in subjective receptivity for the Divinity of Christianity; and what finally emerges is that the Divinity of Christianity is most fully revealed where the subject has the greatest receptivity for it.

Since religion in general is essentially subjective, the subjective standpoint can only be assumed as well in the history of the manifestations of Christianity. Indeed, for Neander the absolute standard by which historical manifestations are judged is really religious feeling, or the subjective Christian consciousness. There quite naturally emerges, for Neander, a concern lest the divine imprint in phenomena be clouded as soon as those phenomena are not merely considered subjectively, according to the religious feeling or consciousness in which they are rooted as the immediate expression of this imprint, but are objectively conceived in their essential reality. In that event, many things have to be taken into consideration, e.g., that which immediately shows itself to be very one-sided, limited, and singular, with which one cannot sympathize. In order to eliminate all this—to be able to hold, on the contrary, to what in historical persons can be regarded as the divine imprint manifested, and in order to rediscover in persons that in which the true nature of religion and of Christianity can be recognized—everything making for a specific historical manifestation and individuality must be traced back to religious feeling and consciousness. This feeling is the original and immediate reality in which everyone lives in the sphere of his own subjectivity, and by which the claims of that subjectivity are validated; it is also the common element through which each can sympathize with the other. As a result, such a presentation as is clearly recognizable in Neander contains a strong tendency to dull the cutting edge of phenomena that emerge with very specific features and in general to level and neutralize everything as much as possible. The most important thing, for such a presentation, is always that by which it is able to rediscover the vantage point of its own theory of feeling, its *pectus, quod theologum facit* [heart, which makes the theologian], its rational supernaturalism, the incompleteness and instability that hover somewhere between faith and knowledge. The soul of history is this element of feeling, with its universality tending to merge into the infinite; it is the substantial element to which in the final analysis what is dogmatically determined and objectively defined can be related only as a mere accident, depending on whether it is clearly indispensable.

From this point of view an authentically Christian character can be attributed even to the religious piety of a Julian,[27] so long as it is not believed necessary to analyze its heterogeneous elements more closely. Neander's *Julian*, the first subject he chose for a special portrayal, can best serve to reveal the innermost aspect of its distinctive character. Neander's obvious predilection for Julian did not allow the erroneous and unfortunate aspects of his spiritual tendency and historical position to escape him. He begins his portrayal as follows: Just as every new epoch in the history of mankind is usually preceded by special signs, and just as every new truth that takes a deep hold on the life of humanity has its scattered forerunners, who proclaim it to a still unreceptive age, so on the other hand it happens that some individuals attempt to restore the human race to a condition no longer suitable, giving a strong expression once again to that which can no longer maintain its predominance over men. Aware of the impossibility of making decayed things newly fresh in themselves, these men look for a spice or a salt—which, for a religion that has become stale, is customarily found in philosophy. The philosophy that offered its services to a dying paganism was Neoplatonism. The inner revelation of God in man, or the Platonic theory of ideas in its poetical-mystical version in the *Timaeus*, would here be brought into union with the old religious traditions and with the cultus of the fatherland in such a way that the latter would be animated by the former, and the former would be given an objective popular foundation by the latter.[28] All this does not prevent Neander from acknowledging that in Julian a true piety, as distinct from abject superstition, sought to realize the ideas that animated him, and that in what he did he was submissive to the will of the gods, confidently leaving the outcome in their hands. Belief in the divine origin and destiny of man, and in the ancient wisdom, gave him an enthusiasm that raised him above the temporal and did not leave him until his final moment. This faith Neander himself called divine; for faith can be divine even if at the same time the dogmas in which it takes shape are human.[29]

27. [ED.] The Emperor Julian (331–63), frequently known as "the Apostate," was the son of a younger stepbrother of Constantine the Great. In 351 he became a convert to paganism through contact with Neoplatonic philosophy and mysticism in Nicomedia, Pergamum, and Ephesus. During his short reign as Emperor (361–63) he sought to restore Hellenism and to establish paganism as a state religion. To this end he was obliged to use force, although he rejected it as an aid to conversion.

28. David Friedrich Strauss thus aptly summarizes the major elements of Neander's portrayal in his *Der Romantiker auf dem Throne der Cäsaren, oder Julian der Abtrünnige* (Mannheim, 1847), 16 f.

29. Neander, *Über den Kaiser Julian*, 96, 170.

If we restrict ourselves to this divine faith of Julian's, we can cheerfully overlook what otherwise we might find perverse and blameworthy. But though Julian may be understood and evaluated in this fashion, how must he appear from the standpoint of objective historical consideration? Strauss was not of the same opinion. The amalgamation (acknowledged by Neander himself) of old and new in order to restore or more adequately to preserve the old he described as romantic; and he explained Neander's benevolence toward Julian as a scenting in him of one after the same mold as himself. "Indeed, not a Christian but a romantic; he is our man; if he did not have the true faith objectively, he had it subjectively; furthermore, faith can be divine in its content even though the dogmas in which it is embodied are human." [30]

To take offense at this would be merely to show that one did not understand in what the objective historical standpoint consists. If in the final analysis everything is only subjective, a matter of feeling, of immediate consciousness, of a faith supposedly divine, then is it indeed possible, by this theory of feeling, to stir together paganism and Christianity in a single brew? How in general is an objective historical consideration still possible? History never changes; there is always the same monotony which Neander's presentation, with its fixed categories, its constant appeal to feeling and consciousness, cannot conceal. Even though history spreads before us the greatest multiplicity of individual forms, there is not to be found in them that true life of history which it is our task to establish. Rather, all those forms are repeatedly dissolved and carried back to the subjective element of feeling, which alone is the true, inner ground of the life of history.

But if we cannot remain satisfied with this indefinite and general situation, we naturally want to know what that feeling, that longing for the infinite, that divine faith is, not merely subjectively for him who has it, but in its own objective quality. If we should analyze it, and demonstrate the contradiction between its various constituent parts, who can blame us? Only he who would thereby do harm to his own religious feeling could hesitate to do this.[31] Since Neander did not do this, it becomes

30. Strauss, *op. cit.*, 19.

31. Only in this sense can K. R. Hagenbach, in his "Gedachtnissrede über Neander's Verdienste um die Kirchengeschichte," *Theologische Studien und Kritiken*, XXIV (1851), 571, have called the term used by Strauss regarding Julian—"romanticism"—a ridiculing of Julian's religious piety. Hagenbach himself feels such an injury to his religious feeling. He could bring no objection against the correctness of the matter itself, since he had just declared the historical survey of earlier evaluations of Julian, on which Strauss's term "romanticism" rests, to be the best part of the latter's book. With the same justification one could call every criticism by which the defi-

evident that he had not so unbiased a view of a Julian's religious piety as to be able to describe its nature openly and candidly, without any participation by his own religious consciousness. This is also the reason why in

cient, inadequate, and contradictory elements of a historical phenomenon are demonstrated and analyzed an act of ridicule. Surely the historian must stand at a point from which he can look freely and without prejudice upon the persons and phenomena before him, and assign to each his due place in the continuity of the whole. However, this is not wanton mockery but rather the objectivity of historical standpoint, to prove the lack of which in Neander must equally be the task of an evaluation that is not one-sided and superficial. The weakest side of Neander is that the highest and absolute element in his mode of historical consideration, in the final analysis, is always the subjectivity of feeling. He never becomes more touchy, irritable, or passionate than when he believes himself confronted by the necessity of emerging from the interiority of his theory of subjectivity and of placing himself at a vantage point where there is a question not of indefinite, unclear feelings and expressions of consciousness but of specific, objective concepts. His whole personality proceeds so completely from this element of feeling that, with every step toward a standpoint outside that indefiniteness, he believes himself to have neither heaven above nor earth below, and sees nothing but atheism and nihilism, the demonic powers of the abyss.

In this connection, a passage in the Preface to the second edition of *Antignostikus* (Berlin, 1849), viii f., makes a not unimportant contribution to the characterization of Neander and his view of history. He here looks back to the time of the first appearance of this work in 1826 and says that it "was a time of darkness, self-called enlightenment, which, in the contraction and obscurity of unconscious mental poverty, looked down with an air of pity on the greatness of earlier ages; it could not understand so striking a phenomenon as that of the new world of Christianity revealing itself to this man of rugged, wayward spirit, and fancied that by taking some paradoxical expressions of this eminent father on philosophy and reason, torn from their connection, it could form an estimate of his whole character, thus judging of the fruit by the hard shell that protects it. But this time has passed away. We look upon Schleiermacher, that great teacher of our nation, from whom it has still much to learn in reference to the development of the future, as the great man, one of whose multifarious merits it was to have contributed materially to this issue. And the true German spirit, of which one essential tendency is to penetrate deeply into divine things, after throwing off the foreign yoke and awakening to self-consciousness, turned away from the poverty-stricken superficiality of the period that had just closed, with earnest longing for the inspiration of a nobler spirit in the earlier ages of the church. It showed itself capable of understanding the manifold phases of Christianity, even those which bear the least resemblance to the spirit of our own age and country, and of contemplating them with affection. In that morning-dawn of a better time, to which, through that common fault which requires each one of us to smite upon his breast, the succeeding development did not correspond, this book first appeared. Since then that standpoint to which we have alluded, though apparently overcome, has come back still more poverty-stricken, though with imaginary wealth, and assuming a far greater boldness of dogmatism on everything that surpassed the comprehension of little, commonplace, cloddish souls. In place of that so-called vulgar rationalism, in which there was still an honorable remnant of a recognition of the supramundane and divine—some sense of the religious and the

his historical portrayal sharpness of judgment and precision of conception are so often lacking, as well as a standpoint from which the historian inquires after the objectivity of the subject matter itself and the elements ensuing from it, independently of any such subjective concern.

4. *Gieseler*

With Neander we stand at the summit of modern church historiography; but the more concrete and comprehensive the image in which Neander's view of history is presented to us, the less can the obtrusive subjectivity of this historian be denied. Two other works that especially deserve to be placed at the side of Neander's church history, those of J. K. L. Gieseler and Karl von Hase, are chiefly distinguished from his in that they are much more rigorous when it comes to permitting history to speak for itself in the pure objectivity of the facts, so far as possible, and

---

moral—from a consequential carrying out of the same principles, there has proceeded what would designate itself as more sublime, but which is, in fact, a far more vulgar thing—the gospel of the apotheosis of humanity, which is only another name for atheism, and of which, after several decenniums have been spent in constructing its theory, the mischievous effects might easily be foreseen; and at last, entering more into actual life, ever since the outrages of the disgraceful 8th of March [1830], it has, to the shame and injury of our nation, been continually making fresh manifestations of its destructive and pernicious effects, which threaten to annihilate all the higher goods of humanity." [ED. Baur paraphrases this passage. I have quoted it in full, with some minor modifications, from the English translation, *Antignostikus, or the Spirit of Tertullian*, II, 195–96.]

More equitably and consistently, Neander might have blamed all the things he has so atrociously confounded not merely on rationalism but also on its opposite, on which he is otherwise accustomed to pronounce the same anathemas. But it is a melancholy spectacle when a mind that has surveyed so many ages filled with rich content retreats so thoroughly within itself that in the gloomy present a slim ray of light appears to it only where it sees its own ego shining. Before the *Antignostikus* nothing but spiritual darkness; after it, once again nothing but a still greater poverty of spirit! In between, the bleak dawn of a better age, which never breaks: such was the briefly happy time in which Neander's spirit seemed to find its full recognition. A high degree of self-confidence is needed to say this of oneself, to make one's own ego to such a degree the standard of greatness for an entire age. It is a peculiar contradiction in Neander's nature that he is as intolerant of the present as he is liberal and open-minded toward the past; but this is only the natural culmination of his principle of subjectivity. One can peacefully contemplate the greatness of previous centuries as a thing of the past; but when it comes to acknowledging in the present something else to be equally justified as oneself, then the reminder of the limits of one's own individuality are too near to be so easily dismissed.

to restraining everything that belongs merely to the subjectivity of the historian. Gieseler's church history,[32] which can justifiably be called the most useful among the more recent of such works, has its greatest excellence in the abundant and aptly chosen documents, which, based upon a new, basic, and critical study of all the historical materials, serve as a running commentary from the source writings on the very loosely constructed text of historical narrative. In the Preface to the first edition, Gieseler explains his method by saying that, in church history especially, no age can rightly be understood if it is not allowed to speak for itself; for the ideas by which it was ruled can least of all be portrayed with full purity in their distinctive form through a foreign language. The work as a whole is directed toward this quest for an objective presentation. Gieseler is concerned only with the factual; and he permits his own judgment to be expressed only in so far as it arises of itself from the preceding development of the subject matter.

When we compare this with other presentations at those points where the sympathies and antipathies of historians are likely to be most vividly expressed, it would almost seem as though subjective interest had withdrawn too completely from the object of presentation. It is exceptional in Gieseler when he dares to express such views as these concerning Gregory VII: If he is considered not as a statesman but as the head of the church and as the apostle of truth, his purely political actions are distinctly repulsive. In order to acquit this Pope, through whom the church was completely stamped with the character of a secular state, and indeed with an encumbering self-delusion, it is necessary to plead an unavoidable

---

32. *Lehrbuch der Kirchengeschichte* (Darmstadt, 1824); the fourth edition of the first volume appeared in 1844. The first division of the third volume, appearing in 1840, contains the first two chapters of the first part, from the Reformation to the Peace of Westphalia.

[ED.] The fifth and last volume, containing posthumously published lectures and treating the period after 1814, was published at Bonn in 1857. Cf. The English translation of the fourth German edition by Samuel Davidson, revised by Henry B. Smith, *A Text-Book of Church History* (5 vols.; New York, 1876–80). Johann Karl Ludwig Gieseler (1792–1854) attended the University of Halle and in 1819 became professor of theology at Bonn. In 1831 he moved to Göttingen, where he remained until the end of his life, lecturing in church history, history of dogma, and dogmatics. In addition to his major work, the *Lehrbuch der Kirchengeschichte*, he published *Versuch über die Entstehung und die frühesten Schicksale der schriftlichen Evangelien* (Liepzig, 1818; against the hypothesis of an Aramaic proto-Gospel); *Über den Reichstag zu Augsburg im Jahre 1530* (Hamburg, 1821); *Symbolae ad historiam monasterii Lacensis* (Bonn, 1826); *Rückblick auf die theologischen Richtungen der letzten fünfzig Jahre* (Göttingen, 1837); and *Über die Lehninsche Weissagung* (Göttingen, 1849).

influence by the prejudices of the age on the morality even of outstanding men, to a degree that the moral nature of the man himself is thereby placed in doubt. Here the historian's own view is expressed with at least a more active interest; but how conditioned, how cautious, how ambiguous the verdict is!

However much we may make it our task to permit history itself alone to speak, there are questions of principle of a general sort such as no church historian can completely circumvent. We cannot merely note the objective character of history; we must also know whence it comes and whither it tends; we must discern some purpose in the church's historical development, some general conception of the nature of church history. Surely, if we define the task of church history as no more than to describe pragmatically the whole course of change and development through which the Christian church has moved, and its effect on other human circumstances, in order to arrive at an ethical and teleological evaluation of this development—then what is said will be worthless unless we know in what the pragmatism of that description and that teleological view ought to consist. "The . . . church . . . is a religious-moral society, connected together by a common faith in Christ, which seeks to represent in its united life the kingdom of God announced by Christ. . . . This kingdom it hopes to see at one time realized, and strives to prepare itself for becoming worthy of having a part in it." [33] But what, then, is Christianity, by origin and in essence? Gieseler's church history hovers so completely between the rationalistic and the supernaturalistic view of this question that from the outset its grounds are extremely uncertain and precarious. The basic view of the historian shows through clearly enough; but it is only a feeble and colorless rationalism, which dares not come to any decision on the most important questions, and deems it most advisable again and again to adhere to the miracle theory of supernaturalism.

In order as little as possible to relinquish the traditional view, there are assertions so uncritical that it would not be possible on such assumptions to bring a more deeply grounded continuity into the history of the first centuries. So little can Gieseler abandon the obsolete and now largely discredited belief in a second Roman captivity of the Apostle Paul that for him the authenticity of the Pastoral Epistles, despite their completely shattered credibility, still remains firm enough that they become the

33. [ED.] Gieseler, *Lehrbuch der Kirchengeschichte*, I (1st ed.), 1–2 (*A Text-Book of Church History*, I, 13).

material for a history of the earliest church. It is very natural, then, that the martyrdom at Rome of the Apostle Peter is likewise still accepted —the only doubt being whether the apostle, present in Rome, had also formally been a bishop there. Once such legends are made the ground-work of history, there can be no denial of credibility to others of the same kind; thus, also for Gieseler, Bishop Ignatius wanders without hesi-tation from Antioch to Rome, there to cover himself with the glory of a heroic martyrdom.[34] Such assumptions go so deep into the continuity of history, and at the same time contain in themselves such doubtful conse-quences, that it is out of no mere suspicion of hitherto valid sources of the earliest history of Christianity, as Gieseler maintains,[35] if we are more than usually rigorous in asking questions to which the response is still so unclear, and in the critical testing of evidence on which depend such doubtful results; and if on the whole we recognize no permanently valid sources.

As for the origin of Christianity and the early development of the Christian church, so in Gieseler a more specific and sharply constructed view of its further course is also found wanting. Gieseler divides church history into four periods: the first (up to Constantine) covers the devel-opment of the church under external pressure; the second (up to the beginning of the iconoclastic controversies) covers the development of Christianity as the prevailing religion of state; the third (up to the Ref-ormation) covers the development of papal dominance over the state; the fourth covers the development of Protestantism. But these four periods are very superficially related; no underlying point of view is to be found in such a division. What is epoch-making in the various periods? To what end does Christianity develop in the first period? If in the second period Christianity is seen as the prevailing religion of state, and if the third is characterized by the subordination of the state to the Papacy, then it would accordingly seem that the fourth period, that of Protestantism, must be epoch-making in redefining the relation of Christianity or the church to the state. But what constitutes this new relation? Indeed, even in the second and third periods the relation of Christianity to the state is not entirely clear. If Gregory VII completely stamped the church with the character of a secular state, then the state has not been subordinated to

---

34. Cf. my "Kritische Beiträge zur Kirchengeschichte der ersten Jahrhunderte, mit besonderer Rücksicht auf die Werke von Neander und Gieseler," *ThJ*, IV (1845), 212 f.

35. Gieseler, Preface to *Lehrbuch der Kirchengeschichte*, I (4th ed.), iv.

the church, but the church to the state. If the church itself has become a state, then the conception of the state has devoured that of the church; but how, then, is the third period distinguished from the second? This shows how difficult it is, from the sparse hints he gives, to abstract the general and basic vision on which Gieseler's church history rests, and to bring it to specific conception. For the same reason, it is not possible to enter into a further analysis of this extensive work, since details can be taken into consideration here only in so far as they are expressions of the general idea determining the whole.

5. Hase

For the same reason Karl Hase's *Kirchengeschichte* [36] does not offer for evaluation the material that one might expect. Of its kind, it is no less

36. First published in Leipzig, 1834; 6th edition, 1848.

[ED.] Karl August von Hase (1800–1890) studied at Leipzig and at Erlangen, where he was deeply influenced by Schelling. In 1823 he lectured in Tübingen; for eleven months, shortly afterward, he was a political prisoner at the Hohenasperg because of his agitation for the freedom of student corporations. In 1826 he went to Leipzig; but a few years later he was called to Jena as professor of theology, and he remained there until his retirement in 1883. He traveled often and made frequent journeys to Rome, where he became intimately acquainted with Roman Catholicism. He was not an innovator in either theology or church history, but became famous through his breadth of interest, acuteness of observation, and artistic treatment of themes. Although he shared Schleiermacher's conception of religion, he belonged to no party or school, but rather considered himself a free theologian, able to pursue his scientific investigations without restriction. One of his great-grandsons was Dietrich Bonhoeffer, whose conception of the church as Christ existing in community bears a similarity to Hase's view of the church.

Among his numerous publications, in addition to the *Kirchengeschichte*, are his *Lehrbuch der evangelischen Dogmatik* (Stuttgart, 1826); *Gnosis oder protestantisch-evangelischen Glaubenslehre* (3 vols.; Leipzig, 1827–29); *Leben Jesu* (Leipzig, 1829); *Anti-Roehr* (Leipzig, 1837; a polemic against rationalism); *Handbuch der protestantischen Polemik gegen die römisch-katholische Kirche* (Leipzig, 1862); and *Geschichte Jesu* (Leipzig, 1875). A collected edition of his *Werke* in 12 volumes appeared in Leipzig, 1890–93. An English translation of the 7th edition of the *Kirchengeschichte* was published under the title, *A History of the Christian Church*, trans. Charles E. Blumenthal (New York, 1855).

Among his contemporaries in church history, Baur probably regarded Hase the most highly, and the feeling of respect was mutual. In 1855 Hase published *Die Tübinger Schule: Ein Sendschreiben an Herrn Dr. Ferdinand Christian von Baur* (Leipzig), occasioned in part by Baur's *Epochen*, in which he raised questions about Baur's treatment of the Johannine question, his hypothesis concerning the opposition between Paulinizing and Judaizing elements in primitive Christianity, and his periodization of church history. Hase's questions were put in a positive and con-

excellent a work than Gieseler's *Lehrbuch,* and for a number of years has
proved so useful and attractive to the German public that its value for the
literature of church history needs no further testimony. Just as Gieseler
made it his task to survey as comprehensively and completely as possible,
in footnotes, the sources and the major data concerning them, Hase did
his utmost to compress the greatest possible range of contents into a
connected presentation of the briefest span. But at the same time the
fullness of life, as it speaks to us from the original monuments of each
age, was also intended to shine forth from this condensed survey. Therefore it was Hase's endeavor to describe the most thoroughly individual
and specific aspects of each age, instead of the general and unspecific, as
are customarily found in textbooks; and, where a general and sweeping
characterization was required, to point to such specific facts as would
thereby force one to think for oneself about the most individual details.
In the same way that, by the stimulus of Neander's example, biography
became the foundation of history, here each age displays itself directly in
the lives of individual men, in its spiritual leaders and representatives.[37]

Hase carried out the idea of his church history with masterful art and
skill; and he merits all the greater recognition because his textbook, when
it first appeared, was the only one among the more recent and independent treatments of church history that from the beginning actually attained its projected goal, and treated the whole content of church history
from the earliest age up to the most recent in accord with a single plan,
rigorously adhered to. From beginning to end, one detail is joined to
another in an artistic sequence. Everything is worked out with exact and
meticulous care. Great and small alike are treated with the same unwaver-
ing fidelity to the subject matter. Because the material is placed before the
eye so clearly and vividly, and in such multiplicity of detail, an infinitely
rich content is disclosed to the thoughtful and knowledgeable reader by
the many skillfully interwoven characteristics, the well chosen, piquant,
and striking expressions (although these are often too much weighted
with sentiment or decorum), and by a mass of ingenious hints and
allusions.

------

structive fashion, and Baur's response, in his *An Herrn Dr. Karl Hase: Beantwortung des Sendschreibens "Die Tübinger Schule"* (Tübingen, 1855), is one of his most
illuminating essays, helping to clarify his position on a number of points—e.g., his
treatment of the historical Jesus, his theological and philosophical position, his
understanding of the relation between Idea and manifestation in the historicity of
the church, and his periodization of church history.

37. Hase, *Kirchengeschichte,* Preface to the first edition.

It must be acknowledged that whatever concerns the particular is here both methodically planned and treated, and precisely thought out, and that the basis and essence of things has been profoundly examined. On the other hand, we can only regret that the whole is not in the same measure permeated spiritually by an Idea connecting and controlling the particulars. Despite its easy handling of form, Hase's textbook on the whole still has too material a character. It may be wondered whether there is not too much rather than too little material for its purpose and plan. Nevertheless, it may be that the breaking up of the contents into the many divisions that compose each of the larger parts works still more against the lucidity and spiritual mastery of the whole. The work is not lacking in reflections and guiding ideas, but the factual, the special, and the concrete are urged forward too much in advance of the general point of view from which they first can be rightly understood. More general considerations are mainly provided only in short, aphoristic statements, rather than in a connected and conscious development; and the particular and the universal (which only in their reciprocal permeation allow us to peer more deeply into the continuity of historical development), are frequently kept apart by division into separate sections, which must then be combined once more.

The reason Hase not only gives special attention to many previously neglected subjects in church history, such as the history of Christian art, but also goes back much further than is customary into the history of peoples and religions before and outside of Christianity—including the Germanic, Slavic, and Indian—is an unusual effort toward enrichment of the content of his work. There can be no objection to this so long as it is not placed in a merely external relation to the purpose and content of church history. But we read what his textbook has to say about Greek folk life, the limits of Greek humanity, Greek religion, the relation of philosophy to popular religion, Rome as a republic, the fall of Greece, the rise and fall of Rome, the decay of popular religion; and even about the popular religion of Judaism, the Jews in dispersion, Hellenism and the Jewish sects; and we ask whether we can adequately find our way from these brilliant considerations and beautifully refined statements to the point at which Christianity enters into the general history of human development.

The more a church-historical work aims toward enrichment of its content, drawing to itself everything that touches even remotely upon the ecclesiastical sphere, the more it must also tend toward concentration and achieve a self-conscious integration in order not to lose itself in a sea of details. It is just here, however, that this church history is least satisfying. What, according to Hase, is the Idea of the Christian church? The church, says Hase, is a continual becoming, i.e., a striving to be the Christ living on in humanity, or to represent his life ever more perfectly and extensively, partly through struggle with the world and partly in alliance with it. The church is therefore the Christ coming into being in humanity. But to know what, through Christ, humanity is to become, we must above all know what Christ himself is, i.e., what Christianity is. On this question, Hase nowhere explains himself any more fully, nor does his periodization of church history make the matter any clearer. The hitherto essential developments of the Christian Spirit are Catholicism and Protestantism; its chief organs are the Greco-Roman and the Germanic folk Spirit. Accordingly, church history falls into three periods: (1) the ancient, up to the establishment of the Holy Roman Empire of the German nation; (2) the medieval, up to the Reformation, characterized by the predominance of Roman-Germanic Catholicism; (3) the modern, up to the present, characterized by the struggle between Protestantism and Catholicism. Thus Charlemagne once again appears as the initiator of a new period in the history of the Christian church! If we could only know in what his greatness for the church consists, and what inner ecclesiastical significance there is in the outward event of the establishment of the Holy Roman Empire of the German nation! If the entire previous development of the Christian Spirit is divided into Catholicism and Protestantism, then Charlemagne must have had an epoch-making importance for the development of Catholicism; but what, then, drives the Christian Spirit into the antithesis of Catholicism and Protestantism?

Hase attempts to abstract a conception of the moving principle of church history from the general survey he has placed at the beginning of every period of history. Striking though individual features may be, they are not sufficient to provide a clear picture of the whole. If the essence of Catholicism is grasped when the church of the Middle Ages is described as the ruler of nations—and thus by nature the greatest power of the age, having as its exclusive treasure all spiritual gifts of grace on earth and in heaven—and if one describes the world-historical Papacy, victorious by the higher power of Spirit, as the bond that holds all peoples and classes together in a great Christian family, then does not the negative side, in the nature of the case, belong directly to the positive—namely, the cause for the self-destruction of the Papacy and Catholicism by their own power?

Only in its antithesis to Catholicism can Protestantism be understood; but it is observed of the latter:

For the first time, as the hierarchy opposed the Reformation, the church was divided by the unavoidable pressure of circumstances, and the hitherto suppressed principle of Protestantism, as a special development of Christianity, established an autonomous church. . . . Since the young church was not able to appropriate for itself the claim of the existing church to be infallible and the only means of salvation, the eternal authority of the Idea was grasped in the struggle against positive authority, and the perfect church was described as an ideal, represented in the existing churches according to the measure of their various faiths, but nowhere perfectly attained, so that the true believers of all places were bound together in that invisible church. Through this the conception of Protestantism—a later word resulting from the elevation of a particular fact to a general concept—unwittingly developed, in part as a continued protestation against the presumptions of Catholicism, and in part as the recognition of a common Christianity wherever a devout heart is bound together with Christ, and therefore as the Christianity of freedom.[38]

Do we learn from this what the principle of Protestantism is? Is it not a degradation of Protestantism when it is exiled, with its invisible church, to the realm of the ideal, and when, in contrast to Catholicism, it is denied the capacity to be what the true church in itself must be—the infallible and only means of salvation? What is left of the principle of autonomy when Protestantism is a mere ideal and is limited in its outward existence to the piety of the heart?

But we now see to what everything in this church history finally leads. "As the quarrels of the Reformation subsided," according to the survey of the most recent period,[39] "the previously initiated secular tendency of public life, of art and science, asserted itself, as it had every right to do. . . . The church was deeply affected by political convulsions, no longer as the first mover in the power struggle among nations, but as the second. Through conflict, suffering, and consolation, it was the bearer of the world's destiny in the struggle between religious autonomy and patriarchal conventions. That struggle passed through three turning points: the undermining of conventions, which brought it up to the middle of the eighteenth century; the overthrow of the existing order, which brought it up to 1814; the renewal of the struggle in earnest and the beginning of a settlement, bringing it up to 1847—yet the mathematical limit of spiritual potencies was no more significant than that which

38. Hase, *Kirchengeschichte*, 355, 423 f. [Cf. *A History of the Christian Church*, 358, 437–38.]

39. Hase, *Kirchengeschichte*, 463. [Cf. *A History of the Christian Church*, 483–84.]

vitally emerged in this period or succeeded to complete effectiveness." At
the end of all this, how weak and fragile the church remains! Once the
first power in the world, it is now explicitly reduced to second place. It
can only look on, struggling and suffering, or at best consoling, while the
secular, in all its variety, asserts itself alongside with complete authority.
Nothing is left to it but to permit the fulfillment within itself of the
world's destiny; its tragic fate is to be the bearer of a form of Christianity
which we know not whether to greet joyfully as the principle of religious
autonomy, or to regret and deplore as the undermining of convention and
the overthrow of the existing order. With these elements of a contradictory existence, the church can only be disintegrated through a presentation of its history which from the beginning gives it no substantial core
and no focus, not even any moving inner principle of historical
development.

So we can indeed rejoice in rich measure over the content and the form
of a presentation that not only gives the general material of church history the appeal of a tasteful modern elaboration, but that also knows how
to add the beauty and charm of aesthetic detail to the major contents,
especially concerning the romance of the Middle Ages—crusaders wan-
dering uncensured beneath the palms, the nightingales of minstrelsy, the
wonderful design and symbolism of the Gothic cathedrals and all the
splendor of the visual arts, the sublime beauty and charm of women, and
so much that moved the hearts of nations and individuals to joy or sor-
row. But such a presentation leaves much to be desired; for along with its
beautiful rendering of detail, it might have been just as rich in those lofty
perspectives, ideas, and summaries, those guiding points of view, and
those deeper insights, by which the whole course of history, the inner
continuity of particulars and the process of movement in general, are
disclosed to thinking Spirit.

The three church historians considered here as the major representatives of recent historiography are characterized by the difference in their
attitude toward the three major periods of the Christian church. While
the major strength of Neander and Gieseler is in the history of the
ancient and medieval periods, Hase, who alone has managed to press
forward into the present, is the historian of the modern church *par excellence*. In the Middle Ages, which are as much an object of scholarly
research for Neander and Gieseler as they are of aesthetic understanding
for Hase, the three authorities have a common point of contact. On the
other hand, Hase cannot be commended, at least in the same degree, for

balance or depth of penetration into the spirit of the ancient church, especially into its dogmatic development, despite his quiet dialogues with the critics of this period.[40]

6. Gfrörer and Niedner

The most recent period is rich in church-historical writing and research; yet, in regard to general histories, besides these major representatives, only two historians, each quite different from the other—A. F. Gfrörer[41] and C. W. Niedner[42]—can here be mentioned with special distinction; and once again, their general view of history does not allow any closer scrutiny. With Gfrörer, to be sure, even in the period before Gregory VII the full significance of the Catholic Church, in itself as well as in its political and national connections, comes to the fore after a fashion hitherto not recognized. But since the work has not yet advanced beyond this major epoch, to characterize the underlying general view at this point would be to prejudge the whole.

Niedner's work not only stands before us completed, but also shows itself to be the fruit of very serious spiritual labor, accomplished, however, with too visible an effort. If there is one of the more recent church historians who has endeavored to penetrate the material in its full scope

40. Cf. *Kirchengeschichte*, Preface to the 6th edition.

41. *Allgemeine Kirchengeschichte für die deutsche Nation* (3 vols.; Stuttgart, 1841–44).

[ED.] August Friedrich Gfrörer (1803–61) studied theology in the evangelical faculty at Tübingen. After 1830 he left the parish ministry to devote himself to historical studies. In 1846 he was appointed professor of history at Freiburg, and in 1848 was elected to the German parliament. In 1853, after failing in an attempt to unite Protestants and Catholics in Germany, he joined the Catholic Church. A fourth volume of his *Allgemeine Kirchengeschichte* was published in 1846. Other works include *Philo und die jüdisch-alexandrinische Theosophie* (2 vols.; Stuttgart, 1831); *Geschichte des Urchristentums* (3 vols.; Stuttgart, 1838); *Urgeschichte des menschlichen Geschlechts* (2 vols.; Schaffhausen, 1855); and *Papst Gregorius VII. und sein Zeitalter* (7 vols.; Schaffhausen, 1859–61).

42. *Geschichte der christlichen Kirche*, a textbook (Leipzig, 1846).

[ED.] Christian Wilhelm Niedner (1797–1865) studied theology at Leipzig, where he became professor in 1838. He was interested not only in church history but also in the history of philosophy. In 1844 he became editor of the *Zeitschrift für die historische Theologie*, in which he later published two important studies on dogma and dogmatics. In 1850 he resigned his professorship in Leipzig and settled in Wittenberg; in 1859 he was called to the chair of theology at Berlin, where he remained until his death.

with all the energy of rational reflection, that one is Niedner. However, the abstract conceptual formalism that gathers everything into the net of its artificial categories and its peculiar terminology has not been very conducive to the carrying-out of the general idea. Moral Spirit, says Niedner in his "Introduction to the Theory of the History of the Christian Church," is the principle that has given to the ages their essential purpose, enduring content, and unconditional value. With Christianity, moral Spirit has entered fully into the sphere of what is possible for man through God, and has placed man as an individual under its Idea. We thus expect the entire history of the development of Christianity to be understood from the point of view of the moral Idea. On the other hand, although much that is appropriate is said in the general survey as well as in the special implementation, nothing in the account of the church through its three periods contains elements that are derived from a general principle and condition the inner progress of development in such a way that the major Idea could be clearly and comprehensively traced through the whole. The unity of the whole is immersed in the variety of contents, and the total vision cannot, therefore, here at least, be set forth more precisely in its specific features. Moreover, since nothing of the general church-historical literature that remains is significant enough to be of special interest for this investigation,[43] we are justified in halting it at this point.

43. In 1883 J. G. V. Engelhardt and H. E. F. Guerike each published a *Handbüch der Kirchengeschichte* (Erlangen and Halle). Guerike's work, in which the rigorism of the old Lutheran confession is linked with Neander's basic perspective, by 1849 was already in its seventh edition. See also the *Vorlesungen über die Geschichte der christlichen Kirche,* edited from Schleiermacher's literary remains and the notebooks of students, which is found only in the *Sämmtliche Werke* (Division I, Vol. XI). In addition to these, the following general portrayals of church history, to mention briefly only the most recent German-Protestant literature, have appeared within a short span of time: W. B. Lindner, *Lehrbuch der Kirchengeschichte, mit besonderer Berücksichtigung der dogmatischen Entwicklung* (Leipzig, 1848–49; 2nd division, only up to the Reformation); Eduard Zeller, *Geschichte der christlichen Kirche übersichtlich dargestellt* (specially reprinted from the *Neuen Encyklopädie für Wissenschaften und Künste,* Stuttgart, 1848); G. A. Fricke, *Lehrbuch der Kirchengeschichte, erster Theil, bis zum entscheidenden Übergang der christlichen Kirche an die germanischen Völker im 8. Jahrhundert* (Leipzig, 1850); J. L. Jacobi, *Lehrbuch der Kirchengeschichte* (Part I, Berlin, 1850; up to 590); J. H. Kurz, *Lehrbuch der Kirchengeschichte* (Mitau, 1849; 2nd edition, much revised and enlarged, 1850; according to the modest remark of the author, Preface, iii, it is intended as before for beginners in church-historical studies) [ED. English translation of the ninth German edition by John MacPherson, *Church History* (3 vols.; New York, 1889)]; H. F. F. Schmid, *Lehrbuch der Kirchengeschichte* (Nördlingen, 1851).

VII

CONCLUSIONS AND SUGGESTIONS

1. *The Idea of the Church*

We have still to ask what is the result of our survey of all these attempts, from the most ancient up to the most recent times, to portray the history of the Christian church. The materials are available in greater abundance than ever before, since the historical data, both in content and in scope, have been investigated thoroughly and from many points of view, and have been studied critically. Furthermore, it has long since been acknowledged that the historian can be equal to his task only in so far as he transposes himself into the objective reality of the subject matter itself, free from the bias of subjective views and interests, whatever they may be, so that instead of making history a reflection of his own subjectivity, he may be simply a mirror for the perception of historical phenomena in their true and real form.

Nevertheless, there is still a lack, even in the most recent treatments of the history of the Christian church, that prevents them from achieving greater perfection. That lack, put briefly, consists in a wrong relation of the Idea to the manifestations in which its historical development is to be presented. The Idea still hovers indefinitely and at a great distance over the manifestations to which it must be related. It is not yet strong and vital enough to penetrate and vivify the historical material, as the soul animates the body, or to become, through such an organic unity, the moving principle of the entire series of manifestations in which the history of the Christian church takes its course.[1] Or should there still be any doubt as

---

1. To put the same thing another way, a progression from the pragmatic standpoint of historiography to the universal is still lacking. Since church history at last came down from the transcendent heights of abstract dualism to the empirical soil of history, it has become pragmatic; but in essentials it has still not moved beyond the pragmatic mode of treatment. Schelling very aptly distinguished and character-

to whether the history of the Christian church is the movement of the Idea of the church, and therefore consists of something more than a succession of changes following one another at random? If it is right to speak of an Idea of the church, then that Idea, like any other, must possess within itself the living impulse to go out from itself and to become actualized in a series of manifestations that can only be regarded as various aspects of the relation that exists generally between the Idea and its manifestion.

But it is not even necessary to take the standpoint of the Idea. Even the most fleeting glimpse into the history of the church can show how significant and radical a turning point the Reformation is, and how church history after it takes a wholly different course from what went before. The church is so deeply involved in the antithesis between Protestantism and Catholicism that we cannot but believe its history to have been guided in that direction, as though intentionally, from the beginning.

------

ized the two vantage points that confront each other here in his *Vorlesungen über die Methode des akademischen Studium* (Stuttgart and Tübingen, 1803), 213 ff.; and a reminder of these brilliant ideas about history generally is all the more appropriate here since of themselves they apply especially to church history. "The opposite standpoint to the absolute," says Schelling, 216 f., "is the empirical, which in turn has two components: the pure perception and determination of what has occurred —a matter for the historical researcher, who represents only one side of the historian as such—and the combining of the empirical materials into an intellectual identity [*Verstandes-Identität*], or (since the latter cannot be found within the occurrences as such, which from an empirical perspective can only appear contingent and unharmonious) an arrangement designed by the subject in accord with a purpose, which thus far is didactic or political. This treatment of history with a quite specific, non-universal intention is, in accord with the word's ancient meaning, called pragmatic. . . . Modern men are inclined to regard the pragmatic spirit as the highest in history, and among themselves to assume it as though it were the highest praise. . . . Among the Germans, as a rule, it is with the pragmatic spirit as with Famulus in Goethe's *Faust:* 'What they call the spirit of the times is their own spirit, in which the times are reflected.' . . . History with a pragmatic purpose of itself excludes universality and also necessarily demands a limited object. The purpose of instruction demands a correct and empirically based linking of occurrences, by which the intellect [*Verstand*] is indeed enlightened, but the reason [*Vernunft*], without another ingredient, remains unsatisfied. . . . It is clear that since the mere linking of occurrences according to empirical necessity can never be anything but pragmatic, and since history in its highest Idea must be independent and free of all subjective connection, the empirical standpoint could not on the whole be its highest representation. . . . For the first time, then, history is completed for the reason when the empirical causes, while satisfying the intellect, become the tools and means of manifestation for a higher necessity. In such a portrayal history cannot fail to be the result of the greatest and most astonishing drama, such as can only have been composed in an infinite Spirit." And where should it have lacked this result least than in the field of church history?

This is at least the Protestant view of history. The high significance of the Reformation for the entire conception of the history of the Christian church is shown by the fact that concerning it the historical views of Catholicism and Protestantism stand in an irreconcilable antithesis. The Catholic is unable to imagine how, from within the bosom of the Catholic Church, an opposition could arise which the church with all its might cannot suppress and reassimilate to itself, and on this account he is likewise unable to connect the Reformation and Protestantism with a view of history whose foundation is the unchanging church in the unity of its principle of an unbroken tradition. Conversely, the Protestant sees in the same phenomenon so epoch-making a transition from an obsolete form of the consciousness of the church to one newly emerging that for him the whole historical process of the church remains an unsolved riddle, if he cannot regard it as a continuous development, progressing from moment to moment, and if he cannot understand the Reformation itself as simply one of the moments in whose interaction the course of development of the church consists.

If we ask what is epoch-making about this point of transition, then the difference between pre- and post-Reformation periods of the church can only be described as a difference in the relation between the Idea and its manifestation. Is it not then self-evident that during the entire epoch of the church up to the Reformation, the Idea of the church as a whole tended to enter into the reality of the world of manifestations and to merge with it in an inseparable unity, whereas since the Reformation the development of the church strives just as much to retract the Idea from the reality of the visible church and to separate Idea and manifestation to the full extent of their distinction?[2] Everything that constitutes the distinction between Catholic and Protestant conceptions of the church lies

2. [ED.] On the basis of this statement Karl Hase, in his *Die Tübinger Schule: Ein Sendschreiben an Herrn Dr. Ferdinand Christian von Baur* (Leipzig, 1855), charged Baur with arguing that for Protestantism the Idea soars far above the opaque positivity of the historical church and that for it the only authentic church is the ideal or invisible one. Baur replied that Hase had overlooked the adverb "just as much" (*ebensosehr*), which, he said, binds these two statements together equally, "so that Protestantism, in the same proportion that it seeks to introduce the Idea into the reality, must also withdraw it, and so that it does this indeed as Catholicism does, but not one-sidedly, rather only so that in the relation of Idea and reality these two sides, which belong together, may be well distinguished and set in the right relation to each other—the unity of Idea and reality and the incongruence of both." *An Herrn Dr. Karl Hase: Beantwortung des Sendschreibens "Die Tübinger Schule"* (Tübingen, 1855), 83–84; quotation from 84. This further clarification of a statement that Hase justifiably found obscure is important for a precise understanding of Baur's position.

on the boundary between the two great epochs into which the history of the church is divided.

If this of itself suggests a consideration that takes into account only the most general elements, then the further question surely arises as to what content the Idea of the church intends to transpose from itself and to realize in the visible church, or, since it can realize nothing other than itself, what it is essentially. The church is the real form in which Christianity is made manifest. If we inquire about the Idea of the church, we inquire, therefore, about Christianity itself. Difficult as the response to this question seems to be, it becomes obvious, as soon as we proceed with it, that Christianity can be essentially nothing other than that which the Christian consciousness of all times, in whatever form it may have occurred, has perceived in the person of Christ: the unity and union of God and man.[3] However else we may conceive the essence of Christianity—as everything it is intended to be for man in its various aspects, such as the revelation of Absolute Truth, the establishment of redemption, reconciliation, blessing—it has its absolute conception and expression in the unity and union of God and man, as that unity is perceived in the person of Christ, and in this perception becomes a fact of Christian consciousness. The substantial content of the historical development of the Christian church is therefore nothing other than this unity. All things can aim at realizing this unity for the Christian consciousness in the various forms in which it can be grasped only in such fashion that they are themselves but forms of this absolute content. Are not the major components in the historical development of the church themselves really to be placed under this guiding point of view? The two major forms in which the Idea of the church realizes itself are dogma and polity. In both, the development of the church proceeded to realize the Idea of that unity in such fashion that Christian consciousness could find in it the adequate expression of its Idea.

In the area of dogma, this happened above all through the doctrine of the Person of Christ, which, together with all the doctrines belonging to it (the Logos, the Trinity, the two natures of Christ and their relation), was the object of so much theological and ecclesiastical activity during the first centuries. Nothing is seen more clearly from all the controversies

3. [ED.] "Die Einheit Gottes und des Menschen." *Einheit* carries the meaning of both "unity" and "union" in English. It suggests a unity achieved by union, rather than a sheer identity on the one hand, or an outward combination of factors on the other. *Einheit* will be translated by either "unity" or "union," or by the hendiadys "unity and union," depending on the context.

and proceedings connected with that doctrine than the great impulse, which dominated the entire age, to objectify its innermost Christian religious consciousness in the christological dogmas. The endeavor to develop dogma in its various aspects from the focal point of Christology and according to the analogy of the basic conception given in it, is the essential content of the church history of the first six centuries, in which the dogmatic system of the church obtained all those essential determinations that since then have remained unchanged. In no other period did dogma have so predominant an influence as in the first, which brought it forth and fixed it for the total consciousness of the church. A portrayal of the first major period that does not permit its dogmatic character fully to appear can therefore only give a very unfaithful picture. It would merely adopt for itself without justification the now customary separation of the history of dogma from church history; the setting apart of the dogmatic for special treatment must not be intended in such a way that it thereby ceases to be an integral component of church history. The more closely dogma is joined to dogma, and the more uniform the characteristics with which all dogmas are developed together into a system, the less it can be misunderstood that the church in this whole period of its theological activity only follows an inner tendency of its nature. It has in itself the irresistible impulse to bring the unity and union of God and man, which is the absolute content of its consciousness, to firm conception and expression in all the dogmas of the Christian faith, and to set it forth in this definite form.

2. The Church before the Reformation

Just as the first period is that of the development of dogma, so the second, which embraces the whole of the Middle Ages up to the Reformation, is above all that of the history of the hierarchy, or more specifically of the Papacy. This is the same movement of the Idea of the church that, once it has arrived at a particular stage of the church's historical development in the area of dogma, moves in the same direction to another area. The formation of the hierarchy goes hand in hand with that of dogma. Dogma is first given more specific form by the bishops, but the bishops themselves exist only for the sake of dogma. They are the preservers, witnesses, and interpreters of dogma, the representatives of the church, whose total consciousness, illuminated by the Holy Spirit, is the highest source and authority for dogma. Through their decisions it obtains the form in which it is universally and unconditionally valid as holy, untouchable truth.

Just as the bishops are the main pillars of the hierarchical system, so the Papacy is simply the acme of the same, to which it mounts step by step. The Pope is the absolute bishop; and the Idea of the church realizing itself in the form of the hierarchy already possesses in the earliest foundation of the bishopric a predisposition toward everything it attains through its complete realization in the Papacy. The bishop, as the head of his congregation, already represents Christ, and is related to a single congregation in the same way that Christ, as its universal head, is related to the church as a whole. Similarly, the Pope in absolute fashion is the representative of Christ, the deputy of God and Christ. The same unity and union of God and man, which in Christology, as the epitome of the dogmatic system of the church, is the absolute content of religious consciousness brought to specific conception, has in the Papacy the absolute form in which the realized Idea of the church is perceived. Everyone who has faithfully accepted the dogma of the church, and who faithfully and willingly subordinates himself to the Pope as the representative of God and Christ, is aware of the beatifying union with God through this mediation. All the humanity of the Catholic Church is joined in absolute union with God through both dogma and Papacy. The Idea of the church, as it sought to realize itself from the earliest development of the church, is realized in the Papacy as the acme of the hierarchical system. The Catholic Church in its visible manifestation is the wholly adequate and concrete representation of the Idea of the church. God and man have become one in the two major forms in which this unity finds specific, concrete expression.

If the whole historical development of the church up to the Reformation, so considered, is divided into two periods, in which the Idea of the church has objectified itself in the two major forms of dogma and of hierarchy, then it automatically follows that the transition from the first period to the second can be located at the time when the still incomplete hierarchy takes the decisive step toward its fulfillment in the Papacy. That happened at the same time as the great transition from the ancient world to the Middle Ages. At this boundary between periods stands Gregory the Great, like an ecclesiastical Janus, since on the one hand, looking backward, he brings to an end the succession of church fathers, while on the other he initiates the succession of the medieval Popes,

whose prototype is already clearly to be seen in him. Therefore, to make
Charlemagne the beginning or terminus of a period is to assume an extra-
ecclesiastical standpoint alien to the subject matter. The iconoclastic controversy also becomes secondary; and since in any event Gregory VII
heralds himself as epoch-making, there is no reason to fix upon Innocent
III in particular as the culmination of the Papacy. The entire age with
which we are here concerned can in a general way be conceived only as
the period of absolute power for the church, which spared no effort to
become in outer manifestation what it was implicitly in Idea. As though
the Idea could have reality only to the degree that it actualized itself in
definite forms of outer, sensible existence, it is intent only on taking form
in the world of manifestation with all its power, and on expanding and
establishing itself there to its full extent. The further the church progresses in its development, the more unconditionally must everything be
subordinated to it. There is no existence independent of it; and if there is
still something beyond its power to reach and suppress absolutely, then
this has its basis only in the impossibility of the matter itself.

Implicitly, in the nature of the case, the Idea and its outer manifestation
cannot be unified in such fashion that they are related only as two mutually superimposed quantities. But this was unable to hinder the church
from asserting itself as the absolute power of the age. From it everything
proceeded; it was, for that age, the absolutely determinative form of consciousness. Even scholasticism, attempting to encompass dogma with intellectual categories, followed, in the service of the church, the same
systematizing tendency of the age, which had been organized by the
hierarchy into a well-articulated system. We can therefore understand all
manifestations characteristic of that age only in so far as we are able to
transpose ourselves into the consciousness of the time as it was filled by
the Idea of the church and of ecclesiastical religion. This form of consciousness was to remain dominant until it brought about its own destruction. But this it had to do, as surely as there was no intrinsic possibility
that the visible church could be the adequate representation of the Idea of
the church and of Christianity.

3. The Church after the Reformation

The Reformation is the great transition point, after which the Idea of
the church seems only to exhibit a tendency to unravel the fabric it has

woven. Whereas hitherto the development of the church has only moved forward in a straight line, now it seems with one stroke to reverse the trend, to turn backward and in upon itself. The spirit now animating the church is one of opposition and protest, antithesis, negation of what is. Since on all sides negation confronts the previous affirmation, its wish seems to be to move only backward—not, surely, so as to arrive at an absolute nullity but rather all the more strongly to affirm the true and enduring by a new absorption in itself, in the absolute content of the Idea, and in the denial of what is acknowledged as untrue and void. No one can deny that the moving forces of the Reformation, its causes and its effects, lie far beyond the controversy over Luther's theses and their immediate consequences, even though in many accounts the epoch-making character of the Reformation period still seems to depend solely on the person of Luther—who loses none of his significance if we regard him as the particular vital point at which various converging rays ignite into a blazing flame.

But if we bring together the various factors under consideration, where else can their unity of principle be more correctly recognized than in the concept of the church? That the perception of the church has become essentially different as a consequence of the Reformation is already shown by the distinction that since then has become customary, between a visible and an invisible church. The meaning of this distinction becomes clear if we bear in mind that, although before [4] the Reformation Christian religious consciousness in general found no offense in perceiving the true church in the visible church, or in regarding the visible church as the manifestation adequate to the Idea of the church, since then it has become increasingly evident that this awareness of unity between the church and its Idea has been badly and irreparably shattered. The Idea of the church is torn away from its manifestation as the visible church; it is in itself the driving and moving principle of progression away from one form of consciousness, in which as an untrue existence it can no longer remain, to another form, in which it is freely related to the manifestation in the same proportion that it stands above it.

The period in which the intent of the church was to set forth the absolute content of its Idea in visible manifestation, and to regard the Idea as absolutely one with its manifestation, is the period of the absolutism of the church. Of necessity, that absolutism conflicted with twin interests, the recognition of which was forced by the inner necessity of the matter

4. [ED.] Reading *vor* rather than *von*, as printed in the text.

itself upon the consciousness of mankind in its progressive development—the interests of the individual and of the state. Where the church rules with absolute power, the focal point of the individual's existence and consciousness is to be found only in the unity of the whole into which he is incorporated, in the objective reality of the church, and in everything that makes the church the essential mediator of his salvation, external and contingent though it may be. The externalization of that which possesses its truth only in an interior relation with the subject—since it exists for the subject, and the subject possesses himself in it and is directly aware through it of his salvation and his unity with God—sooner or later makes inevitable a turning point at which the subject draws back into himself from this externalizing of his religious consciousness, becoming aware that he himself is the absolute subject for everything that makes up the essential content of his religious consciousness. Protestantism is the principle of subjective freedom, of the freedom of faith and conscience, of the autonomy of the subject in opposition to the heteronomy of the Catholic conception of the church.

Just as only in Protestantism can the subject come to the right of his individuality, his free self-existence, the true consciousness of himself, so it is with the state. The absolutism of the church had removed from the state in advance the ground on which it could have arrived at an independent existence. Only when the church finally withdraws from this domain, with the acknowledgment that it is not in a condition to realize its Idea in the world of outer manifestations so as to be the power permeating and dominating everything, can the state claim for itself the area released by the church and assert its absolute right against the church. Where the church cannot or may not rule, the state appears with its full authority. Thus for the state, also, the claim to autonomy—an existence independent of the absolute power of the church—is established for the first time by Protestantism, or by the principle of subjective freedom that comes to its outer recognition only in Protestantism.

Even after the bond of unity between the Idea of the church and its outer manifestation, as established in the Catholicism of the Middle Ages, was dissolved by Protestantism, the church could not cease to aspire toward the realization of its Idea. Two factors now stand as the absolute condition under which alone the church can be recognized in manifestation as the Idea of the church, corresponding to Christian religious consciousness: the freedom of the subject and the autonomy of the state. No matter how the Idea of the church may otherwise be realized, as long as these two factors do not remain an absolute right, the existence of the church will become as false and self-destructive as before. In these two equally essential principles Protestantism has broken permanently with the Papacy, denying it every right to exist in the Protestant domain because of a certainty that the unity and union of God and man, which is the absolute content of Christianity and of the church as the form of its manifestation, cannot be recognized in a form of the church such as is represented by the Papacy. Accordingly, from the standpoint of the Protestant principle, man can know himself to be one with God and therefore certain of his salvation only when he is aware also of being free in himself, and sees himself placed in the state in the sphere of an existence free from the absolutism of the church.

However, in regard to the past, justification for Catholicism and the Papacy is by no means hereby denied; rather, for the first time it is now truly recognized, since only by means of it could the Idea of the church progress to a new form of realization, and Christian consciousness to a higher level of development. From a higher level one can understand for the first time the true significance of a subordinate level, because it now appears for the first time for what it really is—not the whole and complete truth, but only a momentary aspect of the same, through which the Idea in the course of its development must first pass, or a form of consciousness that must first be fully lived in order to be able to move on with the awareness of having the maturity for a higher level.[5] Therefore,

5. What is to be said here cannot be elucidated more simply and strikingly than by the words with which Hegel in the *Philosophie der Geschichte* (*Werke*, IX [Berlin, 1837], 398) concludes his treatment of the period of the Crusades. "At the grave of Christ the same answer is given to the Christians as to the disciples who sought his body there: 'Why do you seek the living among the dead? He is not here; he is risen.' The principle of your religion you have to seek not in the sensible, in the grave among the dead, but in the living Spirit in yourselves. We have seen the tremendous Idea of the union of the finite and the Infinite made spiritless; the Infinite is sought in a wholly isolated external thing. Christendom found the empty grave but not the union of the worldly and the eternal, and therefore lost the Holy Land. To all practical purposes, it is disappointed. . . . This, however, was the ultimate result of the Crusades. Here begins the period of self-reliance, of independence; at the Holy Sepulcher the West has taken leave of the East forever and grasped its principle of subjective, infinite freedom." [ED. Cf. *The Philosophy of History*, trans. J. Sibree (New York, 1956), 393.] This is equally true of the whole medieval period of the church. The Spirit that became conscious of the true Idea of the church through the Reformation took leave forever of the Papacy and the papal church, with a conviction that grew to certainty during the entire previous course of the same, but also only in this sense, that from now on it was no longer to seek the true essence of Christianity in this visible existence of the church.

even though Protestantism may have demonstrated clearly and convincingly to the Papacy and Catholicism the whole body of conclusions, false in principle, on which they erected their bold edifice, they nevertheless retain their full historical right, but only for the past. Protestantism itself must remain an unsolved riddle if it were to imagine another way of becoming what it has become than that by which its self-consciousness was mediated to it through the Papacy and Catholicism.

The opposition raised by Protestantism against Catholicism above all concerned the Papacy as the form in which absolutism must evoke well-justified opposition. But once the bond that brought the Idea of the church into union with its visible manifestation had been severed in only one of the two major forms, the same incongruity between Idea and manifestation necessarily became evident in the other as well. Dogma could likewise no longer serve as an adequate expression for religious consciousness of the Idea that should have been the absolute content of dogma. And just as the realization of the Idea of the church in Catholicism progressed from dogma to hierarchy and its completion in the Papacy, so the dissolution of the unity that Catholicism perceived in the visible church proceeded from the denial of the Papacy to the denial of dogma. What was denied in dogma concerned first of all only the elimination of elements introduced into dogma by the hierarchy and the principle of tradition on which it rested. But once ignited, the process of dissolution had here as well to pursue its further course, and it did so in the same fashion as with the Papacy.

It is generally agreed that the period from the Reformation to the present should be divided into two parts. But what should be the point of division? The Peace of Westphalia, from which Hase dates the most recent period, has merely too political a significance, since it did not bring about an essential change either in the inner nature of Protestantism or in its position with respect to Catholicism. Unquestionably, the epochal point can be located only in the general revolution of dogmatic consciousness during the course of the eighteenth century. Here for the first time Protestantism accomplished the same analytical criticism of dogma—which had remained unchanged since the ancient church—that it had already brought against the Papacy in the time of the Reformation. It was the same process of dissolving a unity whose elements could no longer be unified in the consciousness of the age. Just as the Papacy was overthrown when in the person of the Pope the person of Christ himself, the God-man, the representative of God and Christ, the infallible head of the church, could no longer be recognized, but only a weak and fallible human being; even so, faith in the authority of dogma disappeared completely once the consciousness of the age was no longer prepared to accept a form of dogma in which the person of Christ was to be perceived as the totally adequate and exclusive unity of the divine and the human. The reshaping of the ancient ecclesiastical system came about largely because all those ideas, principles, and teachings by which Socinianism first criticized and polemicized against the doctrine of the person of Christ also gained entrance and acceptance in the Protestant Church, and were carried out to a far greater degree and with more rigorous consistency of principle. In opposition to the Papacy the intention of Protestantism was to allow what man is in himself, as a self-constituted individual, as a free, self-conscious subject, to come into its own, and to set him free for himself from the complex of the hierarchical system in which he was entangled by the sacrifice of his independence and personality. Similarly, in the realm of dogma the major task concerning the doctrine of the person of Christ was to posit the true humanity of Christ in place of a transcendent supernaturalism in which the human was only a disappearing moment of the divine, and to grasp his entire manifestation as much as possible from the natural historical continuity in which it belongs. It was now regarded as a first principle that if the unity and union of God and man, which is the absolute content of Christianity, were to be perceived in the person of Christ, this could occur only under the assumption that his humanity remained in its full integrity and was regarded as the essential, substantial foundation of what he is as a whole.

Thereafter, the whole conception of Christianity followed a course corresponding to this basic perception. The humanization, rationalization, subjectivization, interiorization, and spiritualization of Christianity was, in different forms and directions, the watchword of the time. Just as it was believed that the Papacy had not been transcended as long as it was not analyzed into the basic elements out of which it came, so likewise there was no specific terminus in the criticism and analysis of dogma. Everything that at one time or another had been dogmatically defined must be sharply and precisely scrutinized to see whether it was not already a moment of the process in which the Idea of the church objectified itself in order to enter into union with its visible manifestation. Here even the canonical writings could not set any firm limits. Historical criticism would have labored in vain in the investigation of Christianity's historical origin had it not at least established that within this first historical sphere Christianity was already involved in a process of development so closely connected with the history of the first centuries that the view of the process of the development of Christianity held by the most recent criticism could not but differ essentially and at many points from previous views.

On the whole, can history have a higher task than the ever deeper investigation of the historical continuity linking all phenomena that lie before it as given objects? Thus its natural endeavor is to penetrate with all the means at its disposal into that which still confronts it as a solid, closed mass—as much by investigation of particulars as by subordination of particulars to a guiding higher point of view, from which alone they first obtain their firm position in the whole—in order to melt and dissolve this mass and to draw it into the general flux of historical becoming, a flux in which, in the endless concatenation of causes and effects, one event is always the presupposition of another, in which all together are mutually supported and maintained; and what alone must remain forever incomprehensible is that which could in advance make the claim to stand in the midst of history outside of all historical continuity.

4. *The Periods of Church History and the Arrangement of Its Material*

If we survey the entire course of the Christian church from the beginning to the present, the Reformation in every respect represents a turning point too crucial not to be the pivotal event upon which the whole of historical understanding turns. On the one side the church exists as a unity, on the other as cloven and divided; or, since the two parts of the divided church are related as the church of the past and the church of the present and future, the former is the church emerging from itself and the latter the church returning to itself. The era before the Reformation is further divided, in the fashion already noted, into two periods, the ancient and the medieval, which correspond to the two major forms of the church. In the period of the ancient church we can designate the epoch of Constantine in particular. If the period prior to the Reformation represents an attempt by the church to realize its Idea in the visible world and to constitute itself in it as the absolute power, then the first step toward this absolute monarchy of the church was the elevation under Constantine of Christianity as a victorious power over the whole Roman Empire. In the second step the church, through the fixation of dogma, provided its spiritual power with the solid form and consistency it needed as the foundation of its absolute rule. For the external completion of the spiritual hegemony of the church, the third step furnished the head through whom the church, with its absolute divine right, took the reins of world rule into its hands. With the Reformation, a new consciousness arose in the church, a recognition of having built on too material a foundation and having depended too much on the finite forms of the visible, sensible world. It now did everything to reduce itself once again to the elements from which it had arisen, but only for the purpose of beginning, after the exclusion of all material and mortal components, a more spiritual and immortal structure on an eternally enduring foundation.

Also lacking is a more rigorous method for the arrangement of historical material within each of the periods. The major forms in which the Idea of church history explicates its content are dogma and the hierarchy; but alongside these are others, variously arranged. The division, still maintained by Gieseler, into an external and an internal church history is untenable because of the incongruity of the two major parts. In addition to the history of the expansion and curtailment of the church, the history of its relation to the state is also considered a part of external church history. But a state existing outside the Christian church would only be a pagan state—such as the Roman Empire was before Constantine—coinciding with the pagan world that confronts Christianity. The Christian state is not outside but rather inside the Christian church. On the whole, it seems that the category of the relation of state and church has not found its proper place. Before the Reformation there is, strictly speaking, no state alongside the absolute church. Questions concerning the relation of state and church are identical with the question concerning the extent to which the papal monarchy has asserted itself. In the Protestant Church, out of the recognition that the visible church is always only a very imperfect realization of the Idea of the church, another form of Christian existence has assumed its place alongside the church—the Christian-moral state; but its relation to the church belongs under church government. Since for external church history only the expansion and curtailment of the church would remain, everything else being internal, the entire distinction has no more significance.

The distinction between internal and external is called into question because the church is itself an externalization of the internal essence of Christianity, and therefore every element in the concept of the church serves only to emphasize the internal essence of Christianity in external manifestation, to fix it and objectify it for consciousness. In this regard, the first element is the history of the dissemination and the curtailment of Christianity. First of all, Christianity has to establish itself in the world. Once it is established, that component is subordinated; it is of greatest importance in periods when a new principle must first be introduced into the world, as in the earliest age and in the age of the Reformation. The second component can only be the history of dogma. Dogma is the true substance of the church; for every religious community there must also be a specific, dogmatically fixed form of religious consciousness.

In addition to dogma and the other major form, polity, much else is to be found—with dogma, to be sure, as its presupposition. But it is inappropriate to conceive—as Gieseler also does—the history of church doctrine (which, together with the history of worship and the history of the internal constitution of the community, makes up internal church history) as (1) an object of knowledge: history of dogma, history of moral conceptions, history of the theological sciences; and (2) a living and effective social influence: history of piety and morals. Worship is a special component by which Christianity is objectified in the form of the church. Since worship is a form of action, religion in general gives to the life of man a specific practical direction, a distinctive religious-moral character. To the component of worship is thus joined the component of moral life. What Gieseler too narrowly describes as the social influence of piety and morality accordingly belongs here. Only from this point of view does the history of monasticism—in regard to whose position church historians for the most part vacillate—fall into place. Gieseler separates the history of monasticism from the history of morals; Neander connects it in the fourth period with the history of church polity, to which it does not belong; in the same period Hase, quite without justification, has a separate chapter on the nature of orders. Since monasticism originally arose out of asceticism, and thus out of a religious-moral motive, it was subsequently a very characteristic manifestation of the moral life. Only when it is seen from this point of view does it become immediately apparent that Christian moral life has an essentially different character in each of the various periods of church history. If the Idea of the church has been objectified in all these components, then the whole now obtains for the first time its firm support and continuity in the history of the constitution of the community or of the hierarchy. Since all these components, as elements in the concept of the church, are thus internally connected, their position cannot be arbitrarily changed. Therefore, in the otherwise correct arrangement of Neander's church history, his giving of the history of doctrine only as the last part of the history of each period is not to be approved. And it is even less appropriate to connect dogma so closely with ecclesiastical scholarship and literature that it cannot emerge in its full and independent significance—as is true of Hase, whose church history in general treats dogma too externally.

5. General Church History

Finally, we must still ask in what sense we can talk of a general or universal church history.[6] Neander called his work a "General History of the Christian Religion and Church"; Gieseler gave his the title, "Text-book of Church History"; Hase wrote simply a "Church History." Without doubt Gieseler and Hase also wanted their works to be considered as general church history, even if they did not expressly designate them as such. Every presentation of church history that does not exclude anything special from its scope, and undertakes to recount the history of the Christian church from the most ancient times up to the most recent, is thus of itself a general church history; but the conception of general church history is not thereby exhausted. In whatever form church history provides the universal that belongs to its content—whether on the broad foundation of a narrative that goes into every detail as exhaustively as possible, or in the compendious brevity of a compressed, pregnant expression—something relative always still adheres to general church history, beyond which it cannot move, and from which the conclusion can only be drawn that the conception of the universal can here be defined on the whole not quantitatively but only qualitatively; for no presentation can deal in more than a limited way with the infinite multiplicity of details.

Just as the universal differs from the particular not merely quantitatively but qualitatively as well, so also church history can arrive at the

6. [ED.] The German allgemein embraces the meanings of both "general" and "universal" in English. An allgemeine Kirchengeschichte is general in the sense that it embraces all aspects and periods of church history; at the same time it is universal or cosmic in perspective, since it is concerned with the underlying unity and meaning of church history. In the following section, both English terms have been used to translate allgemein. As a rule, when the word is used adjectivally, it is translated by "general"; when it is used substantively, it is translated by "universal."

universal inherent in its concept not by mere abstraction from the particular but only from the Idea of the church itself, in that as an Idea it must contain in itself the principle of a vital development proceeding from the Idea. A history of the Christian church can rightly be called "universal" only when the historical material, which must be accepted as the given, is so permeated by the Idea as the moving principle—in accord with the particular moments to which the Idea ordains itself—that the universal appears as determinative in the particular. The conception of the universal also establishes the double task, based on the reciprocal relation between universal and particular, of comprehending and perceiving both the universal in the particular and the particular in the universal. In Neander's view of history, too, the singular and the manifold are two equally essential basic forms of church life; but we must also think of the two in an immanent relation to each other such that the singular opens itself to the manifold and the manifold is comprised of the singular. In proportion as the historian must, on the one hand, become absorbed as deeply as possible in the particular, individual, and concrete aspects of historical phenomena, in order to attain the complete reality of historical life, so on the other hand he must also raise himself to the heights of the universal Idea, in order to grasp the particular from the universal and to see in it only the particularity of the universal. The task of historiography is completed only in the union of these two mutually complementary methods, which make up the two aspects of the same process—moving from the particular to the universal and from the universal to the particular.

PART TWO

❖

Introduction to
Lectures on the History
of Christian Dogma

I

THE PLACE OF THE HISTORY OF DOGMA IN THE
REALM OF THE THEOLOGICAL SCIENCES

1. *The Relation of the History of Dogma to Church History*

The significance and importance of the position occupied by the history of dogma in the body of the theological sciences is a function of its relation to church history and to dogmatics, for it has the closest connection to both of these disciplines. Since Christianity belongs to the succession of historical phenomena, what it is in its essence can be determined only in a historical fashion. As a historical phenomenon, Christianity existed from the beginning in the form of the Christian church. Everything that is connected with Christianity as a historical phenomenon is included, therefore, in the history of the Christian church, which can be divided into several major parts in accordance with the various components into which church life is divided. One of these components has as its object the "doctrine" in its historical development on which the Christian church rests, or "dogma" in the widest sense of the term. The history of dogma is thus properly a part of general church history. That it has been separated from the general content of church history and made a theological discipline existing in its own right, is partly because of the importance that dogma has in comparison with the rest of the content of church history, and partly because of the special difficulties bound up with its historical treatment.

The history of dogma is related to church history, accordingly, as a part to the whole, and here the significance of church history in contrast to it can readily be seen. But it is also possible to understand the relation of the history of dogma to church history in such fashion that it emerges from the subordinate position of a part related to the whole and stands alongside church history as having equal significance. If dogma is re-moved from church history, then the latter, with respect to the content that remains its special concern, is occupied chiefly with those phenom-ena in which the activity of church life is directed wholly outward, and in which the ecclesiastical realm is closely bound up with the political, such as in the history of the Papacy. Thus the histories of dogma and of the church can be distinguished in such fashion that the latter is seen to be concerned with the outer aspect of church life, whereas the former turns to its inner aspect; and if the two, so considered, stand on the same level in relation to each other, then the history of dogma is elevated above church history to the same degree that the internal must be placed above the external. Everything external has its basis in the internal life from which it proceeds. The condition of the church in its various epochs has generally been determined by the attitude that ecclesiastical consciousness assumes toward dogma, by the various forms it takes in relation to dogma (according as Spirit relates itself to the latter more or less freely and in it obtains to the freedom of its self-consciousness), and by this inner pro-cess of development, as the history of dogma has portrayed it. The his-tory of dogma, therefore, is that discipline which enables us to see into this inner aspect of church life and which acquaints us with the course of the spiritual movement to which the external phenomena are attributable as their ultimate basis.

2. *The Relation of the History of Dogma to Dogmatics*

In this fashion, the history of dogma as *history* has the closest connec-tion to church history; as the history of *dogmas* it has no less close a connection to dogmatics. Dogmatics is the system of dogmas that deter-mine the content of Christian faith, ensuing as the result of the entire preceding historical development of dogma. Dogmatics itself is thus only the result of the history of dogma, or the point at which the historical movement of dogma stops and fixes itself in the consciousness of the time, in order firmly to establish as an enduring truth for the present what has turned out to be the highest point of development from the past. How-ever, this happens for a present that will itself become a past, and that cannot prevent the same enduring truth from becoming engulfed also in the continually moving flux of history—a flux in which every result exists only to become itself a moment in a newly initiated sequence of development. From this situation, the importance that the history of dogma holds for dogmatics becomes immediately clear. If the history of dogma is, at its starting point, only a part of church history, then, at the terminal point of the history of dogma, dogmatics itself is only a part of it, a part distinguished from the whole to which it belongs in that the movement that is the element of the history of dogma seems for subjective consciousness to have ceased, as if everything preceding had taken its course in order to issue in just this result.

To assume its vantage point, dogmatics can only place itself in the movement of the history of dogma. It does this, however, by attempting as far as possible to bring to a halt the ever elapsing movement of dogma; it does so in order to arrive at a clear awareness of the constant element in the true Christian consciousness, of its immanent substantial content within the variable forms of the changing consciousness of the times. The more it succeeds in establishing itself thus in relation to the history of dogma, the more adequate it is to its task. But the more it allows itself to be carried away by the unending flux of the history of dogma in motion, the more it can only perish in that flux. As evidence for this, we need only to recall all those treatments of dogmatics that are not to be distinguished essentially from a historical portrayal of dogma, since, in accord with their entire structure, they proceed to enumerate and collect a greater or lesser quantity of dogmatic opinions and assertions, and perhaps to accompany them with a comparative judgment. A work in dogmatics maintains its peculiar character, as distinguished from a merely historical treatment of dogma, the less it is satisfied to proceed in merely historical fashion or to bring together a mere aggregate of historical materials—as has often enough been done—and the more it is able to bring whatever has obtained a certain consistency in the dogmatic consciousness of the time to specific conceptualization and expression. We need only to compare Schleiermacher's dogmatics, which distinguishes itself in exemplary fashion by the exclusion of all unnecessary materials from the history of dogma, with a *Lehrbuch der Dogmatik* such as the one by Hase.[1] What Schleiermacher says in a somewhat different connection is also applicable here. It is well for everyone to admit that a structure not at all connected with the language employed in ecclesiastical expressions of piety, even though consisting of pure and wholly characteristic ideas and views, and even though of a truly Christian nature, can

---

1. [ED.] Karl August von Hase, *Lehrbuch der evangelischen Dogmatik* (Stuttgart, 1826).

be regarded only as a private confession and not as a dogmatic statement. In general we can also say that the less there is in such a statement of what is publicly accepted, the less it corresponds to the conception of a dogmatics.[2] Here again the distinction is to be found between dogmatics and the history of dogma. The publicly accepted, which is the foundation of every dogmatic statement, is whatever has merged into the common consciousness of an age so that it obtains a periodic validity and endures for the time being.

Although the history of dogma remains unperturbed by the circumstance—and indeed regards it as essential—that everything belonging to its content passes into constant motion, pressing forward, as it were, in wave after wave, dogmatics has the opposite interest of bringing what is released from the constant flux of history to a stable shore, there to anchor it against the constantly changing element. Thus the highest task of dogmatics can only consist in securing, as far as possible, what at one time has emerged as true and valid for religious and scholarly conviction, and in mobilizing everything by which it can maintain itself for as long as possible against the assault of opponents. Dogmatics would in no way be able to stand by itself without the awareness that something firm and enduring exists in the midst of what is constantly changing and moving. Although the history of dogma should not be completely lacking in this awareness as well, the overriding dependence of dogmatics on the history of dogma can nevertheless be seen in the acknowledgment, which repeatedly obtrudes itself upon dogmatics, that everything permanent and enduring is only temporary, and that what for the present seems to have a still firm solidity must sooner or later revert to the flux of history, against which for the moment it seems to hold fast.

The awareness within dogmatics of battling against a stream whose pressure cannot be withstood for any length of time, despite all efforts to halt its course, is most openly expressed by the one recent dogmatician who has most rigorously excluded the foreign material of the history of dogma from his dogmatic system, and who has most clearly preserved the character of a dogmatic statement. Schleiermacher has assumed this relation of dogmatics to the history of dogma in his definition of the concept of dogmatics; he defines dogmatic theology as the science that systematizes the doctrine prevalent in a Christian society at a given time.[3] He

---

2. Friedrich Schleiermacher, *Der christliche Glaube* (2nd ed., Berlin, 1830), I, 127 [*The Christian Faith*, ed. H. R. Mackintosh and J. S. Stewart (Edinburgh, 1928), 90].
3. *Der christliche Glaube*, I, 125 f. [*The Christian Faith*, 88–89].

further remarks in this connection that every dogmatic statement should limit itself to the doctrine that exists at a particular time; to be sure, this is not often directly admitted, but it would seem to be self-evident, and the great quantity of dogmatic statements following one upon the other can be explained in large part only on this basis. It should be quite obvious, according to Schleiermacher, that the textbooks from the seventeenth century can no longer serve the same purpose now as they did then; that much now belongs only to historical description; and that now only new dogmatic statements can have the same ecclesiastical value as those had in their own day. Such a time will also come for contemporary works in dogmatics, except that great alterations in doctrine can of course only proceed from the more universal foci of development, whereas constant changes occur so gradually that they become noticeable only over a long period of time.

The inescapable fate of dogmatics is that it continually reverts to the history of dogma, which here discloses itself in its all-embracing power —a power that masters dogmatics. But dogmatics already appears in a dependent relation to the history of dogma because it cannot be oriented to its substantial content—namely, what is publicly received and fixed in the total consciousness of the time—except from the standpoint of the history of dogma. It must have sufficiently broad recourse to history to obtain a firm basis for itself. The whole consciousness of dogmatics rests on the foundation of the history of dogma. Only one who has followed the entire course of the development of dogma, and who has rightly understood the moments of the inner process of its movement, can assume a firm standpoint in the present; and only thus can the temporary be distinguished from what ought to be of more universal value, or what determines the fundamental character of the consciousness of an age from that which, being without significance, swiftly passes away and disappears.

The relation of the history of dogma to church history and to dogmatics has thus been specified, and the place it assumes in the context of the theological sciences as a whole has in general been designated.

THE OBJECT OF THE HISTORY OF DOGMA

1. *The Meaning of the Word "Dogma"*

The object of the history of dogma consists of dogmas, from which this discipline, like dogmatics, derives its name. Therefore the question arises as to what is understood by "dogmas," and what significance the word δόγμα [dogma] has obtained in Christian linguistic usage. Originally and etymologically, it was used by the Greeks and Romans—along with the terms "decree," "ordinance," "rule"—to refer especially to the opinions and propositions of the philosophers. For example, Cicero writes: "It is [wisdom's] duty not to doubt herself on her 'decisions' [*decretis*], which philosophers term 'dogmas' [δόγματα], any of which it will be a crime to abandon; for the surrender of such a 'decision' is the betrayal of the moral law. . . ." [1] This last remark already shows in a general way the sense in which the term is used: for the ancients the notion conveyed by the word δόγμα was of definitions whose character was absolutely given, and which demanded unconditional and universal acknowledgment. This sense of the word δόγμα is especially to be found in Stoic usage. In his *Meditations*, Marcus Aurelius Antoninus says, as a conclusion to his reflections: "Let these reflections suffice thee, let the principles [δόγματα] exist forever." [2] Likewise, Seneca writes: "It is the doctrines [*decreta*, which, as Seneca also remarks earlier, are equivalent to the δόγματα of the Greeks] [3] which will strengthen and support us in peace

1. Cicero, *Quaestiones academicae*, II, IX. [ED. *Cicero: De natura deorum; Academica,* trans. H. Rackham (*Loeb*, 1933), 502–3.]
2. Marcus Aurelius Antoninus, *Meditations*, II, III. [ED. Baur follows the reading of Codex Palatinus and Codex Parisinus 319. Cf. *The Communings with Himself of Marcus Aurelius Antoninus,* trans. C. R. Haines (*Loeb*, 1930), 28–29: "Let these reflections suffice thee, if thou hold them as principles."]
3. [ED.] Baur's insertion.

and calm, which will include simultaneously the whole of life and the universe in its completeness [in the practical sense of 'the principles essential to life' [4]]. There is the same difference between philosophy's doctrines and precepts as there is between elements and members; the latter depend upon the former, while the former are the source of the latter and of all things." [5] Thus, δόγμα contains the notion of the essential and necessary, the fundamental and normative, which is to be acknowledged absolutely as such, and which possesses absolute validity. The word has this significance even when that which makes a claim to this sort of validity is in itself only arbitrary and subjective, and can only appear as such.

In the New Testament the word δόγμα appears a few times, some in a political and others in a religious sense. It is used politically in Luke 2:1 to refer to the census decree of Caesar Augustus, and also in Acts 17:7, concerning the δόγματα καίσαρος [decrees of Caesar]. Political ordinances that are absolutely authoritative and must be obeyed are to be so understood. The religious usage of the word in the New Testament is closely connected with this meaning. In Ephesians 2:15 Christ has abolished "the law of commandments and ordinances [δόγμασι]"; in Colossians 2:14, God has "canceled the bond which stood against us with its legal demands [δόγμασι]." Cf. Colossians 2:20: "If with Christ you died to the elemental spirits of the universe, why do you live as if you still belonged to the world, submitting to regulations [δογματίζεσθε]?" The decrees of the Mosaic law were called dogmas not so much in the sense of being arbitrary and positive, as in the sense of commanding absolutely, requiring an absolute obedience. The "law of commandments and ordinances" is the Mosaic law as consisting of regulations that claim absolute authority and therefore ought to be observed unconditionally. In a like sense the ordinances of the apostolic resolution regarding Gentile Christians are called δόγματα in Acts 16:4—not as "decrees agreed upon by the church" [6] (as they were wont to be taken), and not as arbitrary, purely external decrees (which would be completely inappropriate in this context)—but as that which, once prescribed, was to be valid once and for all.

4. Cf. Marcus Aurelius, *Meditations*, I, IX; VIII, I. [ED. Baur's insertion. This is not a direct quotation; cf. *Loeb*, 6–9, 198–99.]

5. Seneca, *Epistula* 95. [ED. *Seneca ad Lucilium Epistulae Morales*, trans. Richard M. Gummere (*Loeb*, 3 vols., 1925), III, 64–67.]

6. [ED.] *Placita ab ecclesia sancita.* I am unable to locate this saying, which apparently represents a later interpretation by the church.

2. Ecclesiastical Usage; Dogma and Ethos; Dogma and Kerygma

With respect to ecclesiastical usage, which concerns us more directly, such church fathers as Chrysostom and Theodoret understand by the term δόγματα, as used in Ephesians 2:15 and Colossians 2:14, the doctrines or teachings [*Lehren*] of Christianity in contrast to the Mosaic law. The expression δόγματα already appears in the letters of Ignatius with this meaning: "the ordinances [δόγματα] of the Lord and of the apostles." [7] As a rule, the earlier church fathers refer to Christian doctrine generally as τὸ δόγμα, τὸ θεῖον δόγμα [the teaching, the divine teaching], [8] in the same sense. The doctrine of the Christian faith can be designated as δόγμα or δόγματα (the plural) in this sense only in so far as it is understood to be that which is unconditionally authoritative and is to be acknowledged absolutely. Christianity is τὸ δόγμα in so far as it consists of absolutely valid truth as divine revelation.

There also appears in the word δόγμα the distinction between the dogmatic and the ethical. According to Cyril of Jerusalem, "the way of godliness consists of these two parts, pious dogmas and good works." [9] According to Chrysostom, "Christianity requires both correctness of doctrine and an upright life." [10] Here, however, dogmatics [*Glaubenslehre*] is not opposed to the teaching of ethics [*Sittenlehre*]; rather, faith and actions alone are contrasted. But it is another matter when Gregory of Nyssa says of Christ that "having divided the life of Christians into two parts—an ethical component [τὸ ἠθικὸν μέρος] and a scrupulousness about doctrines [δόγματα]—he established the saving dogma [τὸ σωτήριον δόγμα] in the ordinance of baptism, on the one hand [cf. Matthew 28:18–20, where the question is both of μαθητεύειν (teaching) and of τηρεῖν τὰς ἐντολάς (keeping the commandments)],[11] while he exhorts that our lives be made upright through the keeping of his commandments [διὰ τῆς τηρήσεως τῶν ἐντολῶν], on the other hand." [12] In distinction from

7. Ignatius, *Epistle to the Magnesians*, XIII [cf. *LCC*, I, 97].

8. Cf. Origen, *Contra Celsum*, III, xxxix; Eusebius, *Historia ecclesiastica*, VII, xxx.

9. Cyril of Jerusalem, *Catechesis*, IV, II [*LCC*, IV, 99].

10. Chrysostom, *Homily* 28 on Jn. 3:19–20. [ED. *PG*, LIX, 164B; *The Fathers of the Church: A New Translation* (New York, 1947 ff.), XXXIII, 273. Baur cites *Hom.* 27.]

11. [ED.] Baur's insertion.

12. Gregory of Nyssa, *Epistula 6* (A. Gallandi, *Bibliotheca veterum patrum*, VI, 631). [ED. This passage is not found in the Greek text of the epistle in either *PG*,

the δόγματα, the ἠθικὸν μέρος, [ethical component] represents in general the ethical side of Christian life; but not merely ethical actions are intended here, since the δόγματα stand alongside the ἐντολαί [commandments] of Jesus as the object of τήρησις [observance]. In Socrates' church history, where it is said of a bishop that "he at first avoided all doctrinal discussion, confining his discourses to ethical teaching,"[13] the ἠθικὴ διδασκαλία, or ethical teaching, is opposed to the διαλέγεσθαι περὶ δόγματος, the doctrinal discussion. But no scientific separation of dogmatics [*Glaubenslehre*] and ethics [*Sittenlehre*] is thereby intended; rather, the διδασκαλία ἠθική is not so much ethical teaching proper as it is instruction for practical life.

Also worthy of note is the peculiar distinction Basil of Caesarea draws between δόγμα and κήρυγμα: "Dogma [δόγμα] and proclamation [κήρυγμα] are two distinct things; the former is observed in silence; the latter is proclaimed to all the world. One form of this silence is the obscurity employed in Scripture. . . ."[14] Δόγμα and κήρυγμα are distinguished as the inner and the outer, the esoteric and the exoteric. Κήρυγμα is the publicly expressed doctrine, δόγμα the implicit content of doctrine, still resting in its silent source, which has yet to be spoken but which is implicitly valid without being expressed in specific propositions; it is the immanent content of Christian consciousness. However, this distinction between δόγμα and κήρυγμα has no wider significance; it was much more common to link with the word δόγμα the concept of a publicly advanced and acknowledged doctrine.

3. *The Concept of Dogma as the Object of the History of Dogma*

On the basis of this ecclesiastical usage, therefore, the term "dogmas" means the doctrines or teachings [*Lehren*] of the Christian faith, in so far as they contain the absolute Christian truth. If what is to be regarded as absolute truth must be stated as exactly as possible, then the same applies to the concept of dogma. Dogmas are the doctrines of the Christian faith in so far as the latter exist in propositions in which they have obtained as

---

XLVI, or Georgius Pasquali (ed.), *Gregorii Nysseni Epistulae* (*Gregorii Nysseni Opera*, ed. Wernerus Jaeger, VIII:2 [Leiden, 1959]), 34–36.]

13. Socrates, *Historia ecclesiastica*, II, XLIV. [ED. Cf. *NPNF* 2, II, 73. The reference is to Meletius, Bishop of Antioch, at his installation in the See.]

14. Basil of Caesarea, *Liber de spiritu sancto*, XXVII [*NPNF* 2, VIII, 42].

much as possible their specific ecclesiastical doctrinal form, as, e.g., one cannot speak of a dogma of the Trinity without thinking at the same time of a specific form of this doctrine. If dogma is Christian doctrine in general, then dogmas are the more exact determinations of the same—the content of dogma explicated in its entirety. If therefore one speaks not merely of a history of Christian dogma but of a history of Christian dogmas,[15] it is thereby presupposed that the doctrines of the Christian faith are the object of this discipline—more specifically, the way in which the content of these doctrines has emerged through their gradual development, and in which they have been brought, as far as possible, to their precise conception and expression.

The historian of dogma can take his position only from the standpoint of the most recent dogmatic consciousness. His task is to follow Christian dogma from its first origins through all periods and moments up to the most recent point of its development. Whence, however, can he obtain a precise conception of the object whose historical movement is the problem with which he ought to concern himself, but from the consciousness of the present? The historian can move back into the past only from the present. His whole task is to move backward along the same course by which the subject matter has come down to him, in order to complete in his own consciousness the movement which the subject matter has completed objectively. To make the origin and progress of the subject matter the object of historical reflection, he is obliged to understand it from that point in its historical development at which it enters the consciousness of the present. Herein lies the inner, essential connection of the history of dogma with dogmatics. Only when the historian of dogma has before him the whole system of dogmas, as its entire content has been explicated in the dogmatic consciousness of the present, can he follow the movement of dogma from its beginning in such a way as to transpose himself into the movement of the subject matter itself, thereby following it from moment to moment. Only thus will he be able to recognize in its earliest beginnings the elements of its entire subsequent development, in which everything that goes before can only be the necessary presupposition of what follows. Only when he knows the essence of the subject matter and what is included within it, does he also know what he is to look for in history so as to include everything that belongs to the subject matter it-

15. [ED.] The German term for the discipline known in English as "history of dogma" is *Dogmengeschichte*—literally, "history of *dogmas*."

self, and not to overlook anything that represents a moment of its development.

4. The Scope, the End, and the Beginning of the History of Dogma; the Teaching of Jesus and the Apostles as the Point of Departure

The more the historian of dogma has assimilated the entire dogmatic consciousness of his time, and the more his own consciousness is filled by it, the more capable he becomes of understanding and expressing for subjective consciousness the whole wealth of material that is objectively contained within historical development. Furthermore, if the historian of dogma can orient himself only from the dogmatic consciousness of the present with respect to the beginning of the movement whose course provides the content of the history of dogma, then for this reason the object of the history of dogma can only be dogma in its entire scope and content, as it runs through all ages, including everything by means of which its content has been explicated. Just as history in its own objective course is a never-resting movement, so historical reflection and presentation cannot stop at any point until it has reached the final phase of development in the present. To terminate the whole at any earlier point that might be established would only be an arbitrarily determined suspension which in the nature of the case could not be justified.

Therefore, the object of the history of dogma is not correctly determined when J. G. V. Engelhardt [16] stops with the year 1580 and devotes his third period (1517–80) merely to treating the formative activity of the Reformers with respect to dogma, and the preparations for concluding the doctrinal systems of the three separated Western Churches. From this termination itself he provides (i.e., sets forth) information as to the form of individual dogmas in the symbolic writings of the Lutheran, Catholic, and Reformed Churches. But even if the symbolic systems of doctrine came to an end in the period designated, this termination is not that of the history of dogma itself. In so far as they are viewed as something closed, the symbolic systems can only express the consciousness of their age. They have their own history. The dogmatic movement has gone beyond them, and new forms of dogmatic consciousness have emerged from the

16. In his *Lehrbuch der Dogmengeschichte* (2 vols., Neustadt-an-der-Aisch, 1839). [ED. See below, 357.]

continuing movement that are no less important for the history of dogma than the earlier forms. They also represent a content that dogma has developed from itself. The object of the history of dogma would therefore not possess the scope that properly belongs to it were it to be restricted to those doctrinal systems. They represent only a point in dogmatic development beyond which the dogmatic consciousness has continued to develop. The same is true of every other point that might be similarly established for the history of dogma as a whole. Thus can be seen how inconsistent it is with the nature of the case not to be willing to consider as an object of history of dogma all the determinations [Bestimmungen] obtained by dogma in the continuity of its historical development. If dogma in its entire scope and content is the object of the history of dogma, then the terminal point of the latter can only lie where it has established itself in the dogmatic consciousness of the present and has set forth the whole wealth of its content. Since it is concerned with the history of *dogmas*, the discipline of the history of dogma should consider dogma as the object of its presentation not merely in its yet undetermined unity but in the distinction between its individual parts, with all the determinations by which alone it has obtained its specific content. It would not completely master its object if it did not pursue the whole temporal course of dogma as far as it has continued to develop through new determinations.

Just as the object of the history of dogma is defined by the terminal point up to which it has continued, so also with its beginning, which can only be the beginning of the movement of dogma itself. The sole question is where the beginning of this movement is to be found. Does it lie in the New Testament itself, or only where the New Testament ends? Concerning this question there are two different views. According to the first, the history of dogma ought to have as its presupposition a beginning that lies outside the movement of history and the temporal variability of dogmas. If the history of dogma is the movement of dogma, then—since there is no becoming without being—at the basis of the constantly moving and changing must lie something that exists from within itself [*ein an sich Seiendes*], and that, as self-identical, substantial truth, remains untouched by everything history produces in the continuing stream of changing human opinions. According to this view the intention is to distinguish the teaching of Jesus and the apostles from the proper content of the history of dogma, and to set the beginning of the latter at the end of the apostolic age. Hence the object of the history of dogma would only be the changes that followed upon the teaching of Jesus and the apostles; and these two factors—the object of the history of dogma and that which it has as its presupposition, the teaching of Jesus and the apostles—would be related to each other as the changeable and the unchangeable. This is what W. K. L. Ziegler means when he writes [17] that it is not the intention of the history of dogma to know what Jesus and the disciples taught, since that investigation belongs to completely different theological sciences —exegesis and dogmatics. Rather, we need merely to know what is found in the religious teaching of Jesus and the apostles for doctrines of the church—what has been taken from this teaching, what has been regarded as important, and what has been changed. The history of dogma can therefore only begin when the church is left to its own resources after the departure from the scene of the authentic interpreters of Christian teachings, the apostles—i.e., at the end of the first century. Here we ought to look for the first alteration in the Christian doctrines of faith, and this first alteration after the death of the apostles is at the same time their ecclesiastical origin.

On the other hand, Wilhelm Münscher asserts [18] that what Jesus and his disciples taught is also a historical question, and that in a history of Christian doctrine a lacuna always remains when the teaching of the founder is passed over in complete silence; this lacuna becomes all the more noticeable the more frequently later Christians call upon the sayings of Jesus and the apostles in confirmation of their own views. On this basis Münscher prefaces the first period of the history of each dogma with a short sketch of the teaching of Jesus and the apostles. Here Münscher is absolutely right: the teaching of Jesus and the apostles, upon which the entire history of dogma depends, cannot be excluded from the content of a history of dogma. But a further question is whether the teaching of Jesus and the apostles stands at the beginning of the history of dogma in such fashion as to represent the unchangeable element in relation to the changeability of dogma in the history of dogma. This is the view ex-

---

17. "Über den Begriff und die Behandlungsart der Dogmengeschichte," *Neues theologisches Journal* (1798), 337.

[ED.] Werner Karl Ludwig Ziegler (1763–1809) was professor of theology at Göttingen and Rostock, and lectured in church history, history of dogma, and New Testament exegesis. He was a frequent contributor to the rationalistically oriented *Neues theologisches Journal* and *Journal für theologische Litteratur*, both edited by J. P. Gabler.

18. In his *Handbuch der Dogmengeschichte* (4 vols.; Marburg, 1797–1809), I, 7. [ED. See below, 354–55.]

pressed by Engelhardt at the conclusion of his *Dogmengeschichte:* [19] he does not, indeed, expect "that all opinions and views of men will coalesce, or that doubt will give up its restless questioning, the inquisitiveness of its presumption, and the pride of its dark prejudice, or, in similar fashion, that seriously and honestly intentioned thinkers will be united in the results of their thought at all points on the way to the goal set for them; but on the other hand [he expects] all to agree that, in a science that has as its goal the salvation of man, a given—and indeed a given from the source of truth itself—can be the sole point of union, and that this given is deposited in the Word of Scripture and in it alone." The exegesis of this Word will set forth its meaning (which is implicitly clear at all points) still more clearly and explicitly in every aspect and detail; criticism will show its external credibility with ever greater and more convincing power; history will demonstrate ever more comprehensively how the whole of the more recent era—in statecraft, science, and art—has proceeded from this Word, and would be unthinkable without it; and thus philosophy will find in this Word its inexhaustible source, base on it its deepest thoughts, in it investigate its origin, and seek its necessary connection with it. In a certain sense this can be granted, and the biblical Word can be considered the substance at the basis of the whole content of dogma, so that the Word of Scripture is rightly explained only as the unchangeable source related to the changeability of dogma. But that it is possible by means of exegesis to eliminate all differences in regard to the content of Scripture must rightly be doubted.

5. *The Relation of the History of Dogma to New Testament Theology*

The question here is of the view one has of the teaching of Jesus and the apostles contained in the writings of the New Testament. If the teaching of Jesus and the apostles is considered as a single whole, in such a fashion that everything forms one and the same unity and nowhere displays any essential differences, then it would be highly superfluous to dwell on a point that shows no historical movement for as long as would be required to describe the teaching of Jesus and the apostles as a whole. If the teaching of Jesus and the apostles is a totality in this sense, the

19. J. G. V. Engelhardt, *Lehrbuch der Dogmengeschichte*, II, 378.

history of dogma would be completely justified in presupposing it absolutely as that which in itself is unchangeable and which only later, via a sequence of changes, passed into the soil of purely human history. However, it is another matter if one regards the writings of the New Testament as already permitting within themselves the distinction between various conceptions of the original teaching of Jesus and various tendencies and types of doctrine. Then it is self-evident that the beginnings of the same movement that has taken its further course in the history of dogma can already be detected in the New Testament. Therefore the content of the New Testament cannot merely be made the presupposition of the history of dogma; that content in itself is already the beginning of historical movement. The same differences can be seen here that have subsequently developed to an ever greater degree.

Since, however, this beginning of the historical movement is delimited by having its sphere consist of the writings of the New Testament, it can be detached as an autonomous whole from history of dogma proper. This is the proper relation between New Testament theology and the history of dogma. New Testament theology is the essential presupposition of the history of dogma; in it lie the first beginnings and elements of all dogmatic development, in so far as various doctrines are already to be distinguished in the writings of the New Testament, or at least the skeleton of the same is to be found there. Therefore, one cannot follow the course of the history of dogma without exact knowledge of New Testament theology. The formative concept of a history of dogma—that it regards its object from the point of view of a historical development—also constitutes the authentic concept of New Testament theology. The latter is the presentation of New Testament doctrine, but only in so far as a diversity of tendencies and doctrinal forms can be detected in it; and just this is what places it in the closest connection with the history of dogma.

At the same time this is what distinguishes the history of dogma from dogmatics, despite all the connections between the two. What dogmatics would regard as permanent is already, for the history of dogma, the first member of a new progression. To be sure, there is also a point in biblical theology (the seat of the origin of the history of dogma) that does not belong within the sphere of movement; but the concern of the history of dogma is to push that point as far back as possible and to acknowledge it only in the teaching of Jesus, which is the unqualified basis and presupposition of apostolic teaching. Thus there can be no doubt that the teaching of the apostles—if not also the teaching of Jesus itself, in so far as it is not immediately given [20]—already belongs to the sphere of the historical movement of dogma. But whether the history of dogma should engage in a closer discussion of the teaching of Jesus and the apostles is another question, since the wealth of material that here lies before us has made it necessary to limit this subject to the independent field of biblical theology. The extent to which the history of dogma can also be biblical theology must be left undecided; the major point, in regard to the object of the history of dogma, is that an area is here acknowledged which the history of dogma can rightly claim, in so far as it is justified in appropriating to itself everything embraced by its concept.

6. The Unity and Multiplicity of Dogma

In the discussion above, the object of the history of dogma has been established with respect to its points of origin and termination; and within these two termini it has been given as broad a scope as possible. Accordingly, the object of the history of dogma is everything that has happened with respect to the development and more exact determination [Bestimmung] [21] of Christian dogma from the earliest period of Christianity and the Christian church down to the present. But in the development and determination of dogma itself, where is the real object of the history of dogma to be found? It has already been pointed out that, in so far as the history of dogma derives its name not from dogma in general but from the plurality of dogmas, the development of dogma can be thought of only as the process by which the one implicit dogma [das an sich Eine

20. [ED.] That is, when it is mediated, interpreted, and modified by the tradition. Only the direct and authentic teaching of Jesus—in so far as it can be established critically through investigation of the Synoptic Gospels—would, according to the author, transcend the sphere of the historical movement of dogma.

21. [ED.] The translation of Bestimmung by "determination" here and elsewhere (as in part 4 of this section) is not fully satisfactory; but the alternatives, such as "definition" (which conveys too restrictive and formal a meaning), are even less satisfactory. Bestimmung derives from stimmen (lit., "to tune"), which in turn is related to the word for "voice," Stimme. The prefix be- often has the effect of changing an intransitive to a transitive action. Hence the root meaning of Bestimmung seems to be that of the "tuned," focussed, unified self-expression of something, in which the whole is contained implicitly; by its various "tunings" or self-determinations, a thing achieves progressive self-actualization. The "tunings" or "determinations" of dogma are accomplished by what the author here describes as the various "focal points" (Mittelpunkte) or "points of unity" (Einheitspunkte) which make up the body of Christian dogmas.

Dogma] [22] increasingly divides and cleaves itself in order to produce and to bring into clear consciousness the distinction within it. A series of determinations, which can be considered not only as separate dogmas but also in their relation to one another, emerge from this constant distinguishing movement of dogma—a movement by which now this and now that particular dogma is established, made the object of reflection, and brought to more or less adequate expression. The more important and essential the determination obtained by dogma, the more what in itself is only a determination of dogma actually becomes dogma; the determination is set forth with a significance independent of dogma in order to obtain its own existence. The more that dogmatic determinations of this sort parallel one another in equally independent significance, claiming recognition as moments into which each of the focal points of dogmatic consciousness can equally fall, the more the substantial unity of dogma is divided into a multiplicity of dogmas, each of which is in itself a special point of unity. In this fashion the one substance of dogma is transformed, as it were, into a multiplicity of monads, each of which in its distinction from the others also contains in itself the unity of dogma and is a substantial focal point of the whole.

Let us take dogmas such as the doctrines of the Trinity, the person of Christ, sin, grace, and the sacraments; each of these major dogmas is in itself so full of significance and so rich in content that from each one dogma can be developed and conceived as a whole, in the inner continuity of its parts. Each major dogma contains an essential and basic article of the Christian faith. Just as in the ecclesiastical symbols of the earliest period it was customary to establish the content of the Christian faith in a series of distinct articles, and to emphasize that content by means of their special significance, so likewise dogmas are the determinate, more or less scientifically constructed, didactic form of these basic articles of the Christian faith. Here we can see with what justification the history of dogma derives its name not merely from dogma in general but from the plurality of dogmas. Its object is dogma in its self-diversification; at each

22. [ED.] *Das an sich Eine Dogma* could perhaps better be translated by another term found in this same paragraph, "the one substance of dogma" (*die Eine Substanz des Dogma*). The "one dogma," "the one substance of dogma," is the "Idea" of Christianity—the reconciliation (or "unity and union") of God and man in the person of Christ (see above, 244). But this unitary substance remains implicit until it achieves concrete historical form in the various *dogmas* (the "tunings" or determinations) of the Christian faith. We have here, then, an instance of the dialectic between (unitary) Idea and (plural) manifestation, discussed by Baur in the last chapter of the *Epochs*.

of various points it obtains a new, substantial focal point from which to portray dogma in its totality.

7. *The Focal Point of Dogmatic Consciousness*

The historical movement of dogma consists in the various expressions of the substantial unity of dogma in the major dogmas that can be distinguished within the one implicit dogma, according as the focal point of the dogmatic consciousness of an age is to be found in this dogma or that. The fact of this movement is to be incorporated into the determination of the object of the history of dogma. Accordingly, it can be said with justification that the object of the history of dogma consists of dogmas that give expression to the dogmatic consciousness of an age by the changing relation in which they stand to one another. As a quick glance at history shows, it is quite natural that in the various periods of the Christian church now this dogma and now that should obtain an especially prominent and commanding significance, and that in the course of time each dogma comes, as it were, into its own and gives an entire period its determinate character. The more that this happens, and the more the entire movement of an age is concentrated in a specific dogma, proceeding from it in various directions and thus impressing its own dominant tendency upon the entire content of the Christian faith, then the more we must see such focal dogmas as expressing the total consciousness of an age. Accordingly, there can be no doubt that dogmatic determinations are properly the object of the history of dogma the more there can be recognized in them not merely the view and opinion of an individual but a common consciousness as well. If history is faithfully to reproduce and portray what every age contains in itself objectively, since every age has its determinate character, so likewise every dogma can be taken only as expressing the consciousness of an age.

8. *Conciliar Proceedings; Writings of Church Teachers; Opposition between Orthodoxy and Heterodoxy*

The especial significance for the history of dogma of public deliberations on dogmatic questions, and of conclusions established through common discussion by representatives of the Christian church, is self-

evident. They are a major object of the history of dogma precisely because they express the dominant tendency of an age in the form of
unambiguous documents. Accordingly everything else that is to be an
object of the history of dogma must be evaluated with these in view. The
more a thing is to be regarded as expressing the total consciousness of an
age, the more important it is for history. Of course this is not to say that,
in comparison to what is made the object of common deliberation and
action and is deposited in the acts of the councils, all else has little or no
significance. The proceedings of the councils are themselves only the
result of a movement that is more deeply enmeshed in the spiritual life of
an age. Therefore they cannot be rightly understood in their deeper
significance if we do not also return to the origins and causes out of
which their present significance first developed.

Councils are by no means the only way in which dogmatic determinations obtain more general validity. Independently of all authority of the
councils, the writings of distinguished church teachers over many centuries have achieved a very determinative influence, which is to be explained only by the fact that in such writings a specific tendency of an
age first has found its adequate expression. This alone can be the standard
by which everything else of greater or lesser significance for the history
of dogma is to be judged. The more deeply a thing is enmeshed in the
common consciousness of an age, and the more universal its validity, the
more justly it is to be viewed as an object of the history of dogma.

Viewed thus, the opposition between orthodoxy and heterodoxy
emerges of itself as an object of historical consideration. If the fact is
considered that the concepts of orthodoxy and heterodoxy are highly
relative, and that what was once heterodox often became orthodox,
whereas what was regarded as orthodox often later lost public support,
then there can be no claim of a greater right for orthodoxy to be an
object of the history of dogma than for heterodoxy. Rather, their mutual
conflict and strong opposition serve as an important object to which
history should direct its full attention.

9. The Systematizing Tendency of Dogma; Relation of the History of Dogma to the History of Dogmatics

Thus the various forms of dogma, as the common consciousness of an
age is given expression in them during the various periods of the Chris-

tian church, are the major object of the history of dogma. Everything that concerns dogmas, as a whole and in detail, has its unity in the total consciousness of an age. In this fashion we see attempts made from one perspective or another, during the process of dogmatic development, to obtain a focal point to which the entire content of dogmatic consciousness can be attached. The more significantly such a point emerges, and the more deeply it is enmeshed in the total continuity of dogma, the more it provides the basic form of a whole system of dogmas. We can think in this connection, for example, of the Augustinian doctrine of sin: despite close proximity to many other dogmas, it also contains in itself the foundation of a system. It is quite natural that the development of dogma —even if at first it has been oriented toward individual dogmas and has tried to exhaust the entire content of dogmatic consciousness in the emergence of those dogmas—should proceed increasingly from the individual to the total and universal, and should hold in view the systematic connection of dogmas with one another.

This systematizing tendency also belongs to the object of the history of dogma; accordingly, that history must demonstrate not merely how each individual dogma has been brought to scientific conception and expression, but at the same time how dogma in its development has also striven to gather all dogmas into a continuous scientific whole. This is called the "history of dogmatics"; and from everything that has already been said about the relation of the history of dogma to dogmatics, it is obvious that the history of dogmatics is also a part of the history of dogma. Ordinarily, however, historians of dogma have been of the opinion that the two disciplines should merely stand next to each other and that it would be good and appropriate, although not necessary, to connect the history of dogmatics with the history of dogma, since, as Wilhelm Münscher says,[23] the material and the form of the doctrines of faith have a constant effect on each other, and since the knowledge of the one would be incomplete without the other. In a later work,[24] Münscher distinguishes between an external and an internal history of the Christian doctrine of faith. The former, which would have as its object the structure and implementation of the doctrine of faith, is called the history of dogmatics; the latter, which would present the variations in doctrine itself, is called the history of dogma. The two are so completely enmeshed in each other that it

---

23. *Handbuch der christlichen Dogmengeschichte*, I, 5.
24. *Lehrbuch der christlichen Dogmengeschichte* (Marburg, 1811), 2.

would be well to join them. Similarly, Leonhard Bertholdt [25] bases the distinction between the history of dogma and the history of dogmatics on the difference between essence and form. The history of dogma is equally concerned with both; the history of dogmatics is concerned only with the *form* of doctrine as it develops, but this, however, only in general, in so far as it provides what has always been sought in the effort to join Christian dogmas into a connected, scientific, and systematic whole, and to cast systematized Christian doctrines into various forms.

According to Ludwig Baumgarten-Crusius,[26] the history of dogmatics, in so far as it may be distinguished from the history of dogma, is concerned either with the continuity of the doctrine of faith and its formation into a whole, or with its scholarly and scientific form, and the means by which it has emerged in the church, as well as how it has changed. In the first instance it could indeed exist independently alongside the history of dogma. However, there would be great advantage in joining it to the history of dogma; many phenomena belonging to the latter can be explained only by means of the history of dogmatics. In the second instance, the two disciplines can be separated only with difficulty, for the expansion and determination of Christianity by means of dogmas happens to a significant extent through the influence of philosophy and scholarship; and the form and content of ecclesiastical ideas and views cannot ordinarily be separated from each other.

All these explanations of the relation of the history of dogma to the history of dogmatics, which in the main do not differ greatly from each other, are based on a false conception of the relation between form and content. Form is everywhere conditioned by content. If in regard to dogmas, in so far as they constitute a scientifically connected whole, form is neatly separated from content, then it is impossible to see what the history of dogmatics might have as its object other than something completely empty and insignificant. The form of the relation of one homogeneous dogma to the other changes whenever there is a sweeping change in the basic dogmatic point of view. The dogmatic systems that have been established in the various periods have always had a significant influence on the form of dogmas and their combination into a scientific whole; for the principle that is the basis of a system must penetrate all its parts and

25. In his *Handbuch der Dogmengeschichte* (2 vols.; Erlangen, 1822), I, 9. [ED. See below, 356.]

26. In his *Lehrbuch der christlichen Dogmengeschichte* (2 vols.; Jena, 1832), I, 15. [ED. See below, 356–57.]

modify them in a distinctive way. If therefore the history of dogmatics ought to have as its object the form or the arrangement and combination of dogmas, then it is by no means an empty discipline but rather deals with the content as it corresponds to and necessarily conditions the form —if indeed, as its concept requires, it is also a history of dogmatic systems. The specific formation that dogmas have received cannot be rightly understood without a return to the general and comprehensive principle that is their basis; but it is just this that fashions the substance of related dogmas into a system.

Therefore, all historians of dogma who place the history of dogmatics in a merely external and arbitrary relation to the history of dogma have an incorrect or at least an unclear notion of the task of the latter. They take the history of dogma to be that only of individual dogmas (which, to be sure, it is to begin with, by virtue of its name [27]); as a result, individual dogmas constitute the material and their combination the form. But one must not forget that the history of dogma is at the same time the history of dogmas in their unity, and that this unity of dogma itself is not merely formal in character. Rather, there exist a multiplicity of dogmas only because the one implicit dogma [*das an sich Eine Dogma*] has divided and explicated itself in its distinction—in a series of dogmas that are the distinct elements of the total concept. The object of the history of dogma is thus dogma in its multiple elements as well as in its unity of concept; in this way the relation of the history of dogma to the history of dogmatics is automatically expressed. The history of dogma should discern how individual dogmas, one after another, have been fashioned into their own independent life and have claimed their right to exist, but also at the same time how they coexist only as parts of a whole, elements of one and the same concept, members of an organic system.

27. [ED.] See above, 270, n. 15.

III

THE METHOD OF THE HISTORY OF DOGMA

1. *The Nature of Method*

The object of the history of dogma concerns the *what*, whereas its method concerns the *how*; or, to put matters differently, the method of the history of dogma concerns the manner in which the objectively given in dogma also becomes subjectively known. A true historical method can only be one that holds to the object itself, pursues the movement of the subject matter itself, and transposes itself into it wholly, excluding everything merely subjective and arbitrary, everything that is not based on the subject matter itself but belongs only to the mode of representation [*Vorstellungsweise*] of the [knowing] subject. Historical presentation [*Darstellung*] should not merely arrange things one after another externally; it should also penetrate the continuity of causes and effects, so as to disclose the inner web of history before us. The manner in which this is done constitutes the nature and essence of [the historical] method: a method that should disclose events in their continuity, their movement and development. That movement, however, should not be merely fabricated or imagined, but should be immanent in the subject matter itself. Consequently, the method of the history of dogma can only be the movement of dogma itself. Dogma contains in itself the driving and moving principle through which it has become a historical given. The whole history of dogma is nothing other than the concept of dogma dividing itself into and proceeding out from its elements, explicating itself in ever wider scope.

The concept is the thought of Spirit; only from the nature of Spirit can the movement immanent to the concept of dogma be recognized. It is obvious that method has the important task, on which a great deal depends, of establishing in the nature of Spirit itself the movement of dogma, the universal moving principle through which dogma becomes a history of dogma. Customarily it is not denied by historians of dogma that their concern is above all with the principle—the universal—by means of which the individual is to be grasped. The point is simply that precisely here the history of dogma must exert the greatest effort to bring the true conception of its nature to consciousness. To be sure, certain universal causes related to the internal aspect of the emergence of dogmas in the Christian church, and to their diversity and alteration, are commonly mentioned, as are the principles that have been applied in regard to the spirit, matter, and form of thought; but all of this constitutes a very arbitrary and disorderly aggregate.

2. *Münscher; Baumgarten-Crusius*

Wilhelm Münscher [1] derives the change in dogmas from the following four general causes: (1) The nature of human Spirit in general, as shown in the propensity for speculation, in an oscillation between progression, cessation, and retrogression, and in the emotions of men. (2) The external conditions under which Christians have lived—especially climatic variations, as reflected for example in the antithesis between East and West; the fortunes of Christians (for example, periods of oppression have produced spiritualistic sects); the polity of the church; whether the teaching office has been entrusted to ignorant or enlightened teachers; the ecclesiastical and linguistic usages that have served, in the expression of religion, to inquire into the state of freedom and to communicate one's thoughts; and the nature of the religions displaced by Christianity. (3) The changing needs of the time, such as the necessity for defending the faith against opponents and the zeal for preserving its purity, which has been the source of many controversies. (4) The various aids to the work of dogmatics, especially such auxiliary sciences as biblical exegesis, philosophy, and history.

How externally everything here is collected! How superficially everything is related to a cause that is itself only the effect of a deeper cause! For example, that the teachers of a certain period are either ignorant or enlightened must surely have its determinative cause only in the spirit of the age.

1. In his *Handbuch der christlichen Dogmengeschichte* (4 vols.; Marburg, 1797–1809), I, 14 f. [ED. See below, 354–55.]

Equally striking is the illogical procedure in the enumeration of such elements, and above all the lack of a general principle for connecting the particulars, on the part of Ludwig Baumgarten-Crusius, in whose *Lehrbuch der christlichen Dogmengeschichte* [2] the so-called universal, inner history of dogma is concerned entirely with investigating these questions. Among the influences that have awakened and promoted the dogmatic spirit and dogmas generally, those that arose out of apostolic Christianity first come under consideration, in so far as the various discussions and applications of primitive Christian ideas provided by the apostles allow for dogmatic investigation and the construction of dogmatic concepts and systems. Likewise Holy Scripture—as a result of misunderstanding and intentional misinterpretation, as well as of forced literal exegesis—must have called forth and demanded the dogmatic spirit and a variety of dogmas. More significantly, the universal and natural aspiration of human Spirit has served to move from feeling to conception, from mere faith to knowledge, from practice to theory, and from particulars to systems; this has also been occasioned by the common desire of men, especially in religion, to proceed from what is simple and human to the arena of speculation, fantasy, and learning. To all of this is added the spirit of certain ages, and of the religions that came into contact or conflict with the newly founded religion. In addition to the above-mentioned causes, the general history of mankind and of nations during the Christian era has been of special importance for the formation of dogmas. The development of Christianity and the church itself has necessarily shaped dogmas in various ways. In addition, we are reminded of the influence that climate and custom or national character have had on the variations and formation of ecclesiastical dogmas; likewise, political systems and legislation, the religions with which Christianity and church have had contact (Judaism and paganism), philosophy and the philosophical schools and systems, and finally individuals such as teachers and leaders of the church.

There is no need to demonstrate more fully that in all these components, which could easily be added to if one wished, a clear conception of the development of dogma has scarcely been obtained, since a firm criterion is lacking throughout. Some of the elements are dreadfully contingent, arbitrary, and insignificant, as for example the influence of Scripture through misinterpretation of certain passages! And why, once Scripture is introduced into the series, should only its misuse be mentioned in

2. *Lehrbuch der christlichen Dogmengeschichte* (2 vols.; Jena, 1832), I, 53–57. [ED. See below, 356–57.]

connection with dogmatics, and not also its proper use? For what is said simultaneously about the beneficial moral efficacy that Scripture has always shown [3] cannot be considered a proper judgment of the place of Scripture in the development of dogma. It must appear strange that in the enumeration of these elements greater weight is not accorded to Scripture, since there is a very important theological school for which Scripture is the highest and indeed the sole basis for dogma. Why, therefore, is Scripture not mentioned in this more general connection? But even were it to be mentioned, what is unsatisfying about this entire mode of consideration would be disclosed, since in the first place it would be necessary to inquire why only the authority of Scripture should be taken into account in the determination of dogma. The majority of these elements are dreadfully vague, indefinite, and trivial in their generality. What is one to think when it is said, for example, that the general history of mankind and of nations, indeed of Christianity itself, has been of influence on the formation of dogma? How can there be any part of the history of Christian dogma that does not fall under the influence of Christianity? Equally trivial is the proposition that individuals have always been important as teachers and leaders of the church; for an individual can be thought to have an effect only under the influence of more general elements and in light of the circumstances of the time to which he belongs.

It can readily be seen what a distorted and self-annihilating concept lies at the basis of this entire universal, inner history of dogma so-called; for these elements are almost purely external, whereas it is supposed to have been an *inner* history of dogma whose construction has been undertaken on the basis of these elements. There is only one exception: the universal and natural aspiration of human Spirit. But it is astonishing how little this element is in harmony with the others, especially in the position given it; and its determination as a whole shows how superficially its subject matter has been handled. In addition—even granting that the elements are all laid out quite properly and with exhaustive completeness—nothing is indicated to give an understanding of the sequence and reciprocal connection of their influence on the history of dogma. One does not know whether and why one or another of these elements was of influence in this or that period, and it can just as well be imagined that all have been at work simultaneously as that only one of them has.

How little in general the history of dogma is considered from the point of view of a progressive development can be seen from what is said about

3. *Lehrbuch,* 55.

the development of Christianity, and its inevitable and manifold influence on the shaping of dogmas.[4] Baumgarten-Crusius says it is obvious that the history of dogma takes no part in dogmatic controversies over the actual or potential perfection of Christianity, in so far as it is a historical object. This means that it does not have to consider whether a perfection is to be located in the Idea of Christianity. But Christianity as a phenomenon must go and have gone its way toward gradual perfection. But how can something be asserted about Christianity's historical development that is denied concerning the history of dogma? If the history of Christianity shows a gradual perfection, i.e., a steadily progressing development, then the same cannot be denied to dogma. Just for this reason, the history of dogma cannot remain indifferent to the question of how the progressive development of dogma is related to the Idea of Christianity.

In Baumgarten-Crusius' *Compendium der Dogmengeschichte* (Leipzig, 1840), there is no longer a question of a universal, *inner* history of dogma, but only of a *universal* history of dogma. The division into a universal and a special history of dogma is intended solely to provide a sufficiently broad basis for the universal character that a history of dogma ought to have. As Baumgarten-Crusius defines it, the universal is Spirit, thought, the inner life of individual periods, conceived both externally and internally, positively and negatively; and thus the question is one of the influences on the Spirit and thought of the church in individual periods, as well as of Spirit and thought in themselves and of the dogmatic tendency and dogmatic controversies in the church. Now there is good cause for the distinction in the history of dogma between universal and particular; the question is whether the universal and the particular are placed in the right relation to each other. As Baumgarten-Crusius says in the *Lehrbuch*,[5] the history of dogma should treat the emergence of dogmas in general and the most prominent causes from which they and their permutations derive; it should specify the times and the men through which this comes about; here it joins hands with the history of dogmatics. In the second part [of the *Compendium*], the views that have been expressed concerning individual ecclesiastical topics are arranged one after the other with a few more titles and in a somewhat different order. So treated, scientific thought justifiably requires the designation of a universal and a special history of dogma. For, without regard to individual dogmas, the first part specifies the general influences on and conditions of doctrinal development and determination.

But, as the treatment clearly shows, this is nothing more than a purely

4. *Lehrbuch*, 63.   5. *Ibid.*, 25.

external combination of the two methods that are customarily distinguished in the treatment of dogma—the chronological and the systematic—without any inner, organic connection between the two. The concepts of the universal and the particular are used here in a completely arbitrary fashion. At no point is it evident why the first part is called the universal, for its one distinction consists in the use of the chronological method as a basis. Nor could anything in the conception of this method lead to a distinction between the universal and the special; and the treatment itself shows that the universal part contains a large body of very special information. Indeed, a comparison of the two parts shows that the amount of particular information in the universal part is greater than in the part devoted to special history of dogma. If the latter is so called merely because it arranges various opinions on individual dogmas one after the other, whereas the section on universal history specifies the times and the men responsible for changes in dogma, one might just as well reverse the point of view and say that the universal history consists of opinions advanced concerning individual dogmas, whereas what is concerned with times and men belongs to the special history. For, once this distinction is made, clearly the question of *what* is taught is of greater and more universal importance than the question of when and by whom individual doctrinal determinations have been advanced. Moreover, such a combination of the two methods is very disconcerting in that what belongs together and therefore ought to be joined is divided and treated in two different parts that are fundamentally self-contained. It is certainly to be expected, after all, that when dogmatic determinations are stated and developed there should also be information as to when and by whom they have been advanced, and that in dealing with the times and the men responsible for the changes in dogmas, there should be information as to their nature.

To conclude, what is shown here is the same lack of a comprehensive inner unity that has been so difficult a problem for the history of dogma hitherto. We have here a universal that is related to the particular, whose universal it is supposed to be, in a purely external fashion; on the whole, we are given only the outward aspect, without penetrating into the inner principle, the universal, from which the sequence of historical phenomena is to be conceived. Despite all the endeavors to penetrate the internality of the subject matter, we are not carried past the outward and superficial aspects of phenomena.

3. Neander

August Neander [6] does not move beyond this point either; and the same deficiency increasingly overtakes him the more he leaves behind the outwardness of customary historical understanding and presentation. Neander fully acknowledges that the dogmatic controversies, especially of the ancient period, are concerned with a very essential element, which belongs to the nature of the subject matter itself; he is far from seeing in them only empty subtleties, the queries of an idle curiosity, a tangle of ingenious views and opinions. In order not to ascribe too much to external circumstances or to the influence of individual men, we must—Neander very emphatically urges—always place ourselves in the total continuity of dogmatic development and perceive doctrinal controversies as a natural result of antitheses that have grown out of the understanding of Christian dogma over a period of time.

If, however, every age is conditioned by what precedes it, we must go back ever further; and the question must finally be raised as to what is the ultimate starting point for the course of dogmatic development. Neander's answer to this question is found in the general categories of realism and idealism. These are the universal antitheses from which all particular antitheses are derived—the various interests, tendencies, and points of view out of which Christian dogma, capable in itself of as yet indefinite and diverse conceptions, takes definite shape for the unfolding Christian consciousness. But in what do these categories themselves have their ultimate foundation? According to Neander, the answer can only be: in the universality of human nature. Therefore Christian dogma, in the course of its temporal development, assumes various forms as the nature of single individuals of itself tends toward a more realistic or a more idealistic manner of thinking and perception.

But just here is the weakness of Neander's standpoint. Since human nature exists only in single individuals, history consists only of individualities, determined by all those elements that make of each a determinate human subject. Neander's standpoint is purely psychological. For him the universal, which is the principle of the movement of history, is a mere abstraction: it is human nature, whose universality is only an abstract

6. In his *Geschichte der christlichen Religion und Kirche* (6 vols. in 11; Hamburg, 1825–52). [ED. See above, 207, n. 6.]

concept, not the concrete universal, thinking Spirit, whose immanent moving principle is in the nature of thinking itself, and which strives toward the freedom of its self-consciousness in the single individuals who are the living members of the organism of history. So it is with Neander too that despite all his attempts to understand them in their significance, the elements of dogmatic development are for him only the beliefs, views, and subjective reflections of individuals, not thoughts of Spirit, by which the concept of the subject matter itself is determined—thoughts that contain in themselves absolute truth, independent not only of all subjective believing and thinking but also of the contingent form they assume in the consciousness of the individual, and that therefore can be grasped only from the general standpoint of speculative reflection. What makes this weakness in Neander's view of history especially noticeable is that in him the immanent progress of history is nowhere to be found. Only new individualities emerge, never those new epochs of development, those moments of the continuing course of development, that are produced out of the inner necessity of the subject matter itself. Nothing intrinsically new occurs; the old is simply repeated; new antitheses are merely different forms of the old ones that existed long before. Even in the antithesis between Protestantism and Catholicism brought about by the Reformation, we can detect only a renewal of the old struggle between Augustine and Pelagius. Everything is divided into supernaturalism, mysticism, contemplation, and speculation on the one hand, and into intellectualism, sober rationalism, and the one-sidedly conceptual and dialectical on the other. Everything falls either to the right or to the left and is classified according to the major categories and their several modifications; hence we have, to be sure, a number of parallel spiritual tendencies, but no central movement of Spirit.

The greatest antithesis, on which everything finally depends, is between Christianity, which permeates humanity like a leaven, and human nature, which is variously affected by this ferment, according to individual diversity. The total view does not move beyond the sphere of such antitheses; hence we always find ourselves within that sphere. It is completely beyond the ken of this view of history that Christianity or Christian dogma, and human nature or human Spirit, should not have the merely external relation of an antithesis but should be at the same time implicitly one; for Christianity itself is grounded in the nature of Spirit, and Spirit cannot as a consequence have a merely external relation to it. Thus we still have no universal that contains in itself all antitheses, as a true universal must, and that can allow those antitheses to issue from itself. Thus the method of the history of dogma is still not the movement of the subject matter itself, and for this reason it does not yet come upon a living process. There are only various contributing elements or factors, but the unity of principle, and thus also of movement, is lacking.

4. Rosenkranz

J. F. K. Rosenkranz [7] has made an attempt to understand the history of dogma from the standpoint of a progressive development, conditioned by the inner connectedness of its moments, and to establish principles for each period. He defines these principles (which predominate in the development of the history of dogma in every period of ecclesiastical life) as *analytical, synthetic,* and *systematic* cognition. In the Greek Church—the church of substantial feeling—dogmatic cognition is analytical; i.e., it resolves faith, which is the given, and which implicitly is knowledge and thought, into its various components, and gives expression to these distinctions as general principles. Thus it joins dogma to dogma until the major determinations of the Christian faith collectively emerge. In the Roman Church, synthetic cognition replaces analytic. It is dogmas that are given. Cognition presupposes their truth, but takes pains to provide proofs for them anyway. Thus arises the definition of individual, abstract concepts, as well as reflection upon the connection of individual concepts with one another, and finally the proof of dogmatic propositions. But even if synthetic cognition is vindicated through logical proof of what is accepted on faith, it still suffers from not having obtained its material from itself but having merely appropriated it as given. It has, to be sure, an advantage over analytical cognition, which remains satisfied with an abstract conception of the material, in that it derives its reflection from

7. In his *Encyklopädie der theologischen Wissenschaften* (Halle, 1831), 249 ff.

[ED.] Johann Karl Friedrich Rosenkranz (1805–79) was professor of philosophy, theology, and literature at Halle (1831–33) and Königsberg (1833–79). As a student at Berlin and Halle, he came under the influence of Hegel through the efforts of Henning and Hinrichs. He was also a student of Schleiermacher at Berlin, and reviewed the latter's *Glaubenslehre* in the Hegelian *Jahrbücher für wissenschaftliche Kritik,* 1831. In the *Encyklopädie,* he attempted systematically to implement the viewpoint of Hegel's philosophy of religion, in opposition to Schleiermacher and romanticism. Thus in Baur's treatment, Rosenkranz stands in contrast to Neander, as representing a Hegelian idealism rather than a Schleiermacherian romanticism. His other theological writings included a *Naturreligion,* published in 1831.

the relation of content to form; but content and form are still externally related to each other. Thus in its totality it only arrives at a more or less felicitous aggregate of various dogmas and their proofs.

Then the Protestant Church—as the church of ideal objectivity—makes the transition from the premises of synthetic and analytic cognition to systematic cognition, whose soul is the self-moving concept. Analysis lacks reflection in the universality of its determinations; synthesis lacks the freedom of the subjectivity of the concept in its reflection upon the particular. This freedom is attained in the theology of the Protestant Church, in which, for this reason, there is a question not so much of individual dogmas, as in the Greek Church, or of rigor and precision of logical explanation, as in the Roman, but rather of the establishment of principles, which, in the struggle occasioned by their one-sidedness and consistent elaborations, are absorbed into the same organic unity, and which scientific thought alone can satisfy through a vital self-development. Method is recognized for what it truly is, namely the movement of the content itself; and with this recognition the long dispute between theology and philosophy is resolved.

Here indeed the attempt is made to place the method of the history of dogma within the movement of the content itself; the moments in the movement of the content of dogma consist of the various modes of cognition—analytical, synthetic, systematic. But against this way of understanding it can rightly be objected that it determines the movement of dogma only according to the formal activity of Spirit. If, in the movement of dogma, Spirit is seen to be related to itself analytically, synthetically, and systematically, then from the beginning the object of cognition is approached from without. Only what is already given in its totality can be analyzed; and it can only be resolved into the distinctions that are already implicit and that are to be explicated for consciousness. But the question is, where does analytical cognition obtain its object? If the object can rightly be said to be given with the content of faith, and the content of faith can be said to be explicated only in dogmas, nevertheless this action by which faith objectifies itself in dogma should not be regarded as a merely formal, analytical process. Faith is encountered as a unity and totality when it explicates itself in dogma as an objective thing, externally given.

Just as improperly, Rosenkranz designates as synthetic cognition the externalizing activity of Spirit in the second period. If synthetic cognition consists in providing a logical proof of the truth of dogma, why should it be called a synthesis? At bottom, it is also only an analytical procedure; the proofs of dogmas that are provided in this period are only analytical discussions of the characteristics of the determination of dogma. What is missing above all, however, is a demonstration of the necessity for a transition from analysis to synthesis. How does it come about, one must ask, that knowing Spirit is now concerned with the proof of dogma? The same goes for the transition to systematic cognition. If systematic cognition is the self-moving concept, a cognition that produces its material out of itself, then the question must be further asked, on what is the possibility of this absolute knowledge based, if from the very beginning the object of cognition was merely given to Spirit? If systematic cognition is to be the self-moving concept, then that which precedes it—namely, analytical and synthetic cognition—must also represent the same self-movement of the concept, and the implicit identity of subject and object must also be presupposed.

Hence, although the process of movement has in general been properly determined, the relation of the three moments of analytical, synthetic, and systematic cognition in this conception of the development of dogma is still too external, since these moments are not derived from the nature of thinking Spirit or conceived as the immanent movement of thought itself. That analytical, synthetic, and systematic cognition make up the process by which Spirit comes into harmony with itself is not sufficiently emphasized, although on the whole the attempt here made deserves recognition for locating the principle of movement in knowledge itself. For, as Rosenkranz says, no external motif can be dominant in history of dogma—neither climate, nor nationality, nor the unique character of a man as the true director of its movement. Only thus is it possible to transcend the superficiality of a view that would see in the history of dogma a bare aggregate of fortuitous opinions, and that has no inkling of the desire of Spirit to perceive its own internality, no idea of the hidden alliance to which all the actions of Spirit belong.

5. Kliefoth

Here we should take into account a similar effort that has taken as its sole task the challenging of a raw empiricism in the field of the history of dogma—an empiricism that can never uncover the Spirit behind the external manifestation—and that seeks to understand the history of dogma according to its inner nature. I have in mind the work by T. F. D. Klie-foth, *Einleitung in die Dogmengeschichte* (Parchim, 1839).[8] Kliefoth says of Rosenkranz that he wrongly places the development of all dogma in the first period.[9] The development of dogma in the Roman Church is by no means involved in the same development as the Greek Church. The East has had no part in Roman development, which was entirely unique. The subsequent development of the medieval church cannot be separated from that of the Roman, but rather forms an essential continuation of it. To be sure, it is not proper to say that all dogmas arose in the earliest period; it could be said that they continued to arise, especially if the earliest period is limited to the Greek Church. But on the other hand we cannot agree with Kliefoth that new dogmas arise in every period—that, for example, the particular dogmas of justification, faith, repentance, conversion, Scripture, etc., first arose in the early periods of Protestantism. There is no question but that these doctrines also existed previously. From these two assertions, both of which are equally true and equally false, it follows that on the whole the question is not one of dogma in and of itself, nor of the extent to which dogma in itself is always the same, but rather of the relation of consciousness to dogma. In every period this relation varies; and if one proceeds on this view, then the Roman Church of the ancient period cannot be related to the church of the Middle Ages but rather only to the Greek Church.

Kliefoth describes the differences between the periods as follows:[10] The Greek Church could not rise above the analytic form, because it developed dogmatically only one component of Christian knowledge [namely, theology]. The second component [anthropology], had to be expanded by means of reflection[11] and indeterminate reasoning. The

8. [ED.] Theodore Friedrich Dethlof Kliefoth (1810–95) was a leading figure in the Prussian Lutheran Church. Following his education at Berlin (under Schleier-macher, Neander, and Hegel) and at Rostock, and a period in the pastorate, he assumed important administrative functions in his church. He was chief ecclesiastical councilor and later president of the superior ecclesiastical court. The *Einleitung* was an early work, written at the height of his Hegelian orientation; later he became strongly Lutheran, seeking to perpetuate not only the doctrine but also the polity of Lutheranism, in independence of state control, but with a strong focus on central authority. He was also opposed to the movements toward church union. In addition to the *Einleitung* he published writings on church polity, liturgy, worship, and catechetics, as well as several commentaries on books of the Bible and collections of sermons.

9. Kliefoth, *Einleitung in die Dogmengeschichte*, 112 ff.

10. *Einleitung*, 108.

11. [ED.] For Kliefoth, "reflection" apparently designates a pre-systematic mode of thinking, one which represents a transition from unreflective life to dogmatic formulation. See two paragraphs below.

Roman Church, which appropriated Greek dogma and developed the other component, then possessed two correlative components that had to be conjoined; hence the dogmatic form of the Roman Church was synthetic. With Protestantism, mediating dogmas came into consciousness as well, and the specific concept of a system soon arose: mediating soteriological dogmas stood between theology and anthropology. The Roman Church and Protestantism both offered distinctive additions to dogma, and both joined individual dogmas together in an organic fashion. In other words, there are three cycles of dogma: that of the first period, or of the Greek Church, is theology; that of the Roman Church is anthropology; and that of Protestantism is soteriology.

The major error in this conception is that the periods of dogma are considered only from the point of view of a quantitative relation. Dogma constantly increases quantitatively; but in fact what seems to be added to dogma has its basis only in the variety of ways consciousness has been related to dogma. Hence, if we consider the matter not quantitatively but qualitatively, we cannot separate the Roman Church from the Greek. If the various periods are to be regarded merely quantitatively, if they consist merely in the addition of a new cycle, then dogma—once it exists, forming a specific cycle—would always have to remain the same; it could be altered only quantitatively (through new dogmas), not qualitatively. But just this is a false view of dogma. The variation in dogma consists not in its quantitative growth from period to period, but in the fact that *everything* in each period—including what already exists—becomes different.

From establishing the general periods of dogmatic development, Kliefoth moves on to the further task of describing the inner development of these periods and their laws. Thus, in the genetic unfolding of dogma, various phases are to be distinguished whose succession constitutes the general unfolding of each period. Under specific historical conditions, a distinctive Christian life develops. This life becomes reflective; then the contradictions and indeterminateness of reflection seek dogmatic formulation. Hence the individual articles of the cycle of dogma given in the life of a particular period arise out of reflection into dogmatic formulation. The activity that comprises this part of a period constitutes its first phase, the phase of the formation of dogmas. Once these individual articles are formed dogmatically, they are then joined together; and as a general result, the whole of dogma emerges in all its articles, and is acknowledged by all as representing a period; this is the phase of symbolic unity. From this synthetic unity, the symbol endeavors to move toward a systematic and organic unity. But this completion of dogma is at the same time its dissolution. Although dogma strives generally to realize itself in life from the moment that it becomes clear symbolically, Spirit has now done with it. Life and feeling gradually are freed of what is completed and hasten imperceptibly toward what is new. But dogma can no longer appropriate this new content; it becomes obsolete; opposed by a new age, it falls apart; and the scientific spirit turns away from it to a Christian life that in the meantime has been renewed, once again seeking to comprehend the particular components of that life, and so forming the transition to a new period. The third phase thus entails the completion as well as the dissolution of dogma.

The first phase, characterized by the formation of dogmas, is determined by the two elements of difference and agreement (or settlement of controversy). The second phase is characterized by harmonious unity, peace, inner satisfaction, and accomplishment. The third phase has two parallel strands with wholly diverse tendencies. The first strand consists of the gradual dissolution of symbolic dogma; this strand is constantly oriented toward the past, moves from traditional adherence to the symbol up to the criticism that annihilates it, and thus embraces the conflict between heterodoxy and orthodoxy. The second strand consists in the gradual emergence of a new period of dogmatic development. This strand is always directed toward the future. The tendencies that develop in this fashion are traditionalism, scholasticism, and pietism, from whose dissolution spring indifferentism and rationalism. From these tendencies proceeds a new tendency, emerging at a different point, toward mysticism, which, although formless at first, in its further development becomes philosophical mysticism. Rationalism is thus ultimately transmuted into philosophical mysticism. On the whole, there emerges from each tendency a gradual, ever-increasing appropriation of what is true in the other tendencies. Thus from supernaturalism the other tendencies appropriate a traditional historical element; from mysticism a vital element of Christian spirituality, and from rationalism a scientific element. The strict separation of individual tendencies begins to come to an end; their closed character and isolated position in contrast to one another begins to dissolve; and there is inaugurated a period of widespread syncretism and general collapse. The different tendencies subside finally into a harmonious unity according to the principle of the new period, whose development is then carried out in the manner already described.

In terms of what has just been brought out, this way of understanding goes so far that it demonstrates its own error. A theory that finally permits everything to subside into a general syncretism, and that views such a syncretism as the highest result of the developmental process of dogma, is a contradiction of itself. On this view, there is no progress and no accomplishment; rather, if everything subsides into a general syncretism, everything must begin anew, and the cycle of history eternally repeats itself. Thus, according to Kliefoth, all the moments mentioned above are merely various phases of one and the same period; there are, to be sure, a number of periods, but each takes its course through the same phases. Even though Kliefoth has much to say that is true and appropriate about all these moments and their relations to one another, nevertheless we do not obtain from him the conception of a historical process of development. Each period always takes the same course; thus there is no progress and no achievement, but rather an eternal sameness. If, as Kliefoth asserts, all these moments are phases of one and the same period, then as a consequence the whole of the history of dogma can only be a single period. The only alternative is to regard the phases themselves as periods; and at the same time, as has already been indicated, the process itself must be defined not quantitatively but qualitatively.

6. The Process of History; the Course of the Development of Dogma in General

The major weakness in all these attempts to arrive at a conception of the history of dogma, and thus to trace its development, is that the historical process, the exposition of which constitutes the true method, is not brought clearly into view. The true method can only be the movement immanent to the subject matter, the self-moving concept. The self-movement of the concept, however, is the self-movement of Spirit, in so far as thinking is the activity or movement of Spirit. Hence we must return to the nature of thinking Spirit in order to understand the concept of dogma. Since the concept in itself, as a vital and moving thing, is only Spirit engaged in the activity of thinking, then the concept of Christian dogma, considered in regard to its content, can be known only from the nature of Spirit. Indeed, Christian dogma, as well as Christianity itself, can be placed only under the higher conception of religion. Religion itself, however, is essentially a relation of Spirit to Spirit, in which Spirit mediates itself with itself through the activity of thinking. All thinking is the mediation of Spirit with itself, in order to be for consciousness what it is in itself, and thus to become thinking, self-conscious Spirit through the mediation of thinking. In thinking, Spirit becomes objective to itself. It distinguishes itself from itself, issues forth from itself by means of that distinction, confronts itself as an other distinguished from itself; but only in order to know itself to be one with itself in that self-distinction, to take itself back into itself from the distinction, to integrate itself with itself, and in this unity of objective and subjective Spirit to be free, self-conscious Spirit. This double activity of Spirit—this issuing forth from itself and returning into itself, this distinction-in-unity and unity-in-distinction—is the principle of the movement of Spirit, by which all the moments of its spiritual activity are determined.

The movement of Christian dogma is also to be considered from the general point of view of the activity of Spirit manifesting itself in thinking. Christian dogma has as its presupposition Christian revelation. Revelation is an act of Spirit in which an objective reality confronts subjective consciousness as an immediate given, and becomes for the subject the object of a faith whose content is the Absolute Idea. Moved by the power of the Absolute Idea, the entire thinking activity of the subject feels the compulsion to become absorbed into this objective reality, given as an immediate divine power, in order to bring its content into consciousness—as it were, to lay it out in all its components for the representative consciousness. Thus far, such explication of a given content can be called an analytical activity. But it is not as though the determinations given to the content of faith in this analytical fashion have the same character of objectivity as does faith itself, in so far as faith has in itself the content of the Absolute Idea. It is only the *subject* who in this fashion explicates and analyzes the content of faith, who transposes himself into that content by means of his thinking and representation, and who thus becomes objective to himself in the determinations that appear to emphasize only the objective content of faith. The representations, judgments, and reflections into which the subject transposes and dissects the content of religious consciousness are supposed to be objective, immediately given determinations of Absolute Truth in the form of propositions and doctrines of faith, whereas what is mirrored in them is only the subjectivity of the representing consciousness.

7. The First Period in the History of Dogma: The Dogma of the Ancient Church

That this was the course of dogmatic development, the first period in the history of dogma, the history of the ancient church, shows clearly enough. No period is richer in dogmatic assertions, doctrinal determinations, and propositions of faith, all propounded as incontestable truths; in no other were so many councils and conciliar proceedings concerned almost exclusively with dogma. This is the period of the greatest dogmatic productivity, in which dogma has as it were an inner compulsion to issue forth from itself, to set forth all its inner components, to unfold and display before consciousness the entire scope of its content. If it can be said of any period that it has formed and produced dogmas by means both of emphasizing and establishing this or that particular aspect of dogma, and of advancing individual definitions in the form of sharply defined propositions of faith, then unquestionably this is the case with the first period above all others. As the subject surrenders himself to the compulsion that moves his religious consciousness, as with all his power he enters into and objectifies himself in dogma, and as he finds himself thereby internally satisfied, he can also—once dogma obtains this determinate form—come to know himself as one with it, for the simple reason that the formation given to dogma is taken entirely from what the subject already possesses in himself. As often as dogma obtains a new, major, and more deeply penetrating determination, it invariably points as well to a positive, subjective interest on which it rests. For the very reason that dominant temporal forms are applied to dogma, such determinations find general acceptance in the consciousness of the time. In this fashion the subject mediates dogma with himself; he places himself in a relation to dogma that is free and in accord with his religious consciousness.

On the other hand, there also emerges for the subject a more or less unfree relation. The more the subject objectifies himself in dogma in order to enter into it, the more he surrenders his own freedom to it. The determinations in which dogma is given specific expression, the propositions of faith that give it a fixed form, obtain an authority that binds the subject, and from which he can no longer withhold recognition. This authority confronts him as an objectivity within himself, which, even if it is only of his own making, increasingly wrests from him an independent power and constricts his free movement to ever narrower limits. In this respect one need only consider the course of events following the Council of Nicaea. Councils and dogmas followed one upon the other until finally, more and more gradually as one after another came to expression, an entire system of ecclesiastical dogmas had been assembled. But what was the result? Since everything that the church had once sanctioned through public proceedings and decisions was regarded as irrevocable dogma, the individual was no longer free to form his own opinions about the doctrine of Christian faith; he had to submit in unconditional belief to the authority of the church. Since dogma confronted him in all the determinations that were regarded as so essential, it became the opposing limit that he was not permitted to transgress, and by which he could only feel himself restricted the more he became aware that it was a purely arbitrary limit. But such an awareness had sooner or later to awaken, for arbitrarily achieved definitions—by means of which an often controversial resolution was brought about only through extraneous motives and interests, and discordant elements scarcely received any internal unity—could not for long possibly satisfy the reflective mind.

Thus considered, the entire history of dogma is a continual procession of Spirit in never-ending conflict with itself, never able to become truly one with itself; it is a constant binding and loosening, a never-resting work in which Spirit, like Penelope, continually unravels its own web, only to begin again anew. No sooner does it impose upon itself a limiting and determining authority, thus binding itself, than it desires to be free, to withdraw from that authority. Whatever, under the compulsion of its internality, it has produced from within in order to become objective to itself, will at just that point have been outgrown. It will have become an external and alien force, and all the efforts of Spirit must now be directed toward reintegrating that force into itself, so as to regain its power and be internally reconciled with itself.

8. *The Second Stage in the Development of Dogma: The Dogma of the Middle Ages; Scholasticism*

Here we have already entered into the second stage of the development of dogma. Dogma stands before the subjective consciousness as ecclesiastical doctrine in the full weight of its external objectivity. But now the subject increasingly has the need and the desire to mediate between dogma and himself, to overcome the externality with which it confronts him, and to find for it a point of contact in his own self-consciousness. The subject has had this aspiration from the beginning. But he first had to draw back from the overwhelming pressure toward objectifying himself in dogma; and he could become acquainted with this aspiration, in so far as it was externalized at all, only in isolated and subordinate manifestations. Since dogma had become so firm and objective a power in the authority of the church, for the first time the subject had now to feel himself driven to oppose dogma with all the energy of his self-consciousness, in an effort to see the extent to which he was in a position to master it. It was thus now legitimate to try to maintain the freedom of the subject against the predominance of dogma. The attempt was now no longer made merely here and there, at isolated single points, but everywhere, in a continuous series of homogeneous efforts, determined by the same principle, and increasingly with a definite awareness of the task at hand. This is what gives the second stage of dogmatic development its peculiar character. This is what essentially distinguishes the dogma of the Middle Ages from that of the ancient church, and gives to scholasticism, as a new form of dogmatic consciousness, so important a place in the history of the development of dogma.

We cannot at this point develop more precisely the nature of scholasticism, how it emerged, and the course it took in its various periods. We can only designate in a general way the place it occupies as a peculiar moment in the course of dogmatic development. The major point of view under which scholasticism must be placed is precisely the endeavor, which lies at the basis of all its major manifestations, to remove dogma from the externality and immediacy it possessed as an absolute given, resting on the bare authority of ecclesiastical faith, and to place it in subjective consciousness, to mediate it with consciousness. The scholastic theologians intend not merely to believe but also to know what they believe; knowledge is to parallel faith. Dogma, to be sure, has its truth in itself; but because it is true in itself, that truth must also be capable of proof. The scholastic theologians wish to comprehend and grasp it rationally, to give an account of what is rational or conformable to reason in the content of dogma. Even though in the mode of argumentation attempted by scholasticism dogma remains exactly what it was from the beginning, and though the result does not differ from its presuppositions, nevertheless the relation of consciousness to dogma has become wholly different. Through the attempt at mediation, it has come closer to *self-*

consciousness. Already it has become one with dogma, if only in a limited sense. Without question, one can see in scholasticism—if it is conceived from this standpoint, in the whole context of the development of dogma—a very significant progression of Spirit. It is an attempt by the subject to free his self-consciousness from the bonds of an authority he has imposed upon himself.

Nevertheless, scholasticism found itself on a path that could never reach its proper goal. Although the moving principle of scholasticism was the liberation of self-consciousness in its relation to dogma, it achieved that liberation to so small an extent as to lead rather to a much greater lack of freedom on the part of the subject. This is the limited, one-sided, deficient element in scholasticism, which made it the particular moment in the course of dogmatic development that it was. Its essential weakness was that dogma never lost the externality that should have been removed from it. It remained always an unmediated objectivity, simply a thing absolutely given, a solid, impenetrable authority into which the subject could never enter with the power of his self-consciousness, a limit that never could be broken and dissolved, an absolute presupposition beyond which Spirit could not move. For this reason, all the attempts by scholasticism to mediate dogma with consciousness were at bottom purely formal in character—a logical analysis and discussion of dogma, a more precise determination of its content through various distinctions, a mode of argumentation in which all possible reasons and counter-reasons, all pros and cons, were opposed to one another. But the truth of the major propositions, which was to have been proved, had already been implicitly presupposed. Rational though the whole tendency of scholasticism was, it could never come to an authentic break with dogma. Even though doubt made itself felt, it never penetrated deeply. Even though dogma was worked over in all its aspects, it nevertheless remained essentially unchanged. Thus the result of all the efforts at a formal clarification and rationalization of dogma was simply that the consciousness of the subject, instead of coming into a freer relation with dogma, was all the more firmly chained to it, drawn all the more deeply into its consequences, and all the more heavily oppressed by the whole mass of materials that scholasticism had produced in order to establish a thoroughgoing system of ecclesiastical faith. Spirit could not have fallen into a greater lack of freedom and a more oppressive servitude than through the spiritless formalism of the scholastics.

9. The Period of Dogmatic Development Introduced by the Reformation

Just at this point arose the necessity for a further step, a transition from the second stage of the history of dogma to a third, in which there might come about for the first time that toward which scholasticism indeed had already aspired, but which it had scarcely been able to initiate. The basic conception by which scholasticism itself was moved—without, to be sure, being able to bring the actual task clearly into consciousness—was the quite correct supposition that an understanding of dogma was possible. An inner bond of unity must exist between the truth of dogma and the self-consciousness of Spirit. But in order to know what in dogma is true and rational, one might not simply presuppose the truth of dogma, as the scholastics did, but must rather above all inquire into the absolute certainty of dogma itself. For this reason, one could assume a standpoint not simply abreast of dogma but rather above it. Nor should one hesitate to break completely with dogma the moment it appeared simply to be untrue and irrational to thinking reason or religious consciousness, or antithetical to religious interests.

That such a break with dogma came about is to be seen chiefly as a consequence of scholasticism. Just as Christianity and religion in general came to have, through the condition of the church as a whole, a form so antithetical to the self-consciousness of Spirit as to cause Spirit in its innermost being to rise up against it, so dogma in particular came to have such a form through scholasticism. Thus there occurred a rift in the religious and dogmatic consciousness, which hitherto had been identical with dogma—a rift through which dogma and the consciousness of the subject were grievously torn apart. Because of the rupture between dogma and the subject, there awoke in the subject an awareness of his subjective freedom, by which he dissociated himself from a form of dogma with which he could no longer feel at one. The principle on which the truth of dogma was supposed to rest could no longer be recognized as true; it would have now to be based on a new principle, essentially different from the one that had gone before. In contradistinction from the earlier principle of ecclesiastical tradition and authority, which alone had been regarded as valid, this new principle consisted in the exclusive divine authority of Scripture—a principle which itself, however, could only rest on the assumption that the subject, in the conscious-ness of his subjective freedom, might acknowledge as true only what was given as true in his thinking reason. Thus through the Reformation the subject obtained for the first time the consciousness of his freedom, or the freedom of his self-consciousness, in relation to dogma. Dogma no longer confronted him in its externality and with the externally imposed author-ity of ecclesiastical doctrine; rather, it derived its significance only from the subject's knowing himself to be internally at one with divine truth, which he recognized as the essential content of dogma.

But even the new period into which dogma entered in its development had its limitations and one-sidedness. The major deficiency was that the principle newly emerging into consciousness could not penetrate the gen-eral consciousness. The new principle recognized the constitutive princi-ple of dogma only in the freedom and autonomy of the subject, whereas the general consciousness held all the more firmly to the old principle of authority, and wanted to know nothing of a liberation of the subject from the bonds of ecclesiastical authority.

Thus, the new period of dogmatic development inaugurated by the Reformation is the period of antithesis between Catholicism and Protes-tantism, in which the religious and dogmatic consciousness shows itself to be divided and split asunder. The progress of dogma took place only in a particular sphere; and the principle of the stability of dogma confronted the principle of progress and movement with the force of a hardened opposition. In this regard, therefore, a limitation already existed; the new principle confronted in the consciousness of the age itself a limit that it could not transcend. Even within the Protestant Church a great deal was opposed to it that restricted its purer and freer development. It had first to undergo various antitheses in order for the full significance of what lay in it from the beginning to be set forth for consciousness. The subject set free by the Reformation still remained bound in many ways in his dog-matic consciousness. He first had to achieve—by means of a process of development that itself took a specific course, and that entailed restric-tions and limitations which first had to be overcome—the full conception of freedom given him in the principle of Protestantism.

How this came about cannot be further developed here. It is sufficient to mention one result of this continuing process of development in the most recent configuration of the dogmatic consciousness, namely that there can no longer be the external relation of philosophy to theol-ogy—which for too long seems to have given theology the upper hand—and that they have increasingly met at the same focal point and have shared one and the same interest. The freedom of self-consciousness, which occupies the highest standpoint of philosophy, is acknowledged more and more generally as the standpoint from which alone theology as well can proceed to a satisfactory solution of its given task in connection with Christian dogma. What in the Middle Ages was for so long held as the highest axiom—that there exists a double truth, one truth for theology, another for philosophy—must increasingly be discounted *de facto* as a false assumption. As certainly as there is only one truth, so must the antithesis between theology and philosophy increasingly be resolved and transcended.

10. *The True Method in the History of Dogma*

If we now return to the purpose for which this survey of dogmatic development has been provided—namely, through it to establish a method for the history of dogma—then the method thus obtained can only follow from the immanent totality of the subject matter itself, and consider the self-moving concept of dogma to be the universal by which all variations occurring in dogma must be conditioned. If, as closer consideration makes ever more evident, the whole history of dogma is an organic process of development, determined by its inner moments, in which everything that goes before is the necessary presupposition of what follows, and everything that follows is only the result of what has gone before, so that all the particular forms of dogma may be conceived simply as the elements of a unity that pervades the whole, then the true historical presentation can only be one that allows this process of development to appear entirely as it is in itself. Thus, the method of the history of dogma is in error to the extent that it perceives in the entire course of dogma only the individual, the contingent, the arbitrary, the disconnected, and is unable to penetrate the external phenomena so as to reach the inner concept of the subject matter itself, the inner moving principle which can only be thinking Spirit as it struggles, in its relation to dogma, toward a consciousness of dogma, as well as toward self-consciousness.

The whole movement of dogma proceeds between two mutually opposing points, which should be brought together in the union of objectivity and subjectivity. On the one hand stands dogma in its objective truth before Spirit, whose task is to assimilate it into its subjective consciousness and to become ever more certain of its content; on the other hand, the absolute truth of dogma can only correspond to the equally absolute certainty of the subject within himself. Between these two poles the entire movement of dogma takes place as the unending work of Spirit struggling with itself, aspiring toward a free self-consciousness in the absolute content of dogma. Every new configuration of dogma is a new attempt by Spirit to become more certain of truth, to take deeper and more comprehensive possession of the content of dogma. However, at every new level of development there inevitably comes to light an inadequate relation of subjective consciousness to its object. Accordingly, the once-inaugurated work can never rest; it contains in itself the driving principle of its own movement; the concept must travel through all its moments; hence there also must be a form of subjective consciousness in which content and form, object and subject, are brought into unity. Without such a goal the work of Spirit would be a process devoid of results, running on into infinity. Therefore, the development of dogma, if it is to be thought of as an immanent process, must rest on the presupposition that even in its point of origin there is nothing in dogma implicitly alien to the nature of Spirit—that dogma itself is simply Spirit become objective to itself and mediated with itself in this antithesis between objectivity and subjectivity.

11. *The Critical Element in the History of Dogma*

Thus the whole history of dogma is a forward-moving process of development; indeed, it is the developing process of Spirit itself. As such it is also a critical process; and in this connection it has rightly been said that the history of dogma is also the criticism of dogma, or that the history of dogma is its resolution into thought. It is the same process whose positive aspect we have considered hitherto, designated now according to its negative aspect, which, however, has an essential connection with the positive. Dogma cannot progress in its development, it cannot move forward as the self-moving concept from one moment to the next, without being related negatively to everything that movement transcends. The progression to a new form of consciousness is possible, therefore, only in so far as the previous form is perceived in its untruth. It is the driving principle of movement that everything produced by dogma always contains implicitly something which has a negative and inadequate relation to the concept of the subject matter itself, and that on this account consciousness is repeatedly driven beyond it, since it cannot rest in the contradiction of which it has become conscious. Everything seems to emerge only to disintegrate once more; and what is distinctive in history is simply that it brings clearly into consciousness—through the constant succession of forms, each of which is transcended as soon as it has been established—the finitude and contingency of all forms of dogma. Hence the result of history as a whole could only be the freedom of self-consciousness in the negative sense of knowing itself to be free from every specific form. Since every successive form in this forward-moving process thus becomes the negation of what has preceded it, and dogma in its own development always labors to remove everything negative and inadequate, the history of dogma is also its criticism; and thus quite naturally the critical consciousness itself appears as an element in history.

There must also appear in the development of dogma a period in which the consciousness of the age can relate itself *only* critically, or much rather only sceptically and negatively, to the content of dogma as it has been shaped in its ecclesiastical development. This is what we have already designated more precisely as the period of the Reformation; and it is self-evident how the Reformation, as the reform of dogma, also contained an essentially critical element. According to its very nature Protestantism is critical; this is its essential distinction from Catholicism. The more clearly the Protestant principle has developed, the greater is the significance obtained by the critical principle that has been an ingredient from the beginning. Thus, in so far as its history is also its criticism, one can describe the course of dogma in its general features as D. F. Strauss does in his *Glaubenslehre:* [12] "[Dogma] exists in Scripture in ingenuous, unspecified form. Through its analysis and more exact determination, the church is torn asunder by antitheses, some of which lead to heretical extremes. Thereupon ensues the ecclesiastical fixation in symbol, and the symbols are converted into ecclesiastical dogmatics. Before long, however, criticism gradually awakens; Spirit distinguishes itself from the reality given it in ecclesiastical life; the subject withdraws himself from the

---

12. *Die christliche Glaubenslehre in ihrer geschichtlichen Entwicklung und im Kampfe mit der modernen Wissenschaft dargestellt* (2 vols.; Tübingen, 1840–41), I, 71.

[ED.] David Friedrich Strauss (1808–74) was Baur's most famous and controversial student. For Baur's criticism of Strauss's rationalistic treatment of history, see below, 354, especially n. 29. On the relation between Strauss and Baur, cf. *The Formation of Historical Theology*, 73–84.

substance of his previous belief and rejects it as no longer true for him. But this is done only because another truth has emerged for him, even if at first only implicitly and in undeveloped form." Already there is an allusion here to the positive element necessarily presupposed by the negative aspect of criticism.

This is expressed still more specifically when it is said that the history of dogma is its resolution [*Auflösung*] into thought. Here the two aspects are held together. "Dogma is resolved by reflection upon its history, in so far as such reflection acquaints us with the fluctuation of its development, the gradualness of its emergence, the sources from which its various elements have been created, the contradiction that adheres to ecclesiastical orthodoxy from the beginning and is pacified in certain ages by external authority, only to erupt again all the more uncontrollably, and the uneasy details in which sore points in its depiction are covered up but not healed. However, it is resolved not into nothing but into thought, in the sense that by looking more deeply into the whole process of emergence and formation—apparently so confused and accidental—one discovers an inner necessity, the impulse of thinking to obtain an ever richer and clearer self-consciousness." [13] Thus, the method of the history of dogma is by its very nature critical. One cannot follow the course of dogma without seeing how it repeatedly cancels itself out [*sich auflöst*]. But it would be very biased to wish to restrict oneself simply to this negative, critical side. History would thereby become only a disintegrative [*auflösenden*] and destructive criticism. Thus, the true method can only be one that is positive as well as negative, and that always sees in history both the mortality of dogma, which can only cancel itself out, and the permanence and immortality of its content.

---

13. Eduard Zeller, *Theologische Jahrbücher*, I (1842), 358.

[ED.] Eduard Zeller (1814–1908), professor of philosophy at Marburg, Heidelberg, and Berlin, was Baur's son-in-law and former student in theology. From 1842 to 1857 he was editor of the *Theologische Jahrbücher*, the chief organ of the Tübingen School during that period. This quotation is from the review by Zeller of Vol. I of Baur's *Die christliche Lehre von der Dreieinigkeit und Menschwerdung Gottes in iher geschichtlichen Entwicklung* (Tübingen, 1841).

IV

THE PERIODS OF THE HISTORY OF DOGMA

1. *The Three Major Periods*

The division into periods of the history of dogma stems from its method. In accord with the inner moments of its development, the history of dogma falls into certain major periods, which for the sake of a historical account must also be fixed. The periods of history may not be set by mere arbitrary incisions here and there in its course. They can be designated only in accord with the epochs that emerge in the objective course of historical development itself. The more definitely a new revolution in the consciousness of an age—a focus of development from which a new sequence of changes takes its beginning—makes itself known, the less it may remain unnoticed in historical presentation. In this regard the significance of the Reformation epoch is self-evident. Also scholasticism, or the history of the development of dogma in the Middle Ages, forms a unique, self-contained whole. Thus there are three major blocks into which the whole body of the history of dogma is to be divided, in accord with the character of the object: the dogma of the ancient church, of the Middle Ages, and of the recent era, beginning with the Reformation.

2. *The Council of Nicaea and Gregory I as the Termini of the Two Phases of the First Major Period*

If these three major epochs and periods are firmly distinguished, then the details within them can be organized more readily in their continuity. Since, however, the division of history into periods also has the purpose of facilitating an overview of the whole and of providing the necessary points of focus and repose for memory, pains must also be taken to subdivide these temporal epochs properly. This too is not to be done arbitrarily; only the more important moments that emerge in the development of dogma are to be singled out—points at which dogma itself achieves a certain equilibrium. In this regard, no other dogmatic deliberations were of greater significance for the history of dogma in the ancient church than those at the Council of Nicaea. Thus that Council is generally to be regarded as terminating the first phase of the first major period, or as the point by which the history of dogma in the ancient church is divided into two equal sectors or periods.

W. K. L. Ziegler [1] alone has objected to this division. The Council of Nicaea, he says, attempted to determine only a single major dogma, and was unable even to settle the controversy over it; rather, it became in fact the occasion of controversy, so that the more exact determination only came about at the general Council of Constantinople in 381. Therefore the Council of Nicaea provides not a point of repose for the history of dogma but rather one of controversy. The debate was then transferred from the Logos to the Holy Spirit, so that the full doctrine of the Trinity obtained creedal stability for the first time only with the Council of Constantinople, at the end of the fourth century.

This objection is of no importance. To be sure, only one dogma was settled at the Council of Nicaea; but this was precisely the one that engaged all the dogmatic activity of that century; and even if the Council did not resolve the emerging controversy, but rather inflamed it still more, the controversy nevertheless had no other result than what had already been established at Nicaea. Thus at Nicaea the development of dogma already reached the decisive point for the history of dogma. Moreover, the Council of Nicaea, as the first ecumenical Council, is epoch-making in that it established a new guiding principle for dogmatic decisions. In this respect, the Council of Constantinople followed it in 381 as the second ecumenical Council and is to be regarded, along with the controversy that produced it, as one of a continuing series of controversies and councils that make up the second phase of the first major period in the history of dogma.

Gregory I, who brings the succession of church fathers to a close, is generally regarded as terminating the second phase of this period. A question could be raised as to whether this second section would not be more appropriately continued to John of Damascus, with whom the dog-

1. In his essay, "Über den Begriff und die Behandlungsart der Dogmengeschichte," *Neues theologisches Journal* (1798), 341.

matics of the Greek Church is brought to an end. But John of Damascus belongs to an age in which a new range of phenomena begins to take shape. The main thing to be established here is not so much a single fact or individual as rather the whole revolution in direction and point of view, occurring at the end of the sixth century and the beginning of the seventh.

3. *The Second and Third Major Periods*

The second major period covers the extensive era of the ecclesiastical Middle Ages, from the beginning of the seventh century to the Reformation. Since scholasticism begins only toward the end of the eleventh century, this period automatically divides into two sections, that of scholasticism proper and that of the transition to scholasticism. One might, if one wished, divide scholasticism itself into several periods—its emergence and first formation, its full blossoming, and its decline. However, for the purpose of a survey it is not appropriate to cut the historical material in this period too thin.

The third major period is temporally the shortest, but the richest in content. For this reason it is suitable to divide it and to begin a new period—the final one—at the opening of the eighteenth century. At this point a very significant change occurs in the realm of dogmatics. To be sure, no essentially new principle appeared in history; rather, for the first time the Protestant principle began to function after a more radical fashion. Thus each of the major periods is divided into two smaller periods.

4. *The Periods of Baumgarten-Crusius*

It is more usual, however, to adopt more than six periods. Indeed, Ludwig Baumgarten-Crusius, in his *Lehrbuch der Dogmengeschichte* (2 vols.; Jena, 1832), offers twice that number, or twelve periods: (1) from the apostolic fathers to the beginning of the struggle between Platonism and Gnosticism; (2) to the controversy between Sabellianism and subordinationism; (3) to the first Council of Nicaea; (4) to the Council of Chalcedon; (5) to Gregory the Great; (6) to John of Damascus and the Council of Frankfurt; (7) to Peter Lombard; (8) to William of Occam and the mystics of the Greek Church; (9) to the Reformation; (10) to

Cartesian philosophy and Cyril Lucar;[2] (11) to the beginning of the conflict between the old and the new faith among Protestants; (12) to the present.

Such a multiplication of periods makes the mistake of cutting the whole too thin; it does not sufficiently distinguish the main points from the many subordinate moments with which they are equated; and it does not reveal any progress in the periods as a whole. Instead of a movement running through the whole, we have here only a colorful diversity, in which it is by no means easy to detect the proper significance of the items herein designated, and which is conspicuous only for the heterogeneity of its arrangement. Baumgarten-Crusius himself seems to have detected this error; in the more recent *Compendium der Dogmengeschichte* (Leipzig, 1840) he adopts, more satisfactorily, the following six periods: (1) formation of doctrine by means of thought and belief, up to the Council of Nicaea; (2) formation of doctrine by the church, up to the Council of Chalcedon; (3) consolidation of doctrine by the hierarchy, up to Gregory VII; (4) consolidation of doctrine by means of Christian philosophy, up to the end of the fifteenth century; (5) purification of doctrine by means of [theological-ecclesiastical] parties, up to the beginning of the eighteenth century; (6) purification by means of scientific thought, up to the present. Formation, consolidation, and purification are thus the three major moments in the history of the development of dogma to be emphasized here. In general, these are the same moments that have already been developed, except that the second and the third are conceived somewhat one-sidedly. If to the Reformation period is assigned the purification of doctrine by means of parties, then the character of this period and the distinctive nature of the Protestant principle have not yet been precisely determined; and even though scholasticism can be considered from the point of view of a consolidation of doctrine, it is not clear how the period from the Council of Chalcedon to Gregory VII can be characterized as the hierarchical consolidation of doctrine. For the leading figures of this period in the area of dogmatics—John of Damascus and Scotus Erigena—have nothing at all to do with the hierarchy. To be sure, in the delineation of these moments the necessity of conceiving the history of dogma as a progression, an immanent movement of dogma, is understood; but the correct procedure is for the most part only hinted at.

---

2. [ED.] Patriarch of Constantinople, 1620–38; proponent of Reformed theology in the Eastern Orthodox Church.

5. The Period Divisions of Hagenbach

K. R. Hagenbach [3] is also unsatisfactory in this respect. In his remarks on the proper division of periods in the history of dogma, he has divided the history of dogma before the Reformation into three periods—an apologetic, a polemical, and a systematic; [4] and in his *Lehrbuch der Dogmengeschichte* (Leipzig, 1840), he has stipulated the following five periods: (1) from the end of the apostolic age to the death of Origen (80–254), the age of apologetics; (2) from the death of Origen to John of Damascus (254–730), the age of polemics; (3) from John of Damascus to the time of the Reformation, the age of systematics, scholasticism in the broadest sense of the word; (4) from the Reformation to the abrogation of the *Formula Consensus* in Reformed Switzerland, and to the flowering of Wolfian philosophy in Germany around 1720—the age of polemical-ecclesiastical symbolics or of confessional struggles; (5) from 1720 to the present, the age of criticism, of speculation, of antitheses between faith and knowledge, philosophy and Christianity, reason and revelation, and the attempted mediation of these antitheses.

Even leaving out of account the last two periods, in which the Reformation principle is not treated with the justice due it, the first three

3. [ED.] Karl Rudolf Hagenbach (1801–74) was professor of church history at the University of Basel for over half a century. He studied under Lücke at Bonn, and under Schleiermacher and Neander at Berlin; he was also greatly influenced by Herder. His theological orientation was that of the Mediating Theology of the post-Schleiermacher school; in later years he moved away from Schleiermacher toward a stronger emphasis on the objective character of revelation in history. Together with De Wette, he helped to bring the University of Basel into closer contact with German evangelical theology of the mid-nineteenth century.

His chief scholarly work was *Kirchengeschichte von der ältesten Zeit bis zum neunzehnten Jahrhundert* (7 vols.; Leipzig, 1869–72), collected from lectures at Basel that were originally published in separate parts. His textbooks were popular among students: *Encyklopädie und Methodologie der theologischen Wissenschaften* (Leipzig, 1833); *Lehrbuch der Dogmengeschichte* (Leipzig, 1840; this and the previous work were translated into English); *Leitfaden zum christlichen Religionsunterricht* (Leipzig, 1850); *Grundzüge der Homiletik und Liturgik* (Leipzig, 1863). He also published works on contemporary theological issues. As a church historian he was not especially original, but he was interested in the connection between scientific theological studies (both historical and dogmatic) and Christian life. He was heavily involved in the affairs of the Swiss Reformed Church.

4. "Über zweckmässige Eintheilung der Perioden in der Dogmengeschichte," *Theologische Studien und Kritiken*, I:4 (1828), 783.

periods are not described very satisfactorily. The first age is supposed to be apologetic because the theology of that period developed chiefly as a defense of Christianity against Judaism and paganism, and also the polemic within the church against heresy was related in large part to the opposition between the Judaizers and the paganizers. The major error is that the period through the death of Origen, which certainly does not constitute an epoch in the history of dogma, is too narrowly delimited. We have here no firm stopping point; hence we must go further. Already, then, this period loses its apologetic character; but not even the major events in the age up to the death of Origen can be brought under the purview of apologetics. The Gnostic systems have nothing to do with apologetics; nor does the Logos theology of Origen, so important from a dogmatic point of view; nor do many other factors, such as the antithesis between πίστις [faith] and γνῶσις [knowledge]. It is clear, then, that to conceive this period simply as apologetic is much too restrictive.

Equally unsatisfactory is the description of the second period as polemical. The history of ecclesiastical controversies from the beginning of the Sabellian controversy to the conclusion of Monotheletism forms a chain that, for the historical consideration of dogma, may not readily be broken: it reaches a conclusion only with the work of John of Damascus. Unquestionably this period, rife with controversy and with doctrinally definitive councils, is the most important one of all for the history of dogma, if we measure importance by the powers that have been summoned to shape that framework which has the previous period as its foundation, and which subsequent periods either built up and gave interior adornment, or now restored and now partially destroyed, with an extraordinary reciprocal effect. If the framework of the ecclesiastical system was erected in the second period, then the character of this period is not so much polemical as it is system-forming or systematic. But why should this period be designated as the only fundamentally productive one, so that everything produced by subsequent periods is viewed only as a more or less insignificant modification of a system already established once and for all?

This view rests on the false notion—evident in other attempts to divide the history of dogma into periods—that the ecclesiastical system remains in essence always the same. That notion can only rest on a predilection for the ecclesiastical system, whereas impartial consideration shows clearly enough how completely the whole form of dogma changes regardless of the system. To this is related the major error, almost always found in treatments of the history of dogma, that only the objective content of dogma is brought into view, or that the conventional dogmatic determinations are still regarded as valid integral components of church dogma. The chief question, however, is not dogma as such, nor that, generally speaking, there is dogma and that it still exists as church dogma, but rather how dogma is thought about, what significance it has for the consciousness of the time. Indeed, it exists only in so far as it is also an object of faith. The more we bear this in mind, conceiving the whole history of dogma as an interaction of consciousness with dogma, the more we arrive at the insight that dogmas are not something existing objectively for themselves; they are not a self-enclosed, self-supporting system, a *Ding an sich*, which exists independently of its manifestation and of its relation to subjective consciousness. Rather, they are forms of consciousness that are always changing, to the extent that every new age has its own consciousness, originating in itself. As has been said earlier, the history of dogma ought to be regarded as the objective movement of the subject matter itself. Such objectivity of consideration, however, in no way conflicts with the necessity for adopting a vantage point from within the consciousness of the subject; subjective consciousness is itself included in the subject matter, since the movement of dogma is nothing other than the self-movement of Spirit whose self-objectification in dogma has both objective and subjective aspects.

6. *The Systematic and the Chronological Method*

In what has been said about the division into periods, a subordinate question concerning the method of the history of dogma has already been settled. We can distinguish between an arrangement according to subject matter and one according to time, or between a systematic-dogmatic-synthetic and a chronological, purely historical method. The former—the arrangement according to subject matter—considers dogmas individually, following the order in which they are connected by dogmatics, and pursues for each without a break the sequence of changes and modifications through all periods from the beginning. In the second method the arrangement is entirely temporal. It presents in chronological sequence the various opinions and systems of church teachers, and ecclesiastical deliberations and determinations. As the presentation moves from one dogma to another, it carries the course of history with it.

The first method provides a ready survey of all the changes relating to a single dogma, although it is always only one specific dogma whose development is traced. There are before one only single and isolated data, and one is not able to view the inner continuity of events or the entire condition of a period. Things that by nature belong together are separated and torn apart. The chronological method, on the other hand, has the advantage of being able to follow the natural continuity of change that the history of dogma ought to describe. It shows how in different periods one dogma after another became the object of theological investigation and ecclesiastical deliberation; and it can develop without interruption the inner continuity of doctrines and systems that came to be of special prominence.

The criticism made by Wilhelm Münscher of this method [5] —that it is too repetitive when it describes often quite similar doctrines of individual teachers, one after the other; that private opinions are not sufficiently distinguished from general church doctrine; that in general it provides only a collection of materials for the history of dogma, not a history of dogma itself—would carry weight only if the method were restricted entirely to an enumeration of individual teachers and writers. It ought to direct itself not so much to persons as to the subject matter; but this is just the difficulty with this method. One can certainly trace the course of dogmatic controversies and describe the changes in dogma that occur in the process; but there are a great many dogmatic determinations that have not been the object of a specific controversy and deliberation and that ought not to be passed over in a historical presentation of dogma. How, then, are these to be incorporated? If one is limited solely to the chronological sequence, how does one obtain a guiding thread for organizing everything of interest to the history of dogma? In order to discuss everything in history in which the development of dogma can be traced, and also to take careful note of still weak beginnings that have not yet emerged in determinate historical form but that already contain the elements of a later important development, we must bring together in historical reflection the concept of dogma, the various elements that belong to its content, and its systematic structure. There is a question here of the previously mentioned connection between the history of dogma and dogmatics, from whose standpoint alone the inner elements of dogma can be distinguished in the manner required for historical reflection. It is just here that the merely chronological method does not suffice, since it must

5. *Handbuch der Dogmengeschichte* (4 vols.; Marburg, 1797–1809), I, 100.

always be interrupted by a great deal of material not provided in the chronological sequence.

7. The Proper Relation of the Two Methods; the Universal and the Particular; the Introduction to Individual Periods

Since each of these methods has its advantages and its weaknesses, and since each seems one-sided and unsatisfactory when pursued alone, it has long been agreed that the proper method can only be a combination of the two. Among historians of dogma, however, this combination ordinarily consists simply in a double presentation of the history of dogma —once according to the one method and once according to the other, with no inner connection between the two. Although they belong together, each of the two forms a self-sufficient whole.

Their relation is rendered all the more superficial by the completely arbitrary distinction between the universal and the special; the chronological first section is called the universal, and the second, organized according to materials, is called the special section. The arbitrariness can be seen from the striking disproportion between the two sections; as is the case even with Baumgarten-Crusius the universal section has a much greater scope than the other.

It is quite clear that what can be related only internally is here externally separated; hence the first task is to bring the two methods into an inner relation so as to constitute a single, essentially coherent unity—the one true method. This is to be achieved by a division of history into periods corresponding to the nature of the subject matter. The history of dogma can treat its object historically only by paying closer attention to chronological sequence, so that what is connected chronologically also appears in history in its natural, chronological sequence. But the chronological arrangement ought at the same time to be one according to subject matter; hence the individual dogmas must appear in historical study in the same order by which together they constitute a systematic whole. This can be accomplished when the entire field of the history of dogma is divided according to periods, and the given material within each period is treated according to the sequence of individual dogmas. In this fashion, the dogmatic determinations concerning each dogma are developed in their unbroken continuity, and at the same time the history of a single dogma is not separated altogether from the history of other dogmas, since in every instance the history of an individual dogma is traced at a single stroke for only a limited stretch of the entire course. As a result of this treatment, the history of dogma of a period provides a true picture of the whole dogmatic consciousness of a specific age, in accord with the various elements that compose it. The respective focal points in the dogmatic consciousness of each age become apparent from the various relations of the dogmas to one another, according as one emerges into the foreground and others retreat into the background, forming new foci of development, at different places and different times, from which a new sequence of dogmatic determinations ensues. All the periods together, considered in their manifold, changing relations to one another, represent the various phases of dogma in the course of its temporal development, showing how dogma repeatedly presents a new form and aspect to the consciousness of each respective age, so that the whole history of dogma is to be conceived as a development, indeed infinitely manifold yet nevertheless thoroughly organic, of the one Christian consciousness, determined by the necessity of the subject matter.

Thus the arrangements according to subject matter and to time can only be so related to each other internally that each has its completion and unity in the other. Likewise, the universal and the particular cannot be related to each other externally; rather, the particular and special can be understood only as the concrete manifestation of the universal. But in order rightly to grasp the universal in the particular, one must hold in advance the concept of the universal. Thus every period must above all be understood and conceived in its general character, in the general moments through which it arrives at this determinate form of dogma, before the course of its movement in particulars can be traced. For this purpose, the description of each period should be prefaced by an introduction, which should restrict itself to the universal in order to give a total picture of the formation of dogma in a specific period and to establish the general point of view from which it is to be considered. It should contain in its unity the still abstract concept, whose various moments are subsequently to be presented and explicated. Moreover, the introduction to each period should provide necessary bibliographical information concerning the teachers and authors whose writings are chiefly to be used as sources.

THE RELATION OF THE HISTORY OF DOGMA
TO THE HISTORY OF PHILOSOPHY

1. *Philosophy and Religion as Forms of Human Spirit*

The history of dogma has a very close relation to the history of philosophy, one that includes the relation of philosophy to religion and theology. Many questions and problems that are the object of the history of dogma have an equal significance for philosophy. Philosophy and theology in general are most intimately engaged; and as the most recent period especially shows, the most important changes that dogma has undergone in its development have proceeded from philosophy. Hence one cannot penetrate more deeply into the course of development taken by Christian dogma without an acquaintance with the history of philosophy, or without practice in philosophical thinking.

The relation of the history of dogma to the history of philosophy, however, presents itself to us under another, more general point of view. The history of philosophy is not merely one of the auxiliary sciences, so called, to the history of dogma. The two disciplines do not merely exist alongside each other, but stand in so essentially internal a relation that they can be conceived only in terms of each other, or only as parts of one and the same whole. If the history of philosophy is the history of human Spirit, or of human thinking about and investigation of the Absolute or of Being-and-Truth-in-itself, then the history of dogma is a part of this history. It is concerned with the same object, the only difference being that in it the thinking and the investigation of human Spirit take the form of Christian dogma. This form itself, however, cannot be considered as something merely fortuitous, coming upon Spirit only externally. It can be conceived only from the nature of Spirit itself, as a form of thinking given by thought itself, a form of consciousness that

319

is essentially conditioned by the general process of development of consciousness.

Another reason for considering the relation of the history of dogma to the history of philosophy from this point of view is that there is a period in the history of dogma—indeed, precisely that in which Christian dogma appears in its greatest productivity and achieves its formation and solidity—in which philosophical thinking merges more and more into theological, making up the content of the history of dogma. In this respect, the history of dogma can be compared with church history. Just as there is a period in church history in which world history itself becomes church history, so that there is nothing great and significant, nothing of world-historical importance, that the church does not draw into its sphere, that does not bear the stamp of the Christian church, so it is with Christian dogma. All thinking is drawn into it, and is subsumed entirely within its forms, so that finally there is no spiritual movement independent of ecclesiastical dogma. All thinking merges into the faith of the church, and for a large part of its extent the history of dogma is only an account of how free thinking is bound to the faith of the church and is extinguished in it. The more deeply these two forms enter into the course of history, however, the more profoundly based this process must be. Accordingly, the only explanation can be that this transition from the one form to the other is a moment in the historical process itself, in whose sphere Spirit moves. In order to obtain a proper view of this fact, we must go back somewhat further.

2. *Oriental Religion and Greek Philosophy*

Religion and philosophy, as two forms of the manifestation of Spirit, are implicitly identical in the nature of Spirit but are essentially different in the form of their manifestation. It is characteristic of religion that Spirit knows the truth which is the content of religion only as something received, something absolutely given—an external revelation which, even though it contains nothing in contradiction to thinking reason, nevertheless has at least its historical origin outside of reason; and on this account it exists only in the form of representation, as something immediate, which is not yet mediated with thinking consciousness. In philosophy, on the other hand, Spirit knows the truth as something immanent to itself, as the result of its own thinking.

The particularism peculiar to the ancient world is to be seen especially in the existence of these two forms of Spirit, religion and philosophy, at first only in separation and outside of each other. The antithesis between religion and philosophy is also the antithesis between East and West. The East, represented above all by the Jewish people, has its entire spiritual being and life in the form of religion, whereas for it philosophy basically never achieved free and autonomous significance. In the West, whose finest flower is the Greek nation, philosophy increasingly assumed the place of religion, which contained from the beginning, for the Greek mind, too many alien, oriental elements, and was finally dissolved into the merely figurative significance of mythical and symbolic forms. In the spirit of the Greek people, philosophy developed in an organic inner continuity, which makes Greek philosophy one of the finest manifestations of human Spirit, of no less world-historical significance than the Old Testament religion of the Jewish people.

If we think of the exclusiveness and mutually opposed self-existence of these two major forms of Spirit in the ancient world, then it can only appear as the greatest progress in the development of Spirit during the pre-Christian era that this particularism should have been shattered, and that the antithesis between two mutually limiting, particularistic forms of Spirit should have been taken up into universalism. This great revolution of Spirit out of the particularism of its previous forms of existence into a more universal mode of thinking and perception was inaugurated by two equally world-historical events: the great dispersal of the Jewish people among other nations, a dispersal begun with the destruction of the Jewish nation and extended ever further thereafter; and the world empire established by Alexander, the Greek conqueror of the East. These two world-historical events each had an equal part in mastering the egotism of the abstract folk Spirit and in stripping the previously existing forms of Spirit of their particularism by overcoming the great antithesis between Greek and oriental world consciousness. Their common result in the spiritual realm was the Alexandrian philosophy of religion, produced out of the fusion of Greek and oriental culture, and finding its most remarkable form in the system of Philo.

3. The Alexandrian Philosophy of Religion

What is distinctive about this epoch-making development is that on the one hand Judaism, previously so isolated, was opened to the influence of Greek philosophy and received a new component, by means of which the religious consciousness of the Jews took a completely new form, whereas on the other hand Greek philosophy was brought to the end of its previous course of development and increasingly obtained the form of a philosophy of religion.

According to the customary view, the collapse of Greek philosophy falls precisely during this period of the emergence of Alexandrian philosophy of religion. The free productivity that had developed a series of autonomous systems and trends was now exhausted; in part it dissolved into a purely negative scepticism, in part it went astray as enthusiasm and eccentric speculation, and in all these phenomena was to be seen a final dissipation of thinking reason. This view can justly be criticized, since, as J. C. L. Georgii says in a recent article,[1]

> . . . it regards that peculiar fusion of earlier, individually separated elements—of Greek and oriental views of the world, of philosophy and religion—simply as the result of spiritual weakness and impotence, the inability to master the spirit of ancient philosophy in its pure integrity and primitive character. The fusion of such antitheses is seen only as an idle syncretism and eclecticism, rather than being recognized as the highest energy of the philosophical spirit, namely, the endeavor to overcome the particularism that was the form of thought, and to transcend, in absolute freedom and identity, the unnatural limitation of Spirit in the separation of philosophical schools and sects, of oriental and Greek life, and of religion and philosophy. Whereas the strongest evidence for Christianity's elevation to a hitherto unattainable spiritual level is to be found precisely in its religious universalism, those elements by which Philo and other non-Christian thinkers constructed a philosophical universalism are regarded as signs of spiritual poverty and depravity. Or, expressed more accurately, the principle that obtained its complete development in Christianity is attributed to the phenomena that first brought it onto the stage of history as something disgraceful and shameful.

Without question, it is one-sided in the extreme to understand the great period with which we are here concerned solely in its negative aspect. One can only recognize in it a new, highly important and epoch-making principle of development. On the other hand, it is not to be overlooked that the elevation of Spirit from the particularity of its forms of existence to the standpoint of a universal principle, which is characteristic of this

---

1. "Über die neuesten Gegensätze in Auffassung der alexandrinischen Religions-Philosophie, insbesondere des jüdischen Alexandrinismus," *Zeitschrift für historische Theologie*, I:3 (1839), 22.

period, was at the same time the transition of Spirit out of subjectivity into objectivity, out of philosophy into religion, out of the immanence of philosophical consciousness into the transcendence of religion and revelation. Since Spirit increasingly lost the productivity and energy of free, self-developing thought in the decline of Greek philosophy, the rebirth of spiritual life ensued in the form of religion and the philosophy of religion. The subjectivity toward which Greek philosophy constantly tended finally disintegrated into scepticism and the negative conclusion that the subject or subjective Spirit does not have the truth within itself. If, however, this was not to be an absolute renunciation of truth—such as is not possible even for scepticism—then that negative view could only be transformed into the positive insight that, since the subject does not have the truth within himself, it can only exist outside the subject; that is to say, it is in God absolutely and thereby can only come from God to man by means of supernatural communication and revelation.

4. Neoplatonism

This is precisely the transition from philosophy into religion; or, to put it another way, the major moment that here comes into view rests on the standpoint obtained by Greek philosophy in its final, Neoplatonic phase, in which the negativity of subjective Spirit changes abruptly into a transcendent objectivity. Hegel also considers Neoplatonism from this point of view.[2] "It is the form of philosophy that is connected most closely with the revolution caused in the world by Christianity. The last stage prior to it was Scepticism—that return of self-consciousness into itself, that infinite subjectivity without objectivity, that purely negative relation to all external existence, to everything determinate, valid, firm, true. This return into subjective consciousness is a form of satisfaction achieved by giving up everything determinate, by a flight into pure, infinite abstraction. This giving up of everything objective is the last standpoint; it is absolute poverty, the complete dearth of all firm and veritable content. The Stoic and Epicurean systems have this same result, but it is in Scepticism that the divestment of all determinate content is completed." In

2. G. W. F. Hegel, *Geschichte der Philosophie,* ed. Karl Ludwig Michelet (2nd ed., Berlin, 1840), III, 3 ff. [Cf. *Lectures on the History of Philosophy,* trans. from the 2nd German edition by E. S. Haldane and Frances H. Simson (London, 1894), II, 374-76.]

Neoplatonism, according to Hegel, philosophy reached the standpoint at which self-consciousness knew itself in its thinking to be the Absolute, and now rejected its own subjective, finite attitude toward and distinction from an external object. Rather, it comprehended within itself the distinction and constructed the truth as an intelligible world. "The consciousness of this, expressing itself as it did in the Spirit of the world, now constitutes the object of philosophy. . . . The idea that has now come home to men that absolute being [*Wesen*] is nothing alien to self-consciousness, that nothing has reality [*Wesen*] for it in which self-consciousness is not itself immediately present—this is the principle that is now found as the universal of the world Spirit, as the universal belief and knowledge of all men; at once it changes the world's whole aspect, destroying all that went before, and bringing about a regeneration of the world. The manifold forms this knowledge assumes do not belong to the history of philosophy, but to the history of consciousness and culture." Here Hegel alludes to the common bond that joins Neoplatonism and Christianity together in the universal consciousness of the age. He further explains: "It is here that Spirit moves on, breaks with itself, and again goes forth from its subjectivity to the objective, but at the same time to an intellectual objectivity, . . . to an objectivity that exists in Spirit and in Truth, to an absolute objectivity, born of Spirit and of veritable Truth. Or, in other words, we see here on the one hand the return to God, on the other hand the relationship between, the manifestation and appearance of, God for man, as he is in and for himself in his Truth, as he is for Spirit."

We can raise the question here of whether Hegel does not regard Neoplatonism too highly when he sees it attaining the standpoint of absolute self-consciousness. In any event, Hegel has not sufficiently stressed the distinctive aspect of Neoplatonism, namely, that in it philosophy possesses the form of religion, that God stands as the Absolute in absolute transcendence over subjective consciousness, hence that all truth is divinely communicated and revealed—a point that surely cannot be harmonized with the Hegelian conception. It is characteristic of Neoplatonism that it sought to attach itself as closely as possible to the religious traditions, symbols, and myths in which ancient divine truth was supposedly deposited, and that it intended to be a reform of the old religion, a revitalization of the religious consciousness. This is the major point of view to be established here. Philosophy itself transcended the limits that separated it from religion. Since the one Divinity was perceived in the various forms of religion and was to be represented, in the infinite multiplicity of its forms and manifestations, as free of all the particular limitations of nationalistic consciousness, consciousness was expanded into the infinite. But it was also encumbered by a presupposition that served as an absolute given for philosophical thinking, namely, the unmediated facticity of a revelation to which subjective Spirit could relate itself only receptively and passively.

5. Jewish Philosophy of Religion

Neoplatonism is one of the two major forms—so long as Christianity itself is not considered—in which the consciousness of the age was expressed; it represents the fusion of Greek philosophy with the religious consciousness of the East. The other major form is Alexandrian Judaism, in which the religious consciousness of the Jews broke away from its nationalistic limitations and felt the attraction of Hellenism. However, it assimilated Hellenism into itself and subordinated it to the principle of Jewish religion, which even in this expanded form of consciousness was absolutely determinative. The emergence of Alexandrian Judaism can be explained only as the awakening of a speculative impulse and necessity on the part of the Jews. In every religion that is by nature positive and traditional, sooner or later in the course of its progressive development and formation an epoch must arise in which Spirit, as it becomes self-conscious, stands over against tradition and seeks to give account of the content of traditional religion by means of reflection and speculation. A Jewish philosophy of religion was, above all, the natural consequence of all those powerfully emerging circumstances of the time by means of which the Jew found himself compelled to move out from his hitherto narrowly delimited and tightly enclosed sphere of nationalistic conceptions and institutions, and to be at home in a broader and freer sphere. To the same extent that he freed himself from his Jewish particularism, there must also have awakened in him the sensitivity for a universal (in particular a philosophical) learning, and thereby at the same time a greater spiritual autonomy. This transformation of traditional Judaism would quite naturally have occurred specifically in Alexandria, in view of the well-known circumstances that made this city a major locus of Greek culture and the center of the world at that time, bringing together such a multiplicity of spiritual elements. Here the speculative interest stirring in the consciousness of the Jews would have encountered such a philosophy as Platonism, whose tendency moved so ideally in the direction of the Absolute.

If we can see the transition from a nationalistic narrowness to a freer and more universal sphere of consciousness, free philosophical thinking nevertheless has as its essential presupposition here the positivity of religion, as in Neoplatonism, and in a far more determinate fashion. Despite all the speculative interests that moved the Jew of Alexandria, he nevertheless remained bound by the sacred authority of the Old Testament canon. If he was not completely to renounce his Jewish consciousness, he could never overstep these limits. Furthermore, he could allow room for the new ideas with which he was filled only in so far as he could become aware of their essential identity with the content of the Old Testament. The great labor with which he struggled, within this constraint of consciousness, to accomplish the task of unifying the two heterogeneous elements into which his consciousness was divided—the religious content of the Old Testament and the speculative ideas of Greek philosophy—is demonstrated most clearly by the allegorical interpretation of the Old Testament, which arose for just this purpose.

6. *Allegory and Allegorical Interpretation*

Allegory served as the mysterious and ingenious bond by which the two elements were joined together into a unity. It was the means by which speculation was reconciled with the Old Testament perspective of the Jew, whose interest in speculation was so awakened that he could no longer ignore it. For as long as the Old Testament was regarded as the highest principle and sole source of all truth, nothing could be accepted into one's consciousness as truth that could not be based on and confirmed by the Old Testament. Hence even the new speculative ideas must be accommodated to the Old Testament. This could be accomplished only if a new spirit could, as it were, be breathed into the letter of the Old Testament, whose content was regarded as a mere form for a meaning quite distinct from it, a meaning that could indeed be legitimated from the Old Testament itself but that in fact was read into it only by the newly achieved speculative consciousness. (We are certainly not to think of an intentional deception, of dishonesty and hypocrisy, as has commonly been imputed to the allegorical procedure.) Thus, by an allegorical treatment, the Old Testament was reduced to the significance of mere imagery. It was merely the figurative form of something else that had only been intimated, that lay hidden under a figurative envelope—a covering which could be stripped off only by the spiritually adept. The two components that must now be distinguished within the Old Testament itself have the relation of spirit to letter, soul to body, content to form, inner to outer. But if the very same speculative element that had been sought and was believed to have been found in the Old Testament was precisely its spirit and soul, its very essence, then clearly Jewish allegory has exceeded the bounds of ordinary Judaism.

On the other hand, the extent to which the entire philosophical and religious consciousness was still captivated by the forms of the Old Testament is no less striking. This is seen from the great arbitrariness that is embedded in allegory, despite all the self-deceiving skill with which the fact is concealed, and from the unnatural compulsion with which it is applied. Everything with which the Jew could consciously identify himself first had to bear the stamp of the Old Testament. Thus it is clear that philosophical thinking, despite all its speculative content, was bound at least in regard to its form. It was bound by religious form, a form belonging essentially to the concept of religion, and thus by an absolute presupposition within the religious consciousness. Thus considered, Neoplatonism and Alexandrian Judaism are two entirely parallel and similar phenomena. Furthermore, the significance of allegory, which is so characteristic of Jewish philosophy of religion, and which reaches its highest development there, is wholly analogous for Neoplatonism, just as allegory is very closely connected with the symbolic-mythical character of the ancient religions in general.

7. The Relation of These Phenomena to Early Christian Theology

The reason we have concerned ourselves with these two phenomena is that, although they obviously belong to the history of philosophy, they also enjoy a very close and essential connection with the history of Christian dogma, as is evident at every point. A system of dogmas can be construed from the writings of the Neoplatonists, as well as from Philo, that is entirely similar to that found in the writings of the church fathers. The Philonic system in particular is so closely related to the system of Christian theology during the first centuries that one might almost be tempted to regard the latter as a further development and expansion of the former. In a word, in the place of philosophical thinking there already appears a form of dogmatic thinking that belongs to the character of Christian theology, i.e., a type of speculation that is not lacking in authentic speculative content, but in which free philosophical thought is bound by a form given to it by religion and is subject to a presupposition that limits thinking and forces it to begin not in itself but only in faith.

Thus we see how the two areas—the history of philosophy and the history of Christian dogma—cohere and merge into each other. The Alexandrian philosophy of religion represents the transition to the history of Christian dogma in such a way that the same current which hitherto had run its course in the history of philosophy is now channeled into another bed, where it moves for many centuries as the history of Christian dogma. Essentially, there is no longer a history of philosophy in addition to the history of dogma. Rather, everything that can be considered to belong to the history of thinking Spirit obtains its form and color from Christian dogma and has some sort of relation, near or distant, to it. All thinking is now determined by dogma and the faith of the church. For a long period this is in fact the visible and evident relation between the history of philosophy and the history of Christian dogma. There remains only the question of how Christianity itself, as the starting point of Christian dogma, is related to it.

If we consider Christianity as a form of consciousness that enjoys the gift of Spirit itself, according to the circumstances of the time in which it appeared, then we can only place it under the same point of view from which the phenomena of which we have previously spoken are to be understood. All these phenomena have their essential focus in the aspiration of Spirit to overcome and transpose into universality everything limited, nationalistic, and particular, and by thus entering into a freer and broader sphere, to obtain its true self-consciousness in the Universal, which unveils itself in Spirit and which alone can be regarded as the true and the essential. If this aspiration toward universality is already the moving principle of the phenomena mentioned above, then by comparison Christianity itself is the purest universalism. It represents the freeing of Spirit from everything particular that adhered to it in all previous forms of its existence. The self-consciousness of Spirit knows its own inner unity only in the Universal, the Absolute, which is the principle of Christianity. Out of the dissolution of all external life, out of the renunciation of everything nationalistic and individual, out of the whole godless, amoral, and lawless world that existed at the time Christianity appeared,

Spirit could only withdraw into itself in order to obtain a new form of existence through an interiorization and self-absorption, by which everything in the subjectivity of Spirit that was untrue and limited had to be excluded. This new form of existence, as a rebirth of the whole of life, could only consist in a revolution out of subjectivity into the objective, into Being itself, i.e., a return to God. Consequently, Christianity appeared in the world not as philosophy but as religion. As divine revelation in the form of religion it was something absolutely given, which in its immediacy could be the object not of thinking and knowing but above all only of faith. Thus Christian dogma has its starting point in faith. It is itself faith in a representational mode; and all thinking connected with dogma has its final, determinative principle only in faith, regardless of how free it might otherwise be.

Here lies the great distinction between the history of philosophy and the history of Christian dogma. Thinking, in the history of Christian dogma, assumes a wholly different form—the form of faith. Its tendency is to become increasingly absorbed in the content of faith, to objectify itself in it until the content of faith is as nearly as possible exhausted and the free, moving flow of thinking has itself become, as it were, a permanent system of rigorously self-contained dogmas, determined by an external authority—i.e., thinking has become transcendent and external to itself.

8. *Ritter on Christian Philosophy*

A different view concerning the relation of the history of dogma to the history of philosophy is advanced if, as has been done recently, one speaks of a "Christian philosophy," the first period of which is considered to be patristic philosophy or the philosophy of the church fathers. August Heinrich Ritter, whose *Geschichte der Philosophie* assumed the title of a "history of Christian philosophy" with the fifth volume,[3] has recently placed special emphasis on this fact, and believes himself, under

3. *Geschichte der Philosophie*, V-XI (Hamburg, 1837-53).

[ED.] August Heinrich Ritter (1791-1869) was professor of philosophy at Berlin (1824-33), Kiel (1833-37), and Göttingen (1837-69). As a student at Berlin, he had been influenced by Schleiermacher; in 1839 he edited the latter's *Geschichte der Philosophie* from manuscript notes. Most of his publications were in the area of the history of philosophy and logic. His *Geschichte der Philosophie* appeared in twelve volumes from 1829 to 1853; a second edition of the first four volumes was published in 1836-38. His own philosophical position was eclectic and inconsistent; in theology he leaned toward Schleiermacher.

this title, to have conquered a new field for the history of philosophy. Ritter intends to counter the false view of those who maintain that philosophy was developed by the church fathers and scholastic theologians in the service of ecclesiastical doctrine. By this view it is understood that the philosophers, so called, of these periods tried to establish a permanent, once-and-for-all system of doctrines with the aid of philosophical propositions, and without permitting a truly free investigation whose only concern was to discover the truth. Hence these periods witnessed no philosophy but only a sophistry. Even if no more than this is asserted —that in their thinking the church fathers and scholastic theologians were so partial to ecclesiastical doctrine as to reduce every turn of investigation simply to establishing the clear meaning of that doctrine—it must still be maintained that philosophy in these periods was wholly abolished, since the essence of philosophical thinking is free investigation. The basic notion here is that Christianity and church doctrine have influenced philosophy only to its disadvantage. But to the contrary [argues Ritter], the faith of the Christian church has not in fact fettered philosophy and forced it into ignominious servitude, but rather has guided and supported it. Christianity has not merely exercised a purifying effect on philosophy, but also has introduced a new movement into it, has shown it new tasks, and has demanded of it new depths of investigation. Just as Christianity in general has awakened a new life in man, so also it has not been able to remain without the most important consequences for philosophy. Of course, philosophy thereby acquired at the outset a dominant tendency in the direction of the religious life of man; and it is not to be denied that this tendency was at first one-sided. But without it there could be no turning point in the life of men.

What Ritter means here by "Christian philosophy" requires considerable correction and understanding. In itself, the rubric "Christian philosophy" not unsuitably designates the new character assumed by philosophy after Christianity appeared. However, this rubric should not be employed to ascribe to the philosophy of the period an autonomy it did not in fact have. If Ritter quarrels with the view he opposes to his own on the ground that the nature of philosophical thinking is free investigation, then philosophy is not to be found where only a subjection of thought takes place, be it unintentional or deliberate. Whoever philosophizes must know that the knowledge he seeks is valuable in and for itself, even though it may also outwardly serve another purpose; and for this reason philosophy in the service of the faith of the church is a contradiction in terms. Hence, up to the time of scholasticism there was in fact no true philosophy. Ritter himself cannot deny this when he reproaches patristic and scholastic philosophy for having been one-sidedly bound to the theological orientation of Spirit, for being devoted to rhapsodic matters, and for having accomplished nothing by way of developing the experiential sciences. Furthermore, the aspiration for ecclesiastical unity perforce restricted it to a fixed canon of doctrine, which had a limiting influence on philosophical investigations. There was a reluctance to extend such investigations beyond the area of what was required by the ecclesiastical community, since free thinking beyond this area, in terms of scientific and logical consistency, could easily have had a shattering effect upon ecclesiastical doctrine. Philosophical thinking was of the highest value in securing faith as a whole against the doubts of scientific thinking, and indeed it was profitable in the advancement of investigation. But when it seemed to exceed the common power of comprehension among the faithful, it resigned itself to general formulas; and it was in danger of a mere external conjoining of the opposite tendencies of faith, a concealment of apparent contradictions rather than bringing them to a fundamental solution.

All of this and more that Ritter says in a similar vein by way of characterizing Christian philosophy indicates that it had its starting point in faith, that it moved only within Christian dogma, and that its orientation was not so much philosophical as theological. Although free philosophical thinking may have emerged with greater purity in certain prominent teachers of the church, such as Origen, even in them it has as its presupposition the facts of Christian revelation. The greater the tension between the philosophical and theological doctrines of Origen, the more clearly it is to be seen how little this freer manner of thinking accorded with the spirit of the times. Thus if one wishes to refer to what was in fact Christian theology, or the development of Christian dogma, as "Christian philosophy," the intention can only be to describe thus a form of thought that does not possess the real character of philosophy, any more than does that designated by the phrase, "Alexandrian philosophy of religion." Christian philosophy, too, was essentially a philosophy of religion. Ritter himself remarks that the alternative to Christian philosophy—a philosophy that has developed from the standpoint of true religion—is actually pagan philosophy. For ancient philosophy, however, this designation must, according to Ritter, be rejected as unsuitable, since the influence of pagan religion on philosophy has been almost wholly negative. From the very beginning, philosophy has tried to elevate itself above the prejudices of folk religion; and although it did not always succeed, we nevertheless observe it struggling almost constantly against polytheism, sometimes openly and sometimes in secret. For this reason, he says, ancient philosophy is a product first of the periods in which ancient religion began to decline, whereas Christian philosophy developed with the rise of the Christian faith. For this reason, Christian philosophy by its very nature cannot be viewed as emerging out of paganism. Rather, it grew up because the development of scientific thought could not be reconciled with popular representations of the polytheistic rule of the gods, and reflective Spirit sought in philosophy a satisfaction that religion could not provide.

But the distinction is rather that ancient philosophy, as pure philosophy, was by no means philosophy of religion, whereas Christian philosophy, so called, cannot be thought of at all without religion as its presupposition. That this was the general course of things, that in place of free philosophical thinking there appeared theological speculation based on religious faith, cannot be better explained than as a general revolution of consciousness. We must return to these more deeply rooted causes in order to understand correctly the differences between various ages and conditions. If one speaks of a history of Christian philosophy, the basic reason for doing so appears to lie in the wish not to lose hold of a continuity in philosophical development. The spirit of philosophy is never to be extinguished; phenomena that at first appear alien to philosophy nevertheless contain a philosophical element and simply represent a new form of philosophy. This interest in a continuity of the manifestations of Spirit certainly has a sound basis, but at the same time one must not lose sight of the essential difference between philosophy on the one hand and religion and theology on the other. The true continuity of the self-identical Spirit is rather to be seen in that philosophy and theology are similar modes of consciousness, expressed, however, in different forms; they are moments in the self-mediation of Spirit. Thus, so far as the subject matter itself is concerned, not only is nothing lost, but also the true conception of unity is first obtained, when we speak of a history of theology or of Christian dogma rather than a history of Christian philosophy. For the history of theology and the history of philosophy can have their common unity only in the history of consciousness and in the formation (or in the history of the development) of Spirit in general.

9. The Interpenetration of Theology and Philosophy in History

It is intrinsic to the nature of Spirit that the history of philosophy merges at a certain juncture into the history of the philosophy of religion and theology, or into the history of Christian dogma. Thus free philosophical thinking is bound to faith, within which alone it moves and develops. But it is no less intrinsic to the nature of Spirit that it also frees itself from this restriction. It emerges out of itself, as it were, in order to objectify itself in dogma, to fashion in dogma a world alien and transcendent to itself, and then to return to itself from this objectivity, which it has opposed to itself. The external form that belongs implicitly to dogma and in which Spirit has divested itself must be removed in order that dogma can be brought back to its inner basis, which resides in the nature of Spirit. This is the same process that has already been elaborated in connection with Christian dogma, except that here the participation of the history of philosophy in the process is especially emphasized. Just as the history of philosophy lost itself and was subsumed in the history of dogma, with the result that there was no longer any thinking independent of dogma, so once again thinking freed itself from dogma, and the history of philosophy from the history of dogma.

Philosophical thinking had already begun to re-emerge in scholasticism. The well-known scholastic opposition between realism and nominalism had a purely philosophical root, from which, to be sure, there was no further philosophical development; nevertheless, the way of thinking shaped on the basis of this opposition had a not insignificant influence on theology. Despite the weakness of this first philosophical movement, nevertheless the history of philosophy again had possession of its own independent area. But philosophy as a whole found its proper and independent beginning only after the Reformation, when, through the force of that great epoch, the general consciousness of the age became freer and more thoroughly self-reflective. A new epoch in the history of philosophy begins with Descartes and Spinoza, an epoch in which philosophy, aware of its inner autonomy, established for itself an area wholly independent of theology, and now seemed to want to pursue a course of its own, one quite distinct from theology. A history of philosophy that could move forward with the inner continuity of its own development, and that could produce its own content, now existed once again. However, it was not long before the two realms of philosophy and theology again came into contact and had a reciprocal influence. Free philosophical thinking became increasingly characteristic of theology, and theology itself could not avoid the task set for it by philosophy, of making its dogmas the object of thinking consciousness. Thus it happened that philosophy and theology both became increasingly conscious of their common content and their common interest in the Idea of the Absolute, which has equal significance for both. Accordingly, the relation of the two disciplines —the history of Christian dogma and the history of philosophy—has taken shape recently in such a way that a history of Christian dogma which was not at the same time essentially a history of speculative thinking in relation to religion and theology would be in contradiction with the whole scientific consciousness of the age. Just as at an earlier time the history of dogma allowed the history of philosophy to be submerged within itself, and spiritual movement could proceed only from a dogmatic interest, so now the reverse prevails, and the philosophical element so predominates in the history of the development of dogma that it is by and large the moving principle. We find represented in this changing relation of the history of dogma to the history of philosophy the same moments of Spirit that have already been established as the guiding general points of view for the history of Christian dogma; these are moments of Spirit as it becomes absorbed in dogma, only to withdraw from it once again into itself, and as it permeates dogma with its own self-consciousness.

VI

THE HISTORY OF THE HISTORY OF DOGMA: ITS EMERGENCE AND FORMATION INTO A SCIENCE

1. *The Subjective Understanding of History*

The history of dogma is by nature *history*. Hence, one must follow the historical movement of dogma, or the course of the subject matter itself, in order to acquire a subjective knowledge of it. The objective aspect of history becomes history in the subjective sense when the subject confronting the object becomes conscious of the object. The subject, therefore, must assimilate only what is objectively given, or permit only the subject matter as it is objectively to be reflected in his subjective consciousness. However, this pure surrender by the subject to the objectivity of the subject matter—in such a way that the subject's knowledge of the object is only the object itself in its subjective aspect—is from the point of view of the subject himself only the result of various possible positions of the subject in relation to the object.

With his subjective freedom, the subject is more or less inclined to intermix his own subjectivity and, instead of allowing himself to be determined by the objectivity of the subject matter, to determine the latter by his own subjectivity. This is the reason why the objectivity of history is understood in so many different ways. The road to an objective historical presentation runs through many detours. That which happens objectively has its own subjective history. The subject must first learn to yield himself to the object, and to deny his subjective interests and to abstract himself from them, in the interests of the subject matter. Thus the more that subjective interests predominate in understanding and presentation, the more erroneous is the historical standpoint, and the more inadequate to its subject matter. Nevertheless, a subjective interest of this sort has existed at various times and in various ways. Thus a history of our science has the major task of tracing the various directions taken by this subjectivity of historical interest, of demonstrating their bias and of showing how the subject gradually emerges from the bias of his merely subjective position in relation to dogma and learns to place himself in a more objective relation to it. But before the subject could come into a definite historical relation with dogma or obtain a historical consciousness of the temporal course of its development, dogma itself must already have run a certain part of its course. A history can first exist only after a series of events has already transpired. Soon thereafter arose the history of Christian dogma.

2. *Dogma and Heresy*

The greater the variation in views and opinions concerning Christian dogma, especially during the first centuries, and the more extreme the antitheses into which these views were divided, the more important was the historical material over which a specific historical consciousness had to be formed, even if there was no interest in a historical presentation as such. The various phenomena that appear in dogma had to be placed in a specific relation to one another, and it had to be explained how, in their mutual contradictions, they are related to dogma itself. A compulsion to do this arose out of the nature of the subject matter, but quickly settled into a quite subjective interest. From the earliest period, the Christian church and especially Christian dogma engendered a very marked tendency toward unity. On the basis of the idea of this unity, the possibility of divergences within dogma from the beginning could not be imagined. Historical consciousness was totally determined by dogmatic interests; throughout dogma as a whole, differences were acknowledged as little as possible. The dogmatic principle of the stability and constant self-identity of dogma, in which nothing could arise that appeared to deviate from traditional doctrine, also became the principle of historical consideration. Accordingly, no conception of a movement and development proceeding from dogma itself was available. Just as in practice care was always taken either strenuously to restore to unity whatever ventured to step beyond it, or totally to exclude it and cut it off, so also it was thought that no such doctrine or opinion had any inner connection with dogma itself. It belonged, in a word, to the broad category of heresy.

The reason for the existence of dogma in varied forms was not, it was thought, to be found in the concept and essence of dogma. Rather, the principle of the various opinions relating to dogma was merely one of subjective arbitrariness, which, in contrast to the constant unity of dogma, falls into constant change and innovation; or, objectively expressed, it is the many-headed Hydra, which raises a new head with each new heresy, or the serpent of old who never ceases to spew forth his deadly poison in every direction. Only the *antithesis* between Catholic truth and heresy was acknowledged. Just as no change was allowed in dogma itself, so also nothing but change was seen in the realm of heresy; and it was the characteristic distinction between Catholic truth and heresy that where the latter predominated nothing stood firm; rather, everything was endlessly divided and separated and dissolved from its own contradiction. Since truth and error thus oppose each other as light and darkness in crude, unmediated antithesis, historical consciousness was itself split into two mutually opposed sides, and historical reflection as a whole became dualistic. This is the posture first assumed by subjective consciousness in relation to dogma. Dogma remains unitary and self-identical, and everything that moves and changes falls outside of it. Consequently, a history of dogma as such does not exist. For one who would proceed historically in this area, there can only be a history of heretical teaching and ideas, since history is found only where something happens and changes.

3. The History of Dogma as the History of Heretics; Irenaeus, Tertullian, Epiphanius, Theodoret, Athanasius; Dualistic Historical Reflection

Thus the history of dogma first came into existence as a history of heretics. The representations given by such church teachers as Irenaeus and Tertullian of the teachings and ideas of the oldest heretics are to be regarded as the earliest attempts at a treatment of this subject. The emerging historical consciousness makes itself felt especially in the way these church teachers return to the past in order to clarify important phenomena of their time and to understand them in their full significance; they trace those phenomena from their beginnings and provide a survey of everything that has happened in connection with them. This is in particular the intention of Irenaeus. The greater the extent to which the procedure was followed, the more this historical consciousness was validated.

The most important works of this sort, in which the history of dogma, as the history of heretics, already emerges with an independent significance, are the heresiologies of Epiphanius and Theodoret [1]—especially the former, who, in his eighty heresies of Christian and pre-Christian times, tries to cover the entire field of heresy—or of dogma in so far as it moves and varies—and, in order to trace it back to its roots, touches even the pre-Christian era. The interest in history is attested especially in the way these historians of heretics, Epiphanius in particular, include in the sphere of heresy or of historical movement even those phenomena that hitherto had not been definitely regarded as heretical, such as the teaching of Origen.

The disproportionate extent to which such historical interest was subjective is to be seen most clearly, however, in that these historical portrayals are not so much an elucidation of heretical teachings and ideas as they are a dogmatic refutation. For they are made the object of historical consideration only for the purpose of being judged, refuted, rejected, and condemned. The historian holds in view everything provided him by the history of dogma only in order to obtain—from the reprehensible character of all teachings and ideas that deviate from orthodox dogma—a confirmation of his own dogmatic convictions. The object with which he is concerned has in itself no right to exist historically, as a moment of historical consciousness. Rather, that right is given to it by the subject alone, on the basis of his subjective interests. Thus he can only apply the standard of his subjective judgment; the object is not permitted to exist or appear as other than what, from his point of view, the subject deems appropriate.

The unity and unalterability of orthodox dogma remained an absolute presupposition. Hence, just as the heretics were considered only for the purpose of illuminating more clearly the truth of orthodox dogma by

---

1. [ED.] Epiphanius (c. 315–403) in 367 was made bishop of Salamis (Constantia) in Cyprus and metropolitan of the island. He became known as a defender of orthodoxy, a supporter of monasticism, and an arch-opponent of Origen, whom he regarded as the father of all heresies. He made the major task of his life the crushing of Origenism, and indeed of all Greek culture and thought in the church. Among his writings, the most important are the *Ancoratus* (374), a compendium of dogmatics that contains an exposition of the doctrines of the Trinity and the resurrection, with polemics against Arius, Origen, and others; and the *Panarion* (374–77), a "medicine chest" aimed against eighty heresies, and useful for the reconstruction of lost writings on which it is based, such as those of Irenaeus and Hippolytus. The *Ancoratus* and the *Panarion* are in *GCS*, XXV–XXVII.

On Theodoret, see above, 66, n. 24.

showing how the teachings of the heretics differed from it, so the interest in the orthodox teachers—when there was occasion to inquire historically into what they taught—was only in order to demonstrate from their interpretations the constant identity of dogma. Historical discussions of this sort are to be found especially in Athanasius. Of special importance here are his writings, *De sententia Dionysii* and *De synodis Arimini et Seleuciae,*[2] from which the stance assumed by orthodox church teachers such as Athanasius in relation to the history of dogma, when there was a question of the relation of their teaching to that of the older orthodox teachers, can clearly be seen. The Arians also maintained that their teaching was not new or completely foreign to previous ecclesiastical tradition. They too appealed to agreement with earlier church teachers. For example, they were not without foundation in their claim that Bishop Dionysius of Alexandria defined the relation of the Son to the Father in a manner similar to their own. Hence, at this point a disagreement over the development of dogma had to be acknowledged. But Athanasius can in no way understand it, and his major argument is that Dionysius died an orthodox bishop, without having been condemned by the other bishops on account of heresy, and is included in the list of the fathers. It is simply calumny to say of orthodox church teachers that they did not teach the same thing consistently. In order to prohibit the appearance of any rifts in this presumed unity of the church, Athanasius went so far as to explain real differences—when they could not be denied completely—as mere appearance. Epiphanius placed Origen among the heretics because of his striking deviations from orthodox doctrine, but Athanasius believed it possible to maintain his orthodoxy, since what he wrote by way of investigation and disputation is not to be regarded as his true opinion; and one must make a distinction between "his personal belief" and "his prolusions against the heretics."[3]

In this way it was thought possible to surmount obvious contradictions. Those were explained on the basis of accommodation—e.g., according to Athanasius, it was a matter of mere accommodation when the seventy fathers of the Council of Antioch [268], which condemned Paul of Samosata, rejected the same word, ὁμοούσιος [of the same being], which

---

2. [ED.] *De sententia Dionysii* (On the Opinion of Dionysius), c. A.D. 352 (*PG,* XXV; *NPNF* 2, IV); *De synodis Arimini et Seleuciae in Isauria celebratis* (On the Councils of Ariminum and Seleucia in Isauria), 359 (*PG,* XXVI; *NPNF* 2, IV).

3. Athanasius, *De decretis Synodi Nicaeni* [On the Decrees of the Council of Nicaea] (c. 351–55), xxvii [*PG,* XXV; *NPNF* 2, IV, 168].

the Council of Nicaea [325] made the slogan of its orthodoxy. Thus if the fathers of two different councils have expressed themselves differently with respect to the word ὁμοούσιος, one is not, says Athanasius, to take offense, but rather to see how they intended the use of the term; and thereby one will discover that the two councils agree with each other completely. The fathers at Antioch regarded the word ὁμοούσιος, which they took in the physical sense, as objectionable only in order to counter the sophistry of the Samosatene. They expressed themselves thus only in view of the circumstances and with the special purpose they had in mind; but implicitly they were in agreement with the Nicene position.[4] It is clear that in this fashion, if it is believed permissible to presuppose a meaning wholly other than that which a word clearly expresses, all the rough spots in history can be smoothed over. Those differences that emerge in history are not real differences but are merely formal and apparent. Such differences are not a serious matter; rather, everything that seems to issue in difference is only an appearance, a mere game. Thus there is no change that can affect dogma itself. Every change relating to dogma is either only apparent or an error, a heresy; there is no history of dogma, but only a history of heresy.

The dualistic view of history held by these fathers is quite naturally connected with a certain form of docetism. Unity on the one hand and variation or movement on the other oppose each other in such sharp antithesis that they are unable to meet at all. Hence every movement within the unity, every difference into which it is separated, can only be docetic, existing merely in the imagination.

But why ought history to consist only of this permanent sameness, this continuing self-identity? Obviously because the subject is fearful of losing the focal point of his dogmatic consciousness if he sees those to whom he believes he must hold as his forerunners not standing firm themselves, or if he perceives deviation, movement, and variation in the teaching approved by the church. Because he does not yet feel sufficiently strong and does not possess sufficient self-confidence, the subject, out of self-interest and in order to stand on his own feet, is unwilling to permit any rupture in history. Everything is to be of a piece, since only so is it to be known as identical with itself. For this purpose, everything possible is done not to permit the occurrence of any division in dogmatic consciousness, and the attempt is made at any price to remove from history everything moving and changing. For this reason alone, precisely where there is authentic movement and change, in heresy so called, the truth of

4. Athanasius, *De synodis Arimini et Seleuciae*, xlv [*NPNF* 2, IV, 474].

dogma is not to be seen, but only error, its opposite. And for the same reason, in the sphere of dogma itself, any differences that might arise ought not to exist at all.

In all of this is displayed merely the bias and limitation, the arbitrariness and obstinacy, the intellectual and moral weakness of the subject. He is fearful of the living reality of history, he dares not see what really has happened in it, and he permits himself, out of necessity and embarrassment, the greatest arbitrariness in regard to it. This posture of historical consciousness in relation to dogma remained unchanged so long as the dogmatic consciousness by which it was conditioned remained unchanged. From the standpoint of orthodox dogma no other view of history could be obtained; such a possibility lay only in another point of view. To heretics, for whom orthodox Catholic dogma did not have the same significance, it did not really matter whether the history of dogma displayed greater or lesser differences and contradictions; indeed, it was in their interest to emphasize the differences.

4. Stephanus Gobarus; Abelard

In this connection it is well to mention the work by Stephanus Gobarus. So far as we know,[5] it contained fifty-two articles, concerned with questions that were brought to expression and defined in the church. In connection with each, he correlated two not merely different but also contradictory explanations of older church teachers. He showed this neither by arguments nor by biblical testimonies, but rather simply by collecting those passages in the fathers where some said one thing concerning what the church taught and others the direct opposite. Since Stephanus Gobarus belonged to the Monophysite party as a tritheist, and hence did not acknowledge the orthodoxy of the Council of Chalcedon and all the authorities upon which it rested, it appeared that he could only have intended, in making such a collection of contradictory assertions, to demonstrate historically that there was by no means the uniformity of dogma of which the Catholic Church boasted. The transition from a history of heretics, in which it is presupposed that dogma remains always

5. Photius, *Bibliotheca*, codex 232 [*PG*, CII].

[ED.] Stephanus Gobarus was a sixth-century tritheist and Monophysite, whose works have been lost. The *Bibliotheca* of Photius (c. 815–c. 897/898), twice patriarch of Constantinople and leading scholar of the ninth century, contained summary accounts or "codices" of 280 books read and studied by Photius, including both pagan and Christian writers.

the same and thus has no history (since all changes affecting dogma are mere heresies), to an authentic history of dogma came about through the recognition that there are indeed ideas and opinions about dogma which despite all their variety have equal justification, and which confront one another with the same right to historical existence. The work of Stephanus Gobarus constituted a feeble start toward this recognition. But we do not know what further conception he had of the history of dogma.

A similar writing from a later period as Abelard's *Sic et non* (Yes and No), only recently edited for the first time, in 1836, by V. Cousin.[6] Here, too, authorities that can be cited for and against various ecclesiastical propositions have been collected, and the interest in history is at least to be seen in the presentation of the contradictions, quite nakedly and baldly, without any attempt to soften or eliminate them. Also, critical canons established in the Prologue are opposed to the customary procedure of reconciling everything, and rest on the presupposition that not everything in the history of dogma is without diversity and contradiction. Here we have already advanced into the scholastic period, but the standpoint as a whole remains the same. Because of their dialectical tendency, the scholastic theologians were lacking in all historical sense; their treatment of dogma had a historical aspect only in that they returned to the older authorities to establish a basis for their Sentences. Even though in general they discussed all the possible arguments pro and con, and also placed conflicting authorities in opposition to one another, they did so only to eliminate the contradiction dialectically, and even for them the identity of dogma remained the presupposition from which they proceeded and to which they always returned. Hence the posture of consciousness in relation to dogma could change only with a whole new revolution of consciousness. This came about through the Reformation.

5. *The Historical Understanding of Dogma Initiated by the Reformation*

What heretofore had been averted in the tendency of the Middle Ages as a whole—namely, a break between the consciousness of the individual

6. [ED.] In *Ouvrages inédits d'Abélard* (Paris, 1836). The *Sic et non* was lacking from the *Opera* of A. Duchesne and F. Amboise (Paris, 1616), published in *PL*, CLXXVIII. Cousin's edition of *Sic et non* was incomplete; a complete text was published by T. Henke and G. S. Lindenkohl (Marburg, 1851).

and the dogma of the church—now came about. In essence the Reformation is nothing other than a great rift in ecclesiastical consciousness, a break with the church and with the dogma of the church. The insight was now obtained that it was by no means nearly so important as had hitherto been thought to agree completely with the dogma of the church, and indeed that to do so was impossible in view of the growing conviction that dogma in its traditional development contained so much that could only be in contradiction to the Christian consciousness determined by the Word of God. Hence for the first time the point had now been reached at which the objectivity of dogma could come into its own. The more free and independent the believer now became, intending, in the consciousness of his freedom and autonomy, to be bound by nothing other than what he could regard as the true and pure Word of God on the basis of his own best conviction, the freer the position he could also assume in relation to dogma. There was no longer the concern always to find in history only the eternal uniformity of an unchanging tradition, as the substance of one's own religious and dogmatic conviction, and not to acknowledge differences between the doctrines and opinions of different periods and teachers. On the contrary, the more these had changed in the course of time, and the greater the contradiction between the original and the reigning doctrine of later times, the less could the justice of the *de facto* separation be denied. Thus the possibility of a purely historical understanding of dogma, and of a history of the same, was first initiated through the Reformation and Protestantism. And just as the Reformation in general first awakened and enlivened the historical sense and instinct, so also it called forth the first historical investigations of the course and alterations of dogma.

6. *The Dogmatic-Polemical Treatment: The Magdeburg Centuries, Petavius, Forbesius a Corse, Gerhard, Quenstedt*

The great historical work that was to give to the work of the Reformation its historical foundation, the *Magdeburg Centuries*,[7] already treated *doctrina* (i.e., church doctrine), and *haereses* in each *Century* in special sections. The greater the importance that Protestantism from the beginning placed on the purification and establishment of doctrine, the more

7. Cf. the author's *Die Epochen der kirchlichen Geschichtschreibung* (Tübingen, 1852), 39–71 [above, 79–105].

significant historical questions and investigations were for Protestant dogmatics.

Hence it is a remarkable phenomenon that, just when Protestantism had awakened a true historical consciousness and interest, the Catholic Church produced its first great work in which the history of the development of dogma was made the object of a special and comprehensive investigation. This is the famous work by the French Jesuit Denis Pétau (Dionysius Petavius), *De theologicis dogmatibus*,[8] which is epoch-making for the history of our discipline. Pétau did not, as Nitzsch correctly points out,[9] call his work *dogmata theologica* [theological dogmas] because he intended to adduce a body of doctrinal opinions of theologians, but because he wished to describe, in accord with historical method, the system of major propositions of Christian theology—i.e., dogmas—as they are known from Scripture and ecclesiastical tradition. The *dogmata* are the absolutely valid ecclesiastical doctrines that remain forever unchanged; they are the ecclesiastical tradition as the self-evident substantiality to which everything that makes up the content of history is related as accident to substance.[10]

8. Five vols.; Paris, 1644–50. New edition: Petavius Dionysius, *Opus de theologicis dogmatibus expolitum et auctum collatis studiis*, ed. C. Passaglia and C. Schrader, I (Rome, 1857).

[ED.] Dionysius Petavius (1583–1652) was professor of positive theology at Paris from 1621 to 1644. His range of scholarship was vast, including classical philology, chronology and history, polemics, patristics, and the history of dogma; his published works number forty-nine. Among his polemical writings were works directed against Claudius Salmasius, Maturin Simon, Hugo Grotius, and the Jansenists.

9. K. I. Nitzsch, *System der christlichen Lehre* (Bonn, 1829), 36.

10. The plan of the work embraces the whole history of dogma, and treats in the first book *de Deo;* in the second, *de trinitate;* in the third *de angelis* and *de sex dierum officio* (in which as an introduction to what follows there appears an essay *de Pelagianis,* a history of the Pelagian controversy); in the fourth *de hierarchia, de inauguratione sacerdotali et poenitentia* (on the sacraments); and in the fifth and sixth *de incarnatione* (on the doctrines of the person and work of the Saviour, as they concern the economy of salvation).

The division [between the first two books and the remaining four] is between (1) God himself and (2) the works of God. The latter consist of both the works of nature and works of grace, since God is the author of nature as well as of grace. The works of nature are in part purely spiritual, as with angels and souls; in part corporeal; and in part a mixture, as with man. This is the doctrine of the world. The works of grace have as their object *deificatio* [deification] or the *communicatio divinitatis* [impartation of divinity]. Such deification can be absolute and internal, as in the incarnation of God. Or it can be merely relative, external, and moral, effected partly by certain *instrumenta* (the sacraments and the law), and partly by inner causes, formally (grace and the infused virtues—faith, love, hope, etc.). In con-

The major excellence of the work is the great scholarship of the author and the rich material embodied in it. In the spirit of the work one could see an involuntary stirring of Protestant consciousness; for Pétau, as he says at the very outset, has the intention "to entrust to these books the whole of theology, not that argumentative and subtle sort, which appeared a few generations ago and now alone has almost taken over the schools, from which it also took its proper name of 'scholastic'; but another sort, more refined and more fruitful, which, being articulated in accord with the form of ancient learning—i.e., recalled from the briar patches of the dialecticians to the open spaces of a freer field of action—reveals its natural and native power solely for its own use and practice." [11] Hence even Pétau felt the need to reform theology and to free it from the scholastic wilderness, with which the dogmatic consciousness could no longer be reconciled. Apart from this, however, the work is truly Catholic, precisely in that, although it intends to be a complete history of dogma, it limits itself chiefly to the ancient period, "because the greater part of theological dogmas are ratified by the decrees of antiquity, . . . and because there is no question, or certainly very little question, concerning the judgment of [the church] today, which speaks for itself, and in a sense publicly." [12] It can scarcely be otherwise if history, in the identity of dogma, is simply a repetition of what has long existed, in contrast to which Protestant dogma can only belong to the category of long-condemned heresies.

Hence there is no question here, either, of any real diversity in the development of dogma. Any deviation must return to the universal content of dogma; or, as Pétau says, it is "evident that the opinions of the ancient fathers—when they stand apart from the councils approved by the church, or from the faith of the apostolic tradition, as they call it—do not have a definite and indubitable power of proof." [13] In order, however, not to relinquish too completely the authority of the fathers, the

---

trast to the *status* of θέωσις [state of deification] stands the *status peccati* [state of sin]. [ED. See *De theologicis dogmatibus*, I, *Prolegomena*, 1 (Passaglia and Schrader ed., I, 3-4.]

The doctrine of the hierarchy and the sacraments is conjoined immediately to the doctrine of the angels and creation, since Petavius, like Dionysius the Areopagite, compares the earthly hierarchy with the heavenly.

11. [ED.] *De theologicis dogmatibus*, I, *Prolegomena*, 1 (Passaglia and Schrader ed., I, 1).

12. [ED.] *Ibid.*, I, *Prolegomena*, 1 (Passaglia and Schrader ed., I, 7). Bracketed insert is Baur's.

13. [ED.] *Ibid.*, I, *Prolegomena*, 11 (Passoglia and Schrader ed., I, 11).

following *cautiones* are established: (1) "That we should preserve toward them a pious and peaceful disposition of the will along with a certain reverence and honor, and not treat them in a contemptuous and uncivil manner if we think they have wavered in any matter, or if we disagree with them in any way." (2) "That we should not rashly accuse them of error, [or, if we do so,] not without great discretion. If ambiguous statements in their books can be explained and excused by reference to other statements by them, let us hold to this latter course rather than ascribe to them any false opinion." (3) "That we should compare them not only with themselves but also with each other; and that we should put the consensus of the others and of the majority above the few who will seem to have departed somewhat from the true and universal doctrine." [14] In a word, no deviation among the fathers themselves or from orthodox dogma must ever be conceded. If, for example, Pétau cannot allow it to pass unnoticed that the previously unsettled dogma of the Trinity was defined for the first time at the Council of Nicaea, so that predecessors to the heretical teaching of Arius were by no means lacking among the church fathers of earlier periods, we are not to see in this any great concession of principle. This is a truly Catholic work, one constructed on so grandiose a scale that Protestant theology of the same period could boast of nothing comparable with it.

The work by the Scottish theologian Johannes Forbesius a Corse, *Instructiones historico-theologicae de doctrina Christiana inde a tempore Apostolorum ad seculum 17*, [15] certainly cannot advance such a claim, as is immediately evident from the plan of the work, which scarcely corre-

14. [ED.] *Ibid.*, I, *Prolegomena*, II (Passaglia and Schrader ed., I, 11–12).

15. Amsterdam, 1645. The work consists of sixteen books, the contents of which are as follows: "(1) on God; (2) on the mystery of the incarnation; (3) on the varied conditions of the churches and many heresies and dissensions, etc.; (4) on Muhammad, his impiety, and his followers, and on the Holy War and certain other wars; (5) on the Monotheletes and on Honorius, Pope of Rome and Monothelete heretic; (6) on the Adoptionist heresy; (7) on the object of religious worship, etc.; (8) on the Pelagian heresy and what remains of it; (9) on the sacraments as a genus, etc.; (10) on baptism; (11) on the Eucharist; (12) on penance and certain related subjects, etc.; (13) on purgatory and intercessions for the dead; (14) on the unity and division of the church; (15) on the primacy of Peter the Apostle; (16) on the successors to Peter and the other apostles."

[ED.] Johannes Forbesius a Corse (John Forbes) was born in 1593 and died at Corse, the estate he inherited from his father, in 1648. He studied theology at Aberdeen, Heidelberg, Sédan, and other Continental universities, and in 1620 was appointed professor of divinity in King's College, Aberdeen. In 1638 he refused to sign the National Covenant and was ejected from his professorship by the General Assembly. In 1643 he was forced to leave Scotland, but later he returned to spend the remainder of his life at Corse. Irenic in temperament, and an advocate of a

sponds to the conception of a history of dogma. It has the special purpose, in opposition to Bellarmine, of demonstrating the agreement of Protestant doctrine with the statements of the ancient fathers—a onesidedness that the Protestant treatment of the history of dogma on the whole still suffered. This treatment had, to be sure, been freed from the Catholic interest in unity; but the standpoint from which history was considered remained equally dogmatic in character, except that it was now connected with the dogmatic interest of polemicizing against the Catholic Church, since the antithesis that emerged brought with it this polemic. What earlier had been the antithesis between dogma and heresy now became the antithesis between Catholicism and Protestantism. The Protestants also could not deny the necessity of being reconciled with ecclesiastical dogma in its historical development; but since they wanted to restore only the pure truth of the Gospel, they looked back especially to the earliest church, which could not yet have been infiltrated by the corruption of later times. Hence it was always a very important matter for the two Protestant parties, in their common opposition to the Catholic Church as well as in their relation to each other, to demonstrate an agreement with the ancient church concerning their major distinctive doctrines. The feeling for historical investigation was aroused above all by this polemical interest. Indeed, the interest was carried so far that the truth now was sought on the side of the heretics persecuted and condemned by the Catholic Church, in whom, it was believed, there existed a continuing chain of so-called *testes veritatis* [witnesses of the truth] to the never wholly extinguished evangelical truth.

Thus the treatment of dogma was thoroughly dogmatic and polemical, for which reason the history of dogma in this period was cultivated chiefly in dogmatic works, which could obtain only from history the polemical material to be used in constructing their dogmatic systems. The great dogmatic works of the Lutheran theologians of the seventeenth century, such as the *Loci theologici* of Gerhard (especially in the edition by Cotta), and the *Theologia didacto-polemica* of Quenstedt,[16] still have

---

project to unite the Reformed and Lutheran churches, he wrote, in addition to the *Instructiones*, an *Irenicum amatoribus veritatis et pacis in Ecclesia Scoticana* (Aberdeen, 1629).

16. [ED.] Johann Gerhard (1582–1637) was a professor of theology at Jena. He began his *Loci theologici* in 1609, at the age of twenty-seven, and completed it in 1622. A 22-volume edition was issued by J. F. Cotta, professor of dogmatics at Tübingen, in 1762–89. Johannes Andreas Quenstedt (1617–88) was professor of philosophy and theology at Wittenberg from 1646 until his death. His *Theologia didacto-polemica sive systema theologicum* was published at Wittenberg in 1685.

a not insignificant value for the history of dogma by virtue of their collection of authorities from the church fathers for the doctrines of the Protestant Lutheran system, and their opposition to all possible parties deviating from the Protestant Lutheran Church. So long as the polemical point of view continued to dominate, historical criticism could only show its influence. Hence it was quite natural that, concerning dogmas that had not become the object of dispute and theological controversy, these theologians adhered completely to the Catholic point of view and attached special importance to the necessity of not deviating at these points from universal church doctrine, in particular the doctrines of the Trinity and the Person of Christ. They could not conceive otherwise than that the traditional doctrines must not only accord wholly with the teaching of Scripture but must also embrace the configurations they obtained in the Catholic Church, so that they could see no occasion, indeed could not even regard it as justified, to go beyond them. Thus the Catholic principle of stability here retained its full force. The movement introduced into dogma by the Protestant principle was not yet thoroughgoing and did not penetrate into the essence of the subject matter itself. There was always a special reason, based on the circumstances of the time, why dogma was considered in this fashion or that. In a word, the standpoint was still chiefly polemical, not critical in the purer sense. Criticism was not totally lacking, to be sure, in so far as the purification of doctrine by distinguishing between original and derived forms, as was occasioned by the Protestant principle, was implicitly critical in character; but criticism was still too heavily dependent on presuppositions and specific considerations.

7. The Critical Treatment of the History of Dogma: Walch, Semler, Mosheim, Rösler

The new epoch in the history of our discipline can be described only as the transition from polemicism to criticism. Generally speaking, the new turn that occurred in Protestant theology around the middle of the eighteenth century had a predominantly critical tendency. Critical endeavors came into view from various directions. In the area of the history of dogma, three men in particular distinguished themselves: J. L. Mosheim, C. W. F. Walch, and J. S. Semler.[17] Historical criticism has various tasks to accomplish, and only when it responds equally to all the demands made

17. [ED.] On Mosheim, see above, 142; on Walch, 163; and on Semler, 153.

upon it, not one-sidedly limiting itself to this or that aspect of its work, can it establish the true historical method. Since its major task is to present the object of historical consideration in its pure objectivity, free of everything that could impede and blur a proper insight into all the details of the subject matter, it arrives above all at the fundamental investigation of sources. On the side of the subject, everything is to be removed that could stand in the way of a pure and objective understanding of the subject matter, especially if one is hindered by prejudices and presuppositions or by thralldom to a controlling theological system. But even if everything is done on both sides—that of the object as well as of the subject—to bring the two as close together as possible and to remove everything that could stand between them as impediment and obscuration, there is still a further important task, that of pursuing the immanent movement of the subject matter itself. For the subject matter is truly perceived for the first time when the concept of it is also obtained; but the concept of the subject matter is the inner dynamic principle that enables the concept to divide and disperse into its elements and to progress from moment to moment, by means of which the concept for the first time actualizes itself and achieves reality.

If we characterize the men named above according to these various considerations, they are distinguished equally both for their comprehensive and fundamental study of the sources and for their meticulous investigation and examination of all the materials that must serve as the foundation for a satisfying treatment of the history of dogma. Walch in particular devoted a rigorous and inexhaustible industry, with persistent attention to details, to the fundamental investigation and study of sources, and made conscientious use of all materials and aids. To this his major work, the *Geschichte der Ketzereien, Spaltungen und Religionsstreitigkeiten bis auf die Zeiten der Reformation*,[18] bears quite credible witness. On the other hand, he was inferior with respect to the second major demand that must be made of a critical student of the history of dogma, namely, freedom and independence of dogmatic presuppositions. Walch was a strongly orthodox Lutheran theologian, who applied everywhere only the standard of Lutheran orthodoxy, and judged everything according to its near or distant relation to Lutheran doctrine, as though dogma had already attained there its absolute point of repose.

18. Published in ten volumes, beginning in 1762, with the eleventh volume edited by Spittler in 1785; it continues only up to the history of the iconoclastic controversy. [ED. See above, 162–67.]

Mosheim was more independent of such dogmatic thralldom and uneasiness, but in this respect Semler was especially distinguished; for him, nothing existed that was steady, permanent, and unchanging. Dogma, for him, was completely liberated from all the bonds by which hitherto it had been connected to the dogmatic standpoint of the subject; but the freedom to which it had now attained was only that of arbitrariness and chance. His standpoint was so much the opposite of the Catholic view concerning the stability of dogma that in fact he went completely to the other extreme. He saw in history only a moving, continually changing element. The whole of the history of dogma consists of an endless multitude of changes. The essence of dogma itself is a never-ceasing change, whose causes are purely subjective and accidental: because one person does something one way, another does it another way; conditions vary at random. Since he saw in history only the free and arbitrary working of subjectivity, he was also much inclined (especially where he suspected the hierarchy had taken a hand) toward suspicion and mistrust of the purity and authenticity of the sources. His criticism is filled with hypotheses suspended in thin air, which, if pursued, would lead one completely to lose hold of the firm ground of history. For all its merit and rigor, his procedure was fundamentally only a vast burrowing in the materials, by means of which everything was indeed shaken up and exposed on every side, but not brought into continuity. Thus all his works in the history of dogma have a striking formlessness. They were basically only raw materials, which he brought to light by means of direct source studies.[19]

In this respect Mosheim has considerable advantage over Semler, for his historical talent is to be seen especially in a penetration of the inner continuity and, with the help of delicate and appropriate combinations, the ability to produce a connected, well-organized whole, which further commended itself by a pleasing and fluent presentation. Mosheim demonstrated this critical sense, which was not merely destructive, but which traced the movement of the subject matter by distinguishing its various elements, grasping it in its organic unity, above all in his investigations of the teachings of the ancient heretics, especially the Gnostics and Manichaeans, on whom Mosheim first shed new light.[20] In Mosheim the idea

19. He embodied his most important investigations in Prefaces that accompanied, as historical introductions, Siegmund Jakob Baumgarten's *Evangelische Glaubenslehre* (3 vols.; Halle, 1759–60), and *Untersuchung theologischer Streitigkeiten* (3 vols.; Halle, 1762–64). [ED. See above, 153, 161.]

20. His most important work in the history of dogma is his *Commentarii de rebus Christianorum ante Constantinum Magnum* (Helmstädt, 1753).

dawned of what must be described as the third element in the critical task. He was aware that in history, and above all in intellectual history, there must also be movement and continuity, life and spirit.

In this regard, no one is more inferior to Mosheim than Walch. Semler brought life into history through the restlessness and vitality of his spirit. But Walch, in his atomistic mode of comprehension and presentation, has so slight an inkling of life in history that in his hands the historical-critical analysis of the richest systems, spiritually and intellectually, becomes a mere autopsy. There is no drier, no more lifeless and spiritless aggregate of statements enumerated one after the other than Walch's heresiology. It has breadth but no depth.

Among these three men, the one who without doubt most influenced the following period, in which the critical element flourished most freely, was Semler, on whom C. F. Rösler [21] was most closely dependent. Rösler deserves much credit for stimulating the study of the history of dogma by his academic writings, his bibliography of church fathers,[22] and especially his *Lehrbegriff der christlichen Kirche in den drei ersten Jahrhunderten* (Frankfurt, 1777), which, in the prefatory critical essay on the rules for investigating doctrinal history, and in its methodical organization of material, offered instructive guidelines for the proper treatment of the history of dogma. The authors of several monographs, and certain dogmaticians who combined the history of dogma with dogmatics—such as J. F. Gruner, G. F. Seiler, and J. C. Döderlein [23]—continued further along Semler's path.

21. [ED.] Christian Friedrich Rösler (1736–1821) studied theology at Tübingen (1755–60), where he was later professor of history from 1777 until his death. Thus he was on the faculty while Baur was a student in the evangelical-theological seminary, 1809–14. In addition to the works mentioned by Baur, he published numerous monographs on the Middle Ages. He was known for his careful source studies and scholarship, and for his opposition to theoretical historical constructions.

22. *Bibliothek der Kirchenväter in Übersetzung und Auszügen* (10 vols.; Leipzig, 1776–86).

23. [ED.] Johann Friedrich Gruner (1723–78), professor at Halle, was a rationalist theologian who sought to distinguish the Platonizing dogmas (such as the Trinity and Logos Christology) from the teaching of Scripture, which was identical with the truths of reason. Cf. his *Praktische Einleitung in die Religion der Heiligen Schrift* (1773), and his *Institutiones theologiae dogmaticae* (1777). Georg Friedrich Seiler (1733–1807), professor of theology at Erlangen, where he also held important ecclesiastical posts, was an opponent of the early rationalists (the "neologists"), and adhered instead to the position known as rational supernaturalism. Cf. his *Der Geist und die Gesinnungen des vernunftmässigen Christentums zur Erbauung* (1769), and *Kurze Geschichte der geoffenbarten Religion* (1772). Johann Christoph Döderlein (1746–92), professor of theology at Altdorf and Jena, sought to relate the work of

8. *Historical Pragmatism: Planck*

This was a time of grossest indifference toward church dogma. For the reason that dogma had lost its substantial content in the consciousness of the age, the history of dogma was readily combined with dogmatics simply to obtain the necessary materials and content for the latter. The less one believed in the ecclesiastical authority of dogma, the more difficult it was to acquire any speculative interest in it. Hence it was believed that one stood at the pinnacle of the enlightenment of the time in deploring the useless ingenuity applied by so many theologians to implicitly meaningless questions, not at all closely related to Christian teaching, which by occasioning controversy brought only endless disadvantages to the Christian church. On the whole, there was seen in history only a boundless arbitrariness and the freest play of subjectivity. Historical subjects and individuals, hitherto wholly suppressed by the overwhelming power of the substance of dogma, now suddenly emerged everywhere, as though freed of that substance now that it had dissolved. They filled the space completely, entering freely and with a will into the course of history, where all human interests, motives, and passions now had the most open of arenas. The more thoroughly one attempted to explore this colorful maze and to examine it psychologically, the more one might boast of having mastered the art of historical pragmatism.

In this period, no one acquired higher renown as a pragmatic historian than G. J. Planck,[24] for his *Geschichte des protestantischen Lehrbegriffs von der Reformation bis zur Einführung der Concordienformel* (6 vols.; Leipzig, 1781–1800), to which was later added the *Geschichte der protestantischen Theologie von der Concordienformel an bis in die Mitte des achtzehnten Jahrhunderts* (Göttingen, 1831). The first work, Planck's *magnum opus*, has great importance for the history of dogma, since Planck described in it very accurately and exhaustively, on the basis of a comprehensive utilization of sources, the doctrinal controversies of the Reformation period. Much as the work excelled in richness of content,

---

the biblical exegete and the dogmatician. He was the only one of the early rationalists to oppose the Wolfenbüttel Fragments published by Lessing; cf. his *Antifragmente* (1778–79). His *Institutio theologici christiani nostris temporibus accommodata* (1780) represents a transition to a more decisively rationalist theology.

24. [ED.] See above, 185.

however, it also bore a subjective character in its historical treatment. The historian did not sufficiently forbear to introduce his subjective views and speculations into history: the persons appearing in history act only out of subjective interests and motives; everything that happens and is brought to a decision depends finally only on contingencies; the objective course of history and the inner necessity with which one moment after the other develops in the area of dogma are nowhere brought clearly into view.

9. Rationalism; Münscher, Augusti

Rationalism emerged out of the same subjective tendency that increasingly spread and became established in German theology during the second half of the eighteenth century. It obtained its more definite form and development through Kant's philosophy—through his moral ideas and principles, which it appropriated for itself. Rationalism, which is based on subjective reason, has, in the nature of the case, no historical sense. The more inadequate and empty a rationalistic dogmatics is, resting merely on the assertions of reason or the products of reflective intellect and on abstract general truths, the more rationalism perceives the necessity of fleeing to history in order to prove how fortuitously the church dogma with which it is at variance has evolved, and how it permits its own critical demolition. Thus it is noteworthy how easily the rationalistic textbooks in dogmatics join the history of dogma to dogmatics, as for example K. F. Stäudlin,[25] *Lehrbuch der Dogmatik und Dogmengeschichte* (Göttingen, 1801), and Julius Wegscheider,[26] *Institutiones theologiae dogmaticae, addita singulorum dogmatum historia et censura* (Hamburg, 1815). In Karl Hase's *Lehrbuch der evangelischen Dogmatik* (2nd edition, Stuttgart, 1838),[27] the historical material is so predominant, moreover, that the work no longer can be called a dogmatics. The one-sided, subjective

25. [ED.] See above, 205–206.
26. [ED.] Julius August Ludwig Wegscheider (1771–1849), a student of Kant, was professor of theology at Halle from 1810 almost until his death. Wegscheider did some work in New Testament, where he defended the authenticity of the Fourth Gospel, but his *magnum opus* is the *Institutiones*, the classic work in the dogmatics of rationalism. He remained uninfluenced by idealism, rejecting the ideas of God advanced by Fichte, Hegel, and Schelling. His popularity as a teacher began to wane after 1826, when the more evangelically oriented F. A. G. Tholuck joined the Halle faculty.
27. [ED.] See above, 255–56.

standpoint of these historians of dogma is to be seen in their use of history merely to supply the material for their rationalistic criticism. The history of dogma cannot gain through such a connection with dogmatics.

This is also true in part of D. F. Strauss's dogmatics.[28] For all the work's imposing and masterful exposition of the view that the history of dogma is also its criticism, it is nevertheless also to be seen that in this linking of the history of dogma with dogmatics, history itself always comes off badly. Not history as such, but rather criticism, is the major concern. Since criticism is negatively rather than positively directed, dogma allows itself to be constructed only to have its structure destroyed, and to show how it contains nothing that can endure. As a result, dogma seems to exist merely for the sake of criticizing itself. Such is rationalism's negative manner of relating itself to the history of dogma.[29]

Nevertheless, the history of dogma can thank the period of Kantian rationalism for a work that is in a certain sense epoch-making in the history of this discipline. Wilhelm Münscher's *Handbuch der christlichen Dogmengeschichte* (Marburg, 1797–1809)[30] was the first work in re-

28. [ED.] David Friedrich Strauss, *Die christliche Glaubenslehre in ihrer geschichtlichen Entwicklung und im Kampfe mit der modernen Wissenschaft dargestellt* (2 vols.; Tübingen, 1840–41).

29. [ED.] A similar criticism of Strauss appeared in the Introduction to the first edition of Baur's *Lehrbuch der christlichen Dogmengeschichte* (Stuttgart, 1847), 42–43: "Rationalism has in itself, according to the nature of the case, no historical sense. The emptier its dogmatics, the more it is devoted to history in order to have an object to criticize. Precisely this, however, is the subjective bias of this standpoint in the historical treatment of dogma—namely, that history of dogma should be conducive only to criticism. In such a relation with dogmatics, the history of dogma can never come into its own. Of this fact, the most striking example is provided by Strauss's dogmatics. Although this dogmatics, in a sense wholly other than with ordinary textbooks, rests on the implementation of the view that the history of dogma is also its criticism, the work also makes clear that history always comes off badly when it is considered only from the dogmatic standpoint. Not history as such, but rather criticism, is the major concern. . . . Rationalism can be related only negatively to the history of dogma." Strauss reacted bitterly to this criticism, especially to the association with rationalist historiography and dogmatics, and the publication of this volume precipitated an open break between Strauss and Baur that was never really healed thereafter. Cf. *The Formation of Historical Theology*, 81–84.

30. Since 1797 it has appeared in four volumes, of which the first two were published in a second revised and partially modified edition in 1802–1804, and the third and fourth in 1802 and 1809.

[ED]. Wilhelm Münscher (1766–1814) was professor of theology at the University of Marburg from 1792 until his death. His theological position was that of a moderate rationalism. His *Handbuch der christlichen Dogmengeschichte* and *Lehr-*

cent Protestant literature to undertake a clearly conceived treatment of the history of dogma in its entire extent. Its four volumes, which to be sure cover only the first six centuries, were equal to their difficult task to a praiseworthy degree in more than one respect. The work's outstanding features are its apt and methodical organization of the whole (in particular, the correct division of the periods and the apt relating of the universal and the particular), the clear, simple, and pleasing presentation, and the effort to treat the object in as comprehensive a fashion as possible. Nevertheless, the work must by and large be viewed as outdated for our time, particularly because of its standpoint. The shallowness of the rationalistic mode of comprehension and presentation is here exhibited fully: the subject matter, instead of being allowed to develop out of its own nature, is merely circumvented in a superficial, rationalizing discussion. The objection often made to such discussions, which as a whole reflect the same standpoint—namely, that they do not hold sufficiently in view the totality of the subject matter (e.g., chronological periods as well as the teachings of individual men), and thus can offer only one-sided judgments—is precisely to the lack of an objective presentation.[31]

Prior to Münscher's *Lehrbuch* (1811) appeared the *Lehrbuch der christlichen Dogmengeschichte* (Leipzig, 1805) of J. C. W. Augusti,[32] which continued through four editions up to 1835. It had the merit of helping to arouse an interest in the history of dogma at a time when there was not much activity in the discipline. However, even in the most recent edition it suffers so many handicaps as to be scarcely usable. The whole

---

buch der christlichen *Dogmengeschichte* (Marburg, 1811) were popular textbooks for many years. He also wrote a *Lehrbuch der christlichen Kirchengeschichte* (Marburg, 1804).

31. A good though far too brief survey of the whole history of dogma is presented in the *Lehrbuch der christlichen Dogmengeschichte*, which Münscher first published in 1811 (2nd ed., by Wachler, in 1815). The *Lehrbuch* was considerably enriched in the third edition (Cassel, 1832–34), which was furnished by D. G. K. Cölln with documents from primary sources, additional literature, historical notes, and a sequel. In this form it serves as a good introduction to source study. The first part and the first half of the second part were prepared by Cölln, the second half of the second part by J. C. G. Neudecker. The latter has the special title, *Lehrbuch der christlichen Dogmengeschichte von der Reformationszeit bis auf unsere Tage* (Cassel, 1838). It is, however, a very superficial and spiritless work.

32. [ED.] Johann Christian Wilhelm Augusti (1772–1841), theologian and archeologist, was professor of philosophy and oriental languages at Jena, and of theology at Breslau and Bonn. In addition to the work mentioned above, he wrote an *Einleitung in das Alte Testament* (Leipzig, 1806), and a widely used *Handbuch der christlichen Archäologie* (3 vols.; Leipzig, 1836–47).

treatment and conception are shallow, vague, one-sided, and lacking in principle; nowhere is there any depth of penetration; nowhere are the general point of view and the constitutive elements advanced from which alone the development of dogma in its inner continuity can be traced.

10. *The Most Recent Literature in the History of Dogma: Baumgarten-Crusius, Engelhardt, Meier, Hagenbach, Neander*

We have now advanced to the most recent period. If we survey the most recent literature in the history of dogma, the following works can be dispensed with quickly because of their insignificance: L. Bertholdt,[33] *Handbuch der Dogmengeschichte* (2 vols.; Erlangen, 1822); F. A. Ruperti, *Die Geschichte der Dogmen* (Berlin, 1831);[34] and C. G. H. Lenz, *Geschichte der christlichen Dogmen in pragmatischer Entwicklung* (2 vols.; Helmstädt, 1834). Bertholdt's *Handbuch* was published by Engelhardt from the lectures of the former on Augusti's *Lehrbuch;* it would be just as well, however, for the publication to go out of print. The *Handbuch* has all the faults of poor organization and superficial treatment. Ruperti's work is a highly superficial survey, and that of Lenz is without any independent study of sources. It is another example of the pragmatism we have already discussed, and its insignificance is proof of how antiquated it is for our time.

This leaves the following works to be considered:

1. The two works in the history of dogma by Ludwig Baumgarten-Crusius.[35] The *Lehrbuch der christlichen Dogmengeschichte* (2 vols.; Jena, 1832) was the first larger work covering the history of dogma as a whole in which the discipline made scientific progress. Undoubtedly, a great treasure of scholarship is contained in it. Almost everywhere

33. [ED.] Leonhard Bertholdt (1774–1822), professor of philosophy and theology at Erlangen from 1805 until 1822.

34. [ED.] F. A. Ruperti, *Die Geschichte der Dogmen, oder Darstellung der Glaubenslehren des Christenthums von seiner Stiftung bis auf die neuern Zeiten* (Berlin, 1831).

35. [ED.] Ludwig Friedrich Otto Baumgarten-Crusius (1788–1843) was professor of theology at Leipzig from 1812 to 1843. He lectured in New Testament exegesis, biblical theology, dogmatics, ethics, and the history of dogma. His theological orientation was that of rational supernaturalism. In addition to the two works mentioned by Baur, he published *Einleitung in das Studium der Dogmatik* (Leipzig, 1820), and *Theologische Auslegung der johanneischen Schriften* (2 vols.; Jena, 1843–45).

throughout are items that testify to unusually extensive reading, as well as penetrating remarks that offer new points of view and illumination on many subjects. It certainly is not to be denied that such a treatment of the entire history of dogma is of great value and profit. The work, however, is greatly harmed by the lack of method and suitable organization and division, which has already been criticized above,[36] as well as by being drawn up in paragraphs and discussions according to the procedure of Schleiermacher's *Glaubenslehre*, which obliged Baumgarten-Crusius to compress and combine abstractly in single paragraphs a great deal of material that is in part quite heterogeneous in character. The whole often gives the impression of vacant and arbitrary abstractions, lacking in the fresh, concrete life and the natural continuity of history. The *Compendium der christlichen Dogmengeschichte* (Leipzig, 1840) is a new, somewhat more lucid treatment, making use of exactly the same method.[37]

2. J. G. V. Engelhardt's *Dogmengeschichte* (2 vols.; Neustadt-an-der-Aisch, 1839) [38] gives itself the task simply of reporting the sources, as far as possible in the original wording. It largely provides excerpts in which the materials of the history of dogma are faithfully and exactly given. This constitutes its major advantage; even in this connection, however, one feels the lack of data concerning the sources. Otherwise, the work has several great weaknesses. It presents an extremely dry, lifeless, monotonous, and wholly superficial narrative; there is no development proceeding from a definite conception. The work lacks, above all, a proper conception of the history of dogma. Engelhardt does indeed define the history of dogma as a series of efforts to apply thought to an understanding of individual dogmas. But not even the remotest effort is made to understand the history of dogma as a process of thinking; and it is impossible to understand what could be the purpose and result of such a process of thinking if religious truth is already so completely contained in the literal content of Holy Scripture as Engelhardt supposes. How lifeless and hollow a conception forms the basis of this work is to be seen from its

36. [ED.] See above, 311–12.

37. Vol. II, ed. by Hase, 1846. The position of both these works on dogma has been discussed above, 258–88.

38. [ED.] Johann Georg Veit Engelhardt (1791–1855) was professor of theology at Erlangen from 1821 until 1855. He did considerable study in patristics and the history of mystical theology, including monographs on Dionysius the Areopagite, Richard of St. Victor, Johann Ruysbroek, and German mysticism. In addition to the work mentioned above, he published a *Handbuch der Kirchengeschichte* (4 vols.; Erlangen, 1833–34).

having concluded the history of dogma with the year 1580, as though with the Formula of Concord the goal of its development had been reached; whereas in this period the scientific movement of dogma had a real beginning for the first time. Engelhardt is no more willing to go beyond this period than Petavius is to go beyond Trent.

3. The *Lehrbuch der Dogmengeschichte für akademische Vorlesungen* (Giessen, 1840) by F. K. Meier [39] is commendable for a not unhappy division and organization of material. It consists of three periods only —ancient, medieval, and modern—and within each period the historical material is distributed into rather large blocks meant to correspond to historically demonstrable levels of development. But a great deal of all this is arbitrary, and to arrange the dogmas only according to their chronological-historical sequence, not according to systematic connections, is an error. In regard to its concept, it is acknowledged, to be sure, that to be scientific the history of dogma must consist in the movement proper to its content; but nothing in the actual treatment achieves such a presentation.

4. K. R. Hagenbach's *Lehrbuch der Dogmengeschichte* (2 vols.; Leipzig, 1840–41),[40] like Meier's, is to be praised for having dispensed with the entirely erroneous distinction between a general and a special history of dogma, and for relating the general treatment to the history of dogma proper by means of an Introduction. The organization of Hagenbach's *Lehrbuch* is distinguished from Meier's in that Hagenbach does not, like Meier, follow the major movement of dogma in each instance, but rather has as his basis a systematic organization, so that dogmas are brought under consideration not merely when they are the object of special deliberations and controversies but in the treatment of every period, and indeed in their systematically connected order.

The general tendency of the three works just mentioned seems to be an attempt to avoid the subjectivity of previous treatments of the history of dogma, since they maintain a purely reportorial relation to their object. The report can take the form of either a simple account of the sources, without the intervention of personal judgment, as with Engelhardt, or a survey of previous investigations in this field (a selection of the most outstanding of these, in the view of the author), as with the other two

---

39. [ED.] Friedrich Karl Meier (1808–41) was professor of evangelical theology at Jena and Giessen, where he lectured in biblical theology, history of dogma, and New Testament exegesis.

40. [ED.] See above, 313–15.

theologians—especially Hagenbach, in whose *Lehrbuch*, besides the
source documents, a large number of quotations are extracted from recent works on the history of dogma. For this reason his work appears in
part to be a mere collection of materials, drawing all the more attention
to the lack of a deeper study of sources and of an independent, productive spirit. Such a merely reportorial presentation cannot satisfy the scientific conception of the history of dogma.

5. August Neander's *Allgemeine Geschichte der christlichen Religion
und Kirche* [41] should also be mentioned here because of its importance
for the history of dogma. In no other church-historical work is this
subject given so independent a position alongside church history. That
part of the work concerned with the history of the conception and
development of Christianity as doctrine constitutes an autonomous whole,
in which dogma is presented not merely as it has become the object of
ecclesiastical controversies and deliberations but in its entire scope.
Neander's presentation is superior to works such as those just mentioned
chiefly by virtue of its comprehensive source-study and special development, but it shares with them the lack of a speculative understanding,
which becomes all the more striking the further the work progresses. [42]

11. *The Catholic Treatment of the History of Dogma: Klee*

The works in the history of dogma just enumerated consist entirely of
recent Protestant literature, not because we have limited ourselves to
them intentionally, but because the Catholic literature has almost nothing
to offer in the field of the history of dogma. In the recent period, only
one work has appeared under that title that deserves to be mentioned, the
Lehrbuch der Dogmengeschichte (2 vols.; Mainz, 1837–38) by Heinrich
Klee. [43] From the explanations Klee gives of the conception of history of

41. [ED.] See above, 207–208.

42. See above, 289–91, and *Die Epochen der kirchlichen Geschichtschreibung*,
202–32 [above, 206–28]. On Neander's *Dogmengeschichte*, ed. J. L. Jacobi (2 vols.;
Berlin, 1857), J. K. L. Gieseler's *Dogmengeschichte*, ed. E. R. Redepenning (Bonn,
1855), and T. F. D. Kliefoth's *Einleitung in die Dogmengeschichte* (Parchim, 1839),
see above, 293–97, and the author's *Lehrbuch der christlichen Dogmengeschichte*
(2nd ed., Tübingen, 1858), 51–55.

43. [ED.] Heinrich Klee (1800–1840) was professor of exegesis, church history, and
philosophy at Mainz from 1824 to 1829, and of dogmatics and exegesis at Bonn from
1829 to 1839. In 1839 he became the successor to J. A. Möhler at Munich. He came at
the beginning of the Catholic theological restoration in Germany, in loose associa-

dogma, it is hard to believe that there is so great a difference between Catholic and Protestant vantage points in the understanding of the history of dogma. For many, says Klee, "history of dogma" has a bad sound, as though the originality and stability of Christian doctrine were being denied. But even church history bears witness that dogmas have actually accomplished their development in time. The substance of dogmas remains always the same; but its dogmatic formation advances through time in accord with the judgment that considers it true and correct, and against the false, subjective aspirations that are opposed to it. That the history of dogma is necessary is as clear as that it is possible. Scholarship should not excuse itself from tracing the development of dogmas and from understanding dogmas in terms of their history. Only thus can there be a veritable scientific awareness of dogmas, one in accord with its object.

All of this—and much more—sounds completely scientific, until one sees how the idea propounded in this work is in fact implemented. One sees the extent to which the history of dogma has become an aggregate of empty propositions assembled without unity or continuity, and the extent to which a spiritless monotony dominates a work rigorously sustaining the principle that dogma always remains the same and that all orthodox teachers of the church have had the same view of doctrine, whereas the heretics are considered only as innovators and falsifiers of dogma. This is by no means true of recent scholarship and its relation to dogma. In modern times, Catholic theologians have protested at every opportunity against the supposition that the history of dogma is chiefly a Protestant science. Up to now, however, the facts are against them, and it cannot be otherwise so long as the old principle of the stability and absolute identity of dogma is maintained. It sounds well to say that one has no scientific consciousness of dogma if one does not trace the development of dogma; but *can* the Catholic, if he wishes to remain consistent, trace the develop-

---

tion with Möhler, who at one time was a colleague of Baur on the Catholic theological faculty in Tübingen. Klee's other important writings include *System der katholischen Dogmatik* (Bonn, 1831), *Enzyklopädie der katholischen Theologie* (Mainz, 1832), and *Katholische Dogmatik* (3 vols.; Mainz, 1834–35). There are some remarkable similarities between Klee's theory of dogmatic development and that of John Henry Cardinal Newman in the *Essay on the Development of Christian Doctrine* (1845), although it is uncertain whether Newman was directly influenced by Klee and other liberal German Catholic theologians of his time. At any rate, Baur's criticism of Klee could in many respects equally well apply to Newman. Cf. *The Formation of Historical Theology*, 22–23, 156–57.

ment of dogma? What does it mean to trace the development of dogma? Apparently nothing other than to understand all the phenomena connected with dogma in their relation to one another in such fashion that we are able to distinguish what is only contingent, mortal, and finite in dogma from its true and substantial nature, and thereby to grasp dogma itself in its essence. In this fashion we can trace the development of dogma in the entire period up to the Reformation: nothing can arise against dogma, regarded as ecclesiastical doctrine; everything that deviates from it and legitimates itself in opposition to it, attempting to maintain an autonomous existence, cannot sustain itself but is suppressed and absorbed by the overwhelming, dominating unity of ecclesiastical dogma, so that everything of this nature collapses as soon as it emerges, never being able to obtain a true and independent existence, and merely representing an antiquated, powerless, and thus untrue and empty phenomenon.

As long as the development of dogma is traced in this fashion, it is thus perceived in its absolute truth, scientifically, and the Protestant can trace the development of dogma thus far completely in accord with the Catholic. But then comes the stumbling block on which this way of understanding dogma must necessarily founder if it remains purely Catholic. The Reformation and Protestantism become the means by which to discover whether this view of the development of dogma can be sustained, whether as a consequence the development of dogma ought merely to consist in the certainty that dogma in its absolute truth remains absolutely self-identical, and that therefore nothing differing from it can arise alongside it and in opposition to it. But this is precisely what is not the case. Protestantism is essentially to be distinguished from all earlier phenomena that came into conflict with ecclesiastical dogma—heresies so called—because, unlike them, it could not be suppressed and absorbed by the absolute unity of dogma but rather overcame it and attained for itself an independent and autonomous existence parallel to it. Thus it is the *de facto* contradiction of the Catholic presupposition that ecclesiastical dogma remains always the same in its development, absolutely identical with itself. The Catholic view of history is here brought to an end with a single stroke and is shown to be limited, finite, and untrue. It ruptures all its categories in the effort to conceive a phenomenon such as Protestantism historically, as a development of dogma; and on this account Catholic historians of dogma such as Klee and Pétau have no choice other than fundamentally to ignore the development of dogma in Protestantism.

How can one trace dogma in the course of its development if one cannot follow it the whole way but must come to a halt midway, as though exhausted? And if a scientific consciousness of dogma is possible only in the course of such a pursuit, then it is quite clear that such a consciousness is not at all possible for the Catholic.

12. *The Speculative View of History*

The necessary conclusion from all this is that dogma in general cannot be expected to remain always the same throughout its development. Its sphere of development may not be limited merely to ecclesiastical dogma. No specific limits may be set for it; the content of its development is not to be prescribed in advance; it must be permitted a free, self-generating movement. However, this freedom of movement can be permitted to dogma only from a standpoint that is itself free, bound to no specific presuppositions. It can be permitted only from the standpoint of free thinking, which is the principle of Protestantism; hence all the evidence indicates that, despite what the Catholics might say, the conception of the history of dogma is possible only from the standpoint of Protestantism, and the history of dogma itself is an authentically Protestant science. Only the Protestant can perceive the free movement of dogma in history. But on the other hand the freedom to which dogma is released by Protestantism from its imprisonment in Catholicism ought not to be the freedom of subjective arbitrariness, but rather a freedom that possesses its own immanent laws—hence, therefore, a freedom that at the same time is necessity, yet is determined not by an external but only by an internal necessity, by the objective concept of the subject matter itself. The truth in the Catholic conception of dogma is that there exists an objective unity to which all subjective arbitrariness must be subordinated; the untruth is that Catholicism regards this objective unity as something merely external, as the unity of ecclesiastical dogma. Catholicism regards this external manifestation of dogma as the essence of the subject matter itself, whereas dogma can have its true, vital unity only in Spirit, which is objectified in dogma.[44]

44. [ED.] The following paragraph, from the author's *Lehrbuch der christlichen Dogmengeschichte* (3rd ed., Leipzig, 1867), 55–58, concludes the section that surveys the history of the history of dogma in that volume. It serves as a somewhat fuller statement of the argument advanced in the preceding paragraph. "That a still incompletely accomplished task lies before the history of dogma can be seen from

One can become aware of this unity based on a spiritual principle only from the standpoint of speculative thinking, for which alone an Absolute Truth exists. If one perceives in history only contingent, subjective beliefs and views, only an endless multiplicity and change, which is the direct opposite of the unchanging unity of the Catholic conception, then no Absolute Truth exists. Everything crumbles into an indeterminable multiplicity; there is no unity, no unity of movement, of moving princi-

---

the survey of its formative history provided above. If the method of its treatment is to be purely scientific, it can be brought closer to its final solution only if it endeavors to move away from the externality and contingency of phenomena to the concept of the subject matter itself; or from the empirical mode of reflection to the speculative—which means holding in view the subject matter as it is in itself; or from particular spiritual tendencies, as the object merely of psychological reflection, to the essence of Spirit itself. If we look back on the course taken by the history of dogma since the Reformation, we can rightly say that the two directions into which it has been divided—Catholicism and Protestantism—have not yet completely attained to and been united in an organic unity. The Catholic view of the history of dogma contains part of the truth, based on the nature of the subject matter itself. A Universal must exist whose unity, identical with itself, is the substantial principle of all forms of dogma. Therefore everything that has developed from dogma must be conceivable as a movement immanent to the unity of dogma. But there exists on the other side another requirement, no less basic to the nature of the subject matter, that a differentiation must also appear in the unity of dogma sufficiently broad not only not to endanger freedom of space for the individuality of the subject but also to permit each moment of the self-moving concept to come into its own and to achieve the reality of its existence. This is the basis of the one-sidedness and limitation that the Catholic view of history, in contrast to the Protestant, implicitly contains. It does not permit freedom of movement to a great deal of material that has emerged from the substantial foundation of dogma; it denies the justification for its existence or declares it heretical. The limits of its historical conception appear where it no longer sees the possibility of resuppressing that which has separated itself, in whatever fashion, from the unity of the Catholic Church. Hence if there are phenomena that maintain the reality of their existence despite the opposition of the Catholic Church, the Catholic historian can at best only remain silent and ignorant. With the epoch of the Reformation, he has reached a point where, owing to the opposition of Protestantism, a limit is established that prevents any further historical understanding and makes it impossible for him to pursue the course of history any further. Just as the Catholic view of history, in conformity with its principle, cannot move beyond the substantial unity of dogma, so on the opposite side the Protestant view could only lose the substantial unity of dogma by dissolving it into the endless multiplicity of individual representations and beliefs; the whole of the history of dogma appears to fall into subjectivity. An objective view of history can therefore only be one that remains equally far from the bias of both extremes and is able to conceive the two divergent tendencies in their inner freedom as two correlative sides of the same spiritual process. The more that further treatments of the history of dogma succeed in detecting this process, based on the nature of Spirit, in the historical course of dogma, and in bringing it to clear perception, the more they will thereby fulfill their scientific conception."

ple. That an Absolute Truth exists, however, and therefore also a consciousness of the Absolute, is the fundamental presupposition of speculative thinking. The Absolute itself must also be the knowledge of the Absolute, for it would not be the Absolute were it not the Absolute for subjective consciousness as well. Hence, from the speculative standpoint, the history of dogma can be considered only as the movement of Absolute Truth, which in that history discloses itself to subjective consciousness. Or the moving principle is thinking Spirit, which strives for consciousness of itself, which wants to become one with itself in the consciousness of itself and of its true nature, and in this process objectifies itself in dogma, becomes external to itself, but also returns to itself from this objectivity in which it divests itself and attains to the freedom of its self-consciousness. The speculative standpoint is concerned with the consciousness of the Absolute; but the subject can be conscious of the Absolute only because it is essential to the Absolute itself to give this consciousness. Hence only from the speculative standpoint can we perceive in the history of dogma and in the multiplicity of its contents a unity, the unity of a moving principle. For this reason, this speculative mode of reflection belongs essentially to the Protestant conception of the history of dogma—but not the Protestant conception as long as it sees in the history of dogma only that which is singular, contingent, arbitrary, subjective, constantly changing and moving in colorful disarray. This is merely the rationalistic view and is no less one-sided—only in an opposite direction—than the Catholic. The one-sided, restricted, and limited character of these two opposing and mutually self-negating vantage points can be transcended only in the Absolute of the speculative conception. This alone can be the goal of the further development of our science. The task of my previous efforts in the field of the history of dogma was to guide our discipline increasingly toward this goal. In these lectures I would also hope to keep the same task constantly in view.[45]

45. [ED.] Two further passages from the *Lehrbuch der christlichen Dogmengeschichte* bear on this discussion of speculative method and the nature of the history of dogma. The first is from the Preface to the first edition (Stuttgart, 1847), ix–x: "Only the coarsest empiricism can think that one should simply surrender oneself to the materials, that the objects of historical reflection could be taken just as they lie before us. Ever since there has been a critique of knowledge, a critical theory of knowledge (one could say without fear of contradiction, at least since Kant), whoever comes to history not entirely naïve philosophically must know that it is necessary to distinguish between things as they are in themselves and as they appear to us, and that they become phenomena for us just because we can reach them only through the medium of our consciousness. Herein lies the great distinction between

the purely empirical and the critical modes of reflection; and the latter—which is called the critical because its task is rigorously to distinguish and to keep separate what in the objects of historical knowledge are either objective or subjective—wants so little to set in the place of the objective something merely subjective that for it everything depends on regarding nothing that is by nature only subjective as the pure objectivity of the subject matter itself. It intends to see the subject matter on the basis of its own nature only with the sharpest eye. On such simple principles (when one knows how to apply them to the historical material, which is of utmost importance), rests the critical—or if one will, the speculative—method."

The second passage is from a concluding section of the Introduction to the *Lehrbuch*, called "The Interest in the History of Dogma." It stands in place of the concluding section of the *Lectures*, "The Speculative View of History," and contains material bearing on the same question. The passage reads in part as follows (3rd ed., 58–59): "After everything that has been said above about the conception and nature of the history of dogma, it would be superfluous to make the question of its value and significance the object of a special discussion. Undoubtedly a great deal that is true and excellent has been said on different sides and from various points of view about the values and uses of studies in the history of dogma, in part for the general purpose of education, and in part for the special call of the theologian, especially in practical matters. But the highest and most direct interest can always only emerge from its conception as a whole. If it is the nature of Spirit itself that is disclosed and laid open in the history of dogma, then the interest in the latter can only be that in it one can trace the paths that Spirit itself, in its development as a whole, has taken in the various directions of its steadily progressive movement, in order to come to consciousness of itself and of the highest interests that condition the spiritual life. What history is in general—as the eternally clear mirror in which Spirit perceives itself, views its own image, in order to be what it is in itself for itself as well, for its own consciousness, and to know itself as the moving power of historical becoming—is concentrated with all the more intensive significance in the more restricted area of the history of dogma. As in history as a whole, so especially in the history of dogma, this general spiritual interest can be modified in two ways—according to whether it is directed chiefly toward the universal, substantial content of historical movement, which remains always the same, or toward the never-resting succession of historical forms, in which everything universal seems to be completely submerged. It is the task of historical reflection always to place the one interest in a relation to the other that corresponds to the nature of the case. . . ."

This is one of the best-known passages from Baur's corpus, but its precise meaning is obscure. In *The Formation of Historical Theology*, 182–84, I suggested that, in speaking of "history" as "the eternally clear mirror in which Spirit perceives itself . . . ," Baur here has in mind the study of history rather than history as a process, and that in this context "Spirit" refers to finite human Spirit, the self-consciousness of the subject, as man comes to greater self-understanding through study of the historical past. This interpretation was based in part on a parallel in language between the *Lehrbuch* and a passage from the Introduction to a lecture manuscript on ancient history dating from the 1820's, "Geschichte des Alterthums" (University of Tübingen Library, Mh II, 166, q, 18): "For this purpose [the practical determination of man, his moral life in community] a thorough study of history is indispensable. This is the inexhaustible source out of which the foundations . . . of moral action can be created; *it is the eternally clear mirror in which human life* in its manifold forms, the moral acts of men in all their connections, *can be glimpsed*" (italics mine). I am now inclined to regard this as a strained interpretation. The formal parallel in language with the ancient history manuscript is probably misleading. We can see here, in fact, Baur's progression from a Schleiermacherian to a Hegelian perspective. A new meaning is expressed in a strikingly similar use of the old formula. It seems more plausible from the context, and especially from the content of the concluding section of the *Lectures,* with which this passage from the *Lehrbuch* has greater *material* correspondence, that Baur is now referring to history as an objective process, and to Spirit as the trans-subjective, infinite foundation of that process. The reason that one *studies* history is that "*in it* [i.e., in history as a process] one can trace the paths that Spirit itself . . . has taken in the various directions of its steadily progressive movement." In the *Lectures,* Baur makes it clear that the moving principle of history is thinking Spirit, or the Absolute, which comes to consciousness of itself, and discloses itself to subjective human consciousness, in the process of history, especially in the history of Christian dogma. Hence the passage from the *Lehrbuch* should be read as parallel in meaning to the following from the Preface to *Die christliche Lehre von der Dreieinigkeit und Menschwerdung Gottes in ihrer geschichtlichen Entwicklung,* I (Tübingen, 1841), xix: "The more important and comprehensive the object with which historical investigation is concerned, and the more directly it belongs to the element of thinking, the more such investigation approaches not merely a reproducing in itself of what the individual thought and did but a rethinking in itself of the eternal thoughts of Eternal Spirit, whose work history is." For further discussion of this aspect of Baur's understanding of the historical process, see *The Formation of Historical Theology,* 145–47.

Selected Bibliography

Inclusive bibliographies, containing books, journal articles, unpublished manuscripts, writings by Baur's contemporaries, and general materials on nineteenth-century theology, are available in Geiger, *Spekulation und Kritik*, 248–55, and Hodgson, *The Formation of Historical Theology*, 285–94. Hence both of the following lists have been restricted in scope. The first includes Baur's major books and only a few of his articles. The second consists of a selection of critical materials bearing directly upon him.

I. WRITINGS BY FERDINAND CHRISTIAN BAUR

(Listed chronologically according to date of original publication)

Symbolik und Mythologie, oder die Naturreligion des Alterthums. 2 vols. in 3 parts. Stuttgart, 1824–25.

"Die Christuspartei in der korinthischen Gemeinde, der Gegensatz des petrinischen und paulinischen Christenthums in der ältesten Kirche, der Apostel Petrus in Rom." *TZTh*, V:4 (1831), 61–206.

Der Gegensatz des Katholicismus und Protestantismus nach den Principien und Hauptdogmen der beiden Lehrbegriffe. Mit besonderer Rücksicht auf Herrn Dr. Möhler's Symbolik. *TZTh*, VII:3, 4 (1833), 1–438. Published subsequently as a book: Tübingen, 1834 (1st ed.), 1836 (2nd ed.). (1st ed. cited in Introduction.)

Die christliche Gnosis, oder die christliche Religions-Philosophie in ihrer geschichtlichen Entwiklung. Tübingen, 1835.

Die sogenannten Pastoralbriefe des Apostels Paulus aufs neue kritisch untersucht. Stuttgart and Tübingen, 1835.

"Über Zweck und Veranlassung des Römerbriefs und die damit zusammenhängenden Verhältnisse der römischen Gemeinde. Eine historisch-kritische Untersuchung." *TZTh*, IX:3 (1836), 59–178.

"Abgenöthigte Erklärung gegen einen Artikel der *Evangelischen Kirchenzeitung*, herausgegeben von D. E. W. Hengstenberg, Prof. der Theol. an der Universität zu Berlin. Mai 1836." *TZTh*, IX:3 (1836), 179–232.

"Das christliche des Platonismus oder Sokrates und Christus." *TZTh*, X:3 (1837), 1–154.

"Über der Ursprung des Episcopats in der christlichen Kirche. Prüfung der neuesten von Hrn. Dr. Rothe hierüber aufgestellten Ansicht." *TZTh*, XI:3 (1838), 1–185.

Die christliche Lehre von der Versöhnung in ihrer geschichtlichen Entwicklung von der ältesten Zeit bis auf die neueste. Tübingen, 1838.

Die christliche Lehre von der Dreieinigkeit und Menschwerdung Gottes in ihrer geschichtlichen Entwicklung. 3 vols. Tübingen, 1841–43.

Paulus, der Apostel Jesu Christi. Sein Leben und Wirken, seine Briefe und seine Lehre. Ein Beitrag zu einer kritischen Geschichte des Urchristenthums. 1st ed. Stuttgart, 1845. 2nd ed., ed. Eduard Zeller. 2 vols. Leipzig, 1866–67. (2nd ed. cited in Introduction.)
> *Paul the Apostle of Jesus Christ, His Life and Work, His Epistles and His Doctrine. A Contribution to a Critical History of Primitive Christianity.* Translated from 2nd German ed. 2 vols. Vol. I, London and Edinburgh, 1873 (1st ed.), 1876 (2nd ed., revised by the Rev. Allan Menzies). Vol. II, translated by the Rev. Allan Menzies, London and Edinburgh, 1875.

"Über Princip und Charakter des Lehrbegriffe der reformirten Kirche in seinem Unterschied von dem der lutherischen, mit Rücksicht auf A. Schweizer's Darstellung der reformirten Glaubenslehre." *ThJ*, VI:3 (1847), 309–89.

Kritische Untersuchungen über die kanonischen Evangelien, ihr Verhältniss zu einander, ihren Charakter und Ursprung. Tübingen, 1847.

Lehrbuch der christlichen Dogmengeschichte. 1st ed. Stuttgart, 1847. 2nd ed. Tübingen, 1858. 3rd ed., identical with 2nd. Leipzig, 1867. (1st and 3rd eds. cited in Introduction and footnotes.)

"Die Einleitung in das Neue Testament als theologische Wissenschaft. Ihr Begriff und ihre Aufgabe, ihr Entwicklungsgang und ihr innerer Organismus," *ThJ*, IX:4 (1850), 463–566; X:1, 2, 3 (1851), 70–94, 222–52, 291–328.

Das Markusevangelium nach seinem Ursprung und Charakter. Nebst einem Anhang über das Evangelium Marcions. Tübingen, 1851.

Die Epochen der kirchlichen Geschichtschreibung. Tübingen, 1852.

Geschichte der christlichen Kirche.
> Vol. I: *Das Christenthum und die christliche Kirche der drei ersten Jahrhunderte.* Tübingen, 1853 (1st ed.), 1860 (2nd ed.), 1863 (3rd ed., identical with 2nd, published under title *Kirchengeschichte der drei ersten Jahrhunderte*). (2nd ed. cited in Introduction.)
>> *The Church History of the First Three Centuries.* Translation from 3rd German edition, edited by the Rev. Allan Menzies. 2 vols. London and Edinburgh, 1878–79.
> Vol. II: *Die christliche Kirche vom Anfang des vierten bis zum Ende des sechsten Jahrhunderts in den Hauptmomenten ihrer Entwicklung.* Tübingen, 1859 (1st ed.), 1863 (2nd ed., identical with 1st).
> Vol. III: *Die christliche Kirche des Mittelalters in den Hauptmomenten ihrer Entwicklung,* ed. Ferdinand Friedrich Baur. 1st ed. Tübingen, 1861. 2nd ed. Leipzig, 1869.
> Vol. IV: *Kirchengeschichte der neueren Zeit, von der Reformation bis zum Ende des achtzehnten Jahrhunderts,* ed. Ferdinand Friedrich Baur. Tübingen, 1863.
> Vol. V: *Kirchengeschichte des neunzehnten Jahrhunderts,* ed. Eduard Zeller. 1st ed. Tübingen, 1862. 2nd ed. Leipzig, 1877.
An Herrn Dr. Karl Hase. Beantwortung des Sendschreibens "Die Tübinger Schule." Tübingen, 1855.

Die Tübinger Schule und ihre Stellung zur Gegenwart. Tübingen, 1859 (1st ed.), 1860 (2nd ed.). (2nd ed. cited in Introduction.)

"Die Bedeutung des Ausdrucks: ὁ υἱὸς τοῦ ἀνθρώπου," *Zeitschrift für wissenschaftliche Theologie,* III:3 (1860), 274–92.

Vorlesungen über neutestamentliche Theologie, ed. Ferdinand Friedrich Baur. Leipzig, 1864.

Vorlesungen über die christliche Dogmengeschichte, ed. Ferdinand Friedrich Baur.
    Vol. I/1: *Das Dogma der alten Kirche von der apostolischen Zeit bis zur Synode in Nicäa.* Leipzig, 1865.
    Vol. I/2: *Das Dogma der alten Kirche von der Synode in Nicäa bis zum Ende des sechsten Jahrhunderts.* Leipzig, 1866.
    Vol. II: *Das Dogma des Mittelalters.* Leipzig, 1866.
    Vol. III: *Das Dogma der neueren Zeit.* Leipzig, 1867.

Ausgewählte Werke in Einzelausgaben, ed. Klaus Scholder. 5 vols. Stuttgart–Bad Cannstatt, 1963—.

II. SECONDARY MATERIALS

(Listed alphabetically)

BARNIKOL, ERNST. "Der Briefwechsel zwischen Strauss und Baur," *Zeitschrift für Kirchengeschichte,* 4. Folge X, LXXIII (1962), 74–125.

———. "Das ideengeschichtliche Erbe Hegels bei und seit Strauss und Baur im 19. Jahrhundert," *Wissenschaftliche Zeitschrift der Martin-Luther-Universität Halle-Wittenberg,* Gesellschafts- und sprachwissenschaftliche Reihe, X (February 1961), 281–328.

BARTH, KARL. *Die protestantische Theologie im 19. Jahrhundert.* 3rd ed. Zürich, 1960. Pp. 450–58.

BAUER, KARL. "Ferdinand Christian Baur als Kirchenhistoriker," *Blätter für Württembergische Kirchengeschichte,* Neue Folge, XXV (1921), 1–38; XXVI (1922), 1–60.

———. "Zur Jugendgeschichte von Ferdinand Christian Baur (1805–1807)," *Theologische Studien und Kritiken,* XCV (1923/1924), 303–13.

BAUR, AUGUST. "Ferdinand Christian Baur," *Protestantische Kirchenzeitung für das evangelische Deutschland,* XXXIX (July 1892), 661–67, 691–99.

BAXMANN, RUDOLF. "Baurs spekulative Geschichtskonstruktion und der Wunderanfang des Christenthums," *Jahrbucher für deutsche Theologie* (1863), 733–58.

BECKH, HEINRICH. "Die Tübinger historische Schule, kritisch beleuchtet," *Zeitschrift für Protestantismus und Kirche,* Neue Folge, LXXIV (1864), 1–57, 69–95, 133–78, 203–44.

BERGER, SAMUEL. *F. C. Baur: les origines de l'école de Tubingue et ses principes, 1826–1844.* Strasbourg, 1867.

BRUCE, A. B. "Ferdinand Christian Baur and His Theory of the Origin of Christianity and of the New Testament Writings," in *Living Papers Concerning*

Christian Evidences, Doctrine, and Morals, Vol. VII. Cincinnati, Chicago, and St. Louis, 1886.

DILTHEY, WILHELM. "Ferdinand Christian Baur," in *Gesammelte Schriften*, Vol. IV, *Die Jugendgeschichte Hegels und andere Abhandlungen zur Geschichte des deutschen Idealismus.* 2nd ed. Leipzig and Berlin, 1925. Pp. 403–32.

FRAEDRICH, GUSTAV. *Ferdinand Christian Baur: der Begründer der Tübinger Schule als Theologe, Schriftsteller, und Charakter.* Gotha, 1909. (Contains a nearly complete bibliography of Baur's writings.)

GEIGER, WOLFGANG. *Spekulation und Kritik: Die Geschichtstheologie Ferdinand Christian Baurs.* Munich, 1964.

HASE, KARL. *Die Tübinger Schule. Ein Sendschreiben an Herrn Dr. Ferdinand Christian von Baur.* Leipzig, 1855.

HEFNER, PHILIP. "Baur versus Ritschl on Early Christianity," *Church History,* XXXI (September 1962), 259–78.

HILGENFELD, ADOLF. "Ferdinand Christian Baur nach seiner wissenschaftlichen Entwickelung und Bedeutung," *Zeitschrift für wissenschaftliche Theologie,* XXXVI:I (1893), 222–44.

HIRSCH, EMANUEL. *Geschichte der neuern evangelischen Theologie im Zusammenhang mit den allgemeinen Bewegungen des europäischen Denkens.* Vol. V. Gütersloh, 1954. Pp. 518–52.

HODGSON, PETER C. *The Formation of Historical Theology: A Study of Ferdinand Christian Baur.* New York, 1966.

―――. "The Rediscovery of Ferdinand Christian Baur: A Review of the First Two Volumes of His *Ausgewählte Werke,*" *Church History,* XXXIII (June 1964), 206–14.

LANG, WILHELM. "Baur und Strauss," in *Von und aus Schwaben: Geschichte, Biographie, Litteratur,* Vol. III. Stuttgart, 1886. Pp. 1–31.

―――. "Ferdinand Baur und David Friedrich Strauss," *Preussische Jahrbücher,* CLX (April–June 1915), 474–504; CLXI (July–September 1915), 123–44.

LIEBING, HEINZ. "Ferdinand Christian Baurs Kritik an Schleiermachers Glaubenslehre," *ZThK,* LIV (1957), 225–43.

―――. "Historical-Critical Theology: In Commemoration of the One Hundredth Anniversary of the Death of Ferdinand Christian Baur, December 2, 1960," *Journal for Theology and the Church,* III (1967), 55–69. Originally published in *ZThK,* LVII (1960), 302–17.

LIPSIUS, RICHARD ADELBERT. "Ferdinand Christian Baur und die Tübinger Schule," in *Unsere Zeit, Jahrbuch zum Conversations-Lexikon.* Vol. VI. Leipzig, 1862. Pp. 229–54.

MACKAY, R. W. *The Tübingen School and Its Antecedents: A Review of the History and Present Condition of Modern Theology.* London, 1863.

PÄLTZ, EBERHARD. "F. C. Baurs Verhältnis zu Schleiermacher." Unpublished doctoral dissertation, University of Jena, 1955. Abstract by the author in *Theologische Literaturzeitung,* LXXXI (September 1956), 570–72.

PFLEIDERER, OTTO. *The Development of Theology in Germany Since Kant, and*

Its Progress in Great Britain Since 1825. Translated by J. Frederick Smith. London, 1890. Pp. 224–32, 284–98.

––––. "Zu Ferdinand Christian Baur's Gedächtnis," *Protestantische Kirchenzeitung für das evangelische Deutschland*, XXXIX (June 1892), 565–73.

RAPP, ADOLPH. "Baur und Strauss in ihrer Stellung zueinander und zum Christentum," *Blätter für Wüttembergische Kirchengeschichte*, 3. Folge, LII (1952), 95–149; LIII (1953), 157; LIV (1954), 182–85.

SCHNEIDER, ERNST. *Ferdinand Christian Baur in seiner Bedeutung für die Theologie*. Munich, 1909.

SCHOLDER, KLAUS. "Albert Schweitzer und Ferdinand Christian Baur," in *Albert Schweitzer: Sein Denken und Sein Weg*, ed. H. W. Bähr. Tübingen, 1962. Pp. 184–92.

––––. "Ferdinand Christian Baur als Historiker," *Evangelische Theologie*, XXI (1961), 435–58.

SENFT, CHRISTOPH. *Wahrhaftigkeit und Wahrheit: Die Theologie des 19. Jahrhunderts zwischen Orthodoxie und Aufklärung*. Tübingen, 1956. Pp. 47–86.

TROELTSCH, ERNST. "Adolf v. Harnack und Ferd. Christ. v. Baur," in *Festgabe für D. Dr. A. von Harnack, zum siebzigsten Geburtstag*. Tübingen, 1921. Pp. 282–91.

UHLHORN, GERHARD. "Die älteste Kirchengeschichte in der Darstellung der Tübinger Schule," *Jahrbücher für deutsche Theologie*, III (1858), 280–349.

Worte der Erinnerung an Ferdinand Christian von Baur. Tübingen, 1861.

ZELLER, EDUARD. "Ferdinand Christian Baur," in *Allgemeine deutsche Biographie*. Vol. II. Leipzig, 1875. Pp. 172–79.

––––. "Ferdinand Christian Baur," in *Vorträge und Abhandlungen geschichtlichen Inhalts*. Leipzig, 1865. Pp. 354–434.

––––. "Die Tübinger historische Schule," *Sybels historische Zeitschrift*, IV (1860), 90–173. (Reprinted in revised form in *Vorträge und Abhandlungen geschichtlichen Inhalts*, pp. 267–353.)

Index